Effective Philanthropy

Effective Philanthropy

Organizational Success through Deep Diversity and Gender Equality

Mary Ellen S. Capek and Molly Mead

A Project of Women & Philanthropy
funded by the W. K. Kellogg Foundation

The MIT Press
Cambridge, Massachusetts
London, England

MIT Press books may be purchased at special quantity discounts for business or sales promotional use. For information, please email special_sales@mitpress.mit.edu or write to Special Sales Department, The MIT Press, 55 Hayward Street, Cambridge, MA 02142.

This book was set in Sabon by Graphic Composition, Inc.
Printed and bound in the United States of America.
Printed on Recycled Paper.

Library of Congress Cataloging-in-Publication Data

Capek, Mary Ellen S.
  Effective philanthropy : organizational success through deep diversity and
  gender equality / Mary Ellen S. Capek and Molly Mead.
      p.   cm.
  "A project of Women & Philanthropy, funded by the W.K. Kellogg Foundation."
  Includes bibliographical references and index.
  ISBN 0-262-03337-2 (alk. paper)
  1. Endowments. 2. Endowments—Case studies. 3. Charities. 4. Charities—
  Case studies. 5. Women—Scholarships, fellowships, etc. 6. Women—Services
  for—Finance. 7. Minorities—Services for—Finance. 8. Sex discrimination
  against women. 9. Organizational effectiveness. I. Mead, Molly. II. Woman &
  Philanthropy. III. Title.
HV25.C36 2005
361.7'632—dc22
                                                          2005049114

For the next generation: Elena, Marlene, Anna, Katie, Leah, Abby, AJ, and Derek

Contents

Foreword

Susan V. Berresford

In 1977 a small group of women funders joined together to found Women and Foundations/Corporate Philanthropy (WAF/CP). They and their female and male colleagues were troubled by funders' inattention to discrimination against girls and women of all ages and by the lack of funding for projects responding to this problem. I was among the funders who set out to create this new organization, expecting that it would directly and indirectly challenge disappointing behavior patterns and also assist women who wanted to advance in jobs in organized philanthropy.

Much has changed since that time, including the name WAF/CP, which is now Women & Philanthropy. While then women were rare in higher ranks of foundations, today they are numerous. In the earlier time period, grant programs specifically targeted to women's opportunities were virtually nonexistent. They are now fairly common, although not sufficient. And, thanks to so many efforts, women have advanced in many professional areas and types of employment, education, and religious and cultural life that influence both philanthropy and the larger society. Women & Philanthropy and the donors the organization mobilized were one small but effective part of the many mobilizations that brought about this change.

Nonetheless, all alert and thoughtful people know that while progress has occurred, we are far short of the ideal of gender equity. Much of the change in women's opportunities to date rests on the flexibility and adaptability of individual women, men, and their families. Individuals and their kin have made enormous personal and familial sacrifices to enable women to move into fields from which they had been barred. But, to their frustration and disappointment, the social institutions around them have made few significant or compensating institutional adjustments. For example, the United States has no national day care system, after-school, or elder-care system; many of our employers expect extensive time commitments from their full-time staff, while others refuse to adopt part-time work patterns to jobs with significant responsibilities; and in many places women still have to struggle for basic equal opportunity. Minority, gay, and low-income women have even greater challenges.

Mary Ellen Capek and Molly Mead's book gives us a way to understand where we are today and what can be ahead if we want to make far greater progress for women and men who believe greater gender sensitivity and equity are desirable. They envision the effort and outcome in broad terms that encompass the many diversities that exist in modern organizations. They focus on institutions and offer an analytic framework, practical steps we can take, and examples from pioneering people and organizations. This is an exceptionally helpful contribution for which we salute Women & Philanthropy. It draws on the W. K. Kellogg Foundation's funding of a cluster of grantees and the Kellogg Foundation's leadership in this area, which is rare and commendable.

Reflection on my own experience at the Ford Foundation helps me see how valuable the Capek/Mead approach can be. Our foundation worked through a number of stages in its feminist grant making, moving toward the ideal the authors call "deep diversity," although we were not conscious of that evolutionary process as it occurred. In the first stage, staff developed a range of grants to support female and male feminist pioneers trying to gain footholds in jobs, education, and religious and political roles from which they had been excluded. At the same time, female and male pioneers in and outside the foundation brought forward these grants and also argued there were important parallels between this work and Ford's earlier and continuing support for minority civil-rights movements. From supporting single pioneers, the foundation moved to funding groups of people in projects and "centers" or "institutes" that began to establish an institutional presence around single innovators. Later, as centers and their counterparts matured, we funded "mainstreaming" efforts, while maintaining a special focus on women-specific work and gender more generally.

In the process, we began also to see proposals that grew less from a desire to integrate women into formerly male domains or vice versa, but rather proposals that brought a gender lens to an entire institution's activities or a broad intellectual field. This meant that we and our grantees explored what was added to our understanding of the problem we were try-ing to solve when we looked at gender patterns in a field, in learning efforts, in daily activity, in successful results, etc. These proposals and the work car-ried out by those who brought them to Ford reminded us of the lessons we had learned working on minority civil-rights challenges. In particular, that when you bring in excluded groups, fundamental changes occur. That is be-cause those who have been "outside" bring different perceptions, different frameworks, different questions to the table. And if people in the institu-tion engage with those ideas, they will see problems from new perspectives, get new information, read into more networks, have greater legitimacy in the broad range of people in society, and be stronger and more effective.

As Ford has continued its work with minorities and women, social-justice and gender issues, our staff composition changed accordingly. We also began to diversify our staff internationally. Once again, the new inter-national staff brought new assumptions, questions, frameworks, and ideas that strengthen our work significantly.

Ford is a stronger, more sophisticated grant-making organization thanks to the "deeper" diversity of our staff and trustees, gained over several decades. We are by no means satisfied with where we are, since we con-tinue to rethink one aspect or another of our activities as time goes along and as new questions emerge. What we have learned is that having facets of the world's diversity inside the foundation helps us to see problems, so-lutions, and ideas from multiple perspectives and helps us to frame grant-making strategies that combine insights in broad combinations that reflect the variety of human experience and our collective sense of the best way forward.

Capek and Mead see these values too, and their book helps us turn the ideas into practical measures.

Susan V. Berresford
President, The Ford Foundation

Foreword

William C. Richardson

Somehow, it strikes me as odd when I hear the term "minority" used to refer to women or people of color. After all, there are 5.5 million more women than men living in the United States, and in six of the country's eight largest metropolitan areas, "minorities" are the majority. But, perhaps it is this shared status as "minorities" that has created the crucible from which authors Mary Ellen Capek and Molly Mead take their deep dive into diversity. Perhaps it is this relentless clinging to yesterday's thinking that makes their work so important today.

In *Effective Philanthropy*, Capek and Mead tell us that by acknowledging and addressing the biggest slice of diversity there is—the difference between males and females—we can raise the bar on the effectiveness of all philanthropy. Starting more than a decade ago, the authors began looking at issues of gender in philanthropy. As researchers, consultants, leaders, and provocateurs, they've observed and listened intently as individuals and organizations have tried to address the continuing needs and opportunities of a diverse America. Through *Effective Philanthropy*, they show us vivid examples of how to use a "gender lens" to help our sector be effective.

Capek and Mead tell us that it just doesn't work to focus on race and class without focusing on gender. Conversely, to truly attend to the needs of women and girls, we must consider the totality of the diversities they represent: race, economic class, sexual orientation, disabilities, and age. Capek and Mead's striking analogy is that using bifocals is good, but using trifocals—a gender lens, a race/ethnicity lens, and a class lens—is even better, albeit much more difficult. The old "melting pot" concept has given way to the reality that we only can address these dimensions by facing them, dealing with them, and celebrating them.

The facts about women in need are undeniable. Seventy percent of the world's population living in absolute poverty are women. Two-thirds of the world's 876 million illiterate people are female. Women earn 76 cents for every dollar earned by men. African American women earn 68 cents on the dollar, and Latino women 56.

Even before the feminists of the 1960s and 1970s raised the gender flag, there were significant moments in history when notable people reminded us that addressing the needs of women and girls was the most effective path to improving the lot of society. There is a powerful shared history between women and others who struggled against oppression. Women activists of the 1950s found themselves inspired by the African-American civil rights movement. In the 1960s, feminist organizations were among the first to stand arm-in-arm with organizations who demanded equal rights for people of color. But well before that time, women were the lifeblood of the abolitionist movement. The feisty and articulate Sojourner Truth, who lived in Battle Creek, Michigan—also home to the W. K. Kellogg Foundation—advocated for the right to vote but made it clear that only by extending the vote to blacks *and* women would America achieve its true potential. She said in 1851:

If the first woman God ever made was strong enough to turn the world upside down all alone, these women together ought to be able to turn it back, and get it right side up again!

Few remember that the first woman to run for president, Victoria Woodhull, tapped Frederick Douglass, a black man, as her vice-presidential candidate, further underscoring the shared social agenda of women and people of color.

History reveals that the chaordic partnership between women and people of color grew from many motivations—a shared sense of oppression, an elevated consciousness about the need to care for others, a political strategy, a personal act of kindness—but, all led to the same path—a quest for equality.

Yet as we begin a new century, it seems again that we overtly address issues of "diversity," all the while keeping the largest "minority"—women and girls—a shadowed population. In our zeal to be "politically correct," many have embraced issues of diversity, while avoiding direct support of "women's issues." Capek and Mead tell us only about 7 percent of all foundation funding goes to programs that focus on women and girls. Development organizations throughout the world—USAID, the World Bank, and the United Nations—subscribe to the principle that an investment in educating women is the best investment in the future. Study after study has shown that educated women provide better nutrition, health, and education to their families; experience significantly lower child mortality; and generate more income than women with little or no schooling. "Investing to educate them thus creates a virtuous cycle for their community," noted one World Bank study.

Capek and Mead's work may well convince you that if you want to change the world, fund women. At the Kellogg Foundation, we recognize the complexity of social issues and work to address issues from multiple pathways. We encourage our staff to tap their own differences and use their rich cultural experiences in their work. We direct grants specifically to discrete disadvantaged populations, and we provide grants that are intended to address communities as a whole. But even as we interact with communities as a whole, we bring along our toolkit for raising otherwise unheard voices at the table.

In recent years, the Foundation's Philanthropy and Volunteerism team has noticed an impressive innovation taking place in six population groups: new wealth creators, youth, communities of color, corporate social innovators, social entrepreneurs, and of particular interest here, women. In a major initiative, Unleashing New Resources, the Foundation is supporting innovation led by women and working to unleash new resources of time, money, and know-how for social good. In our international grant making—focused on southern Africa, and Latin America and the Caribbean—women, girls, and their organizations often are tapped for learning, mobilizing, and constructing new ways of dealing with poverty in their communities. We understand the old adage that "the hand that rocks the cradle is the hand that rules the world."

You may wonder why a fairly senior, white, male university-president-turned-foundation-head would be interested in this cause. I was born and raised in Passaic, New Jersey, the son of an English immigrant who came here in the 1920s. My father emigrated because he could no longer tolerate a caste-oriented society that denied many of its citizens opportunity, with little regard for personal skill or merit. My mother was a woman who, in the 1910s and 1920s, held personal and professional beliefs that were in many quarters considered radical. In Passaic, her forays into suspicious behavior included founding an integrated child-care center for working women and later collaborating with the NAACP on various causes. My father, a conservative, pursued his dreams unfettered. My parents' understanding and belief in democracy and diversity—although they wouldn't have labeled it as such—is a gift to me, yet one that I've often found tested during my career.

So naturally I've looked for opportunities to apply their principles and extend their gift. It was at the Kellogg Foundation—with the support of a board of trustees who themselves reflect this face of diversity—that we've been able to do substantial work. In 1996, the Kellogg Foundation brought together the Global Fund for Women, Michigan Women's Foundation, Resourceful Women, Women & Philanthropy, and the Women's Funding Network to share what they had learned and the barriers they encountered and to craft strategies that would propel them forward. The momentum grew, and from the dynamic and persistent work of these organizations emerged the questions that Capek and Mead explore in this book. The Kellogg Foundation was pleased to be able to support the authors as they began to capture the lessons—and began planting the seeds of this book— in 1999. Recognizing the potential for elevating women in philanthropy, the Kellogg Foundation provided a $4.8 million grant to the Women's Funding Network to strengthen the resources they provide to women's funding organizations across the country. More recently, the Kellogg Foundation provided additional funding to Women & Philanthropy, a national association of grant makers, to elevate further the role of philanthropy by and for women, to strengthen the networks of support, and to advance techniques that engage women and girls more fully in social change.

In recent decades, charitable giving by Americans, including foundations, individuals, and corporations, has equaled about 2 percent of our national income, for a total of nearly $150 billion per year. Yet for all we accomplish, there's still a need to devote more resources to core issues that threaten society. But can the nonprofit sector truly have an impact in the fight against inequality, disadvantage, and racism? I obviously believe we can, and if that weren't the case, I wouldn't be advocating for this work.

When we hear news reports of burned churches, day-care-center shootings in Los Angeles, or hate-speech sites on the Internet, we see the symptoms of challenges that have plagued us throughout our history. To grasp this problem, and ultimately to solve it, we must look deeper and wider than we've done in the past.

Yet as philanthropists, as leaders of nonprofit organizations, we're only fooling ourselves if we believe that it is good enough simply to treat the symptoms. We need to look at the underpinnings of sexism and racism and all the barriers to equality and opportunity that prevent millions of Americans from reaching their full potential. For when they are so denied, our whole society and world suffers from the loss of what could be.

Encouraging diversity of thoughts and the people thinking them is essential for sparking creativity and innovation. Collaboration and civic participation are crucial to improving institutions and assuring sustainable social change.

Capek and Mead's work goes a long way toward shining light on organizations that are doing the right thing, all the while keeping the important questions and challenges on the table. The authors' overarching message is to continue learning. *Effective Philanthropy* shows how organizations can maximize their potential for effectiveness by institutionalizing new research and thinking about gender and "deep diversity." Offering demographics, case studies, strategic funding initiatives, theoretical analyses, and original research, *Effective Philanthropy* describes models for effectiveness that need to take root and grow in all kinds of organizations.

William C. Richardson
President and CEO, W. K. Kellogg Foundation

Preface

Why *Effective Philanthropy?*

The impetus for this book grew from the W. K. Kellogg Foundation's Women's Philanthropy Cluster, a multiyear, core-funding initiative that the foundation launched in 1996. The Philanthropy Cluster brought together the Global Fund for Women, Michigan Women's Foundation, Resourceful Women, Women & Philanthropy, and the Women's Funding Network to share strategies that would strengthen each of the Cluster organizations and develop collaborative long-range planning strategies to improve philanthropy for women and girls.[1] Both authors of this book have written in-depth background monographs for the Cluster, and in 1999 the foundation asked us to expand our work into a book highlighting best practices in the field and collecting in one volume resources needed to make the case for the importance of foundations funding programs and organizations that specifically serve the needs of women and girls.[2]

Kellogg's Philanthropy Cluster is one of the most recent among coalitions that have worked for over thirty years to increase both the amount and the percentage of foundation dollars reaching women and girls as well as to improve strategies for funding women's and girls' organizations and programs.[3] Although these efforts have had some success, the consensus of the Philanthropy Cluster—along with many other philanthropy professionals, nonprofit leaders, and researchers—has been that women and girls still do not receive foundation funding proportionate to their numbers in the population. Nor do most typical grantmaking approaches adequately build on the strengths of women and girls or meet their documented needs and the needs of their families and communities. So we began this project with a primary focus on how philanthropy does and does not work for women and girls.

For the first phase of our research, October 2001 through February 2002, we interviewed sixty philanthropic and nonprofit leaders—polling them, among other topics, about effective funding strategies and roadblocks to increasing and improving funding for women and girls.[4] As we spoke with these leaders about their observations and concerns, it became clear that we had to broaden the focus of our book: among the most frequently mentioned issues that surfaced in these interviews was the need to understand and talk about gender in the broadest possible contexts of race, class, sexual orientation, religion, national identity, culture, disability, and other realities of people's lives.[5] The bottom line according to the people we interviewed is that in order to be effective, foundations must both understand diversity and *institutionalize* that knowledge.

Other frequently cited issues and concerns raised by these leaders are listed below, ranked in order of frequency. We have used these findings to shape the structure of our book.

• The need for talking in more subtle ways about *organizational culture* and the importance of institutionalizing diversity and gendered cultural competence[6]

• The need for better and more accessible demographic data as a key tool of institutionalized diversity and cultural competence

• The need for grantees to focus on effectiveness and target foundations' issue areas when they make the case for funding women and girls

• The importance of relationships and partnerships (between funders and grantees, among funders, and among grantees themselves)

• The importance of applying international understandings of gender to domestic grants programs

• The need to take a closer look at women in foundation leadership positions (constraints, strengths, and the need for leadership on women's issues)

• The need for new language and strategies for talking about effective grant making for women and girls

• The importance of leadership to address and institutionalize such effectiveness

• The need to educate and/or change both foundation and nonprofit boards to be more accountable for effective philanthropy

The most important insight we gained from all the research, conversations, and thinking that inform this book, however, is the link between doing effective philanthropy and funding women and girls. When foundations are effective, they fund women and girls explicitly. They understand, for example, that funding a "youth"-in-science-and-technology initiative in inner-city Los Angeles does not work well for either boys or for girls unless:

• Funders exercise "due diligence" regarding a potential grantee's ability to understand specific cultural differences, including gender, that affect how children think of themselves and their career opportunities

• Both the funder and the nonprofit doing the work account for documented differences in how boys and girls from different cultures relate to and learn science and technology[7]

When foundations understand how much they gain by considering multiple perspectives—all the complex historical and cultural dimensions, including gender, that affect individuals, families, and communities—then gender becomes just one piece of the big picture, and foundations start funding women and girls explicitly. And, not surprisingly, their other funding initiatives also become more effective.

About the Authors

The research and thinking that shape this book come from a variety of sources. Authors Mary Ellen Capek and Molly Mead have years of hands-on experience in philanthropy, nonprofit leadership, and higher education. They are also researchers and leading authors on the subject of women, girls, and philanthropy.

Mary Ellen Capek is a founding officer and former executive director of the National Council for Research on Women. She is a founding board member of the Aspen Institute's Nonprofit Sector Research Fund, a former member of Independent Sector's Research Committee and The Conference Board's Work/Life Leadership Council (formerly Work/Family Council), a founding member of Women & Philanthropy's Action/Research Committee, and board chair of the Equality New Mexico Foundation. She currently works as a consultant to both foundations and nonprofit organizations, delivers speeches and workshops on deep diversity and effective philanthropy, and is a research scholar affiliated with the Anderson Schools of Management at the University of New Mexico.

Molly Mead is Lincoln Filene Professor at Tufts University's University College of Citizenship and Public Service. She teaches courses in leadership, gender and public policy, and innovative nonprofits in the department of Urban and Environmental Policy and the department of American Studies. She is a research advisor to the Girls' Coalition of Greater Boston, a member of Women & Philanthropy's Action/Research Committee, and also works as a consultant to foundations and nonprofits on the topic of women, girls, and philanthropy. She has worked closely with the United Way of Massachusetts Bay to help them develop their Today's Girls . . . Tomorrow's Leaders campaign, a program that raises funds for and develops the capacities of programs that serve girls. She regularly speaks at events around the country where funders and grantees discuss how to serve women and girls more effectively.

Research Informing This Book

The authors' original research informing this book includes interviews and focus groups with more than 250 women and men over the last decade.

• Mead's in-person interviews in 1993 and 1994 with philanthropic leaders in Boston and a six-year research study (1995–2000) on the outcomes for girls who participate in coed youth programs in Boston

• Capek's research in 1997 and 1998 for the W. K. Kellogg Foundation that included in-person and telephone interviews with current and former trustees, CEOs, senior executives, and program officers in private foundations, corporate foundations, family foundations, community foundations, and women's funds; leadership of the identity-based Affinity Groups of the Council on Foundations; heads of women's organizations and other nonprofit organizations; women donors across the age spectrum; consultants, professional fundraisers, and development directors

• Research done in 2000 and 2001 by both Capek and Mead for Chicago Women in Philanthropy: focus groups, in-person and telephone interviews with foundation CEOs and trustees, foundation senior staff and consultants, nonprofit leaders, and researchers in the Chicago philanthropic community

• Sixty "key informant" telephone interviews conducted specifically for this book, some of them re-interviews of subjects in the earlier Kellogg

Foundation research, that included interviews with leaders with significant experience and responsibility in private foundations, corporate foundations, family foundations, women's funds, women's organizations, and other nonprofit organizations

· Thirty-seven interviews conducted for the six "model" case studies (included in chapter 3 of this book) with foundation trustees, staff, and grantees

Acknowledgments

We have many people to thank for this book, beginning with staff and trustees of the W. K. Kellogg Foundation. Stephanie Clohesy, a consultant to the foundation, first approached us about collaborating on a book that would pull together thinking and writings that have informed almost a decade of work since the Kellogg Foundation first funded the Women's Philanthropy Cluster in 1996. The original members of the Women's Philanthropy Cluster helped to shape some of the early ideas that fed into this book: Judy Bloom, Felicia Lynch, Carol Mollner, Kavita Ramdas, and Peg Talburtt. In 1999, Women & Philanthropy became the official sponsor for the book. Kim Otis, President and CEO of Women & Philanthropy, has been an enthusiastic and thoughtful collaborator. Thanks also to Chris Kwak, W. K. Kellogg Program Officer, and Sonia Barnes-Moorhead, Kellogg Foundation consultant, who have overseen funding for this project since its inception. Others at the foundation—among them Robert Long, Gail McClure, Wenda Weekes Moore, and Tom Reis—also provided strategic help, suggestions, and encouragement.

A special thanks to Susan Berresford and William Richardson for their thoughtful forewords. Their leadership and encouragement has meant a lot to us as we worked to complete the final manuscript.

Lynn Burbridge, Michelle Fine, Elizabeth Minnich, Terry Odendahl, Susan Ostrander, and Marie Wilson were an early "brain trust" that helped us think about ways of researching and expanding the original ideas that informed our book. Janet Spector conducted interviews during the first phase of the book's research, and her anthropological skills helped us think creatively about what we were finding. Jake Page edited an early draft of the manuscript, and his suggestion to add case studies and more concrete examples strengthened both our writing and the substance of the book. Mike

Capek edited early drafts of the introduction and provided helpful suggestions for sharpening our ideas. Jean Ramsey and Jean Kantambu Latting both read early drafts of the book and made helpful suggestions. Jean Ramsey also provided valuable background information and work-in-progress about cultural competence and learning organizations and shared intense discussions with us as our ideas were forming.

Michael Ames, Louis Delgado, Mark Dowie, Virginia Hodgkinson, Terry Odendahl, Susan Ostrander, and two anonymous reviewers wrote thoughtful, detailed, and helpful reviews of the almost-final manuscript. Sonia Bettez pointed Mary Ellen to the "deep democracy" literature. And Sue Hallgarth valiantly read and argued through early versions of the manuscript-in-process, helped coin the term "deep diversity," and has been a diligent, demanding, and patient partner in the final editing process.

Vic De Luca, Larry Kressley, John Kostishack, Beth Smith, Andrew Swinney, Gary Yates—and their staff, trustees, and grantees—all provided time, thoughtful responses, and suggestions as we developed the six case studies in chapter 3. And Talia Weiner Bilodeau, Pat Brandes, Diana Campoamor, Nancy Cunningham, Sara Gould, Marcia Greenberger, and Elwood Hopkins all provided help as we pulled together the model funding strategies in chapter 7.

Many other people and organizations also provided insightful, thoughtful suggestions as we talked about our research and shared drafts at both formal and informal conferences and gatherings. The National Council for Research on Women (NCRW) has been a rich source of ideas and experience. Susan McGee Bailey, Linda Basch, Florence Bonner, Charlotte Bunch, Carol Burger, Mariam K. Chamberlain, Alice Dan, Bonnie Thornton Dill, Sharon Doherty, Sara Englehardt, Carolyn Farrell, the late Barbara Finberg, Angela Ginorio, Geeta Rao Gupta, Beverly Guy-Sheftall, Mary Hartman, Heidi Hartmann, Jan Holmgren, Carol Hollenshead, Eleanor Horne, Liz Horton, Florence Howe, Demie Kurz, Ruth Mandel, Shari Miles, Jan Monk, Sandi Morgan, Caryn McTighe Musil, Heather Johnston Nicholson, Jan Poppendieck, Deborah Rhode, Kathy Rodgers, Judith Saidel, Cynthia Secor, Donna Shavlik, Debbie Siegel, Ellie Smeal, Catharine R. Stimpson, Kristen Timothy, Debbie Walsh, Elizabeth Weed, Beth Willinger, Wayne Winborne, Leslie Wolfe—all these and other current and former NCRW center directors and board members have shared fundraising expertise, innovative gender analyses, and collaborative research and policy initiatives for over two decades. Cynthia Secor and Donna Shavlik, especially, have been helping Mary Ellen think about issues of diversity and gender since 1977.

Chicago Women in Philanthropy (CWIP), especially Robin Berkson, Betsy Brill, Amina Dickerson, Sunny Fisher, Pat Ford, Linda Harlan, Deb Hass, Iris Krieg, Valerie Lies, Marcia Lipetz, Celene Peurye, Heather Steans, and other members of CWIP's Research Advisory Committee provided support and good advice as we researched and wrote *Fostering Effective Funding for Women and Girls: A Next Stage Strategy*, which was instrumental in providing baseline data for our effective philanthropy benchmarks. Lowell Livezey was a commited, thoughtful researcher who helped us conduct the CWIP interviews and analyze them.

Boston Women in Philanthropy and the Boston Women's Fund provided the funds for Molly's 1993 study, *Worlds Apart: Missed Opportunities to Help Women and Girls*. Documenting corporate and foundation giving to women's and girls' programs, this study provided essential data and analyses to strengthen an ongoing conversation about gender and philanthropy that continues today. Boston Women in Philanthropy has changed its name to Greater Boston Funders for Women and Girls in acknowledgment that their focus is on using philanthropy as a tool to strengthen women's and girls' lives. Susan Dickler, Renae Gray, Cindy Rizzo, and Amy Segal Shorey have been and continue to be particularly strong voices for grant making with a gender lens. Jenny Russell offered advice about the *Worlds Apart* study in 1993. It would not have been as strong a report without her guiding hand. The Boston Women's Fund continues to be a vibrant funding organization that "gets" how to combine gender with other diversities and does the deep diversity work this book describes. Previous directors of the fund, including Hayat Imam and Jean Entine, deserve special mention. Renae Gray, the current director, has sharpened Molly's thinking about the role of diversity in effective grant making on many occasions. Ellen Remmer of the Remmer Family Foundation and Greater Boston Funders for Women and Girls has been a steady presence in virtually all of Molly's work on philanthropy. Her support—and even more crucial, her questions— have helped Molly think more deeply about gender and grant making.

The United Way of Massachusetts Bay (UWMB), a national leader in raising funds for women and girls, has been especially influential in demonstrating Molly's ideas about how to use those funds to build organizational capacity and develop effective programs for women and girls. In particular, through their Today's Girls . . . Tomorrow's Leaders (TGTL) campaign, UWMB has raised millions of dollars for girls' programs, and United Way programs around the country look to Mass Bay as a model for how to do this work. When Pat Brandes, then chief operating officer of UWMB, first heard Molly present her research on the ineffectiveness of coed youth programs serving girls, she challenged their entire organization to learn about Molly's research and then put Molly's findings into practice. They have done just that. Particular mention should go to Sarah Alvord, Carisa Olivo, and Renate Yssel as well as to Martha Crownenshield for providing the original "venture capital" to launch TGTL.

The Girls Coalition of Greater Boston provided Molly with practitioner perspectives on how to serve girls effectively, which Molly has used in several of her research studies. Katie Wheeler, Jerry Martinson, Laura Watkins, Pat Driscoll, and Marie Turley deserve specific mention. Researchers Sumru Erkut and Janie Ward have themselves done research on girls in all their diversity and have been role models for Molly in doing research that is grounded in deep diversity.

Because of confidentiality agreements, we cannot list names of all the trustees, CEOs, staff, and grantees we interviewed for this book. But there are many we learned from—researchers, experienced professionals on both sides of the "giving desk," and friends—all of whom have shared ideas, suggested resources, provided feedback, and/or served as role models for how philanthropy can and should be practiced. And, not least of all, they reassured and encouraged us at times when we really needed reassurance and encouragement. Thanks to Alan Abramson, Katherine Acey, Rebecca Adamson, Herb Altheimer, Jeanne Argoff, Libby and Martha Atkins-Trolin, M. Carlotta Baca, Tim Backes, Linda and Gloria Bailey-Davies, Lotte Bailyn, Carmen Barroso, Lori Bartczak, Mariette Bates, Ella Bell, Lucy Bernholz, Ellen Boneparth, Elizabeth Boris, Liz Bremner, Eleanor Brilliant, Melissa Susan Brown, Millie Buchanan, Martha Burk, Roxanne Carrillo, Emmett Carson, Denise Cavanaugh, Susan Chambré, Donna Chavis, Elayne Clift, Rick Cohen, Dennis Collins, Pablo Eisenberg, Robin Ely, Kathleen Enright, Cindy Ewing, Allison Fine, Marsha Freeman, Twink Frey, Katherine Fulton, Joan Garner, Elan Garonzik, Tracy Gary, Ruth Goins, Susan Gore, Caren Grown, Chris Grumm, Sitara Harvey-Cook and Sue Gradisar, John Havens, Kathleen and Clifford Hill, Elizabeth Hill,

Sheila Holderness, the late Joanne Howes, Si Kahn, Janice Kando, Ann E. Kaplan, Kate Karpilow, Stan Katz, Joanna Kerr, Virginia Kerr, Barbara Kibbe, Emily Katz Kishawi, Lisa Wyatt Knowlton, Jan Jaffe, Pat Lewis, Judith Lichtman, Jeff Lucker, Jing Lyman, Gloria Mallory, Geri Mannion, Vince McGee, Yolanda Moses, Kim Mulhern, Helen Neuborne, Jean O'Barr, Joel Orosz, Torie Osborne, Francie Ostrower, Susanne Page, Katherine Pease, Patti McGill Peterson, Barbara Phillips, Denis Prager, Jane Ransom, Rhona Rapoport, Tom Reis, Debbie Rettke, Dottie Reynolds, Mark Rosenman, Harilyn Rousso, Tim Russell, Peggy Saika, Mary Beth Salerno, Paul Schervish, Mudge Schink, Deb Schultz, Cinthia Schuman, Joan Scott, Michael Selzer, Vicki Semler, Ed Skloot, Esta Soler, Pam Sparr, Paul Spivey, Lynn Szwaja, Nicki Tanner, Barrie Thorne, Adrian Tinsley, Judy Walzer, Barbara Webster, Phyllis Holman Weisbard, Ellen Wicklum, Candice Widmer, Ann Wiener, Margaret Wilkerson, Anne Wilson, Kate Woodward, and Karen Zelermyer.

Thanks also to Stan Katz and Julian Wolpert, who provided Mary Ellen safe harbor as a Visiting Scholar at Princeton University's Woodrow Wilson School of International and Public Affairs in the late 1990s. And to Jacqueline N. Hood, Helen Muller, and Mary Cromer who have similarly secured her at the University of New Mexico Anderson Schools of Management, where she is currently affiliated. Librarians Laird Klingler, Susan McGee, and Barb Rosen provided fast, reliable assistance. Without Princeton and UNM's support and access to library and online resources, this book would not have been possible.

Dot Ridings, Char Mollison, Judith Kroll, and others from the Council on Foundations were always ready to respond to queries, similarly Sara Englehardt, Loren Renz, Steven Lawrence, and Josie Atienza from The Foundation Center. Thanks also to James Abruzzo and Alex Plinio at the Center for Nonprofit and Philanthropic Leadership at Rutgers Business School for sharing their insights about nonprofit sector leadership and for "thinking big" about effective leadership in the sector.

This book could not have been written without the support of family and friends, many of whom are already acknowledged. We would like to thank our parents: the late Althea D. and John B. Stagg, whose fairness and strong sense of social justice inform Mary Ellen's earliest memories, and Allen and the late Margaret B. Mead who encouraged Molly to say what she believed even when it was controversial. Major kudos go to our respective partners, Sue Hallgarth and Carole Bull. Besides her masterful editing skills, Sue provided Mary Ellen with emotional and financial support over the more than six years of this project, without which it would never have been completed. She was always available to listen and talk through old frustrations and new ideas. Carole was a key member of the Worlds Apart research team in 1993 when she ran the focus groups with funders. Because of Carole's warm and straightforward style, the program officers in those focus groups were forthcoming about how they saw (or didn't see) the relevance of gender to grant making. When the focus groups with heads of nonprofit agencies serving women and girls produced such different results from the funder focus groups, Carole reported that the two groups seemed to live in "different worlds." Out of this came the name of the report. Carole has urged the writing of this book and patiently watched its slow but steady progress.

Finally, thanks to Sherri Eisenpress, who provided pro bono legal assistance as we finalized publication contracts. Thanks to Charlie Capek for eagle-eyed proofreading and for compiling a first-rate index. And thanks to Clay Morgan, Mel Goldsipe, and the MIT Press, who have been thoughtful, professional partners. We are grateful for their expertise and support that have brought this book to press. Finally.

Introduction

Philanthropy is a Greek word whose origins literally mean "love for mankind." Contemporary use of the term refers to voluntary giving by individuals and organizations to promote the common good. Philanthropy is a fundamental human impulse. People of all economic means and cultures develop lifetime habits of donation and service to a wide range of causes—aiding family members and those less fortunate, sustaining communities and cultures, and working for systemic social change. Although public and private philanthropy in many countries at various stages of economic development are increasingly common, the United States has evolved the most institutionalized history of philanthropy—driven at least in part by federal-income-tax exemptions for contributions to organizations certified "charitable" or "nonprofit" by state governments.

This book is about "organized" philanthropy in the United States, philanthropy by foundations: tax-exempt nonprofit, charitable organizations created by individuals, families, and corporations with gifts of money, stock, or other resources invested to generate income used to make grants. In 2004, more than 66,000 foundations with over $476.7 billion in assets gave an estimated $32.4 billion in grants to nonprofit organizations to support a variety of activities, including research, health, education, arts, and culture as well as both systemic and charitable efforts to alleviate poverty and improve people's lives.[1]

Why Philanthropy Matters

Foundations are stewards of resources that would otherwise be added to federal and state treasuries. So given that these assets are managed privately instead of paid into the U.S. Treasury, foundation dollars are, by this definition at least, public money, money otherwise taxed and used for public benefit. For this reason alone, the public should know more about how foundations are managed.

But it is not the size of endowments they manage that make foundations an interesting sector to study. Collectively, foundation endowments add up to large sums, but they represent only a small fraction of the total federal budget, so the dollar value of the sector, while significant and growing, is in fact relative. Most foundation clients—nonprofit organizations—seldom rely on foundations for more than fifteen percent of their annual budgets. Yet foundations have significant influence beyond the dollar values of their endowments or their grants because foundations are a bellwether for both the nonprofit sector and for society at large. A foundation grant is an imprimatur, a "Good Housekeeping seal of approval" that can help a nonprofit organization—new or established—attract a wider donor base. Effective foundation support—or the lack of it—can make or break nonprofits and the well-being of many constituents they serve.

Increasingly, foundations have important roles to play in public policy by funding research and policy analyses as well as working in collaboration with other sectors to implement effective policy. By some assessments, the success of conservative public policy at federal, state, and local levels in the last several decades is largely attributable to the strategic philanthropy of a small group of conservative foundations. In a series of reports, the National Committee for Responsive Philanthropy documents the effective philanthropic strategies that conservative foundations have used to support activities of public policy-oriented right-wing think tanks at the federal, state, and local levels.[2]

Service on nonprofit boards, especially "culture" boards like museums and the performing arts or boards for the "right" diseases that have garnered high-status profiles, provides essential expertise, generous donations of both time and money, and considerable community benefit. But another dimension of this generous charitable service is status: board service on the "right" boards is *de rigueur* for both women and men who are upwardly mobile (or have arrived) in high-status social and business communities and networks, and many elite trustees also serve on private, family, and community foundation boards. While these wider cultural and public-policy dimensions of the philanthropic sector are beyond the scope of this book, it is important to name them because they demonstrate the multi-faceted—and often unacknowledged—weight and influence both charitable giving and foundations hold in our social, political, and economic sectors.

By virtue of their "power of the purse" and more subtle forms of influence, foundations are key players in U.S. social, economic, and public-policy sectors. This is the main reason we have written this book. When foundations function effectively, there is potential for tremendous public benefit. When these institutions, which influence the public good both directly and indirectly, do their work effectively, the impact on the public good is enormous. A quick scan of funding priorities makes this point. In 2003, the largest 1,010 U.S. foundations allocated an estimated 87 percent of their funding, an estimated $12.4 billion, to education (25 percent), health (20 percent), human services (16 percent), arts and culture (13 percent), and public affairs/society benefit (13 percent).[3] Imagine the public benefit if foundations were able to make still more effective grants in all of these areas.

But many foundations are elite institutions, classic examples of organizations with little actual public accountability beyond the narrow constraints of federal and state tax laws. In many instances, foundations have self-perpetuating boards, and they "market" to clients who, for all intents and purposes, are captive customers. While many foundations, especially larger, professionally staffed foundations, work responsibly, collegially, and for "the common good," many more—an estimated five out of six U.S. foundations[4]—are unstaffed and, for want of a better word, *idiosyncratic* because they are influenced by family members on their boards or financial advisors who may or may not have the interests of "the common good" as part of their portfolio.

All of which is why foundations make such an interesting subject for a book about organizational success. Much of what we write about in this book can be equally applied to the corporate sector, to government, and to higher education. The case studies and other examples of effective philanthropy cited throughout this book are models for the kinds of effectiveness that need to take root and grow in all kinds of organizations—large and small, private and public, national and regional, bureaucratic and entrepreneurial. Given their inherently elite status with so few outside pressures to change, foundations are the least likely sector to model cutting-edge organizational effectiveness initiatives. As one of our seasoned CEO respondents observed, "Trying to move the philanthropic sector is like trying to herd cats."

So if foundations can learn to be effective in the ways we describe throughout this book, so too can colleges and universities. So too can multinational corporations and government agencies. So too can both large and small nonprofits. And while we focus throughout the book on philanthropy itself and provide examples specific to foundations' primary work—giving away money—many of our analyses, case studies, and benchmarks can work for any organizations that aspire to be effective.

What *Is* Effective Philanthropy?

So just what *is* effective philanthropy? Effective philanthropy is philanthropy that has impact. It is philanthropy that succeeds at amassing, managing, then allocating financial and human resources in ways that have the greatest positive impact in the sectors that foundations choose to fund. To allocate resources effectively, foundations must have vision and strategies for their grant making that allow them to analyze issues and concerns they want to influence, identifying both challenges and potential resources. They must be able to find the nonprofit organizations most likely to produce the results they intend. They must be able to structure their grants in ways that will be most useful to their grantees. And they must evaluate what they do to ensure they are having the intended impacts.

So how do foundations have impact, and what makes them effective? *The most important findings from our research—and the central theme of this book—are the links between foundation effectiveness and institutionalizing nuanced understandings of diversity, including gender.* Why diversity? As we describe in more detail in chapters 1 and 2, the foundation and nonprofit leaders interviewed for this first phase of our research most often define effective philanthropy in terms that can be summed up as "democratized" philanthropy and "democratized" organizational dynamics. Benchmarks for effective philanthropy (figure I.1) that emerged from the first phase of research for this book replicated findings from our earlier research and helped us frame the concept of "deep diversity."

"Democratized" philanthropy encourages responsive "bottom-up" grant making as well as effective "top-down" funding initiatives that in-

Figure I.1
Benchmarks for effective philanthropy.

- Encourage responsive "bottom-up" grantmaking as well as effective initiative-driven grant making
- Develop mutually respectful relationships between funders and grantees
- Include those working "closest to the ground," grantees as well as foundation staff and trustees, in decision making and priority setting
- Make sure decision makers have firsthand experience and/or breadth of theoretical knowledge in the areas foundations fund
- Encourage risk taking on the part of both foundations and grantees
- Do multiyear, core support grants
- Stick with grantees over time
- Leverage support from other funders on behalf of grantees
- Build collaboratives with other funders that can leverage and publicize for public benefit both grantees' and foundations' own expertise
- Aim for "transparency" with clear guidelines and accessibility
- Establish goal setting and accountability that includes both internal and external evaluations of the effectiveness and impact of foundations' own grant making
- Work with grantees (and covers their costs) to evaluate the quality and impact of grantees' work
- Foster a "learning organization" culture of willingness to learn, accommodate "midcourse corrections," and change

clude stakeholder input and stress the importance of responsible, mutually respectful relationships between funders and grantees. And "democratized" philanthropy makes an effort to include in foundation decision making and priority setting those working "closest to the ground," grantees as well as foundation staff and trustees—all of whom have either (preferably both) firsthand experience or breadth of knowledge in the areas foundations seek to fund.[5]

Benchmarks for effective philanthropy also include risk taking on the part of both funders and grantees; the importance of making multiyear, core support grants and sticking with grantees over time; leveraging support from other funders on behalf of grantees; building collaboratives with other funders that can publicize for public benefit both grantees' and foundations' expertise; and finally "transparency"—clear guidelines and accessibility coupled with internal and external evaluations of the effectiveness and impact of foundations' own grant making as well as evaluations of the quality and impact of grantees' work—all of which enable funders to improve both their accountability and their expertise.

Defining Deep Diversity

While these benchmarks have little to do with gender, as we note in the preface, gender equity in philanthropy is the primary reason we started writing this book. Other than obvious examples like the one cited in the preface about science initiatives for "youth" versus science initiatives for boys and girls, why claim a link between gender and these benchmarks for effective philanthropy? Our interviews with philanthropic and nonprofit leaders about their priorities and perceptions of effective philanthropy made it increasingly clear that effective organizations and "democratized" philanthropy are intimately linked to a more nuanced understanding of gender in all its complexity. This is a three-step analysis.

First, much of what we understand about the social construction of gender in fact applies to a wide range of institutional diversity issues. Second, the converse is also true: any working definition of institutional diversity must also incorporate knowledge of gender and how gender plays out in institutions, often to the disadvantage of women and girls. Third, and most important, as we analyzed patterns emerging from our interviews with philanthropic and nonprofit leaders, another dimension of these issues came into focus that makes this book both timely and essential: *nuanced understanding of diversity that includes gender and gendered cultural competence is a key variable for doing effective philanthropy.*

The term "diversity" is commonly understood to refer to race and ethnicity more than it is to gender or class. But focusing on race or class apart from gender creates false dichotomies. In fact, women and girls are part of every racial and ethnic group from the most privileged to the least: women and girls are included in all economic classes, sexual orientations, disabilities, age groups, and other diversities. And understanding the social construction of gender also means understanding how men and boys of all races and classes are adversely affected by "gender conformity"—the head counselor in an inner city after-school career program, for example, who discourages a Hispanic boy who wants to be a nursery school teacher; a welfare-to-work initiative that offers parenting classes for mothers but not for fathers; or a large nonprofit legal resource agency that offers "family leave" for both men and women but whose woman CEO through teasing and decisions about promotion implicitly discourages men from making use of the policy.

Diversity also works to democratize boards and staffs of foundations. More diverse boards and staffs have a better shot at doing effective philanthropy. Understanding gender in the context of other diversities like race, class, and culture—which also means understanding the insidious, often subtle and unacknowledged preference for "normal," which we define and discuss in the next section—is essential for building healthier institutions and doing more effective grantmaking. Philanthropic and nonprofit leaders interviewed for this book emphasized the need for new language to capture this understanding. To respond to that need, we experimented with terms from other languages (e.g. *verscheiden, mannigfaltig, diversité, diversidad*) to help keep readers conscious and alert to the totality of how we are defining diversity, but we chose an English phrase, "deep diversity," that appears, among other contexts, in the philosophy of education, Canadian political science, and Santa Fe seed catalogs marketing biodiversity.[6]

We intend our use of the term "deep diversity" to parallel and draw connotations from the term "deep democracy," a concept growing out of international grassroots organizing efforts. "Deep democracy" emphasizes strategic transnational networks, collaborations, coalitions, and federations of the poor and disenfranchised at the same time that it highlights a set of traditional democratic principles like inclusion, participation, transparency, and accountability.[7] Throughout our book, we use the term "deep diversity" to describe an institutionalized understanding of diversity that goes *wide* as well as *deep*.

• *Wide* to include the breadth and web of differences that weave through most modern organizations: gender, sexual orientation, gender identity,[8] race, ethnicity, nationality, religion, class, disability, geography, age, learning styles, and other physiological, social, cultural, and economically defined differences that categorize groups of individuals

• *Deep* into an organization's DNA, or to use another metaphor, deep into the taproot of an organization and intertwined in the wide network of roots that anchors and feeds the whole of an organization's culture.

Defining "Gendered Cultural Competence"

Like connotations of "deep democracy," we intend the phrase "deep diversity" to echo the importance of collaboration, networks, and coalitions of those most affected by foundations' work, as well as fundamental democratic principles like inclusion, participation, collaboration, transparency, and accountability. "Cultural competence" is a term in common use in the medical and nursing professions, social-service agencies, counseling, law enforcement, education, and other helping professions that describes the ability of individuals and organizations to offer and deliver services tailored to the complex needs of the culturally diverse populations they serve. The term "gendered cultural competence" emphasizes the importance of making sure gender is consciously included in the concept. As we are defining it here, "gendered cultural competence" describes some of the required skills for doing "deep diversity," skills that enable people to communicate and function effectively across a wide variety of differences.

Defining "Norm"

As the case studies in chapter 3 document, foundations that institutionalize deep diversity fund women and girls. And foundations that institutionalize deep diversity have learned to challenge norms. We define *Norm*, as a capitalized noun, to be the insidious, often subtle, and unacknowledged tyranny of "normal." Webster's *Third* defines *norm* as "an ideal standard binding upon the members of a group and serving to guide, control, or regulate proper and acceptable behavior"—an innocuous enough definition describing a fundamental building block of civil society.[9]

Like HDL and LDL cholesterol, however, there are good norms and bad norms. High-density lipoprotein (HDL), the "good" cholesterol, protects against heart attacks. But too much low-density lipoprotein (LDL) circulating in our blood forms plaque, a thick, hard deposit that clogs arteries. Bad norms get in the way of our health and the health of our relationships and organizations. So the key questions about Norm are: Who gets to decide "proper and acceptable behavior"? Who decides who looks "normal"? Why do these controls and guides so often become blind spots that get in the way of effective philanthropy?

At its most extreme, Norm becomes racism, sexism, heterosexism, homophobia, transgender phobia, classism, fundamentalism, egotism, ableism, ageism, and xenophobia, and abuse of social, economic, and political power. Most of us working in the philanthropy and nonprofit sector have learned to avoid at least the appearance of these egregious manifestations of Norm. But it is the hidden assumptions, the unspoken expectations, and unyielding attitudes that make Norm so dangerous for deep diversity. Norm assumes the face of neutrality, the appearance of "universal"—generic, genderless, objective, colorblind, classless—in determining policies, procedures, and informal cultural interactions and assumed values that in fact are neither neutral nor universal.

We are writing this book to help foundations, nonprofits, and a wide range of other organizations recognize Norm, the arbiter of "proper and acceptable behavior" that too often becomes an unnamed, undiscussable elephant on the table, the invisible dead center of organizations that pushes to the periphery all the group identities included in our definition of deep diversity: gender, race, class, sexual orientation, gender identity, age, disability, geography, nationality, religion, and other diversities—anyone "not Norm." The last decade has seen a wealth of important research that documents how unexamined organizational norms get in the way of effective management. Researchers like Joan Acker, Lotte Bailyn, Marta Calás, Robin Ely, Joyce Fletcher, Evangelina Holvino, Deborah Kolb, Joanne Martin, Deborah Merrill-Sands, Debra Meyerson, Aruna Rao, Rhona Rapoport, Linda Smircich, and others have developed a cluster of helpful analyses and strategies for better understanding these dynamics and how they work to the disadvantage of most people in organizations, women and men of all races and ethnicities.[10]

So this is also a book about dismantling Norm—about how organizations learn to spot and avoid the pressures of convention, those "normal" organizational imperatives that reproduce "the way it's always been done" conventions, the ruts in the brain, the mud in the road solidified by the sun, over-and-over-and-over-again preferences, styles, and comfort zones instead of reaching for innovative and effective governance, staffing, and collaborative partnerships. As we document throughout this book, "Norm knowledge" is essential for effective philanthropy. Of all "normal" group identities, gender is perhaps the most familiar. For better or for worse, in virtually all modern societies, people are identified as males or females, men or women, boys or girls. *So understanding gender and gender identity becomes a key strategy in this book for understanding differences, deep diversity, and Norm knowledge.* Understanding how unexamined assumptions about gender in fact structure relationships and expectations of what's normal and what's rewarded in organizations is key to achieving effective philanthropy. Throughout this book, we use examples of the social construction of gender and gender identity to document how Norm undermines innovation and effectiveness, both in foundations and in their grantees. And how understanding gender enhances and strengthens innovation, especially an understanding of gender framed within deep diversity, the complex textures of people's lives and cultures *and* an understanding of the cultures of their organizations.

Funding Norm doesn't effectively fund Norma—or anyone else, for that matter. But the philanthropic practices that most benefit women and girls are the same practices that strengthen philanthropy generally. This book aims to provide helpful analyses of the social construction of gender and gender dynamics that often get overlooked in discussions of deep diversity and organizational health and well-being. With this book, we offer in one volume theoretical analyses, case studies, model funding initiatives, demographics, and a broad array of resources that help shift the conversation about funding women and girls from the margin to the center of the nonprofit sector's discourse, a shift that serves as a model of how philanthropy can become more effective.

What We Learned from Our Research: The Good News

There is plenty of good news to report. Many established women's and girls' nonprofit organizations are successful. Over the last several decades, many more women's and girls organizations have made serious commitments to practices like deep diversity. Well-managed organizations like Family Violence Prevention Fund, Girls Inc., Girl Scouts of the USA, Institute for Women's Policy Research, the National Council for Research on Women, National Partnership for Women and Families, National Women's Law Center, Legal Momentum (formerly the NOW Legal Defense and Education Fund), and the Wellesley Centers for Women—to name just a few—have produced impressive programs, policy initiatives, and research.

They have learned to make the case for funding their issues and in the process built a wide range of foundation support, individual donor bases, government contracts, and in-kind support. As we describe in chapter 4, some foundations, including women's funds like the Ms. Foundation for Women, are launching initiatives that expand beyond "women only"/ "girls only" to "both/and" frameworks—mainstreaming sophisticated gender knowledge within coed youth programs, for example, as well as funding innovative girls-only organizations and programs. And some nonprofit youth organizations, like those described in chapter 5 that serve both girls and boys, are doing a better job of meeting the specific needs of girls within their programs.

More good news: as described in chapters 4–7, many more funders have developed increasingly sophisticated understandings of gender and deep diversity within their own program areas than they did only a few years ago. Funders are also thinking in bigger, more imaginative frames of reference that go beyond short-term problem solving. "Twenty years ago, all the money we got was to solve a social problem," one nonprofit executive points out. "Now foundations are more aware of the need to invest in the healthy development of young people rather than just fix problems they have. This is a very different orientation." And more funders are implementing strategic funding initiatives that include unrestricted core support and multiyear grants—sticking with grantees for the long haul. More funders also realize that effective social change takes a long time to bring about and sometimes entails taking large risks with no assurance of immediate or even longer-term success. As the case studies in chapter 3 document, funders are "in there" partnering with their grantees for as long as it takes to keep working on mutually defined ambitions.

Still more good news: both the number and size of foundations organized to target support to the specific needs of women and girls have grown exponentially since the early 1970s. By 2005, a handful of U.S.-based funds had grown to more than 100 women's funds worldwide. In the United States and Canada, a sample of 50 funds that belong to the Women's Funding Network reported over $630 million in net assets for fiscal year 1999 and for the same time period, $180.3 million in dollars raised and $21.3 million given away in grants. By 2005, the number of funds participating in the network had grown to 105. Women's funds and foundations, like many women's organizations, also have made important commitments to deep diversity—in the case of the women's funds, they have democratized donors and achieved greater racial/ethnic diversity on their boards and staffs. Over the years, the funds' experiments with less hierarchical structures and grantee-driven grant awards have brought necessary innovations to organized philanthropy. And they are building larger endowments: the Ms. Foundation for Women, for example, one of the largest women's funds in the United States, in 2005 had an endowment of over $22 million. In 2004, the foundation gave away $3.8 million in grants.

We also are seeing that commitment to deep diversity pays off in effective philanthropy *and* more effective institutional cultures. As we noted earlier, results of original research conducted for this book document that much of what we understand about the dynamics of gender also applies to a wide range of diversity issues—in organizations across sectors as well as in foundations and nonprofits—and in fact leads us to deeper understanding about effective philanthropy in general: a foundation's commitment to deep diversity helps democratize its board and staff, and more effective philanthropy ensues. New foundation models are emerging, six of them highlighted in chapter 3, that document the process of democratizing philanthropic boards and staffs, signaling what researcher Mark Dowie describes as a "new covenant between society and philanthropy."[11] An understanding of deep diversity is key to these new models.

What We Learned from Our Research: The Bad News

The bad news is that small-budget and grassroots nonprofit organizations still have a hard time functioning. While many lack the capacity necessary to do more sophisticated fundraising, many more have managed to cobble together effective proposals that they still cannot get funded. In spite of increases in support available from community-based women's funds and women's initiatives within community foundations in recent years, many grassroots organizations do not receive funding adequate to do their work—in many cases critical service-delivery and activist projects. Even larger, multifocused, and established women's and girls' organizations still have to devote too much time convincing funders that their programs incorporating gender are essential to strengthening society and "deepening" democracy.

While philanthropic dollars reaching women's and girls' programs in the last decade have increased, in part because of the surging 1990s economy, the percentage of grant dollars specifically earmarked for women and girls from major U.S. foundations did not. According to figures compiled by The Foundation Center, the percentage of foundation dollars granted to programs specifically targeting women and girls from 1975 to 2003 increased from 0.5 percent to 7.3 percent—an increase but still minor, almost insignificant part of most foundation portfolios. In order to be classified as a grant to women and girls, a grant must meet one of the Foundation Center's four requirements: 1) women and girls make up a substantial majority of the grant recipient's members or clients; 2) the grant is intended to increase participation by, or extend services to, women or girls; 3) the grant recipient addresses an issue or discipline as it affects women or girls; and 4) the grant recipient addresses an issue or discipline whose impact primarily affects women and girls.[12] While the Foundation Center figures obviously do not reflect the total amount of funding that reaches women and girls, they do reflect grants purposely targeted to women and girls, which are grants more likely to be effective because *in targeting specific population groups, funders are more likely to know who benefits from their funding.*

Knowing who benefits is essential to philanthropic effectiveness. Some of those who dispute the Foundation Center numbers argue those numbers are an "understatement" because by definition women get over 50 percent of the benefits of their grant making. But funders need to ask two key questions that are part of any effective grant maker's "due diligence" toolbox.

• Exactly who is being served?
• How does the grant seeker's program or initiative respond to the needs, strengths, and resources of those being served?

Grant makers who argue that grants to coeducational colleges and universities benefit women equally with men, for example, may be overlooking questions of effectiveness.

On the other side of the controversy about the percentage of grant dollars reaching women and girls, advocates miss significant opportunities if they argue that to be effective all grants must be "targeted" to women's or girls' organizations or programs. In 1970, when women were virtually ignored by philanthropy and most public policies, it made sense to argue for targeted philanthropy. There was a pressing need to build an infrastructure of organizations specifically designed to advance the status of women. But that singular focus is now too limited. As we document throughout this book, to be effective, foundations do need to fund organizations specifically designed to serve women and girls. But "universal" programs and organizations also must be challenged to serve women and girls more effectively. Women's funding advocates lose credibility when they limit their arguments to "targeting" or those seven-percent numbers.

As we discuss in chapters 1 and 2, however, much of the "understatement" in numbers arises from exactly the issue that concerns advocates: because it remains controversial to fund women, program officers may frame their grant making for women and girls in more universal terms to ensure it will not be rejected at higher levels of review. This is a resourceful strategy any good program officer knows how to use, but it begs the question. *To be effective, philanthropy has to understand the implications and benefits of how and where its dollars are spent.*

Other bad news: while many foundations struggle in creative ways to develop programs aimed at systemic causes of social and economic disparities, many funders avoid issues of poverty, violence, and other deep-rooted social ills altogether. Or they respond to victims' needs in the short term and ignore the messier systemic roots of social and economic injustice that eat away at the underpinnings of a successful democracy. And often foundations miss opportunities to incorporate innovative thinking about funding women into their larger portfolio of grant-making programs. Many still assume that women are a special interest group deserving some (but not substantial) resources. As noted, segregated grant-making programs for women and girls are typically only a small part of foundations' overall funding strategies. Not only that, but some philanthropic leaders and advocates for women and girls are mired in decades-old "victim" demands or base their requests only on arguments that seek equity, a "fair share" of the grant-making pie for "women's issues."

In our view, the most appropriate goal is not a "fair share" of anything. The metaphor is misleading. As some of us have been arguing for years, "Think yeast, not pie, if you want more dough." The goal is deep democracy—a stronger, more vibrant society in which everyone's diverse contributions are recognized, appreciated, utilized, and funded. We hope in this book to present an analysis that documents persuasively that virtually *all* issues are women's issues and that understanding gender is a key factor in successful deep democracy and effective philanthropy (figure I.2).

Figure I.2
Bad-news problems and good-news solutions.

PROBLEM: Small-budget and grassroots nonprofit organizations still have a hard time surviving. Grassroots organizations do not receive funding adequate to do their work.
SOLUTION: See chapter 7, especially model funding initiatives Hispanics in Philanthropy (HIP), Funders for Lesbians and Gay Issues (FLAG), and Los Angeles Urban Funders (LAUF)

PROBLEM: Even larger, multi-focused, and established women's and girls' organizations have to devote too much time to convince funders about the importance of gender.
SOLUTION: See chapter 7, especially model funding initiatives United Way of Massachusetts Bay, National Women's Law Center and NYC Board of Education, and Ms. Foundation Funding Collaboratives.

PROBLEM: Percentage of grant dollars specifically earmarked for women and girls from major U.S. foundations has not increased.
SOLUTION: See chapters 1–4: funders develop increased awareness of "deep diversity" and "both/and" funding strategies.

PROBLEM: Too many funders still funding "universal" or generic programs, which usually are not effective grants.
SOLUTION: See chapters 1, 3, and 5: funders need more nuanced knowledge of deep diversity and gender in all its complexity; so-called "universal" programs and organizations must learn to serve women and girls more effectively. Philanthropy has to do "due diligence" and recognize the implications and benefits of how and where its dollars are spent.

PROBLEM: Too many funders avoid issues of poverty, violence, and other deep-rooted social ills altogether.
SOLUTION: See chapters 3 and 7, especially HIP, FLAG, and LAUF.

PROBLEM: Too many funders still respond to victims' needs in the short term.
SOLUTION: See chapter 3: core support and long-term grant making.

PROBLEM: Foundations miss opportunities to incorporate innovative thinking about gender into their larger portfolio of grant-making programs. Many still assume that women are a "special interest group," deserving some (but not substantial) resources.
SOLUTION: See chapter 6: model international funding strategies.

PROBLEM: Some advocates for women and girls are stuck in decades-old "victim" demands that seek equity, a "fair share" of the grantmaking pie for "women's issues."
SOLUTION: See chapters 1 and 4: funders need to help sustain deep-diversity organizations, recognizing that *all* issues are women's issues. Understanding gender is a key factor in successful deep democracy and effective philanthropy.

Best Practices and Roadblocks

Another important theme that emerged in the research for this book, in retrospect, is not surprising. As philanthropy has become increasingly professionalized over the last several decades, an increasing need has arisen for foundations to become more effective: strategic and innovative, working within current realities while at the same time aiming to improve both their own and their grantees' accountability and practice. In 1997, Grantmakers for Effective Organizations (GEO) formed as an affinity group of the Council on Foundations to address many of these concerns in foundations themselves, among grantees, and within the larger profession of philanthropy. Michael Porter and Mark Kramer, who founded the Center for Effective Philanthropy in 1999, describe strategic ways foundations can think more systematically about their philanthropic work and how to measure the effectiveness of their funding initiatives.[13]

There is also a growing literature about "learning organizations" that a number of philanthropic and nonprofit leaders interviewed for this book have found helpful in assessing their institutions' organizational cultures. As we describe in chapters 1 and 2, the fundamentals of "learning organizations" are common sense and have been around for a long time. But the concept took off in 1990 with Peter Senge's book, *The Fifth Discipline: The Art and Practice of the Learning Organization,* which launched wideranging literature on the subject as well as the Society for Organizational Learning, a separate nonprofit that started out as the Center for Organizational Learning at MIT's Sloan School of Management. As Senge defines it, a learning organization is one in which "people continually expand their capacity to create the results they truly desire, where new and expansive patterns of thinking are nurtured, where collective aspiration is set free, and where people are continually learning how to learn together."[14] The organizational learning literature concentrates largely on systems thinking, values, dialogue, and feedback, and also stresses openness and shared vision.

As helpful as these resources are, however, neither Senge's "learning organizations" nor Porter and Kramer's "effective philanthropy" strategies have yet to link the dynamic thinking that informs their analyses of effective organizations with the creative insights and thinking involved in deep diversity, gendered cultural competence, and Norm knowledge. Too often, sophisticated quantitative metrics used to track *best* practices offer little more than strategies for measuring *common* practices. To get to best practices, foundations need to look at a broad range of indicators that include assessing how "deep" their diversity goes and how effectively their organizations dismantle Norm and what Senge calls "mental models," as well as more quantifiable measures like positioning and impact. As Porter and Kramer say about one of the foundations they are assessing, they have "done much good, but . . . could do even better."[15]

To cite just two examples, Porter and Kramer talk about the importance of foundations' central role in leading social progress and thinking strategically about creating social value, especially in times of diminishing resources. If foundations miss deep diversity and Norm knowledge, however—if they do not have in their boardrooms or on senior staff people like those they are funding and lack the benefit of diverse perspectives engrained into their organizations—these "shallow diversity" foundations do long-term thinking and goal setting that are seldom strategic or effective. They lack the capacity to define the broadest range of problems they are attempting to solve. This "shallow diversity thinking" is the equivalent of doing cancer research without looking at patients' genetic history. Even the most basic way Porter and Kramer describe foundations' creating value—selecting the best grantees—does not happen if foundations overlook deep diversity. As described in detail in chapter 7, the philanthropists that eventually formed Los Angeles Urban Funders talked about their initial failure to address root causes of problems they were trying to solve because foundation collaboration had failed to include the experiences of people and organizations from the most affected neighborhoods.[16]

Fortunately, new models are developing that document the beneficial learning that takes place when organizations practice deep diversity, when employees are encouraged to tap their differences for creative ideas and to make explicit use of their cultural experiences at work. Researching efforts at the Ford Foundation to increase diversity understanding among the foundation's program officers, for instance, David Thomas and Robin Ely in the mid-nineties developed paradigms for talking about, increasing, and institutionalizing a more complex understanding of diversity in organizations.[17] In analyzing effective philanthropic practice, we use Thomas and Ely's "learning and effectiveness paradigm" in chapters 1 and 2 to highlight essential links between and among deep diversity, gendered cultural competence, institutional quality, and effectiveness. We show that organizations succeed when they incorporate the best ideas and energies of all stakeholders into their institutions. Chapter 3, "Capitalizing on Deep Diversity," highlights how deep diversity strengthens effective philanthropic practice for six foundations.

Gendered Cultural Competence

Another aim of this book is to provide sufficiently broad frames of reference so that both funders and fundraisers—as well as organizational resource people in other sectors—can think creatively about issues of effectiveness that incorporate and transcend gender. As we noted earlier, "cultural competence" is a term used to describe the ability of individuals and organizations to work effectively with culturally diverse populations. "Gendered cultural competence" emphasizes the importance of making sure gender is consciously included in the concept. Using a "gender lens" is no guarantee of gendered cultural competence *or* effective philanthropy. Nor does it guide an institution towards more effective management.[18] On the other hand, *not* using at least trifocals—a gender lens, a race/ethnicity lens, a class lens—makes effective philanthropy that much harder, if not altogether unlikely. A gender lens, a race/ethnicity lens, a class lens, and other appropriate tools like a disability screen—all these are tools of deep diversity that help us better understand the impact funding initiatives have on the population groups we seek to help.

Many foundations' mission statements and funding guidelines describe commendable ambitions to change society, to have direct benefit and visible impact, and to ameliorate economic and social injustices. But compelling evidence suggests that for these ambitions to succeed, funders must see the big picture and grapple with larger issues that have impact—often hidden but nonetheless profound—on those populations both funders and nonprofits seek to help. Put simply, both foundations and nonprofits have a choice of being stuck or being flexible. Especially because so many foundation program initiatives *are* aimed at economically disadvantaged groups, deep diversity and gendered cultural competence—or, as one foundation executive puts it, being "bi- or even tri-paradigmed"—are key to effective philanthropy.

While all these considerations are crucial, gender still is too often overlooked, dismissed as unimportant, or labeled "special interest funding." It defies logic to regard a majority of the population as a special interest group, and the documented needs of women and girls are seldom met if women and girls are considered mere add-ons to traditional philanthropic programs. Well-designed grants supporting the needs and strengths of women and girls both in this country and internationally are essential to effective philanthropy. The women's movement succeeded beyond the expectations, even the imaginations of many people. In our lifetime, women of all racial and ethnic backgrounds have had opportunities their grandmothers never dreamed possible. Indeed, white women now constitute close to a majority of philanthropic leadership. But in spite of middle- and upper-class women's many professional successes, gender-based discrimination is far from vanquished.

Deep diversity in our philanthropic organizations is essential if we are to help build stronger communities and a stronger, "deeper" democracy. As we describe in chapter 6, the awareness that women's rights *are* human rights, a standard assumption in at least some international venues, is key to building thriving, healthy economies and to improving philanthropic effectiveness. Understanding how gender, race, ethnicity, disability, and culture are defining factors in poverty, labor force participation, wage disparities, access to capital, child care, aging, health, and politics—as well as in the development of healthy organizations that practice deep diversity—all of this knowledge is essential for effective philanthropy.

Straddling the "Giving Desk"

In the course of conducting our research for this book, we were struck by the extent to which philanthropic and nonprofit perspectives mirror each other. Among the foundation and nonprofit executives and trustees interviewed for this book, there is little disagreement about what constitutes effective philanthropy, what works to produce high-quality programs and strategic funding initiatives, and what is needed to make the independent sector work better. But many nonprofit leaders and some foundation executives we spoke with talk about a roadblock to effective philanthropy that at least some foundation executives have a hard time naming. Those who do talk about it understand what the process looks like from both sides of the giving desk, which is too often a clunky piece of furniture that divides the sector and gets in the way of effective philanthropy and the health of nonprofit organizations, both the organizations that are funded and those that are not. Understanding deep diversity and democratization of philanthropy helps a foundation call the movers to get rid of that clunky piece of furniture.

Shortly after taking a program officer's position in a large foundation, a former nonprofit executive told her husband, "Wow, I've gotten so much smarter. Contentious old pals who are now potential grantees nod enthusiastically at everything I say." One roadblock that surfaced in our research is this elephant on the table, the too often unmentionable power imbalance between funders and grantees. Another aim of this book is to find ways to write thoughtfully about that divide from both sides of the giving desk. In spite of innovative strategic programming on the part of various organizational meeting grounds between funders and grantees, like Independent Sector, and regional associations of grant makers and nonprofits, this so-called power differential emerged in our research as one of several major roadblocks to more effective philanthropy. And responsibility lies on both sides of the desk. Many nonprofits are not able or willing to risk honest feedback to their funders or seek their considerable expertise and partnerships in shaping mutually advantageous programs. Many funders, stuck too long in staff or board jobs, are not able to share power, acknowledge grantees as peers, or join with them as partners to build stronger programs and funding initiatives.

The reality is that both the philanthropic and nonprofit communities are filled with vibrant, creative people working long hours to do important and often unheralded work. A major goal of this book is to highlight some of that good work and provide thoughtful analyses and resources that will enable us all to do our work better. We intend the ideas presented in this book to be part of an ongoing conversation. Our interpretations—even though informed by a wide range of research and individual perspectives and experiences—are far from the last word on any of these subjects. These analyses and resources are offered as food for thought—and some new thinking and new language, we hope—for what has been a divisive, often contentious subject. Our expectation is that others will join this conversation and help point the way to still more exciting opportunities for effective philanthropy.

1

What Is Effective Philanthropy?

Effective Philanthropy: A Growing, Sector-Wide Focus

In 1997, The David and Lucile Packard Foundation organized a breakfast roundtable discussion at that year's Council on Foundations meeting in Hawaii to talk about how to help strengthen grantees. The sponsors quickly found themselves scrambling to add double the number of tables set for breakfast. Many of the funders who showed up had reached similar conclusions about the importance of helping their grantees function more effectively. They were struggling—on their own or in collaboration with other funders and sometimes with grantees—to articulate broader roles for themselves. They were looking for ways to strengthen grantee organizations by helping with long-range planning and more effective staffing, management, and governance practices. At least some of the funders attending that first breakfast also wanted to get a grip on outcomes and were especially interested in measuring the impact of funded projects, essentially by assessing how well grantees spent foundation dollars. In short, grant makers were—and are—becoming increasingly aware that, in addition to writing checks, they have significant roles to play in supporting the effectiveness of nonprofit organizations.[1]

Representatives from The James Irvine Foundation, The Ewing Marion Kauffman Foundation, and The David and Lucile Packard Foundation, among other funders attending that first roundtable, gave themselves a name and constituted themselves as Grantmakers for Effective Organizations (GEO), an affinity group of the Council on Foundations that by 2002 had merged with the Grantmakers Evaluation Network. By 2004, the expanded organization included over 500 institutional members. Although early emphasis in the organization was on helping grantees, GEO members soon began expanding the definitions of their work to include more assessment of foundations' *own* institutional effectiveness. In GEO's 2003 theory of change, the board decided officially to broaden its focus to include foundation effectiveness along with nonprofit effectiveness as part of its mission and commitment to influence the sector at large.[2]

Foundation effectiveness has a current and central role to play in how the philanthropic sector is thinking about itself. GEO's 2003 *Baseline Membership Survey* describes its organizational goals as "understanding, promoting, and supporting the optimal functioning of community-based and philanthropic organizations so that in partnership they may effectively achieve important social missions."[3] The survey reports that most grant making members of GEO are engaged in supporting grantees' organizational effectiveness and capacity-building activities, and there is a clear assumption that "increased capacity leads to increased levels of effectiveness."[4]

Nine out of ten GEO members support capacity building among their grantees with a range of initiatives, including operational support grants, direct in-kind assistance to grantees through foundation staff, services of management-assistance organizations, capital financing, and venture grants as well as direct grants to researchers and educators. Specific types of capacity building supported by GEO members include (in order of frequency): strategic planning, evaluation, collaboration efforts, staff development and training, board development, technology and information systems, leadership development, fund development, marketing and communications, financial systems, program replication, program design and development, human resources management and training, and social entrepreneurship ventures. GEO member organizations' efforts to improve their *own* internal effectiveness include:

• Redesigning grant making to include organizational effectiveness or adding capacity-building funding

• Adjusting program goals

• Adjusting staff/board roles and strengthening leadership and other skills

• Enhancing internal operations by improving processes, structures or systems

• Developing methods for increasing grantee effectiveness and feedback to funders[5]

As useful as these strategies are, however, the GEO survey reports that "these results also reveal that there is an opportunity to increase members' own internal effectiveness efforts, as well as a need to develop a common definition, or set of standards, for effectiveness."[6] GEO is attempting to model a "causal chain," with links between specific philanthropic activities and "outputs, outcomes, and impacts."[7]

As philanthropy has become increasingly professionalized over the last several decades, GEO is one of the better-organized manifestations of an increasing need funders have articulated to become more effective: strategic and innovative, working within current realities while at the same time aiming to improve their own as well as their grantees' practices and accountability. This is the conversation we hope to join with this book. We are writing this book to articulate an understanding of organizational change and capacity building that fits into the "effective organization" discussions and research already taking place in the sector, with two significant additions: enhancing foundations' understanding of "deep diversity" and enhancing foundations' understanding of how organizational norms and cultures profoundly affect how they do their work.

As defined in the introduction, throughout our book we use the term "deep diversity" to describe an institutionalized understanding of diversity that goes both *wide* and *deep*.

• *Wide* to include the breadth and web of differences that weave through most modern organizations: gender, sexual orientation, gender identity,[8] race, ethnicity, nationality, religion, class, disability, geography, age, and other socially, culturally, and economically defined differences that categorize groups of individuals

• *Deep* into an organization's DNA, or to use another metaphor, deep into the taproot of an organization and intertwined in the wide network of roots that anchors and feeds the whole of an organization's culture

Robert Long, vice president of programs for the W. K. Kellogg Foundation, is quoted in *Agile Philanthropy,* a 2003 review of ongoing research on effective philanthropy: "We think that foundations would be a lot more effective if they were more open and committed to the integration of the differences and richness among us [youth, women, people of color, social entrepreneurs, and corporate social innovators] into how they organize, operate, and so on."[9] Our research confirms Long's impressions: when foundations institutionalize deep diversity, they become more effective institutions and, arguably, they do more effective philanthropy. This connection between deep diversity and effectiveness, however, is not a widely held assumption. In fact, aside from Long's thoughtful quote, there were no other mentions of gender or diversity in any form relative to effective philanthropy that surfaced in the thirty-six interviews conducted for this otherwise useful and important report. As one of the coauthors of the study noted, "That *could* be data in itself."[10]

This book adds to the sector's ongoing conversation on effective philanthropy by pushing us to stretch the common understandings of effective philanthropy and provides evidence that the "causal chain" that GEO seeks to identify includes institutionalized deep diversity as part of effective philanthropy. As figure I.1 in the introduction outlines, our research found many components similar to those identified by GEO organizations and others in *Agile Philanthropy* (most notably foundations' commitment to capacity building and long-term relationships with grantees). But respondents in our research also stressed the importance of stretching the definition of effective philanthropy to include informed innovation, risk taking, and collaboration with other funders and grantees; philanthropy that fosters "learning organization" institutional cultures as well as transparency, accountability, and evaluation in both foundations' own organizations and their grantee organizations; and *last but far from least,* philanthropy that understands and practices deep diversity and Norm knowledge.

As this book documents, without a fundamental understanding of deep diversity, foundations seldom achieve effectiveness. Deep diversity requires more than simply hiring a diverse staff or holding a few sensitivity sessions or making one or two grants to nonprofits that work with diverse constituents. *When foundations have not struggled to understand and institutionalize deep diversity in their own organizational cultures, they are "shallow diversity funders." And "shallow diversity funders" are seldom effective, no matter what fancy metrics and output measurements they use.*

Understanding and institutionalizing deep diversity, however, is not in and of itself sufficient. Theories of effective philanthropy also must account for how organizations function *qua* organizations—how organizational cultures evolve, how organizations tend to perpetuate themselves, how organizations change, and who gets to change them.[11] Without this kind of Norm knowledge, foundations or any organizations—nonprofits, business, government bureaucracies—are seldom effective. To use popular organizational-development language, effective foundations are those that strive to be "learning organizations," especially learning organizations that use diverse people and perspectives as assets. Results of our research also point to this larger picture of institutional innovation as one of the most useful insights for understanding how effective foundations do their best work.

The fundamentals of learning organizations have been around for a long time and add up, for the most part, to common sense. But the concept took off in 1990 with Peter Senge's book, *The Fifth Discipline: The Art and Practice of the Learning Organization,* which launched a wide-ranging literature on the subject as well as an institute, the Center for Organizational Learning, that in 1997 became the free-standing nonprofit, The Society for Organizational Learning.[12] As Senge defines it, a learning organization is one in which "people continually expand their capacity to create the results they truly desire, where new and expansive patterns of thinking are nurtured, where collective aspiration is set free, and where people are continually learning how to learn together."[13] If organizations are flexible, increased productivity can result. If foundations listen openly to grantees, learn from them, listen and ask hard questions of other stakeholders, innovation is possible. If foundations learn to avoid cultural and racial stereotypes—especially those hidden, embedded, and harder to root out—their own institutional cultures becomes more vital, and staff has the freedom to be increasingly more effective. The literature offers case studies and often helpful insights about how learning organizations evolve.[14]

The people we interviewed in our research, however—many of whom have run or have been part of healthy institutions—find it hard to say with assurance just how learning organizations evolve. Is it board leadership, staff leadership, a carefully tended institutional culture, all of the above? One administrator noted that, in his experience, we understand less, far less, about institutional DNA than we now know about the human genome: "Way more complex, way more elusive to pin down. We're still in the dark ages of understanding what makes organizations healthy and keeps them healthy." But that doesn't mean pessimism. The reality is that creating learning organizations is as much an art as it is a systematic science, and the process boils down to some fundamental choices. Another thoughtful observer of the philanthropic scene notes: "It's fundamentally simple: either you're stuck or you're flexible."

As we document in chapter 2, perspectives of organizational culture, management, and change have a lot to offer foundations trying to improve their overall effectiveness. Our interview respondents echo common denominators of the organizational research literature when they talk about common features of healthy organizations: free flow of ideas; knowledge of and respect for differences, comfort with ambiguity and "not knowing," and Norm knowledge's continual reassessment of unspoken assumptions and "normative thinking." Normative thinking is thinking that, often unconsciously, rests on conventional and frequently stereotyped notions about both people and values. *It is Norm knowledge that we hope to interject into the ongoing discussions about effective philanthropy.*

Learning Organizations Think "Outside the Boxes"

Normative thinking is all too often "*not* thinking." Management literature frequently uses metaphors like "thinking outside the box." The image needs to be "thinking outside the box*es*." Humans, all of us, think in boxes, paradigms, frameworks, and mental models—categories of analysis and assumptions that we use to organize the worlds we live in. That's one of the cognitive skills that makes us human. But these boxes all too often are "nested," boxes inside boxes inside boxes. Or, to use another image, Russian dolls, those beautifully carved and painted wooden dolls, each one smaller than the other, nesting sometimes five or six dolls each inside the other.[15] Children often experience both delight and disappointment when they get to the smallest doll—disappointment that there are no more dolls to play with, delight that they can be stacked back together, that they fit so neatly inside each other. When we are trying to get to the bottom of our assumptions, it's disheartening to come up with still another doll, carved and painted just like the first one we twisted open. We can stack them back together again, but they're still the same, just bigger.

As we describe in more detail in chapter 2, it's hard for organizations, perhaps especially hard for foundations, to talk about assumed norms and other seemingly immutable definitions. They are so unthinkingly normal, taken for granted. And pressure on us to challenge them feels destructive, phony, or invasive. ("These ideas are *mine,* part of who I am in the world.") And when someone challenges us about cultural assumptions, one of our first reactions is to be defensive: "But *I'm* not a bad person. *I* don't discriminate." To talk about foundations and nonprofits as effective learning organizations is not to talk about freeing organizations from outright discrimination. Most foundations and nonprofits in recent years have struggled to confront racism and sexism within their own institutional cultures and have evolved beyond any practice that could be labeled blatant discrimination. So this analysis is not about discrimination. It *is* about not thinking clearly, or at least as clearly as we need to be thinking in order to do effective philanthropy. It's about challenging long-held assumptions: what constitutes responsible philanthropic decision making, who gets to sit at the table or "giving desk" where funding decisions are made. Who gets heard? Who listens?

Learning organizations have long discovered that thinking outside the boxes is exciting, not destructive; exhilarating, not punitive. *The alternative to challenging the familiar does not have to be a feared unknown.* Especially when confronting the kinds of difficult social and economic challenges that so many foundations and nonprofits work to ameliorate, new insights, new perspectives, and new thinking can be a source of help. Many foundations now have diverse workforces, but most have not tapped their diverse staff's full potential to assist in new thinking. Organizations that have learned these realities, however—organizations that have figured out how to incorporate continually new thinking on old problems—are often the most effective. As chapter 4 in this book describes, a both/and approach to funding women and girls is optimal—both "universal" funding and initiatives designed specifically for women and girls. But for either universal or targeted funding strategies to work, our research documents the importance of thinking creatively within and about our institutions, about the people who work in them, and about the people and communities we serve.

Diversity: An Essential Resource for Learning Organizations

David Thomas and Robin Ely, two members of the Harvard Business School faculty, have developed new ways of thinking creatively about institutions that are as relevant for foundations as they are for corporations. In a 1996 article entitled "Making Differences Matter: A New Paradigm for Managing Diversity," Thomas and Ely show how the best thinking on diversity produces the most effective organizations.[16] Thomas and Ely describe three alternative paradigms that can inform organizational thinking about diversity, but as they describe it, only the third paradigm fully embraces diversity in ways that make it an asset for the institution. The first paradigm—discrimination and fairness—focuses on the fact that discrimination is wrong: diversity is a response to that injustice. Historically, most foundations and nonprofits have embraced the idea that they should not discriminate in their hiring practices or program activities. Foundations that have diversified both their staffs and their grant making may be proud of the fact that they don't discriminate, but when the only rationale for diversity is justice or fairness, little changes in the organizational culture. Staff members in these foundations, typically expected to follow norms of behavior, are most likely to make universal grants that downplay cultural and other differences. The organization's diversity focus is on recruitment and retention, helping newcomers fit in to the existing organizational culture. Too often gender-blind and color-blind conformism become the implicit goal. An example of the first paradigm is the U.S. Army.

Ely and Thomas' second paradigm—access and legitimacy—exists in organizations that celebrate differences but then marginalize people who are different by failing to integrate people's strengths fully into the institution's culture. White women and women and men of color are hired in "second paradigm" foundations and nonprofits because of their special knowledge about diverse populations, but they then are pigeonholed into grant-making programs for those populations. This paradigm is a step forward from the first because it acknowledges that diversity is an asset. But because it marginalizes the very diversity it has attracted, it is too limited. In "second paradigm" foundations and nonprofits, there is little recognition that *all* the activities of the organization could benefit from the ideas and actions of a diverse staff that fits into the larger organizational culture.

Thomas and Ely's third paradigm—learning and effectiveness—links diversity to organizational learning and shows the benefits of an organization tapping into diverse points of view for creative ideas. It no longer makes historical sense to justify diversity "just" because of blatant discrimination. Organizations who think reflectively about themselves nip most blatant discrimination immediately when they spot it. But even that kind of thoughtful vigilance misses the mark. A diverse workforce is more than a reality that has to be "managed": it can be a positive force for increasing organizational effectiveness. Benefits can include new learning, creativity, flexibility, organizational and individual growth, and increased ability for the organizations to adjust to changing environments. A diverse workforce embodies different ideas about how to design processes, reach goals, frame tasks, create effective teams, communicate ideas, and lead. And members of diverse groups can challenge those unspoken assumptions—normative thinking—about an organization's functions, strategies, operations, practices, and procedures. This is not always comfortable, but the benefits of learning to stretch, challenge, and deepen institutional cultures far outweigh the temporary discomforts. Only when organizations start thinking about diversity as renewable assets—assets that provide fresh and meaningful approaches to work—do they reap the full rewards of diversity.

Gender and Organizational Effectiveness

Gender is at the center of the institutional shifts in thinking that Thomas and Ely describe as most effective. And gender must be understood in all its diversity, within cultures of different communities, for men as well as for women. *Gender* is a term that theorists in the last several decades have refined to talk about socially constructed traits that often masquerade as immutable biological differences. Gender is about men, just as race is about being "white." Along with skin color, gender is one of the most fundamental ways cultures around the world differentiate people.[17]

Throughout this book, we use examples of the social construction of gender to document how Norm undermines innovation and effectiveness. Gender is the scalpel we use to cut away the complexities of organizational norms. Or to frame the issue with another metaphor, without a better understanding of organizational norms and deep diversity that includes gender, trying to understand and measure how organizations are or are not effective is like researching skin cancer without looking at the immune system or investigating family medical histories. Our ambition in this book is to provide readers with an understanding of gender—especially an understanding of gender in the context of deep diversity—that is sufficient to unlock organizational norms that impede effectiveness: those formal, informal, and unconscious ways difference is locked in or (better said) locked OUT of organizational structures and cultures. Framed more positively, we aim to offer insight into how understanding gender enhances and strengthens innovation and effectiveness, especially gender framed within deep diversity, the complex textures of people's lives and cultures *and* the cultures of their organizations.

Effective Organizations Cultivate Wide-Ranging Gender Knowledge

What's the first thing most people ask about when a baby is born? Gender is one of the most familiar ways families, communities, and societies distinguish people from one another. For better or for worse, most of humanity names, divides up, classifies, or characterizes people as males or females, men or women, boys or girls. Perhaps because being male or female is so basic, so "normal," so native to our personal landscapes, gender is often "just there." Especially when people live out the gender identities assigned to them at birth—when they act like "normal" men or "normal" women—gender often manifests itself as a buzz in the background, people wearing red dresses or gray suits, head scarves or yarmulkes: casually noticed but assumed and taken for granted so long as men don't wear red dresses or women pray in the front row of an Orthodox synagogue. Gender is as "normal" as mom and apple pie.

But as we describe throughout this book, gender and the impact of being male or female—especially "not quite" male or "not quite" female— is also a reality of people's lives, a complex reality that has significant impact on men's and women's social and economic lives as well as on their civil and human rights. The point here is that "normal" gender behavior easily can be overlooked and not accounted for—much less subtly analyzed or institutionalized as deep diversity. Not accounting for gender and how gender impacts so many dimensions of our lives creates significant loss of vision. Throughout this book, we use examples of gender to document how this not-seen "normal"—"Norm" as described in the introduction—undermines effective philanthropy. And how understanding gender enhances and strengthens organizational innovation, especially gender framed within deep diversity. Effective philanthropy requires new thinking about diversity. Funding "Norm" doesn't effectively fund "Norma"—or anyone else, for that matter. But the philanthropic practices that most benefit women and girls are the same practices that strengthen philanthropy generally and make for effective philanthropy.

This brief story illustrates the problem. The events are all true, but names and other details have been changed both to provide anonymity and to strengthen the narrative.

An "Ah Ha" Moment

Several years ago the white male CEO of Andrews Foundation, Dr. Martin O'Malley, was at a gathering of foundation executives and board members in a large midwestern city. He struck up a conversation with Samantha Rivers, board chair of the Maxwell Fund, a well-respected regional foundation known for thinking in sophisticated ways about how to do effective community-based grant making. Rivers was excited about a new approach her foundation was taking in community development: identifying and investing in emerging local leadership in a multiracial neighborhood that was home to many newcomers to America, among others Vietnamese, Brazilians, Haitians, and Dominicans. The Maxwell Fund's approach, Rivers proudly described, was most likely to succeed because the foundation had designed its initiative to mobilize the community's resources to address its own problems.

O'Malley had recently returned from his own foundation's biannual board retreat where two outside facilitators had walked the foundation through diversity training, and he was curious about how some of what he'd learned played out in other foundations, especially a foundation like the Maxwell Fund that had such a well-known local reputation for "doing diversity" effectively. So when he heard Rivers describing the new Maxwell community-development leadership initiative, he asked her what had worked in identifying women leaders from the various ethnic groups in the community the foundation was targeting.

There was a long pause in what had previously been a highly animated and rapid-fire conversation. Rivers was embarrassed when she replied, "We have no strategy. In fact, I'm not sure we identified any women. Even worse, until you just asked me the question, I hadn't even noticed that all of the emerging leaders we funded are men." There was another long pause while O'Malley looked at her in some curiosity. "Wow," she went on, "I just can't believe our oversight."

Oversight? Or something else? This story easily could be dismissed as an anomaly, but unfortunately it isn't. More likely, it's Norm at work, a blind spot—a failure, even on the part of a woman board chair, to see that women made up a significant portion of available community workers and had the potential to make important, unique contributions to the initiative's leadership. Once Rivers stopped to think, however, she immediately recognized the absurdity of trying to put into place an effective leadership development strategy without women. As O'Malley and Rivers talked further,

Rivers also realized that her foundation might need to go back to the drawing board to develop different strategies for identifying women who were the backbone of their community. Why hadn't that need been factored into the project's planning? There were senior women on both the board and staff of the Maxwell Fund, even the board chair was a woman, but no one had put the issue on the table; no one was thinking about the needs and contributions of women.

Besides fairness, why should it matter? Without identifying who actually was doing the work in the community, the project would have been dead in the water. While the leaders of all but one of the local community organizations were men, most of the people who kept the neighborhood groups working together were middle-aged and older Vietnamese, Brazilian, Haitian, and Dominican women, a core of whom had gotten to know each other through several small business collaboratives launched three years earlier by a local women's foundation. After seeing around her blind spot—what she later described as a "smack me upside the head, why didn't I think of that" moment—board chair Rivers and the rest of the Maxwell Fund were able to tailor several new successful funding initiatives that reached deep into the community and helped the local community-based organizations strengthen themselves with a broader mix of activists, both male and female, able to work more effectively across racial and ethnic neighborhood boundaries. Men had been seen as leaders and had exhibited what the foundation had defined as "leadership characteristics"; women for the most part had been invisible. Their relational skills in weaving the community together had not been credited as "leadership skills," so the foundation's definitions of leadership also had to change.

Understanding Gender: A Research Summary

Why is gender so invisible yet so pervasive? And just what *is* gender? "It's a boy" or "it's a girl" is one of the first things we say about any newborn baby. But once that basic biological fact is pronounced, virtually everything else is socially constructed. One superficial but telling example of how gender (and color) traits are *not* immutable comes from an exhibit at the Smithsonian's Museum of American History, "Who Wears the Pants?" A 1918 Infants Department description asserted, "There has been a great diversity of opinion on the subject, but the generally accepted rule is pink for the boy and blue for the girl. The reason [is] that pink being a more decided and stronger color is more suitable for the boy; while blue, which is more delicate and dainty is prettier for the girl."[18] This seemingly trivial example helps illustrate the fact that what we take for granted with respect to gender is more likely a product of a given moment in history and a given society.

Understanding gender means understanding how every culture's assumptions about male and female characteristics are slippery and pervasive, and how those assumptions skew our thinking. The bottom line for effective philanthropy, as chapter 2 describes in greater detail, is that ignoring these social and *not* innate constructions of gender means not understanding the different impacts a given problem or solution can have on people of different genders. Understanding gender in the broadest possible context is key for understanding how problems evolve within communities and how organizations can address them more effectively. Women and men, girls and boys all lead diminished lives because of societies' constructions of gender and failure to see the far-reaching implications of distorted gender knowledge that hampers both individuals and organizations. As described in chapter 3's case studies and chapter 5's analysis of youth organizations, effective funders and nonprofits that have done considerable amounts of clear thinking about gender—in effect, learning to take apart and think outside those not-immutable boxes and nested Russian dolls—produce the most effective results.

This section summarizes basic assumptions growing from a wide-ranging body of research on gender and sexuality. Two key findings to emerge from this research are, on the one hand, *a lack of inherent differences between women and men* beyond the obvious and, on the other hand, *the pervasiveness and subtlety of mostly unchallenged, culturally created differences widely and wrongly assumed to be innate.* The third and most important finding of all is that *these culturally created differences serve to create, reinforce, and institutionalize hierarchies in which men, as a group, have more power than women as a group.* Gender, in short, is about power relations.

Obviously these are oversimplifications, but chapter 2 talks more about how these power relations play out in the often-invisible structures of organizations themselves. And these power relations are also relative to people's positions within organizations: in traditional hierarchies, those who hold leadership positions, women and men, more often than not hold the reins of power. And as the case of the Maxwell Fund shows, those who hold the reins of power sometimes miss considerable talent because their blind spots hide potential leaders. The rest of this chapter, however, explains how current research seeks to "deconstruct" gender, to take it apart on the operating table so we get a better glimpse into how it works, most of the time in spite of ourselves.

Reviewing this literature suggests why many foundation staff members and nonprofit executives are confused about how they should think about gender when they design programs. When foundation and nonprofit staff hear about research that shows few inherent differences between women and men, they readily conclude a "one-size-fits-all" approach to program design will work effectively. Only when they grapple with research documenting gender socialization do they have the information they need to design effective programs. The reality is that women and men are *not* significantly different from each other in ability. In virtually every study on gender differences, "within-gender variation is greater than differences between men and women taken as groups."[19] Put simply, the differences among women, or the differences among men, are greater than the differences *between* women and men.

So if there are virtually no differences in ability, then gender doesn't matter, right? Wrong. Despite the lack of documented differences in innate ability, profound differences in power often exist. In every country in the world, men make more money, hold more and usually higher political offices, and have greater control over public and private resources. So while gender is a social construct, it has a major impact on people's social and economic lives. The so-called gender gap is narrowing in many countries, but nowhere has it been eliminated. One way this power imbalance is held in place is through the assignment of social roles and expectations: who are "seen as" potential leaders and who are not, as we saw in the Maxwell case. These are more or less rigid "rules" about how women and men are expected to behave and what opportunities those expectations allow—or do not allow. The research *does* show differences in skills that develop out of inequities in opportunity and experience for women and girls compared to men and boys. Boy soccer-players, for example, are encouraged to play soccer games (on average) two years longer than girls. Why? The greater science proficiency in boys compared to girls is generally attributed to the fact that more boys than girls enroll in physics, chemistry, and advanced math courses and have more experience with science through informal contexts—not differences in innate abilities. Why is it more socially "acceptable" for boys to play soccer into their teens and learn more math and science? Why not girls?

Assumptions and expectations about gender differences have powerful effects on how women and men behave. Gender expectations, especially within race and other culturally defined group characteristics like disability, are lumped together in a set of normative ideas about appropriate behavior and appropriate "roles" and competencies. These assumptions—both sociocultural and psychological—shape, pattern, and evaluate "appropriate" behavior. They create a prism through which behavior not only is evaluated but also is controlled. Most traditional assumptions of gender behavior expect men to occupy the public sector of society, the world of work and politics, and women to inhabit the private sector, holding together families and communities. Even though this delegation of roles is evolving, the primary way men are accorded power over women is to be viewed as the "dominant" gender in the public sector. And one way women are seen as less powerful is to be relegated to family or "caring" work. In most societies, in spite of lip service to equality and political agendas promoting "family values," this caretaking is in fact valued less both literally and figuratively, with disparities in pay and disparities in prestige. Even as women have entered the workplace in unprecedented numbers, they still earn less than men. And even as men are paying more attention to family responsibilities, as a group they take much less responsibility for family and community affairs.

And at least on some levels of unconscious assumptions, maleness still equates with "superior." For example, some research has documented that little boys, by the time they are no more than three years old, know that playing with girls' toys or doing "girl things" equates to lower status, not as important or as much fun as boys' activities and toys. Virginia Valian, in a 1997 book called *Why So Slow? The Advancement of Women,* synthesized over twenty years of social psychology research on what she calls a "drip, drip" theory of discrimination: small slights and biases accumulate over time to the great disadvantage of girls and women. The book explains in painful detail how subtle, how pervasive, and how early in the lives of children these perceptual biases and subsequent discriminations take root in our lives and in our institutions.[20]

These biases are prescriptive and inhibiting—and they are *not* a reflection of inherent biological differences. They exist apart from any inherent capability within an *individual* male or female or even within *groups* of males and females. Assumptions about gender also can override objective reality about actual differences in ability based on gender. As researcher Valerie Walkerdine succinctly puts it, "Femininity and masculinity are powerful fictions imbued with fantasy lived as fact."[21] Societal expectations—assumptions transmitted by family, friends, playmates, employers, the media, religious beliefs, and larger society—can predict and even dictate behavior. Literally, what we think girls and women can and "should" do and what we think men and boys can and "should" do more often than not determines how men and women, boys and girls actually behave or perform. And while these pervasive and often unexamined expectations affect and diminish opportunities for both men and for women, they more often *disadvantage* women. Too many women and girls still are socialized for and restricted to subordinate options, roles, and rewards. Gender expectations also limit and restrict men to narrow definitions of masculinity. Although men face negative sanctions when they defy gender prescriptions, women, especially women of color, face a double bind that most men do not. When women behave according to societal norms and agree to occupy a subordinate role, they receive the most rewards from society, especially if they marry; if they defy those norms, they are criticized and ridiculed for not being "feminine." While men also bear personal and psychological costs associated with their gender limits, when they conform to male norms of competence, they are typically rewarded more than women—socially, economically, and politically as well as personally.

These differences sometimes are subtle, and they sometimes are hard to distinguish from other job-related issues in context, but they have significant implications. Consider, for example, the real experiences that transgender and transsexual men and women shared with colleagues working at a Fortune 50 company. The following are their email exchanges. Edited to assure anonymity, they document the extent to which gender roles are arbitrary, not inevitable. But they also show the consequences of being male or female, one consequence being that each gender is judged by a different yardstick.

From: Allison Ready
Sent: Friday, January 24, 2003 11:19 AM
To: MacKenzie LGBT Listserv
Subject: Gender Benders

I have some interesting observations this year from my performance review. . . . A few years ago, I was an aggressive, confrontational, stressed-out guy engineer. My areas for development were always mostly focused on technical stuff. Then I began my transition from male to female and became way more relaxed. My supervisors that first year said I was much more pleasant to work with, less confrontational, and more willing to accept others' opinions and ideas. Now this is my first full year as a female employee, and my performance review has mostly focused on personality stuff: the need to make small talk, be more thick-skinned, not take things so personally, not be so intimidating. It blows my mind because I am light years more personable than I was in a guy's role. So I am wondering if this is common for females. Do people focus more on how you behave, how much you smile? It may just be a reflection of my shift into a management role, so I certainly am not bent out of shape, just curious. But the irony is that I do have a pretty thick skin: after what I went through [making my transition from male to female], I think I am all thick skin and nothing else.

From: Martha Lewis
Sent: Friday, January 24, 2003 12:28 PM
To: MacKenzie LGBT Listserv
Subject: Gender Benders

That is such an interesting situation, Allison, you having been both sexes and now seeing such a difference in feedback! I believe that people's perceptions really play a role in how they view us. And I feel being female or male DEFINITELY impacts on-the-job feedback! I am sure if you confronted your supervisors with these concerns, they wouldn't know what the heck you were talking about because it is so subconscious. My own performance feedback in the past has been about the kinds of personal stuff that wouldn't have even come up if I had been a man, so I can vouch for your dilemma. It really is strange isn't it?

From: Elizabeth Martin
Sent: Friday, January 24, 2003 12:37 PM
To: MacKenzie LGBT Listserv
Subject: Gender Benders

I agree. I think this is a really interesting observation, although I also think that as we transition from individual technical staff to managers, the feedback changes along with the change in expectations/job description to be more how one interacts as opposed to how we are judged just for our technically driven output. But I used to manage a group of people that were all men. I received feedback that I was being "overly aggressive," and I always thought that feedback was very gender-biased: in my opinion, the men in my group were more aggressive and outspoken than I was, and I often found it very difficult to get a word in edgewise (very uncommon, if you know me at all). Anyway, I have to say that from my experiences, I do think there is a big difference in how men and women interact with each other and how we perceive other genders. The biggest compliment I ever got was when a co-worker was really frustrated with me and said, "You don't act like my mother!" In context, he meant that I wasn't acting like the other "women" he had known and worked with/spent a lot of time with. We joke about it sometimes now, but at the time, it did lead to some open discussion on gender perception. I agree with Allison. Being stuck in my paradigm, I would love to hear more from someone who has lived both sides of the gender fence.

From: Amelia Smith
Sent: Friday, January 24, 2003 12:52 PM
To: MacKenzie LGBT Listserv
Subject: Gender Benders

This is a VERY interesting discussion. Thanks for bringing it up, Allison. As a female who has played both technical and manager roles, I've also found that I received way more personality-based feedback as a manager than an individual technician. What I've found eye-opening as a manager is that when I managed a group of men outside of MacKenzie, I was very well-received. Inside MacKenzie I managed a group made up of all women, and it turned out to be REALLY difficult. I received TONS of feedback about relating to the team, criticizing me for micromanaging and the need to be less confrontational and so forth. It really surprised me, since I didn't get that kind of feedback when I was managing more senior men. I'm back in an individual technical position now, so I get more technical development feedback. I've also found that feedback obviously varies a lot from manager to manager and department to department.

From: Michael Polansky
Sent: Friday, January 24, 2003 2:53 PM
To: MacKenzie LGBT Listserv
Subject: Gender Benders

Hi everyone, first, heartfelt thanks to everyone for their thoughtful, articulate, and VERY enlightening inputs on this issue. If we have any female-to-male people on this list who have completed their gender transition (or are in transition and are now identifying as men), it would be very interesting to hear their perspectives on this. These issues should be part of the training for all managers starting next year.

From: Max Cerrilos
Sent: Saturday, January 25, 2003 3:35 PM
To: MacKenzie LGBT Listserv
Subject: Gender Benders

I can relate to all that has been said. As a female-to-male, before I transitioned, the descriptors I heard were "too aggressive" and "difficult to work with." Now that I have been living and working as male for the last couple of years, the descriptors have changed from "aggressive" to "assertive" (in a positive way) and from "difficult to work with" to "taking charge" and "having a proactive manner." A lot of perceptions do seem to be tied to a person's gender. Occasionally one male who's trying to "dominate" another male in the work place will label a male he can't dominate as "difficult to work with," or "inflexible," but for the most part those types of power plays I haven't seen very often.

From: Sarah Warner
Sent: Wednesday, January 29, 2003 4:09 PM
To: MacKenzie LGBT Listserv
Subject: Gender Benders

I've been following this discussion with interest also. Michael asked if there are ways we could incorporate some of the feedback here into job review training. We have already worked to include in review training some messages that touch on avoiding unconscious bias and how it can play out in focusing on behaviors rather than results. Unfortunately, unconscious is just that, unconscious. So maybe managers don't see themselves as guilty of these differences re: how they evaluate based on gender. We train, but they still can't see how they are doing this. I would also hate to assume that the people who posted are indicative of any kind of norm in MacKenzie job reviews. We have done some studies in specific business groups to see if there were any major differences in the qualitative feedback given men vs. women, and in those groups we did not see any conclusive data to say this was so. However, the anecdotal data continues to come up in many forums, with both men and women commenting on how their "style" is viewed in the context of job reviews feedback. I'm more than willing to entertain and forward on your suggestions about how these practices could be improved. The problem is, there are no sure ways to eliminate subjective evaluations completely. Nor to know whether feedback is a result of unconscious bias or a valid estimation of the employee's behavior. It may come down to the simple question of what definitions a person is using for a term like "assertive" or "team player." But as I said, if you can think of something more we can do, let me know. In the meantime, I will figure out some way to summarize these comments and feedback and share them with our diversity team.

Just these brief reflections on people's perceptions and judgments make more transparent how differently women and men are often judged, even when the behavior they exhibit is exactly the same. The experiences of the transgender employees are particularly telling because they have lived both genders and can name the "subconscious" assumptions that are made about each. The good news is the level of acceptance that transgender and transsexual men and women, lesbians and gays all experienced from their colleagues at MacKenzie. The bad news is that gender stereotypes are still flourishing like weeds in this otherwise "progressive" organizational culture.[22]

Let's take a deeper look at some of these issues in historical context. Socially approved gender behavior is not static. In the last twenty years, we have seen movement by both males and females toward increasingly "male" behavior. An analysis of studies on responses to the Bem Sex Role Inventory, for example, showed a rise in scores on traits socially defined as "masculine" for both men and women; but *no* comparable rise in scores on traits defined as "feminine."[23] This result "reflects a general trend in gender stereotypes which allows women to adopt masculine roles while prohibiting men from taking on more feminine ones."[24] While this shift has some initial benefit for girls and women in that they can choose to behave in masculine ways, in the long term, it reinforces and sustains the male-centered idea that masculine traits and roles are more valuable than feminine ones. And underplays the impact of gender stereotypes on men and boys. Differing expectations typically translate into differing treatment. If it is assumed that women and men "must" behave in certain ways, they will be treated accordingly, and gender assumptions take on a life of their own. Sociologists call this a self-fulfilling prophecy. Since women and men receive significant social pressure to be appropriately feminine or masculine—or risk social censure—most people adapt their behavior to fit social expectations. Obviously, these are the same unspoken norms and expectations that result in more extreme censures like homophobia, hate crimes, and distorted stereotypes about lesbians, gay men, bisexuals, and transgender, transsexual, and intersexed people.[25]

One of the main barriers to clear thinking about gender differences is the insistence on male/female dualities when the reality is much more complex. It is tempting to think of gender differences in stark terms—to assume *either* that men and women are quite different from one another *or* they are just the same. These either/or, different/same dualities are a trap for girls and women because whenever similarity or difference prevails, the model invariably compares women to men. And if girls or women are found to be different, as Virginia Valian documented, they are the ones who are seen as inferior. And if women are seen to be the same as men, those socially constructed differences that really *do* exist are ignored, perpetuating the disadvantages of women and girls. In either case, consciously or not, maleness and masculinity are assumed to be the gold standard.

Gender is not a duality; gender differences do not conform to a simple either/or dichotomy. Research has documented few inherent differences that predetermine behavior, and tremendous variations exist within each gender—much broader than the average differences between genders. Thus any particular woman or man might fit or totally defy gender expectations. Some gender differences are based on life experiences, often deriving from life experiences shaped by gender norms. For example, we expect a girl to cook, so we teach her how to cook, and then she knows how to cook. We expect a boy to use a hammer, so we teach him how to hammer, and then he knows how to hammer. We expect a man to be assertive, and we reward him when he asserts himself; we expect a woman to be caring toward others, and we reward her when she cares. And more often than not, we punish her if we perceive her to be too assertive or uncaring.

Recognizing Intersections of Gender, Race, and Class

Given the pervasive reality of gender expectations—especially the abundant misinformation that informs attitudes and stereotypes about gender—organizations must pay special attention to both hidden and explicit gender biases if they want to be as effective for women and girls as for men and boys. Equally important, however, gender expectations must be understood within different cultures and other socially defined group expectations.

No universal gender definition exists, no *Woman* that subsumes all women or *Man* that subsumes all men. Gender must be considered along with race, class, and sexuality—at a minimum. The weaving together of these social constructions affects our lives. Of course, a whole host of social constructions of identity exist, each of which has the power to shape our lives. Disabilities—both physical and mental, for example—often are the most invisible of all the difference categories. Society has gone through a number of stages in the evolution of its thinking about gender. In the 1970s, as a result of the women's movement of that era, scholars, mostly white women, argued much of our knowledge about human beings was based on an entirely male model. Most social science research was conducted on men, they argued, and the results were then mistakenly universalized to all people. Unfortunately, too many of these scholars repeated a similar conceptual error: they universalized the concept of woman, as though there were one common experience of being a woman. African American scholars like Paula Giddings, Maxine Baca Zinn, and Bonnie Thornton Dill along with other women of color developed the important critique called multiracial feminism.[26] Multiracial feminism moves beyond recognizing diversity and difference among women to examine structures of domination. This branch of feminist thought asserts that race and class differences are crucial, but not as individual characteristics of individual people. Instead, they are primary organizing principles of a society that positions groups within particular opportunity structures. Multiracial feminism addresses how both women and men, especially women and men of color, live within multiple systems of domination.

Kimberlé Crenshaw developed the term "intersectionalities" as a way of thinking about the idea that women have a number of identities that come together to shape and constrain their lives.[27] Gender, she argues, intersects with race, class, ethnicity, sexual identity, physical abilities and disabilities, and other socially constructed characteristics. More recently, the idea of "multiplicities" has been put forward as a way to understand this same idea, adding a layer of interaction: it is not simply that one identity is layered on top of another or that identities "meet" at some intersection. Rather, we all live complex realities that constantly and dynamically interact to shape our lives, even our physical lives.[28] Within gender, the other categories of difference cannot be overlooked because they constrain which women have more power than others. Understanding gender in all its complexities can be daunting. Grappling with these extended analyses can tempt us to dismiss gender as too multifaceted or, finally, too individualized. But the reality is just the opposite. And, as we show throughout this book, effective philanthropy depends on people's abilities to understand and analyze gender in all its complexity.

International studies of gender have shown that profound inequalities persist to the disadvantage of women in both developed and developing countries. While there have been modest improvements in some societies in women's living conditions and structural positions, many countries of the world also have seen a collective worsening of women's lives. Issues include unequal wages, gender-segregated jobs, the feminization of poverty, inequalities in health care, differences in access to old-age pensions, gender-related violence—and overarching all of these, the lack of a gender perspective in human rights' analyses. "Women's rights are human rights" emerged from a decade of research and international grassroots activism, but too often this understanding eludes decision makers at all levels of government and international agencies. These issues may impinge on women but centrally are concerned with men's practices. Questioning dominant forms of masculinity and gender oppression is a necessary step in addressing these inequalities.[29]

And gender is not just a "girl thing." Like "femininity," "masculinity" is also socially constructed, and it's essential that we understand "maleness" as well as we understand "femaleness." Otherwise we run smack into the dilemma of difference again, the irony that focusing on gender simply shines a light on the ways women are "different," and implicitly but very powerfully makes it look like men are the norm, the gold standard. Only when we examine masculinities alongside femininities can we escape that trap. To focus on the female gender in isolation is to ignore the real problem, which is women's subordinate status to men. In an article entitled "Studying Men's Practices and Gender Relations," Patrick White argues that if gender is about power relations between men and women, then men's experiences also must be taken into account.[30] The invisibility of masculinity—the social construction of masculinity, not "innate" masculine traits—reproduces gender inequality, both materially and ideologically. As long as the issue of gender is seen to refer only to women, men will continue to be thought of as the "normal" gender, and women will continue to be defined, if not as "abnormal," at the very least as "other." In addition to stigmatizing women, this also fails to force men to examine their culpability in maintaining power inequalities. The gender gap in voting, for example, only can be understood by looking at both male and female voting patterns. Otherwise, it appears that men are normal and constant, and females are changing. In addition to power inequalities between genders, hierarchies exist within masculinities. The gender order expresses men's power over women *and* the power of some men over other men (by virtue of race, sexuality, class, ethnicity, age, able-bodiedness, and other socially defined characteristics). Once gender is understood to refer to women *and* men, the differential dilemmas of men can receive their fair share of attention.

In higher education, for example, women significantly outnumber men—a difference that may translate into important differences in lifetime earnings. To date, this latter difference has not arisen because men have access to a very different labor market than women. But it is legitimate to ask why so many fewer men than women are enrolling in and graduating from colleges and universities. In 2000, according to the U.S. Census Bureau, 15.4 million women held bachelor's degrees compared with 14.8 million men.[31] The gender gap in education is most pronounced in blacks and Latinos. But while in other racial groups the gap is significant, virtually no gender gap exists between white women and men. The United Negro College Fund documents that during the 1990s, twice as many African-American women as African-American men earned college degrees.[32]

Although this gap has narrowed (by 2000, African-American women were 39 percent more likely to have earned bachelor's degrees), these data argue for a very specific approach to understanding why so many fewer African-American and Latino men are going to college—an analysis that requires viewing men as gendered.[33]

Gender is not static. Just the opposite: it is always changing. And both men and women actively participate in defining and reconstituting gender. Gender is not "just" something that is done *to* us. To the extent that we adopt or resist the gender identities that society and our families gave us at birth, we are helping give life to gender as a meaningful category that shapes our lives, whether we intend to or not. Gender or sexual identity or race or poverty or disability—none of these socially defining characteristics by themselves yield an adequate picture of the complexities of people's lives. As noted in the introduction, this complexity was one of the major findings of the first round of research for this book. One nonprofit executive we spoke with in the course of doing this first phase of research put it this way: "Race, ethnicity, poverty, class, how those issues are confounded by gender can't be addressed too much: it's where so much work needs to be done as a practical matter. Who are the kids most in need? Low-income girls of color." To understand poverty, we need sharpened awareness of what it means that the majority of people living in poverty are nonwhite females with children.

Another foundation executive notes, "There is greater awareness now of the range of diversity in race conversations; Asian and Latina are in people's concepts of race now; so is white. Race is not just African American. Conversations are more nuanced now, but class needs to be brought in too. There's more trouble brewing around class. Class is the elephant on the table." But not everyone agrees that we've come very far on this more nuanced understanding of race. Another foundation executive says, "We still define race as a black-and-white paradigm, which is disempowering for so many. Asian Americans are still invisible." Yet another executive notes, "I don't like the word 'intersectionality': it's a good concept but a bad word. What I would like to see is an expectation that we would always have this conversation: that there will always be talk about a range of initiatives that foundations undertake to impact women and girls, men and boys in all of their diversity. We need to not be afraid of the complexity of intersections, to expect explicit discussions, to not be afraid to say we mean white women or Black women or Latino men or Asian women." The head of an affinity group points out, "We've made enormous progress; I've been part of a generation provided enormous opportunities because of the various movements. But when I work with women and girls, particularly in immigrant communities, there are still so many society *and* community barriers. And then low income is added to the mix. I can't find the words to describe the condition; it's so deep." But it is so important to see all its complexities. *And effective philanthropic and nonprofit initiatives must take into account all these complexities.*

In addition to gender, it is also important to understand that other socially defined categories are not static: they constantly undergo change as part of new economic, political, and ideological processes, trends, and events. Those who are allowed to shape meaning within a culture, those with more power than others, often define categories of people as dualities, as polar opposites—white/black, rich/poor, men/women, heterosexual/homosexual, abled/disabled. In other words, people are parceled out into opposites that are not neutral—not infrequently for political gain—and these dualities are invariably labeled "good" and "bad." Many of the value judgments contained in these concepts often are linked to biology, with implications that the distinctions are fixed, permanent, and embedded in nature. Or, ironically, even where there *is* evidence of some biological and genetic factors at work—for example, in sexual orientation—the differences are demonized: homosexuality as contrasted to heterosexuality is labeled an abnormal lifestyle choice. But the culturally powerful ignore research and positive values like fairness and tolerance, and—consciously or unconsciously—use these good/bad categories for power and political gain.

In reality, these categories are neither polar opposites nor biologically determined: these distinctions are more often human-constructed hierarchies of domination and discomfort. And gender cannot be separated from descriptors of other socially defined traits. All dimensions of people's lives shape their experiences and their opportunities, and effective organizations must understand these complexities, this deep diversity, and monitor organizational culture as well as design programs and products with this kind of understanding at their core. What is key is that organizations *cannot* look through any single lens, such as gender or race or class, to ensure effectiveness. A gender lens by itself is no assurance of effective philanthropy. Instead, effective foundations must ask nuanced, pointed questions about both their own grant making and the programs and organizations they fund. How does gender impact the experiences and opportunities of the constituents of their grant recipients? How does race impact experiences and opportunities? And what about class? Sexuality? Physical ability? Due diligence requires funders continually to shift lenses and ask many specific questions of grant recipients: Who are most affected by the issue(s) we care about? How do gender, class, race, ethnicity, culture, sexuality, and ability shape them? What are their specific needs and interests? What are their concerns and issues? How do their identities affect (and how are they affected by) what this grantee recipient is trying to accomplish? How can foundations' stakeholders be actively involved in shaping initiatives to which we are all committed? Nonprofits must ask similar questions of their constituencies.

Effective organizations continually look for the bigger picture. As chapter 5 describes, a foundation with smaller funding capacity, and therefore not in a position to handle employment or housing, can collaborate with others who have that expertise. As the head of one of the Council on Foundation affinity groups puts it:

Somehow we have to dig deep inside ourselves and learn that our survival rests with everyone else. Get the long-term view. We will succeed to the extent we can work collaboratively, strategize with other foundations and nonprofits, and figure out how these issues can be approached on a bigger scale. The metaphor I've been using is the handwritten manuscript vs. the printing press: in my lifetime, I'm aiming for the printing press. Better still, a computer with access to the Internet and a color printer with many different fonts.

Understanding gender is crucial to seeing that bigger picture. As another foundation executive points out, "We need to work to strengthen our own analyses, need to convince people that investing in women and girls—women and girls of diverse backgrounds—is good for the community." Another notes that "you get results in investments in young girls, women. . . . You get liftoff with it. There's a strong case to be made, a lot of data that proves it's a good investment."

Having women at the center of the analysis can help foundations better understand and disrupt the cycle of poverty. Women who lived in public housing in Chicago, for example, were the real leaders who brought about lasting change in one foundation's work in a major urban area. Another foundation executive that funds welfare-to-work talked about programs with moms and young kids as their focus. "If we ground gender in family, we've got lots of consensus. We focus on women's leadership roles in their families. Nowhere are we promising we'll have nuclear families, but we acknowledge women as family leaders. . . . And that's crucial for better understanding needs like safe child care and job development tailored to women's needs." As the World Bank's *Engendering Development* report documents, society as a whole makes progress only when women's status improves. Funding with a focus on women is not about women as a special interest group. On the contrary, funding with a focus on women in the context of all their other socially defining characteristics is essential to the success of development initiatives in countries around the world.

Understanding Gendered Cultural Competence as Assets and Innovation

As chapter 6 documents, understanding the way international funders have used a strategic gender lens successfully for decades is invaluable for helping foundations and nonprofits that seek to develop new thinking about funding U.S.-based initiatives. But essential to both international and more effective national funding is a strategy as simple as asking new questions.

A foundation executive interviewed in the first phase of our research, for example, talked about how an agriculture program in his foundation never took women into account. It was focused on technical questions: Are we doing the research that's producing better strains of rice? Then someone in the foundation asked, "How do you know that rice is actually feeding people?" This new, simple question led to a more probing analysis of who was or was not benefiting from the foundation's work. As the person recounting the story pointed out, "We're not into food distribution, but we had to think about distribution. Our archetypical image for the program soon became 'the woman on the hill': a woman in rural Kenya, baby on her back, other children at her side, eking out a living in hardscrabble dirt." This recognition led to related questions: Who are these people we were trying to reach: rural widows whose husbands died of AIDS? Or were they living in the city? Who grew the rice? Who used it to feed the children?

Understanding gendered cultural competence goes beyond the concept of women as victims and leads to insights into the complex reality that gender stereotypes so often mask. Funders had to realize that in rural Kenya, where women do the farming, giving men tractors as part of the food program did not increase production of rice. But providing seeds and technical assistance to the women who do the farming did increase food production. Unless funders learn to look at who's actually doing the work—which means better understanding gender roles and class roles and social roles and how they play out in specific cultural circumstances—funding will fall on barren ground. These were not conscious gender or class analyses, per se, but rather efforts by people, trying to do their work better, who kept asking the question, "How do we know we reach the people most in need?" The Kenyan farmers were not female victims but agents of their own productivity. With their work supported, they became agents of change within their families and communities.

Such understanding of the role of gender as it plays out in different dimensions and contexts of people's lives is critical to achieving funding goals. Where investing in women can get us closer, investing in women with explicit analyses of all their needs and differences can get us closer still. As one affinity group head noted, "We sometimes don't realize we're overlooking women." But another funder who seeks to strengthen both philanthropy and the nonprofit sector describes his role in helping his foundation better grasp these insights.

Part of our work is to locate more assets by and for women and girls. We also care where the money for women goes. It should go to those who are most marginalized and least advantaged. We are focused on where the need is the highest. But we don't start with need. Starting with need makes you look like you are whining. . . . We start on what women in all their diversity bring to the table, what women can contribute to society, and then we focus on where resources should go.

In short, a fuller understanding of gender leads funders to new resources, new assets, and new strategies for innovation.

This process is neither simple nor necessarily comfortable. It takes strategic planning by program officers who are clear about where they are headed. To counter resistance from sometimes skeptical staff, effective program officers have learned to "back into" funding specific population characteristics like gender.

We recognized there was a huge reluctance both at our own foundation and within the rest of philanthropy to invest in [certain] populations. Our strategy to counter this had several parts. First we [identified and] linked the other population areas that we fund. No one questions funding youth or new wealth creators, for example. This allowed us to get funding for women without any problem. I don't know that we could have gotten as much funding for women if we had not linked it to other, less controversial, populations. We also put an emphasis on the innovations that come from all of these population groups. We have succeeded in this approach, and our work has gone from marginal to mainstream because of this focus on gender.

Because so many women and men in foundations still consider funding women to be controversial or resist funding any specific population groups, it is all the more important to reiterate how shifts in thinking and values are essential for effective philanthropy. Once foundations "get it," they are in unique positions to help shift or at least profoundly refocus the embedded biases and distorted values in the larger society that continue to have negative impacts on both men and women. To understand what happens in the family, for example, and to fund significant changes in attitudes toward family, foundations must understand gender in all its complexity: gender linked to race and class and sexuality and physical ability. In families gender roles play out in their most obvious forms. And within families, dysfunction that emerges from unbalanced, gender-based, and culture-based power roles often plays out in violence, depression, and missed opportunities for children, mothers, *and* fathers. But family and community dysfunctions have by far the greatest impact on children and women, especially poor women of color. And all of that mutates into larger cultural patterns of subtle and not-so-subtle bias that work against foundations' best efforts to fund change and workable solutions to complex problems.

According to one nonprofit executive:

All the research shows that if you grow up in a home with violence or substance abuse you're going to burden the justice systems and the mental-health systems. You're going to grow up to be vulnerable to a whole host of societal issues. We have to make this case over and over again. To the extent that we've been successful and persuasive, we make the case that the home as a social unit has to be healthy if we're going to deal with any social program. If you have a foundation interested in social problems, what happens in the family has to be central.

Another executive says:

I would argue that sex discrimination and gender bias (I use those terms interchangeably) happen because we're women. Then there are all the intersections: women with children, women encumbered by family responsibilities, women who are poor and African American, women and disability, etc. There's clearly a glass half-empty, half-full. We've come very far and have very far to go.

Gender biases are still rampant in the society at large, even though they've taken some new twists and turns as children of the seventies and eighties grow up. One nonprofit executive reports some social-science research on young men whose preference is to marry women who want to stay at home. "We've yet to revolutionize a culture of work, and that's a huge roadblock to women's equality. . . . I don't think we've changed much the belief that young men can work differently. I think until we begin to tackle what it means to be a family-centered society, we're stuck."

As negative as these hidden and not-so-hidden effects of gender discrimination can be, effective foundations have figured how to use gender knowledge as assets by learning to think outside the boxes. Putting families—and work values that support families—at the center of philanthropic and nonprofit interventions turns these seemingly immutable problems on their heads and gives effective organizations crucial ammunition for creative solutions. Understanding gender and gendered cultural competence as assets leading to innovation is certainly no panacea. But a more nuanced understanding of gender is essential for organizational effectiveness and effective philanthropy.

2

Institutionalizing Deep Diversity as an Asset

Norm Knowledge and Stereotypes

Chapter 1 describes the importance of gaining more nuanced understandings of gender and other intersecting, socially constructed "identities" for funders who aspire to effective philanthropy. Better understanding of how we all live socially constructed lives offers the potential for increasing philanthropic innovations and as well as help for nonprofit grantees. The examples of the social construction of gender in chapter 1 set up our discussion in this chapter of how organizations succeed or fail to *institutionalize* that knowledge and understanding.

Institutionalizing new knowledge is not easy, especially new knowledge about differences that often trigger discomfort. Even the most thoughtful people and the most agile of learning organizations fall prey to Norm. Being both researchers and practitioners has left us with few illusions about the difficulties of sustaining organizational cultures with Norm knowledge when that knowledge continually calls into question how we govern and manage ourselves. There are limits to patience and downsides to change. Like model but occasionally exasperated parents, even the most thoughtful leaders of learning organizations sometimes just want to do it the way they've always done it without need for lengthy justification.

We have few illusions about how hard this work can be and how frustrating it can feel. But for any foundation that aspires to effective philanthropy and any nonprofit that aspires to effective programming, institutionalizing deep diversity is an essential process to undertake. And like many elite organizations, the philanthropic sector has a long history of ignoring difficult conversations. Respondents in earlier research commissioned by the

Kellogg Foundation, for example, expressed frustrations about foundation culture that are probably little different from critiques leveled against other institutions.[1] And although many of the examples cited in this chapter focus on foundations, they are equally applicable to other organizations, especially larger and more established nonprofits.

As the case studies in chapter 3 document, foundations that have learned to institutionalize deep diversity, however imperfectly, and understand this work to be a lifetime process, have learned to challenge Norm. We're using "Norm" as shorthand for all the formal, informal, and unconscious ways difference is locked in or—better said—locked *out* of organizational structures and cultures, the insidious, often subtle and unacknowledged effects of "normal." Webster's *Third* defines *norm* as "an ideal standard binding upon the members of a group and serving to guide, control, or regulate proper and acceptable behavior"—an innocuous enough definition describing a fundamental building block of civil society.[2] But at its most extreme, Norm becomes racism, sexism, heterosexism, homophobia, transgender phobia, classism, fundamentalism, egotism, ableism, ageism, xenophobia, and abuse of social, economic, and political power. The hidden valuing, the unspoken expectations, and unconscious, socially constructed stereotypes and assumptions make Norm dangerous for deep diversity.

For those "native" to an organization's culture—those most in sync with their organization's values, styles, and structures—many of these assumptions and conventions seem so opaque as to be inconsequential. And those not native to the organization's culture, who stumble over these conventions, often are marked as ineffectual and easily marginalized. Many of these conventions boil down to what to say or not to say to whom about what. Or they appear in subtler details, like the office equivalent of which fork to use with the salad: who gets mentored and has access to the informal advice and knowledge, the invisible "grease" that makes the organization run. The following example shows how nonnatives sometimes get excluded from this often invisible but essential learning.

New England Telephone

At the time of the AT&T Consent Decree, New England Telephone had to get women into supervisory positions. New England Telephone had always taken their supervisors from the ranks and had a very elaborate—and very expensive—supervisor training program.

The men who went through this training worked extremely well as supervisors. But when New England Telephone trained the women in this way, they were not successful. At that time, they had a very forward-looking manager who did not blame the women but called in a sociologist to look at the problem. The sociologist discovered that the reason the men were doing so well had nothing to do with the wonderful training they were getting but had to do with informal on-the-job help they received once they were supervisors. The women weren't getting this help. With that insight, the company saved a lot of money by not having to do this very expensive training any more. They could put into place what was really effective—helping people on the job. Once men and women had the same on-the-job assistance, they both performed well.[3]

Most protocols within specific organizations can be learned, especially with the help of experienced mentors. At New England Telephone, these protocols were the informal knowledge and advice, the invisible "grease" that makes the organization run: on-the-job shortcuts and how-tos that made the difference between success and failure for these new supervisors. These components of informal culture are often different in different organizations. They are the dialects that nonnative speakers can master to enable them to fit in with different organizations' language, rituals, and styles of communication that Rosabeth Moss Kanter defined in her still relevant 1977 study, *Men and Women of the Corporation*. More subtle, however, are the implicit cultural norms that for many people are much harder to spot: what to say or not to say to whom about what. Or what to wear to board meetings? Who asks whom to lunch? Who gets included on which committee? Which vice president to copy on which type of memo? What types of jokes are permissible in whose company? These are the norms we use to judge those who misstep, and we often silently misjudge them because most of the time we are unaware we are holding such expectations. As we saw in chapter 1, these assumptions often are internalized, even among those not born to Norm. And they are usually gendered. As we also saw in chapter 1, both men and women are handicapped by gender norm expectations. And because of the differential power and status assigned to traditional gender roles, especially when these are combined with the differential power and status assigned to race and ethnicity, it is women, particularly women of color, who often find themselves in double binds because of unchallenged assumptions about acceptable gendered behavior that also is tied to different racial or ethnic stereotypes—for example, black women branded aggressive if they push too hard, weak if they don't.[4]

Women obviously have made significant strides in philanthropic leadership, but too often, especially in elite foundations with large assets, women rarely are seen as potential leaders. One experienced foundation executive interviewed for the 1997 Kellogg Foundation study, for example, observed that women can "do the work, carry the load, even get praised for the work, but we don't get to be at the helm." Another funder interviewed in the course of our research refers to a Women & Philanthropy report on the difference it makes to have women on boards: "If a male grant maker who went to Princeton recommends funding for Princeton, it's seen as fine. But if a woman who went to Princeton recommends the funding, it will be viewed as taking advantage of her being an alum."

And what does it mean that black male program officers are more likely than black female program officers to be involved in setting policy?[5] For that matter, what does it mean that an articulate black male foundation executive must continually check his creativity and energy at the meeting room door: "Do you have any idea how much I just hold myself in?" he asks. "Just speaking too strongly will do you in. You're then an 'angry black male' and threatening, totally unacceptable." With some exasperation, he noted, "This gets to be a real obstacle, making it hard to do your best work." When others in the foundation ask tough questions, they are praised for their solid professionalism. But this man had learned that showing his intellect makes people uncomfortable: a black male asking tough questions is labeled "attacking"—another gender/racial stereotype that seldom is discussed but difficult to shake.

Extensive analyses of these complex dimensions of institutional life and organizational culture are beyond the scope of this book and best not undertaken without more in-depth applied research, especially as it pertains to both foundations and nonprofits. But the last decade has seen a wealth of important research that documents how unexamined organizational norms get in the way of effective corporate management strategies. Researchers like Joan Acker, Lotte Bailyn, Marta Calás, Robin Ely, Joyce Fletcher, Evangelina Holvino, Deborah Kolb, Joanne Martin, Deborah Merrill-Sands, Debra Meyerson, Aruna Rao, Rhona Rapoport, Linda Smircich, and others have developed a cluster of helpful analyses and strategies for better understanding these dynamics and how they work to the disadvantage of most people in organizations, women and men of all races and ethnicities.[6]

Translating to philanthropy some of the insights these researchers discovered in their work with corporations helps us better understand why so many women and men in foundations have such a hard time making the link between deep diversity and effective philanthropy. Although we leave more extensive analyses of foundations' organizational cultures for future work, it is crucial here at least to name Norm, crucial to talk about how that arbiter of proper and acceptable behavior becomes the unnamed, undiscussable elephant on the table, an invisible dead center that pushes to the periphery all the group identities included in our definition of deep diversity: gender, race, class, sexual orientation, gender identity, age, disability, geography, nationality, religion, and other diversities—anyone not Norm.

Chapter 1 described the importance of understanding the complex intersections of deep diversity for making effective funding and nonprofit program decisions. But these intersections also play out within a foundation's *own* culture. The phenomenon is complex because it can be both hidden and well-meaning. As one senior foundation male executive noted erroneously in Capek's earlier Kellogg Foundation research, "We *don't* discriminate against women; that's why we make 'generic' grants. . . . Women are equally considered in every way. We *don't* need a special program to make sure women get their fair share." But other respondents in that research disagreed. While quick to acknowledge significant changes in philanthropy, especially the advances women have made in the profession, many respondents interviewed—male and female senior program staff, foundation executives and trustees, and heads of the organizations they fund—were candidly critical. And theirs were not just criticisms of men in philanthropy: "Sometimes Norm wears a skirt," one woman of color executive quipped, "and often she's white."[7] White women collude, for example, by not raising issues faced by women of color in the foundation *and* in the grantee community.[8]

Women in Foundation Leadership

In 2004, according to the Council on Foundation data, a projected 53 percent of full-time, paid chief executive officers/chief giving officers were female (table 2.1) and 73.6 percent of all program officers were female. Corporate philanthropy has the highest percentage of women executives

Table 2.1
Women and men as percentages of full-time paid CEOs of foundations with different asset sizes, 2004

	% women	% men	Total	# of women	# of men	Total
$100 million and over	39.2	60.8	100.0	93	144	237
$50 to $99.9 million	47.5	52.5	100.0	57	63	120
$10 to $49.9 million	59.1	40.9	100.0	159	110	269
Under $10 million	71.9	28.1	100.0	87	34	121
All	53.0	47.0	100.0	396	351	747

Source: Council on Foundations. *2004 Grantmakers Salary and Benefits Report.*

(78.2 percent); the lowest percentage (43.2 percent) is in independent private foundations (table 2.2).[9] Breakdowns of gender within racial/ethnic categories show that 22 women of color head up foundations reporting data to the Council on Foundations (table 2.3), and overall 5.1 percent of CEOs were minorities (table 2.3), with 19.9 percent of program officers women of color. Tables 2.4–2.5 show those breakdowns according to the foundations' asset sizes. While women and men of color have not made the same inroads into philanthropy leadership that white women have, it is safe to argue that the face of philanthropy has changed significantly from what it was even a decade ago.

Yet the increase in the numbers of women program officers, CEOs, and trustees of foundations has had no marked effect on funding for programs for women and girls, to no small extent because of the pervasive reach of Norm. Organizational culture, taken for granted and unexamined, steers the course. Women and men who move up the ranks in most organizations are promoted because they fit in to existing organizational norms and traditions, because they are unlikely to rock the boat. In interviews for this book, women staff indicated that several factors affect how or whether they advocate for programs for women and girls. Some women reported their reluctance to argue strongly for funding for women's programs because they feared they would be labeled "single-issue funders" and marginalized within their foundations where gender did not function as a category of analysis. This is Norm at work, Norm overwhelming Norma. Within the group of women program officers we interviewed, some abandoned their interest in funding programs benefiting women and girls to advance their

Table 2.2
Women and men as percentages of full-time paid CEOs of different types of foundations, 2004

	% women	% men	Total	# of women	# of men	Total
Corporate	78.2	21.8	100.0	43	12	55
Community	56.8	43.2	100.0	163	124	287
Public	52.1	47.9	100.0	38	35	73
Family	49.0	51.0	100.0	72	75	147
Independent	43.2	56.8	100.0	80	105	185
All	53.0	47.0	100.0	396	351	747

Source: Council on Foundations. *2004 Grantmakers Salary and Benefits Report.*

Table 2.3
Women and men within racial/ethnic groups as percentages of full-time paid CEOs, 2004

	% women	% men	Total	# of women	# of men	Total
Asian/Pacific Islander	57.1	42.9	100.0	4	3	7
Black	62.5	37.5	100.0	10	6	16
Hispanic	50.0	50.0	100.0	7	7	14
American Indian	100.0	0	100.0	1	0	1
Other	0	0	100.0	0	0	0
White	52.8	47.2	100.0	374	335	709
All	53.0	47.0	100.0	396	351	747

Source: Council on Foundations. *2004 Grantmakers Salary and Benefits Report.*

own careers; others chose to argue quietly wherever possible to fund women and girls. Still others reported that they had no particular focus on funding for women and girls and resented that anyone might automatically assume they would have an interest in the issue. Finally, others argued they had little control over funding decisions, an argument borne out in research conducted in the Greater Boston area, which showed that boards of trustees set funding criteria in 70 percent of the Boston-area foundations.[10]

Too many foundation trustees, executives, and staff—both men and women—still lack knowledge of deep diversity. Nor do they acknowledge the role Norm plays in dictating the way it's always been done. Nor do they

Table 2.4

Women and men within racial/ethnic groups as full-time paid CEOs of foundations with different asset sizes, 2004 (assets in millions)

	$100 or More			$50 to $99.9			$10 to $49.9			Less than $10			All		
	Women	Men	All	Women	Men	All	Women	Men	All	Women	Men	All	Women	Men	All
Asian/Pacific Islander	2	2	4	0	0	0	2	0	2	0	1	1	4	3	7
Black	7	6	13	0	0	0	1	0	1	2	0	2	10	6	16
Hispanic	3	2	5	0	0	0	2	4	6	2	1	3	7	7	14
American Indian	0	0	0	0	0	0	1	0	1	0	0	0	1	0	1
Other	0	0	0	0	0	0	0	0	0	0	0	0	0	0	0
White	81	134	215	57	63	120	153	106	259	83	32	115	374	335	709
All	93	144	237	57	63	120	159	110	269	87	34	121	396	351	747

Source: Council on Foundations. 2004 Grantmakers Salary and Benefits Report.

Table 2.5
Women and men within racial/ethnic groups as full-time paid CEOs of different types of foundations, 2004

	Family			Public			Community			Independent			Corporate			All		
	Women	Men	All	Women	Men	All	Women	Men	All	Women	Men	All	Women	Men	All	Women	Men	All
Asian/Pacific Islander	0	1	1	0	0	0	1	2	3	2	0	2	1	0	1	4	3	7
Black	0	0	0	3	0	3	0	4	4	3	2	5	4	0	4	10	6	16
Hispanic	2	0	2	0	2	2	3	3	6	1	2	3	1	0	1	7	7	14
American Indian	0	0	0	0	0	0	0	0	0	1	0	1	0	0	0	1	0	1
Other	0	0	0	0	0	0	0	0	0	0	0	0	0	0	0	0	0	0
White	70	74	144	35	33	68	159	115	274	73	101	174	37	12	49	374	335	709
All	72	75	147	38	35	73	163	124	287	80	105	185	43	12	55	396	351	747

Note: Corporate grantmakers include direct giving programs as well as foundations.
Source: Council on Foundations. *2004 Grantmakers Salary and Benefits Report.*

acknowledge that women's and girls' needs can be different from men's and boys' needs. As a consequence, too many funders still are unwilling to account for gender disparities in their grants—in spite of significant evidence, for example, that accounting for gender-based differences in "youth" programs provides expanded, more innovative resources for both boys and girls.

Diversifying Boards and Staff

The board composition of many philanthropic organizations (tables 2.6–2.10)—still predominantly white, middle-class, and male—contributes to the reign of Norm and poses a considerable obstacle to effective philanthropy. But as we saw in the Maxwell Fund case in chapter 1, many white upper-middle-class females also don't get it. If in fact, as the research in Boston-area foundations suggests, trustee boards set the funding criteria for most foundations, it is of significant consequence that boards are also where women and minorities have made the fewest inroads. In 1982, women on boards numbered 834 out of 3,710 at the 417 foundations reporting to the Council on Foundations—just 22.5 percent of all board members. Minorities that year numbered 159, only 4.3 percent of all board members. From 1982 to 2002—a twenty-year period when the total number of board members jumped from 3,710 to 8,481 (and the number of reporting foundations from 417 to 704)—the number of women on boards

Table 2.6
Women and men as percentages of trustees on boards of different asset sizes, 2002

	% women	% men	Total	# of women	# of men	Total
$100 million and over	32.5	67.5	100.0	676	1,402	2,078
$50 to $99.9 million	34.2	65.8	100.0	464	893	1,357
$10 to $49.9 million	35.6	64.4	100.0	1,050	1,902	2,952
Under $10 million	38.8	61.2	100.0	813	1,281	2,094
All	35.4	64.6	100.0	3,003	5,478	8,481

Source: Council on Foundations. *Foundation Management Series, 11th edition, volume I–II: Governing Boards and Administrative Expenses in Private Foundations*, 2004.

Table 2.7
Women and men as percentages of trustees on boards of different types of
foundations, 2002

	% women	% men	Total	# of women	# of men	Total
Family	43.8	56.2	100.0	610	782	1,392
Public	35.2	64.8	100.0	340	626	966
Community	34.9	65.1	100.0	1,543	2,872	4,415
Independent and private operating	29.9	70.1	100.0	510	1,198	1,708
All	35.4	64.6	100.0	3,003	5,478	8,481

Source: Council on Foundations. *Foundation Management Series, 11th edition,
volume I–II: Governing Boards and Administrative Expenses in Private Foundations*, 2004.

Table 2.8
Women and men within racial/ethnic groups as percentages of trustees, 2002

	% women	% men	Total	# of women	# of men	Total
Asian/Pacific Islander	47.6	52.4	100.0	50	55	105
Black	47.2	52.8	100.0	257	288	545
Hispanic	40.6	59.4	100.0	91	133	224
American Indian	54.3	45.7	100.0	19	16	35
Other	33.3	66.7	100.0	7	14	21
White	34.2	65.8	100.0	2,579	4,972	7,551
All	35.4	64.6	100.0	3,003	5,478	8,481

Source: Council on Foundations. *Foundation Management Series, 11th edition,
volume I–II: Governing Boards and Administrative Expenses in Private Foundations*, 2004.

increased to 3,003 (35.4 percent of all trustees whose foundations report
to the Council on Foundations), and the number of minorities increased to
930 (11 percent of all reported trustees). While obviously an improvement
over 1982 levels, these 2002 data still fall short of numbers needed to ensure leadership opportunities for people of color and white women at the
tables where philanthropic decisions are made. As we describe throughout
the rest of this chapter and the next, these numbers document boards at
risk, ones lacking the diversity needed to ensure board effectiveness.

Table 2.9
Women and men within racial/ethnic groups on boards of foundations with different asset sizes, 2002 (assets in millions)

	$100 or More			$50 to $99.9			$10 to $49.9			Less than $10			All		
	Women	Men	All	Women	Men	All	Women	Men	All	Women	Men	All	Women	Men	All
Asian/Pacific Islander	24	23	47	7	6	13	14	12	26	5	14	19	50	55	105
Black	88	113	201	56	73	129	83	75	158	30	27	57	257	288	545
Hispanic	42	34	76	20	36	56	20	50	70	9	13	22	91	133	224
American Indian	6	7	13	2	0	2	3	5	8	8	4	12	19	16	35
Other	1	5	6	0	2	2	5	4	9	1	3	4	7	14	21
White	515	1,220	1,735	379	776	1,155	925	1,756	2,681	760	1,220	1,980	2,579	4,972	7,551
All	676	1,402	2,078	464	893	1,357	1,050	1,902	2,952	813	1,281	2,094	3,003	5,478	8,481

Council on Foundations. Foundation Management Series, 11th Edition, Volume I–II: Governing Boards and Administrative Expenses in Private Foundations, 2004.

Table 2.10
Women and men within racial/ethnic groups on boards of different types of foundations, 2002

	Family			Public			Community			Independent			All		
	Women	Men	All	Women	Men	All	Women	Men	All	Women	Men	All	Women	Men	All
Asian/Pacific Islander	5	9	14	11	8	19	17	25	42	17	13	30	50	55	105
Black	10	9	19	41	38	79	147	172	319	59	69	128	257	288	545
Hispanic	4	3	7	9	28	37	52	79	131	26	23	49	91	133	224
American Indian	0	1	1	9	4	13	6	8	14	4	3	7	19	16	35
Other	1	0	1	1	3	4	4	8	12	1	3	4	7	14	21
White	590	760	1,350	269	545	814	1,317	2,580	3,897	403	1,087	1,490	2,579	4,972	7,551
All	610	782	1,392	340	626	966	1,543	2,872	4,415	510	1,198	1,708	3,003	5,478	8,481

Council on Foundations. *Foundation Management Series, 11th Edition, Volume I–II: Governing Boards and Administrative Expenses in Private Foundations*, 2004.

Another often overlooked aspect of diversity is age. A number of the people interviewed for this book stressed the importance of involving younger people both on staff and on boards. A respected consultant who was asked her advice for more effective organizations replied, "Make sure you have staff under thirty-five. They've had more integrated experience across gender, more assertive perspectives. . . . I don't always agree with them, but there's a truth there." Another nonprofit executive talked about her experience with a young woman she met at an international racism conference who is now on her staff: "I have learned a tremendous amount from her. We need to open spaces for young people and share leadership; we can't stay stuck. They don't need to reinvent the wheel, but they help us get unstuck."

In fact, without using the term, many people interviewed for this book stressed the importance of deep diversity—those nuanced, complex understandings of differences that are also *institutionalized*. One former corporate executive observed, "You'd have to be half dead not to see it's in a foundation's interest to have diverse populations in their organization and in their funding priorities—that their organizations and agendas need to mirror our world. But it's more than 'add a few and stir': these people need to be woven into the fabric of the organization." Another former program officer notes, "The more people there, the more debate, the deeper you can go. . . . Without more diverse staff, you're really limited. Those foundations that broaden have richer conversations. That doesn't mean the conversations go any smoother—they can in fact be more difficult—but that's what you need." And these differences make the difference between superficial add-ons to the "same old same old," the dead weight of tradition, and an organizational culture that is flexible and able to ask critical, new questions of itself and its stakeholders.

And diversity, even deep diversity, must go beyond skin deep. Here's where Norm comes into play again. People who look different still can act the same. As we saw in the previous section, having a majority of women in leadership positions has not had a significant impact on either foundation culture or increased amounts or quality of funding for women and girls. People of any gender or race can buy into the nested Russian dolls of a foundation's culture. As the head of an affinity group interviewed for the 1998 Kellogg Foundation research quipped, "Foundations can be multiracial but monocultural."

Although difference does not guarantee deep diversity, you can't achieve deep diversity without difference. One foundation CEO notes that bringing different voices onto the board, especially more diverse women in larger numbers, contributed significantly to his board's renewed energies.

We had a rocky beginning like many new organizations: the initial board was all white males chosen by the founder. Many things transpired; at first we added just one woman (on a six-member board), but five years ago the board was rebuilt. This was a rare opportunity. We consciously set out to diversify on every level of the organization. We now have a significant group of women of color on the board, and they play an important leadership role. . . . On our board, women have made a difference. They don't want to be the squeaky wheel all the time, but they have been effective leaders. They have done such a good job at leadership that they have gotten men to step up to the plate and speak out on gender issues. . . .

Willingness to speak out on gender issues is also important. As one nonprofit executive pointed out, nonprofits and foundations need to vet prospective board members, both men and women, about their awareness of gender issues.

I remember taking over "the woman's seat" on our judicial nominating committee, a very prestigious appointment. My predecessor warned me that she was in the middle of a big fight. Our nominating form for potential judicial candidates asked about military service, but she wanted a question on the form to ask if candidates were parents because being a parent, after all, affects your worldview. I inherited the fight. These guys could not incorporate into their worldview that it was at least as important to acknowledge parenting as it was military service. I won, but it took me a very long time. They just got bored; I wore them down.

While this executive did not advocate the "wear down" strategy as a model for how to diversify boards, the point is important to make: having diverse people on boards can provide more diverse perspectives that directly affect work outcomes.

More diverse boards also can empower themselves to be "bi- or even tri-paradigmed," as another foundation executive put it. Understanding positive differences in other cultures and the negative impacts of gender or racial dynamics in ways that go beyond superficial markers is a complex process that requires us to suspend stereotypes, or at least entertain concepts that are not in our standard frames of reference. This executive talked about the importance of cultural competence, recognizing something as simple as the fact that not everyone frames their worlds alike. The communitarian nature of many American Indian cultures, for example, contrasts starkly with the individualism of many non-Indian cultures. So the challenge is to create spaces in organizations that allow, indeed foster, understanding of these differences and integrate people who think differently. And not to expect people not born to Norm to fit in and adapt to the dominant institutional culture. The organization needs to be flexible enough to accommodate different styles, and be intentional—and selective—about what people *must* do to "fit" the dominant culture.

As we saw in chapter 1, these are the same strategies that David Thomas and Robin Ely describe as their learning and effectiveness paradigm for making differences work for an organization instead of against it. As Thomas and Ely describe the process, we have focused on diversity mainly because discrimination is wrong. But a diverse workforce embodies different ideas about how to do work, and they can challenge basic assumptions about an organization's functions, strategies, operations, practices, and procedures. The benefits of learning to stretch one's own institutional culture far outweigh the temporary discomfort of doing things differently.

To recap, effective learning organizations are not stuck in Thomas and Ely's first paradigm of "discrimination and fairness," where all staff members are expected to fit neatly into the institutional culture's norms of behavior. Nor are they stuck in Thomas and Ely's second paradigm of "access and legitimacy," where foundations celebrate differences but marginalize different people's strengths without integrating them into the institution's culture and where people of color, for example, may be hired because of their special knowledge about diverse populations then pigeonholed into grant making programs for only those populations. In this instance, people of color should be recognized as resources for bringing new perspectives and expertise—resources foundations miss out on if they don't create the time and space for struggling with differences and empower all stakeholders in the organization to change as they learn new knowledge and different ways of working. Our model of deep diversity and Thomas and Ely's "learning and effectiveness" strategies are all potential power tools for Norm busting, not just academic notions or cultural niceties. They have direct impact on how both philanthropy and nonprofits do business. One executive cited population planning in China to make his point:

Take the one-child policy, for example. That hasn't worked because [the Chinese leadership planning the policies] haven't dealt with cultural values that only value boys and men; girls are thrown away. This is a huge gap in understanding. What role can philanthropy play in that? We have to institutionalize cultural competency: we have to have cultural competency in our capacities within our foundations. If we don't have that understanding, we can't do our jobs.

That foundation actually had to have *gendered* cultural competence, because without understanding how Chinese culture undervalues girl children and why, there is little philanthropy can do to positively change people's lives.

In another example, one foundation conducted an evaluation of a project funded in Africa.

We found a lot of backlash, a lot of teachers angry because resources were perceived going just to girls, not to boys. Families didn't want to send their girls to school. So the program did some research to find out what was behind the hostility. It turns out families didn't want to send girls to school because of sexual harassment. Also backlash. So we've retooled the program: now it's focused on strengthening primary education, with a special emphasis within the program on girls, but it's not billed "just for girls." We're trying to improve access to education, remove barriers for girls. We're not moving away from a focus on girls, we're just trying to be more strategic.

Institutionalizing Deep Diversity

A major goal of this book is to expand discussions about the importance of "naming Norm" and, in the process, *institutionalizing* knowledge of deep diversity and thinking outside the boxes. We chose to embed this notion explicitly in our definition of deep diversity.

• *Wide* to include the breadth and web of differences that weave through most modern organizations: gender, sexual orientation, gender identity,[11] race, ethnicity, nationality, religion, class, disability, geography, age, and other socially, culturally, and economically defined differences that categorize groups of individuals

• *Deep* into an organization's DNA, or to use another metaphor, deep into the taproot of an organization and intertwined in the wide network of roots that anchors and feeds the whole of an organization's culture

Because the intersecting dimensions of race, ethnicity, gender, class, and culture go so deep, it becomes all the more important for foundations to embed gendered cultural competence throughout formal institutional processes and structures as well as throughout informal organizational interactions, e.g., formal value statements and reward mechanisms as well as informal valuing transmitted by how leadership listens and interacts with staff. And it is important to embed both formal and informal strategies at the board level, in staff leadership and management levels, and in program and support staff as well as in program initiatives themselves. Having a program within a foundation's urban poverty initiative devoted to the needs of Native American women and children is important, for example, but it is even more important that cultural and gender understanding specific to Native-American communities be infused throughout the entire foundation.

As some of the people interviewed for this book pointed out, however, often it may be easier to make the case for race/ethnic awareness than for gender. Funders assume they reach women and girls because females are more than half of the population. One funder describes this experience as trickle-down confidence and says, "It's harder to make the case when people feel there's so much progress. But if understanding of gender dynamics is not built in and institutionalized, it'll be dropped when a sympathetic program officer leaves."

Institutionalizing diversity, especially institutionalizing gender awareness, takes persistence. One program officer describes her foundation's progress:

We started funding women as a category, but we also needed to move that gender awareness into all program areas, and we did that. We integrated gender with race as well. This often started with staffing in the foundation (getting more women and minorities in important positions) and then moved into priorities set within program areas. In general, there is a larger pool of gender-informed people now. If one person leaves, the agenda doesn't drop. People who understand gender dynamics are now on boards—both men and women—and they have integrated important perspectives. . . . In some areas, small groups of gender-informed people are building collaborative portfolios with people in other program areas. This is a good move. When I was doing funding on domestic violence, for example, I encouraged communication with program officers working with low-income fathers. We worked together. Our grantees began to understand each other better. The domestic violence groups didn't always understand issues for low-income dads. This effort has changed both projects.

The most important step is the "interactive" embedding just described. A lot of foundations talk about cultural competency at a learning level—taking in new information about diverse cultures—but as important as it is to master cultural competency at a learning level, the process stalls unless it gets taken higher and transforms the organization's own norms and culture. An affinity group head reports:

I hear stories from so many in the field: the systems are just not established. Holidays are still based on the Christian calendar. As people from diverse backgrounds come into philanthropy, they are expected to shape themselves around the field, but the institutions don't accommodate them, much less really integrate their cultural diversities. There's been no cultural integration: that's the next step.

Bringing Boards Along

Any discussions of institutionalizing deep diversity and gendered cultural competence within foundations, however, must circle back to board membership. This book is not a manual for foundation or nonprofit board and staff management. Many other thoughtful books on the subject are on the shelves. But some of these issues need to be addressed here because so much of what we've described about foundations as organizations institutionalizing learning and effectiveness paradigms—which we are arguing is key for doing effective philanthropy—seems to depend on fundamental governance and management issues: suffice it to say here that lessons from generations of classic board advice apply. These tried-and-true board strategies help to create the proper learning climate for an organization to evolve and thrive, for an organization's culture to be more pliable and reflective of new ideas and experiences.

- Ask hard questions of themselves
- Probe their own assumptions
- Diversify and renew their board membership with well-searched new appointments
- Work with staff to develop targeted mission statements and flexible guidelines
- Hire independent CEOs
- Understand the difference between boards' fiduciary responsibilities and policy-setting roles, management roles, and decision making

Yet to achieve effective philanthropy, foundation boards often present special roadblocks. With little accountability and not much pressure for self-evaluation, many boards have problems built into their governance responsibilities. For instance, few private foundation boards have term limits. Most are self-perpetuating, without pressure to diversify beyond "people like us." Even when boards do make attempts to diversify membership, there is an inevitable centrifugal force, as several respondents pointed out, pulling them back to "the way we've always done it." Some of these difficulties seem built into organizational DNA. A monocultural, hierarchical leadership model is still the norm in many foundations and larger nonprofit organizations. "Organizations are like silly putty," one experienced administrator notes. "You can pull and tug them into shape for a while, but once you let go, whammo, back to the original blob."

Change is hard. So long as the basic legal requirements of asset distribution and reporting are met, private foundation boards, family foundation boards, and corporate boards are under no pressure to do their work differently, and often there is little incentive to rethink business as usual. With less professionalized foundations, those without professional staff for example, there is also tendency toward a self-image of generosity that can undercut any pressure to change. After all, if they are giving away money they could have spent on other, more selfish pursuits, they see critics as merely ungrateful. Those people who question the often complex motives behind the establishment of foundations (e.g., tax incentives, social standing in the community, support of cultural institutions that perpetuate class and differential power) are deemed troublemakers or downright rude. One researcher who published a controversial study of philanthropy in the early 1990s actually was booed out of the room at a major national philanthropic conference. It was considered neither nice nor a sign of appropriate respect or gratitude to suggest that foundation boards need to evaluate how they work and even worse to suggest that they change.

These concerns about accountability and change obviously go beyond the gender of the person who is in charge of the foundation. As one longtime male foundation executive noted, "Some years ago, we couldn't envision that by now women would be heading up more than 50 percent of foundations. And if we had, we would have expected that this would have made huge changes." He went on to explain why he thinks so few changes have occurred in philanthropy in spite of large numbers of women moving into leadership: boards of directors: "Boards determine the CEOs who determine the staffs. I think everyone is educable, but in fact we still need to educate people who have a lot of money. They don't have social change as their priority. Why change since they benefited from the system as it is?" Expanding the number of women on boards will help, according to many observers, but as we saw with the statistics describing women in foundation leadership positions, even with higher numbers, change does not necessarily happen. As a former foundation program officer and trustee notes, the issue is more than numbers: "The question is to what extent we can really engage a foundation board in meaningful ways in its own grant making work." He points out:

The more distant the board is, the more we as board members can draw our own conclusions because no one's going to confront or debate us on it. If we're out there in the community, we have to make tougher decisions. It's tough to say no when you're there. It's a challenging bit of work, but it's the style needed for foundations to be more effective and meaningful. It's important to have people familiar with/from those populations we're trying to serve on our boards.

Even when boards are more diverse, bringing them along is the job of the CEO, at least in part. An effective CEO understands that his or her job includes working to develop the board, educating them about the best new thinking about effective philanthropy. Even the most active board works less and thinks less about the organization than the CEO and other senior staff who are on the job five or more days a week. And effective boards encourage CEO and senior staff guidance. So while this strategy of the CEO "bringing the board along" is not necessarily politic to discuss or openly acknowledge, many of the respondents interviewed for our book share a common understanding that primary responsibility for refining and maintaining a healthy, dynamic organizational culture rests in the hands of the CEO and senior staff. For both boards and their organizations to succeed, boards must keep moving and growing, and effective CEOs and senior staff understand that process. As one long-time foundation executive described:

What was revolutionary [for our board] five years ago, they [the board] now brag about as our decade of successes. Bring them along, get them to take risks, see results and take credit for it. . . . It's an ongoing thing, not a formula. . . . We've tried to . . . engage board members on something they know about or think they know about . . . and bring them along from there.

As to the nuts and bolts of institutionalizing differences, smart staff members learn to see where board members "are" and work from there. One senior staffer described insights he gained trying to implement ethnic-specific funding in higher education. His board kept resisting, arguing strenuously that ethnic-specific funding was divisive. After months of frustration, it finally occurred to him that many board members were of the generation that felt strongly that assimilation was key to a stronger America. Immigrants wanted to become Americans as fast as they could, and

these now-established immigrants and children of immigrants saw targeting specific populations as fragmenting, leading to ethnic divisiveness.
Once he recognized where his board members' thinking was coming from,
he could make the argument that it wasn't either/or and then convince his
board of the importance of funding people within their communities to
strengthen their skills and *then* begin integrating: "They can't integrate if
they're not up to speed. We start strengthening, then we connect. We don't
want women to go off and forsake their families. We want to strengthen
them, then connect them better to their families, their communities, *and*
the larger society."

Boards can and should be brought along, and everyone is the better for
it. A corporate program officer described the importance of talking about
things that are sometimes hard, one of the first steps in naming Norm. His
board was having a hard time with domestic violence as a proposed new
priority for the foundation. He describes the importance of addressing the
issue of discomfort directly:

I witnessed it taking place. It was one of our board members, a woman on our
board, who actually named the problem. "You know what," she said to the board
at large, "there's an issue of discomfort here." It was easier for the board to talk
about glass ceilings than domestic violence. I think there was this feeling of "all
you men are batterers." Once she raised the issue, though, people started talking
about their discomfort quite personally.

Leadership Is Key

In addition to helping shape effective boards, leadership is also key to creating healthy organizational cultures that institutionalize deep diversity.
Of the leaders we interviewed for this book, the most effective are curious
and positive and inspire both board and staff in their visions for the organization. They see the big picture. A major private foundation board member notes, "If you have enlightened leadership, you know you can't ignore
women. It took the World Bank a long time to understand this; they failed
in development projects because they ignored women. But the Bank's leadership was finally able to provide a crucial gender analysis that made all
the difference."[12]

Leadership empowers staff and trustees alike. When a CEO "gets" deep
diversity and communicates that in explicit and implicit ways to everyone
in the organization, change happens. A program officer at a family foun-

dation notes, "It isn't just staff moving it forward, it's top leadership. It's crucial that they believe diverse women's funding is important, women's positions are important." In another instance, a male CEO is seen as giving permission to his staff to raise a range of issues involving gender and race questions: "What a difference that makes that he's an advocate in his institution. My sense is that it raises awareness among a huge sweep of staff, but he also implicitly provides permission for a large staff of young women to look at things, do some work that they might otherwise find difficult."

At least some aspect of effective leadership has to do with timing. An executive observes that, so often, important decisions come down to having key people in place at the right time:

Our founder would turn in his grave to see what the foundation does now. We need to institutionalize and mainstream what we do—when you have the right leadership, they need to work on the institutionalization part: seed the field, support younger people, and bring them on board, especially people who are challenging us. We need to trust in the ability of people to organize on their own behalf with the right resources. Then get the leadership to move on and give new people opportunities to lead.

This kind of leadership, which also knows when to push and when to back off, how to get the right people in place on both board and staff to make these organizational cultural shifts happen—these are all crucial components of the hard but essential work involved in institutionalizing deep diversity. Without it, effective philanthropy doesn't happen.

3

Capitalizing on Deep Diversity: Case Studies of Successful Foundations

As we saw in chapters 1 and 2, naming Norm and understanding and institutionalizing deep diversity are key strategies for doing effective philanthropy. This chapter explores how these skills play out in the settings of actual foundations: how foundation staffs and boards learned about the "Norm" elephants on their desks; how they deepened their understanding of a broad range of diversities, including gender; and how they institutionalized that knowledge and in the process transformed their organizational cultures.

For this phase of our book's research, we conducted thirty-seven interviews with CEOs, staff, trustees, and grantees of six private, family, and community foundations—Otto Bremer Foundation, The California Wellness Foundation, Hyams Foundation, Jessie Smith Noyes Foundation, The Philadelphia Foundation, and Public Welfare Foundation—foundations selected because they have reputations among their peers for effective funding of women's and girls' organizations as well as for institutionalizing deep diversity that includes gendered cultural competence within their own organizations.

In selecting these six, we opted for foundations based in different regions of the country, for a range of foundations that are themselves diverse: diverse in the size of their endowments and annual grant making awards, diverse in the size of their staffs and boards, diverse in their missions and the constituencies they serve. We also wanted to include different types of foundations (e.g. private, community, family) as well as foundations that were at different stages in their own institutional development. We interviewed corporate philanthropy CEOs and staff for the first phase of our research for this book but chose not to include corporate funders in this chapter for two reasons: we wanted to highlight foundations within the range of the majority of foundations in this country so our examples could be more easily replicated, and governance structures of corporate foundations usually are dependent on parent corporations so issues like diversifying boards have to be addressed differently.[1] Corporate foundations like Wells Fargo, Sara Lee, and the Prudential Foundation have institutionalized valuable lessons about deep diversity and share many of the qualities of effective philanthropy described in this chapter, but describing how corporate foundations apply deep diversity and gendered cultural competence to their organizations is out of the scope of consideration for this book.

Because this chapter aims to provide case studies describing funding and management strategies that can be replicated easily by the majority of foundations in this country, we limited our selection to private, community, or family foundations with less than $1 billion in endowments in 2001 (when we started this research), with fewer than fifty full-time staff, profiles that mirror a considerable majority of U.S. foundations.[2] Those selected have founding dates that range from 1918 to 1992. The smallest had an endowment of $60 million, the largest an endowment of just over $1 billion in 2003 dollars. The number of grants they each awarded in 2003 ranged from 120 to 935, and the annual total dollar amounts of each foundation's grants in 2003 ranged from $2.76 million to over $40 million. Collectively in 2003, they held $2.338 billion in assets and gave away more than 2,856 grants worth just under $113 million.

Although a common denominator of these six foundations is their commitment to various facets of social-justice funding—which may make them more attuned to diversity issues—their organizational cultures are in fact quite different from one another, and they offer a range of strategies that all organizations, regardless of their funding priorities or mission statements, can learn from in assessing their own institutional cultures. The point here is that institutionalizing deep diversity helps strengthen organizations, whether those foundations fund the opera, an upscale hospital, or a homeless shelter.

Deep Diversity Works

We began the research for this chapter looking for how-tos that could nail down the more theoretical analyses laid out in chapters 1 and 2: how did these funders get national reputations for funding gender unabashedly and for institutionalizing deep diversity so effectively? As you will see throughout this chapter, there are a variety of answers. As we moved through interviews for these case studies, however, other distinct patterns began to emerge that proved a happy bonus for one of the basic themes of this book and answer the question of what difference "difference" makes. Deep diversity works. Deep-diversity organizations do effective philanthropy.

These foundations—all of them committed to institutionalizing a nuanced understanding of deep diversity in their organizational DNA—hit most of the benchmarks for effective philanthropy that surfaced in our first round of interviews and early research: core support, multiyear grants, sticking with grantees over time, grantee-driven and community-based (responsive) grant making, balanced "power" relationships with grantees, and so on. Typical of other foundations with similar goals, these funders manifest understandings of deep diversity that reflect multifaceted awareness of gender and diversity issues that clearly strengthens their grant making and their institutions. In these foundations, gender is understood to be a piece of the puzzle, not avoided, not a source of discomfort to boards and staffs, whether in their interactions with each other or their priority-setting and grant-making decisions. None of the funders, trustees, and grantees we interviewed describe their work as universal or generic grant making. Instead, most of them describe using a gender lens and exhibit functional understandings of gender that reflect much of the analysis described in the first two chapters of this book.

Interestingly, however, a gender lens is only one of the diversity lenses these foundations use, and most of those interviewed speak of diversity in much more nuanced terms: diversity is *diverse,* not "just" gender, race, and ethnicity. And issues related to gender, race, and ethnicity get more traction to the extent that they are part of a larger, more complex understanding of the importance of diversity that includes a working knowledge of how age, disability, geography, class, culture, learning styles, and other diversities impact grantees as well as their foundations. As one staff member defines it:

Real diversity is just the opposite of Norm and the expectations so many foundations have that those of us "not Norm" fit in like clones. Even if we look different, even if we're multicultural or have diverse gender identities, there's still this pressure to be "monocultural." That's not only boring, it really gets in the way of innovation. More than just "tolerance" for different perspectives, real diversity shows enthusiasm for difference, a push to think outside the box—the flip side of

Norm. Diversity's exhilarating. There's a kind of spontaneous, creative, collective energy that bubbles up when the filters are off, and all kinds of differences are respected, when people are valued and listened to.

And this kind of diversity makes for more effective, innovative philanthropy that meets the needs of diverse communities. Gary Yates, CEO of The California Wellness Foundation (TCWF), talks about being at the foundation before their push to institutionalize diversity and the difference a diverse staff has made for the effectiveness of their grants:

The foundation's diverse program staff brings intimate knowledge of underserved communities . . . and these values inform their grant making. For example, a program director who is an immigrant herself and a former executive of a women's foundation brought to the board's attention the specific health concerns of indigenous Oaxacans [Mexicans], many of whom are migrants and seasonal farmworkers. There is a high incidence of upper respiratory illness, infectious diseases, tuberculosis, domestic violence, and alcohol addiction. Oaxaqueños are often isolated because of language barriers that separate them from both English- and Spanish-speaking people. In Oaxaca alone, there are over sixteen indigenous languages including Mixteco, Zapoteco, Triqui, and Chatino. While the grant was risky because of the sponsoring organization's fragile infrastructure, the program director was able to make a strong case for support because of her familiarity with immigrant-focused organizations and their specific health issues. The organization successfully leveraged the TCWF grant attracting additional funding from national foundations.[3]

More Than Multiculturalism

This deeper understanding of diversity that permeates the entire organizational culture and changes the kinds of grants a foundation makes emerged as one of the key findings in our research. More than multiculturalism, in most cases, this multifaceted understanding of diversity grew as a consequence of foundations' "intentionality" and constant vigilance (not just "add a few and stir," as one trustee emphasized). These foundations took intentional steps, both historically and ongoing, to pay attention, to get comfortable with "fluidity," to let their institutional culture as well as individual trustees and staff members change and be changed by each other and by new people and new ideas.

All of the staff, trustees, and grantees interviewed for this chapter stress that diversity does not happen overnight. Diversity is an ongoing process that requires looking for new ways of bringing on board more diverse employees, for example, like hiring people from professions outside philanthropy and using both alternative media and ethnic networks to advertise for employees. All of these foundations also stress the importance of communication across differences, and they have devised a variety of ways to make more effective communication happen. Perhaps hardest to achieve, they also work to embed these values into their organizational cultures, cultures very different one from another among the foundations interviewed. Even accounting for differences among these six case studies, the foundations shared common denominators that include valuing differences among all components of the foundation, differences on the board, differences across staff—including leadership, program and support staff—as well as differences among grantees themselves.

And as important, ongoing processes used to diversify and institutionalize deep diversity reflect intentionality. Diversifying boards, for example, means looking for trustees who bring a range of expertise and cultural experience to their boards. In family foundations, the processes emerged as especially thoughtful: adding outside trustees, working together to learn to take risks, learning to be comfortable with change and difference, and setting those attitudes as visible values for staff to emulate. Both board and staff leadership play a key role in making these changes happen, and most of the trustees stressed the importance of their foundations' not just paying lip service to diversity but going after the messier dimensions of diversity like undoing racism and bigotry and homophobia. For trustees and staff members alike, accessibility is seen as a key strategy: staying available and being responsive to the communities they serve.

Gender a Key Piece of Deep Diversity

Gender is a key piece of this bigger picture of deep diversity. Funders interviewed do not see gender pitted against race or ethnicity, vying for tight dollars. Nor do they cite universal or generic funding: no one claims they fund girls, for example, when they fund youth programs. Instead, they describe gender, including sexual orientation and gender identity, as essential lenses that give them integral, detailed knowledge—including demographics and patterns of more subtle discrimination—that play out in the organizations they fund. Like other differences, gender is understood as a variable often overlooked but essential for teasing out the most detailed, thoroughly documented knowledge of priority areas and institutions funded. In the California Wellness example cited earlier, for example, because the program officer was using a gender lens, she could see domestic violence as one of the indigenous Oaxacans' health risks.

Not that any of this comes easily. One program officer talks about the importance of keeping the pressure on to find ways to make a gender lens automatic:

> I think, for the most part, all of us embrace our work using a gender lens, but I think more can be done. For some, it's a part of who we are, for others not necessarily; they don't use that lens around aging, for example. So the question for me is how we can better institutionalize that knowledge, that perspective, so that it's more tangible. How do we do it? What's the benefit? I'm rather careful, always being one of the first people to bring that up. But it needs to be more institutionalized. We need to find ways to make it come alive so it's automatic, part of the angles we use to see our work.

When asked how use of a gender lens showed up in her foundation, another program officer talked about a deliberate decision her board made in the early 1990s when, having decided to find a new trustee with good finance skills, the board made a real effort to find a female to fill that slot: "That could only have happened with a gender lens ingrained. We had a female chair of the board then, and the finance slot for a female was the last hurdle for the board. To me, sitting on staff watching the board, they had a struggle to decide a female could make those decisions."

So even in our model case studies, inevitable gender discomforts had to be to overcome. A family trustee described how her board had some difficulty understanding sexual orientation as part of their diversity agenda: "There was fear that all of a sudden we'd have lesbian issues pushed, but that didn't happen. Instead, our new appointment brought a different perspective, someone speaking from experience about prejudice and discrimination." And some of the "model" boards still have to struggle to get past an "old boys' club" history. One female trustee observes that in spite of a history of good appointments of women staff and grants to women's organizations, her board "still has some difficulty recruiting women trustees. Although I never get the sense that women aren't welcome on the board, conversation at board meetings can sometimes be 'boyish.'" And there are more subtle hurdles to overcome: "The men on the board want to invite more women trustees, but they seem to be stumped by some sense of who they don't want. . . . A lot of potential trustees, for instance, who are 'strong women' and may be the kind of women they're worried about inviting on board"—a classic case of unexamined assumptions about "gender nonconformity" tripping up otherwise thoughtful and well-intentioned trustees.

Commitment to Deep Diversity Pays Off

Most of the funders interviewed have learned to get past these kinds of unexamined assumptions and speak about the importance of a deeper understanding of gender and diversity as key for more effective grant making. Intentionality and sustained attention can create new sources of funds for foundations that raise money to give it away—expanding donor-advised funds, for example, and educating donors. Intentionality also can lead to strategies for more effective grant making: responsiveness to grantees, community-based solutions to intractable community problems, funder-grantee partnerships and respected peer relationships with grantees, risk-taking, and so forth.

When a foundation diversifies its board, diversifies its staff, and institutionalizes diversity—especially when it defines diversity broadly—the power balance between funders and grantees shifts and not coincidentally, more effective grant making results. But the process takes commitment and patience. One executive interviewed describes an instance of internal tension continuing to play out in the organization as a consequence of the organization's shift from "initiative-driven, targeted, prescriptive, complicated laid-out funding initiatives" to grantee-driven, community-based responsive grant making: "Moving away from prescriptive grant making has required an unlearning and relearning for program officers, and that's been a source of some internal tension. Program officers had been doing initiatives, had power bases established, and now the main focus is around due diligence, doing all the upfront work, less around monitoring. It's a power shift." And some have a hard time adjusting to such shifts.

But it is precisely this kind of struggle that makes for more innovation within the foundation's own institutional culture as well as externally. Our case study foundations extended their understanding and awareness of diversity in their own institutions to their grantees, promoting a consciousness of diversity among grantees and an accountability that rewards both results and the process of achieving them, even when results are not immediately apparent. These foundations also are committed to working across the larger field of philanthropy itself, modeling accountability by making outside evaluations public and taking on responsibility for translating their institutions' experiences to other funders. Unlike philanthropy that mirrors a "gentleman's agreement" not to comment on other foundations' work, these funders are active in philanthropy field activities and do not hesitate to speak out about issues such as the importance of maintaining levels of funding in hard times, even when it means upping the level of foundation payouts (the percentages of foundation endowments used for grants).

How Consciousness Starts

How does consciousness of diversity start in a foundation that hasn't paid much attention to such concerns in the past? Most of those interviewed point to a combination of leadership and openness to change. One program officer recalled a former CEO:

I don't know how this evolved. Our ED certainly didn't get diversity in his bones, but he was intellectually committed to the process, and he trusted the people he hired. He himself was hired because the board liked him, and he looked like a lot of people on the board. But he had the wisdom to hire program officers who were more diverse. As a CEO, he insisted that all staff members interview any new candidates for staff positions. And once you hire one person who understands diversity lenses, you're more likely to get others.

Another CEO argues how important it is that the perceived leader, board or staff, give a stamp of approval or remain neutral in the face of change:

Some family members on our board were slower in accepting that we needed more diversity. Others were stronger in pushing it. Sometimes responses were subtle, for example, questions like "are we moving too fast?" But because some family board members felt it was important to have a really diverse board as fast as possible, that message allowed staff and nonfamily board members to push the issue, helped make them comfortable in challenging others on the board to push. I think if the family had opposed in unison, it would have been more difficult. At least half of the board members sent strong signals and empowered our staff to push.

Another CEO described some discomfort expressed by a foundation staffer but emphasized the need to acknowledge the concerns but put them in context:

This process has a lot to do with the culture of the foundation and its leadership. We had an agreement of neutrality from informal [board] leaders. Most of our staff was with us. Maybe there was one early on who felt "It's ok but . . . there are only so many slices of the pie." But we'd argue that picking one out of three in any job search means you're always losing good people, by definition. So was it possible our being so "race conscious," so focused on race and ethnicity, meant we were going to lose opportunities to put strong, skilled people on the board? Sure, but we just needed to keep working to find people who had *all* the qualities we were looking for, including diversity.

And the process sometimes got tense. A board leader stressed, "Look, I don't want to sugarcoat this process. We've had board members say, 'I just don't understand this race stuff.'" The bottom line for this foundation was that they persisted, responding clearly to board concerns and discomforts, but kept looking and looking until they found the diversity they sought. To reiterate a point made earlier, they looked for trustees in places that they had not looked before: grantee communities, minority law and accounting professional associations, networks of other funders who had successfully diversified boards, and so forth. The point here is that the process was intentional—and involved thinking in new ways about how to find trustees for their board. And the intentionality pays off. As one relatively new trustee notes, "Diversity is a plus. Before coming on this board, I had not fully understood issues of diversity and inclusion as being a benefit. But it makes the work that much richer, more likely to be successful."

Bumps in the Road and Roadblocks

But no one claims it's an easy process. People interviewed for this chapter spoke candidly about a range of issues that got in their way as they evolved more diverse organizations. The difficulties are many and range from people who "just don't understand this race stuff" to the problems of starting with unreflective organizational cultures that viewed diversity as worth little more than lip service. These unreflective organizational cultures felt stagnant to the people who worked in them, both staff and trustees. Without meaning to, the foundations had evolved cultures and styles of interacting that didn't tolerate a lot of difference, spoken or unspoken, and they were fraught with style and class issues that easily triggered discomfort without effective institutional mechanisms in place for improving communication. Difficulties also included covert or subconscious homophobia and racism and the dangers of tokenizing people who are "different."

Larger Culture

Organizations do not exist in isolation. Even the most progressive foundations mirror the culture of their larger communities and the nation at large—neither of which have solved entrenched problems of racism and difference. In fact, in recent years, differences have been exacerbated for political gain and religious ideology, e.g., marriage equality used as a wedge issue in the 2004 presidential campaign, appeals to narrow segments of voters based on their ethnic or racial identification—all of which make it even more difficult for organizations struggling to diversify their own boards and staffs. The new board member quoted earlier explains:

I think people are most comfortable with folks who are like themselves. The reality is that most people in their everyday lives tend not to be exposed to a broad kind of swath of America. People are not interacting regularly with people who are of a different race, ethnicity, or sexual orientation, certainly not living with people who are different, not living or praying with them, so they don't have the opportunity to become comfortable. So even with people of good will, I think there's resistance. There aren't enough opportunities for people to interact regularly in an unpressured environment. Debates about diversity can be pressured. But even in less pressured settings, people are inclined to resist.

Institutional Cultures

Institutional cultures themselves can be roadblocks. One CEO describes what happened when people of color who themselves had risen through the ranks resisted change. When he pressed for better understanding of organizational cultural issues in collegial coalitions, he got some negative feedback: "As a white guy, I was dismissed as 'you don't know what you're talking about,' and I got some pretty racist reactions. Leadership in this group has been people who've made it by 'going along, getting along.' I come from ornery stock, and I recognize I've got privilege. Maybe it's easier for me to see it, say it." Blindness to such manifestations of Norm usually is unintended, not explicit or even conscious most of the time. As a gay trustee points out, "straight white culture is never seen as having an agenda." Unquestioned cultural norms and the "ways it's always been" dominate organizational cultures that don't push to change, and that blindness, however unintended, can be a significant roadblock.

Style and Class Issues, Especially Class

Style and class issues also can be roadblocks. A new trustee recalls:

I came here thinking the South is so innately polite, and others often don't understand that politeness. I used to think "politeness" was the source of communication glitches. Women from the South, after all, do things very indirectly. I used to think that was a peculiarly Southern style, but since coming to this foundation, I now see it's a class thing. I watched the women on this board do exactly the same thing as my relatives, and they're certainly not Southern. Some of them have a politeness that makes it hard to have the tough conversations necessary to make things work. . . . When new people came onto the board, there were tensions about people being too plainspoken, and we had to guess what other people were thinking.

These are class issues dressed up as "style" or regional differences, and without efforts to confront them directly, they pose significant roadblocks to diversifying boards and staffs as well as dead weight for flexible organizational cultures. "Class" is not a conversation easily shared in our larger culture, much less in more intimate settings like boards. A trustee from another foundation recollects, "The brick wall we hit when looking for new trustees? Social-economic status. We had some trustees who weren't comfortable that we could add board members who weren't 'like the rest of us.' The one thing we don't have on our board is a lot of class diversity."

Another program officer notes, "I think the class lens is . . . the bear. It's easy to work with an Ivy League educated person of whatever color or gender." It's especially easy when a common educational level always has informed the organization. It's also relatively easy when everyone shares comparable professional credentials. As another trustee points out, "Although our trustees' backgrounds are quite different, we're all operating at a professional level in our workaday lives." But this trustee's foundation ran into trouble when they started looking for trustees who didn't fit their educational/professional/class mold: "We ran into opposition from several board members. . . . One of the concerns voiced at the time was our fiduciary responsibility. There were assumptions that someone without our class advantages could not understand budgets. Which is kind of ironic since the market has decimated the endowment on our watch. And we're all still professionals."

What *does* work to make people from different walks of life work together? At least in one foundation, it wasn't training: "We did a diversity training, but some of the board and staff hated it. I don't think it was successful. We didn't have the right combination. It was embarrassing to say you didn't want to do it, but some people just weren't ready for it and felt attacked." What did work was building close relationships and continuing to strengthen commitments to make it all work. Several foundations, for example, spoke of trying different strategies for improving explicit, intentional communication across differences—even to the point of asking all staff members in meetings to repeat in other words what they thought they had heard and understood. They were amazed by how often the words they used carried different meanings for different listeners.

As boards and staff diversify, these are predictable discomforts, assumptions, and confusions. And they are tricky because the discomforts are not always what they seem. Another dimension of "class" discomfort surfaced as the "are we going to have quality people" question—and more often than not the discomfort was class intimately linked with race and ethnicity. As noted in the example of Ivy-League trained folks of whatever race or ethnicity, such caveats, in fact, are more often about class than about race. A CEO described board discussions:

Are we just going to put people on because of their color or backgrounds or will they "fit"? The natural, first reaction . . . is "are we giving up other things we care about?" That was a challenge. Boards tend to perpetuate themselves; you work in the circles you are working in. That makes it difficult to nominate different kinds of people on the board. We work really hard to broaden the pool for both board and staff members. We cast a wide net out there, bring in a large number of people to interview. We consciously make sure the pool is diverse.

While more complex diversity, including class diversity, is important it is equally important that boards struggle to avoid "multiethnic but monocultural." As one CEO said, "I think the problem is people who get uniformity in spite of diversity. What they really get are clones who just look different. . . ." Such unintentional assimilation is understandable because in any institution, there is a sense of leveling. "A new person doesn't want to be a pain in the ass, a one-note person. So it's uncomfortable for some folks, some make an effort to find a common middle ground." But as the same CEO says, "Bring on people who speak comfortably from their experiences and find ways to make the process safe so everyone can listen. The last thing we want to do is to homogenize."

A CEO's enthusiasm for difference may be a necessary push for innovation, but how does staff deal with such discomforts, especially discomforts among people from different socioeconomic backgrounds? One program officer says it takes patience and vigilance:

In our foundation, it's still touchy—I'd confront someone, but . . . Especially when you work with liberals or progressives, people don't want to hear they're not "getting it." They can easily shut down. What works? Keep reminding yourself that these changes take a long time. It takes time for people to unlearn. Stereotypes are hard to dismantle.

It's also important to keep checking one's own assumptions, as this same staffer points out: "Just when you think on a personal level, wow, I feel so much better about not judging, then I come up short. You have to give yourself a checkup. It's hard to do. We get comfortable, find a comfort zone, stay there."

Trustee "comfort zones" are another example of class and sometimes age issues that seldom are named but always grab onto the status quo. A family trustee recalls:

I think there were people in the older generation really concerned whether they'd have anything to say to people different from themselves. They were comfortable giving grants, but that was a circumscribed relationship. They were concerned that grantees on our board or people not from our same background would be able to fit in. Certainly there are generational differences re: comfort level with conflict and different ways of expressing disagreements that have been uncomfortable for some people.

A trustee of color recalls hearing, "Oh, we tried but we just haven't found anyone that's qualified," which is virtually a synonym for maintaining the status quo. But he says, "Well, I'm pretty persistent. And it's not just me; others on the board also understand and cut through those arguments. But some trustees just don't get it. The light bulbs just don't turn on. . . . Sometimes it's quite sad for me."

Racism and Other "Not Norm" Prejudice

Besides class discomforts, racism, homophobia, and other prejudices are still significant roadblocks, if subtle ones. A number of those interviewed talked about the difficulties of acknowledging a range of hidden and not-so-hidden biases when people are well meaning and struggling with these concerns. Sometimes raising the issues, naming the elephants on the table, is best done by someone who looks like most of the board or staff. As one trustee responded, "What will it take for the board to institutionalize diversity? People pushing it who look like the power elite on this board: straight, white people pushing it. Who does the asking does make a difference."

Well and good, but foundation cultures that make it hard to acknowledge subtle and not-so-subtle racial and ethnic stereotypes means trustees and staff of color pay a painful price. A program officer of color said this sometimes hits her in the solar plexus:

When you're a person of color and you do your work well, e.g., write well, you get a "wow" reaction and this big compliment. This happened to me, and I'm going "Why are you surprised? That's what I'm supposed to be doing." The racism in all of this is very subtle. You can't ask, "Why are you surprised?" If you do, they'll say, "Well, I was trying to give you a compliment." It's the experience question: if you're looking for experience, I've got it. Don't be surprised.

Another foundation executive of color adds that liberal organizations can be uncomfortable with minorities and display that discomfort in subtle ways: "Sometimes liberals or so-called progressives are harder to deal with than conservative groups. As a person of color, I see that there's less accountability for people of color. It doesn't allow for a level playing field. I'm sure these organizations would say it isn't the case, but I can tell you it really is." Good intentions perhaps, but cultural incompetence nonetheless.

Real cultural competence means getting beyond the superficial starting points and reaching "got it" competence. Another program officer of color explained:

I have to say that personally I'm so sick of talking about diversity, particularly race and gender, but especially race. It's hard to sit in meetings where I will be judged, but I have to edit my reactions or my grantees will be the ones who suffer. It's so disheartening that we still have to keep talking about race in such simplistic terms. Diversity's an asset, for goodness' sake. But I keep seeing the differential criteria in other foundations' programs, and it's even worse. So many have such a low level of cultural competency. They still don't get it.

But even when people do get it, there's the danger of tokenizing others who are "different," forcing them to do all the hard work of diversity. Another program officer of color says:

I don't want to be the conscience for people. Others have to do this. Mainstream folks don't do enough. If you go to a workshop on how to bring in more people of color, for example, the audience will mostly be people of color. White folks don't go. Personally I'm very conflicted: I've done this for so many years. It's been a given that these issues get raised, but not everybody takes responsibility for raising them.

Another trustee of color says, "Everywhere I go I have the feeling that I'm expected to speak for the Asian community." These examples of subtle and not-so-subtle racism explain how everyone gets tired of the "diversity problem." Exhaustion kills the sheer joy of learning from differences and represents a significant roadblock that foundations aspiring to do effective philanthropy ignore at their peril.

Case Studies

Following are six case studies that place issues discussed throughout this book inside foundations' own histories and development. Trustees, CEOs, program staff, and grantees all spoke candidly about their work and efforts to understand and institutionalize deep diversity. In different voices, these six foundations all spoke concretely about how they came to more nuanced understandings of deep diversity, including gender, and how they institutionalized that understanding on their boards and on their staffs using intentionality, recognition of process, and leadership. They also talked about the impact their deep diversity work has had on their grants and on their relationships with grantees as well as on their commitments to the larger field of philanthropy. And not least of all, they shared an array of different strategies and benchmarks they evolved for defining and evaluating effectiveness. Table 3.1 presents in summary form a list of the issues they addressed. The numbers refer to how many of the six case study foundations mentioned the summary descriptors, all of them strategies and benchmarks these foundations used for achieving both deep diversity and effectiveness.

Table 3.1
Summary Descriptors of Case Study Foundations

Descriptor	Number
Leadership is committed to achieving deep diversity	6
Leadership works to add diverse trustees on board	5
Leadership and staff work to add diverse staff members	6
Gender is understood to be a key piece of deep diversity	6
Board and staff understand how differences like race, class, and gender "intersect"	6
Board and staff use a "gender lens" in grant making	6
Leadership allows organization to change to fit new board and staff members	6
Board and staff committed to learning new skills to communicate across differences	6
Board and staff committed to "institutionalizing" gendered cultural competence	6
Board comfortable taking risks	6
Staff comfortable taking risks	6
Staff partner with grantees where possible	4
Leadership seeks external input to grant-making guidelines	5
Leadership seeks external input to grant-making decisions	3
Leadership committed to do more "responsive" grant making, fewer requests for proposals (RFPs)	4
Staff encouraged to provide core support	6
Foundation can fund some grantees longer than three years	6
Foundation can fund some grantees longer than five years	6
Foundation can fund some grantees longer than ten years	5
Foundation works to leverage other funders' support for grantees	5
Staff monitors grantee diversity	6
Foundation does internal evaluation of grant making	6
Foundation does external evaluation of grant making	3

OTTO BREMER FOUNDATION

Established as a charitable trust in 1944, the Otto Bremer Foundation defines its mission as promoting human rights and creating opportunities for economic and social justice. The foundation's assets, which in 2003 totaled over $455.4 million, are invested primarily in the Bremer Financial Corporation, a privately held $5 billion regional financial-services company owned by the foundation and the corporation's more than 1,700 employees. As the corporation describes their relationship with the foundation, "this unique ownership structure, the only one of its kind in the nation, fosters an environment of caring and commitment to the communities we serve like no other." The foundation reinforces the corporation's commitment to the region (Minnesota, North Dakota, Wisconsin, and Montana). In fiscal year 2003, the foundation gave away 728 grants totaling over $19.3 million and 7 program-related investments of more than $3.6 million. Affiliates of the Bremer Financial Corporation also donate hundreds of thousands of dollars annually to community causes, and corporation employees give thousands of hours of their time and skills.

Foundation History

The Bremer legacy began in November 1886, when Otto Bremer arrived in America as a nineteen-year-old German immigrant whose travels eventually brought him to St. Paul, Minnesota. A banker's son who had served an apprenticeship in a German bank before he immigrated, Bremer eventually followed in his father's footsteps, pursuing a career in banking that started only six months after he arrived in America. Beginning as a bookkeeper, he rose over the next thirteen years to chief clerk and major stockholder in a St. Paul bank. Bremer's success as a trusted local businessman helped get him elected Treasurer for the City of St. Paul, where he served five terms.[4]

Even before entering politics, Otto Bremer began to invest in community banks, including the American National Bank, and in 1913 he was elected to its board of directors. By 1921, he was asked to preside as chairman of the bank. His association with what he called his "countryside" banks, however, was the work nearest to his heart. One of his banking creeds was "banks should be home banks, independently operated by people of their communities."

When the Great Depression hit, Bremer stuck with his community banks. Dipping heavily into his own personal assets, he invested in many of these small local banks and kept them afloat until the waves of panic subsided. His community-oriented commitment shaped the future of both his corporation and his foundation. When Otto Bremer carefully outlined the issues and concerns he wanted his foundation to address, one of his primary concerns was to "relieve poverty in the city of St. Paul." Today, the foundation continues to invest in human rights and economic and social justice issues throughout a four-state region. Establishing his foundation enabled Bremer to channel a significant share of his earnings back to the communities served by his banks while at the same time securing the future of his banks in their communities.

With Bremer's own life and vision as a legacy, his foundation has developed a national reputation for innovative grant making and a special awareness of the needs of women and others who have limited access to resources. What is especially interesting in this case study is that the foundation built this national reputation with the smallest board in our sample, three trustees, all white, one woman. The head of the foundation is John Kostishack, who has been with the foundation for 22 years. Kostishack points to an early start with grant making to promote access: "When the foundation trustees began grant making in 1969, they wanted to start by serving rural communities. From the beginning, that experience meant dealing with barriers in accessing other resources. It brought out a whole sense of equity and justice in funding. Although that wasn't expressed at the time, that experience led to the foundation giving to organizations that have less access."[5]

Peer Relationships with Grantees

Program Officer Karen Starr recalls these early experiences as essential to the foundation's own organizational culture, especially the fact that many of their grantees "were not trained to have a cultural connection with philanthropy." She talks about how the grantees' assumptions—or lack of assumptions—about philanthropy taught her how to do a different, more responsive kind of philanthropy.

They expected much more of a peer relationship. Respectful, more honest, these relationships challenged me to do this work as a peer. We got to work with grantees that didn't buy into the existing culture of philanthropy, so we started acting the way we would probably have wanted to anyway. We were accountable, we kept going back to the same town, and if we made mistakes, we heard about them.

This sense of responsibility as peers also helped staff to grow, a key attitude mentioned by a number of those interviewed for the case studies. Without being open to learning from grantees and each other, staff members seldom improve their grant making. Starr says:

One of the things that helps is working as a team, working with colleagues and allies who are constantly pushing and prodding you not to go back to old ways of thinking. Going on site visits is an example: I might approach a site visit with certain assumptions about how nonprofits work, but I get pulled back. And I'm always reminded that many of us are operating out of white privilege.

Importance of "Intentionality"

The foundation is small: three trustees with no term limits, four program people, and four support staff, plus additional consultants that the foundation brings in as needed. They attribute their success over time both to their history of "operating in a family-like way" and the importance of intentionality. The foundation's history is alive to all still involved in the foundation: both board and staff describe going back and frequently revisiting their history, especially when a new staff person is hired. Board member Charlotte Johnson also traces their success to being more conscious about their work, especially as they moved into the foundation's fifth decade:

What's happened in the last decade is more intentionality, more thinking about "why we do it," giving it more shape. And that's always changing, that sense of equity, of access. How can we be more intentional for women and others? Rather than focusing on specific groups, we focus on equity, on broader issues like human rights.

This intentionality early on resulted in a residency program for local women of color in philanthropy. As program Officer Karen Starr describes its inception, they modeled their residency program in Minnesota on Women & Philanthropy's national initiative:

We led our program with a lot of help from women of color organizations, and we housed women of color in the foundation who helped us see things differently. Working with a lot of other local foundations, we also joined with community women, many of them nonprofit executive directors. They were paid residencies; this was a paid leadership program. And the women residents were surrounded by other women of color. We had three women residents working here in our offices, all of them seen as leaders within their respective communities. We were trying to demystify gaps between foundations and nonprofits.

A Complex Understanding of Difference and Walking the Talk

Like other foundations profiled in this chapter, the Otto Bremer Foundation has benefited from their evolving understanding of diversity and difference. This understanding is reflected in their funding priorities as well as in their own staff. CEO John Kostishack describes their history:

In our grant making, we're looking at issues where others haven't gone. With our staff, we're looking for values and differences that are strengths. Valerie Lies, who was one of the first woman executive directors of a Minnesota foundation, a founder of Women & Philanthropy, and currently the President of the Donors Forum of Chicago, hired me to replace Joyce Yu, a program officer who went on to the Ms. Foundation. When Valerie moved on, we hired Karen Starr. Trustees have also provided ways of exploring, insisting that we should really "walk our talk." They pushed us: when we're concerned about serving communities with little access, we need to have them represented on our staff.

So how did this sense of difference evolve? Especially with such a small staff and so little changeover in trustees (one trustee has served for forty years, the son of one of the original trustees, another eleven years, the "newest" seven years). John Kostishack says, "There's this assumption that we don't have the answers. Because of that, we have to be open to other points of view."

Program Officer Karen Starr talks about experiencing the organization's positive attitudes toward difference and openness to new ideas—and how the small staff interacts with each other and with the board:

There's a tone here. I credit Valerie and John with establishing it. This is not a hierarchical place. There are functional distinctions among us based on what we do, but we're a group of human beings working together. . . . There's a sense of respect and trust, that what you say is important. Everyone comes to the planning meetings, including support staff. We all talk. Dispelling assumptions about hierarchy and class has established a way of working.

Board member Charlotte Johnson describes this culture as promoting individual growth, a culture that from her perspective as a board member is both intentional and nonhierarchical:

When people are hired, there's an assumption they won't stay in that position but will have opportunities to shift and grow in the job. There's a sense of fluidity. We used to be smaller, and it was easier to have everyone in on the conversation. With trustees and staff, we now number eleven. We worry about this. We bring everyone to our retreats, including families.

For the last five years, the Otto Bremer Foundation has invited Margarita Rubalcava, Program Director of the Funders' Collaborative for Strong

Latino Communities, who previously worked with the foundation as a communications officer, to prepare and facilitate its annual retreat for trustees and staff. She provides the foundation with ways of looking at its work that have helped build its commitment to human rights and its ongoing challenge to complacency.

An Active, Hard-Working, Hands-On Board

Although the board accepts most of the staff's recommendations for grant awards, the board itself is involved actively in all funding decisions. The staff and trustees work via a consent agenda, putting together a full book that includes background details with recommendations, and the board meets every month, alternating between grants-decision meetings and meetings with a wider-ranging programmatic focus. (The board used to do a grants-decision meeting every month, but as John Kostishack describes, that can "get in the way of being intentional.") Still, as Karen Starr points out, "We gave 732 grants last year. That's a lot for a small foundation. Up until last year, the trustees had seen every one of those proposals."

If the amount of work involved made the board change its mechanics for approving grants, it did not lessen their commitment to diversity. Charlotte Johnson describes the board's work and their efforts to keep learning about the issues they fund:

We do a lot of reading. One of the changes we made is that we have more selected information coming to us, not full-fledged proposals, but we haven't lost the diversity. In the months alternating with grants decisions, we bring in someone to discuss broader programmatic issues: affordable housing or Native American land tenure, for example, and we look at how all of these issues work together, how they interact with other sectors.

Combined with the proposal documentation the board reads, these meetings teach the board about the universe in which they operate. "Those proposals represent a lot of diversity. The legacy to the trustees is seeing that there are many, many ways to solve problems."

Bremer consultant Margarita Rubalcava adds that she thinks the foundation's success is a result of their visiting the communities the foundation serves: "Everybody, including the board, gets out on the road. This has been really important. Encouraged to be active in the community, their ears are closer to the ground."

A Learning Organization that Focuses on Institutionalizing Change

In the early 1980s, the foundation started the annual planning process described earlier that also has helped them to "reflect and think about what we're doing and intentionally institutionalize it." John Kostishack says, "We're trying to build a culture here where change is something that people embrace. This is a major challenge. We change things. We change ourselves." The foundation's staff has gotten so comfortable with change as a vital part of the organization's culture that they can tease about it: one staff member, who is in charge of computer support, showed up at a foundation retreat wearing a tee shirt that read "I FEAR CHANGE."

Site visits are an important part of institutionalizing change. Karen Starr says she is constantly learning something from grantees and feels her role is to get beyond the superficial niceties in the grantee/grantor relationship in ways that give her deeper knowledge of the grantees and then communicate that to the rest of staff and board: "I get to walk through a door and a world opens up. My job is to understand what's written on paper but also beyond that, to get a feel for the organization. And my job is to communicate. An ongoing challenge is to capture new thinking and insight and pass that on. This is what keeps this job new after twenty years."

The foundation also actively seeks out advice from grantees, even setting up special situations to encourage candid responses from grantees. Karen Starr explains:

Last year, each of us (in teams of two) had the job of interviewing grantees prior to our annual planning meeting. We try to do things to counter the sucking up. . . . These are different ways of getting different pieces of the picture. . . . I met with an African American organization head who had loved what we'd written about human rights. He said, "Great, this is different; now here are some other ways you can walk your talk."

All this planning and reflection has carried over to the foundation's grant making. The commitment to working with grantees as partners, for example, has led to more investment in nonprofit capacity building. According to Starr, "This work does take more time (we hired more staff), but all the staff is committed to it. The feedback from grantees has been positive. More nonprofits are recognizing that it's ok to invest in themselves."

Not without Criticism for an All-White Board, But . . .

The Otto Bremer Foundation is especially interesting because over the years their small, white board has garnered a national reputation for understanding and institutionalizing diversity. One grantee notes, "When you go into the community, Otto Bremer is the name you hear most, the one nonprofits look up to, especially on diversity." But this same grantee goes on to point out that the foundation's board is only three people large, two white men, one white woman:

One thing I'd challenge them on is not finding other ways of having a diverse board. They say Bremer can never be other than a white organization at the same time that they are pointing out ways our organization can improve our diversity. That's a problem for me. Not because we don't need ways we can improve . . . we obviously want all the help we can get. But it rankles because Bremer could change their policies on trustees too. Even if they can't legally expand their board, why not have a review panel, or an advisory board? There are ways other foundations have found to diversify.

This same grantee, however, tempers the criticism with more praise for the foundation's commitment to the wider field of philanthropy as well as for their efforts to expand grantees' commitment to diversity:

I just love the Bremer Foundation. I think they're fabulous. Another exemplary thing about them is their funding of diversity within philanthropy. They've always been huge supporters of women working in philanthropy. They house a Midwest branch for Hispanics in Philanthropy in their office and provide them other in-kind support. They've done a lot to raise consciousness of diversity, to keep the pressure on the rest of the field of philanthropy.

More Than Multiculturalism

So how did an all-white board with a white male CEO get so good at understanding diversity, especially their more complex understanding of gender? A foundation consultant, Margarita Rubalcava, says, "It's the people that are there. Starting with the foundation leadership, the trustees and executives, first Valerie Lies and now John. . . . It starts at the top." Another funder notes, "From a very early start, there were women at the foundation. And the men at the foundation understood gender." This peer funder also praises the foundation's intentionality, their consciousness about diversity in hiring new staff: "There's a strong effort to do recruiting to encourage applicants from low-income communities, communities of color, people who've walked in the shoes of people they're supposed to be helping."

Another funding colleague notes how their active cultural immersion in the communities they serve helps Bremer's staff and board members remain open to new ideas and awareness of diverse cultures. They don't rely on superficial knowledge:

Bremer is out in all the small communities. They know where the best Mexican food is, where the ethnic grocery stores are. That helps them get information, exposes them to people who might not otherwise be on foundations' radar screens. In every ethnic community, there are the usual suspects, the known leaders, but unless you're actually out and about in those communities and have culturally aware people on your staff, you don't get to see the ones doing the work.

Bremer consultant Rubalcava points out that the foundation's commitment to diversity and cultural immersion is an outgrowth of its history:

Otto Bremer wrote in his trust in 1944 that no one was to be discriminated against on the basis of race or religion. Minnesota prides itself on being progressive. There's a strong sense of populist democracy. Foundations here are involved deeply in the community. I think a lot of it was Otto Bremer's vision himself. Otto Bremer's commitment is reminiscent of the movie *It's a Wonderful Life* that starred Jimmy Stewart. Mr. Bremer was concerned about small communities and small banks being wiped out during the Great Depression. He kept many of these small town banks from going bankrupt. That commitment to small, rural communities is still present at the foundation.

Rubalcava points to more recent history and the foundation's attempts to deal directly with institutional racism as underpinning its current emphasis on inclusiveness among its staff. As she sees it, the foundation formed with an initiative aimed at undoing institutional racism, which is far more difficult to accomplish than just embracing diversity or multiculturalism.

But when the foundation started this, they didn't have a diverse staff. My sense is that the foundation has learned a lot simply by focusing on undoing racism, then switching to human rights and social and economic justice. Having done this work programmatically may have influenced their thinking. It's a more diverse staff now, ethnically speaking, but programmatically, they've always understood diversity, even with a predominantly white staff and board. For a long time, talking about undoing racism was not popular. People want to talk about the positive, but the Bremer Foundation's work is about undoing institutional racism and bigotry, a much bigger deal.

Undoing Racism and Bigotry: Accessibility Is Key

So if one of the secrets to Bremer's success has been their willingness to tackle the more negative dimensions of diversity work, opening doors to difference is the measure of their achievement. The negative dimensions they have tackled include the use of language, as Rubalcava points out. She also emphasizes the importance of this kind of commitment and how hard it can seem: "It's a negative thing to talk about racism and bigotry. The words themselves describe the roadblocks. A lot of foundations don't want to do what seems to be negative work." Rubalcava also identified another one of the real challenges foundations face, another example of Norm that is seldom discussed, what she labels "white male privilege." According to Rubalcava, the Otto Bremer Foundation has named that particular elephant on their desk and sought out ways to unload it:

Psychologically it's difficult for white men to start with the premise they're part of the problem. We operate in a field [philanthropy] where even though more women are making it to the top, my sense is there's a retrenching, avoiding the issues. It's a huge challenge. Diversity is one challenge, but seeking to undo racism and the legacy of racism, it's much harder. It's not pleasant. It's much more doable to diversify staff, but diversifying staff in and of itself doesn't change thinking. . . . As a field, philanthropy doesn't look enough at the class dynamics, class issues. And a lot of people of color in philanthropy don't represent low-income communities. I think the Bremer Foundation is conscious of that.

Dealing with such elephants and also being active in diverse and low-income communities may have contributed to another real key to their continued success: accessibility. Accessibility is a concrete strategy foundations can use to begin the work of unraveling privilege. It's sometimes seen as inefficient, but accessibility from the top down in a foundation sends clear signals of respect and accountability to both grantees and the communities they serve. Consultant Rubalcava says,

I'm amazed that if you call John, you call him directly. There's no assistant to schedule his appointments. I'm not sure it's the best use of his time, but I certainly know that it makes a big difference that he's that accessible. Some of undoing racism comes from being able to access the institution. It's something the foundation prides itself on. Every year they ask "are we spending enough time?" This foundation has [even] institutionalized listening. . . . They go to all the small places and they listen. They're walking the talk, really have their ears to the ground.

And many of those interviewed emphasized other aspects of the foundation's accessibility, including how they continue to fund smaller grants, increasingly rare in a philanthropic climate that puts more emphasis on accountability without including a commitment to diversity and innovative organizational cultures. Bremer bends over backward to accommodate less sophisticated grassroots organizations. As one grantee put it, "Organizations can submit a proposal on a paper bag." Bremer's staff has a reputation of being willing to work with just about any group. This grantee goes on to say that other foundations have processes in place to smooth the way, but they sometimes get in the way, keeping them from reaching key people: "Grants under $10,000 are not cost effective at all, but sometimes it's those small grants that can have enormous impact. Bremer still makes those grants. In the large scheme of things, it may not make sense, but to those people it makes a huge difference. . . . Common sense is not so common."

But the common sense applied daily by the Otto Bremer Foundation pays off, building on and honoring its unique legacy, working peer-to-peer with grantees, being intentional about diversity, and cultivating a more complex understanding of diversity. Bremer's understanding of diversity models the "deep diversity" we talk about in chapters 1 and 2: a diversity beyond mere multicultural add-ons that tackles the more difficult work of undoing racism and bigotry. They have made deeply held commitments to being accessible and to institutionalizing a culture of change. All these factors combined make for an effective, well-regarded foundation that has over the years garnered a well-deserved reputation among peers and communities served by the foundation.

THE CALIFORNIA WELLNESS FOUNDATION

The mission of The California Wellness Foundation (TCWF) is to improve the health of the people of California by making grants for health promotion, wellness education, and disease prevention. Formed in 1992 with assets from the conversion of California Health Net from nonprofit to for-profit status, the foundation is currently one of the largest in the state, an independent, private foundation with an endowment of just under $986 million.[6] In its first decade, TCWF awarded 2,900 grants totaling more than $378 million, with an average outlay of $40 million in grants annually. Grants in 2003 numbered 486 for a total of $40.1 million awarded. The size of endowment as of the end of 2003 was $1.044 billion.

The foundation defines its vision broadly: "Wellness is a state of optimum health and well-being achieved through the active pursuit of good health and the removal of barriers, both personal and societal, to healthy living. It is the ability of people and communities to reach their fullest potential in the broadest sense."[7] Building on consensus among groups like the World Health Organization, TCWF defines a healthy community as one that includes "characteristics such as a clean, safe physical environment and a sustainable ecosystem; the provision for basic needs; an optimum level of appropriate, high-quality accessible public health and sick-care services; quality educational opportunities; and a diverse, vital and innovative economy." The foundation began by defining health as "a state of complete physical, mental and social well-being and not merely the absence of disease or infirmity." As a result, from its inception, TCWF's goal has been to promote the health of Californians by making grants for prevention, believing that it makes more sense to prevent health problems that result from violence, teen pregnancy, poverty, and other issues rather than focusing solely on medical treatment.

Focusing on the health of citizens and communities at both individual and societal levels, the foundation encourages people to adopt behaviors that will improve their own health but stresses that the pursuit of wellness is more than just an individual effort. While recognizing that individuals must take personal responsibility for their own health—e.g., combating the dangers of smoking and substance abuse, realizing the importance of physical and emotional fitness, and benefiting from the effectiveness of good nutrition—the foundation's funding efforts seek larger impact. For underserved communities, for instance, pursuit of wellness "can mobilize residents to reduce violence and teen pregnancy, confront environmental health hazards, and open up new opportunities for youth." Believing that the most successful approaches to change are those that develop the capacity of local leadership and institutions, their grant making looks for projects that "build on existing community strengths, emphasize the potential of each community, and foster self-determination."

In general terms, TCWF's funding priorities are:

• Addressing particular health needs of traditionally underserved populations, including low-income individuals, people of color, youth and residents of rural areas

• Strengthening nonprofit organizations that seek to improve the health of underserved populations

• Encouraging leaders who are working to increase health and wellness within their communities

• Informing the development of public policies that promote wellness and enhance access to preventive health care

Broad Definitions of Diversity

Perhaps because of its grasp of systemic economic and social roots of health, the foundation early on stressed the need for a broader understanding of diversity within its own institutional culture. According to communications officer Julio Marcial, early in its history, TCWF defined its diversity broadly.

Here diversity means much more than "just" race or gender. Diversity is all about difference. Our staff is so diverse: we have many differences, cultural values, life experiences, thinking styles, personal preferences. This creates a conglomerate of different people and perspectives, an environment that nurtures everyone. Part of our mission, our mandate, is to make sure all of that diversity is integrated in everything that we do, from the top down.

Marcial goes on to point out, "What the foundation is trying to do is empower underserved communities *and* empower staff."

Definitions of diversity also shift with experience. Magdalena Beltrán-Del Olmo, vice president for communications, recalls, "When we started it was more numbers, now it's more an understanding, getting along with each other, having common goals." As it grew, the foundation expanded its definitions of diversity: diversity is *diverse*, not "just" gender and race. When they are part of this larger picture of diversity, understandings of gender, race, and ethnicity concerns deepen and gain more traction.

Importance of Institutionalizing Diversity

So why and how did the foundation choose this path? Gary Yates, the second president of TCWF since its founding in 1992, says it was a conscious decision to institutionalize diversity: "When I became president in 1995, we had to double the staff and rebuild the board, which was down to four people. Because California is such a diverse state, and we fund statewide with a focus on providing grants for the underserved, we made a decision that to the extent possible (this was not a formula), we ought to represent the diversity of the state." The director of administration, Annette Drake, recalls that Yates' predecessor also gave "marching orders" to hire a culturally diverse staff: "Then Gary Yates made it clear that it was very important to understand differences. Core values were discussed at staff meetings over a period of time."

The board, staff, and grantees we spoke with for this case study all reflected the foundation's understanding of and commitment to diversity. If the foundation hoped to reach underserved communities around the state, they felt they had to have the expertise on staff to understand those constituencies, literally to speak their languages. As Gary Yates says, "We have a 'strategic imperative' to understand better in our own organization what we are trying to do in our work. We owe it to our communities."

Board and Staff Leadership Is Key

Leadership is key to understanding diversity, both board and staff leadership. Several of the people interviewed note that the foundations' institutional commitment to diversity starts at the board level, with the selection of board members themselves who take on the responsibility of learning to work together across differences. The commitment and success of TCWF is especially interesting because the foundation started with an all-white, all-male board chosen by California Health Net. As board members left, they were replaced by trustees from different backgrounds, a conscious intention to diversify a board that by early 2003 included six men and three women, with four white board members (three males and one female), one African-American (male), two Asian-Americans (one male, one female), and two Hispanics (one male, one female). From 2001 to 2003, the board was chaired by a Latina, Luz Vega-Marquis, the president and CEO of the Marguerite Casey Foundation in Seattle, who says, "In making the selection of diverse board members, you create a climate where these issues permeate the organization." A majority of the board now comes with diverse nonprofit experience, and as it has evolved over the last decade, the board clearly has become one of the driving forces behind the foundation's commitment to diversity.

Literal diversity obviously played an important role in the evolving board, but another factor emerged in the TCWF interviews (as well as in many other interviews conducted for this chapter): race or ethnicity or gender per se is only one piece of the puzzle. The two people cited as most responsible for stressing racial and gender diversity on both the board and staff—and working in a variety of innovative ways to institutionalize that awareness—are Yates and Tom David, former executive vice president. Both are white males.

Conscious Intentions and Constant Vigilance

Which comes first, board consciousness or executive staff pushing the issues? Chicken or egg? To answer that in any detail, at least for TCWF, would take more historical and observational data than we are able to provide for this brief case study, but on the surface, both appear to be equally important. The process was jump-started by concerned senior staff, but both board and staff leadership are committed to keeping numbers at a critical mass. As board chair Luz Vega-Marquis recalls, "In terms of board replacement, we made a commitment to maintaining a balance in terms of diversity. This isn't a quota, but we are very conscious, vigilant." Their vigilance is not just about numbers, it is about getting a critical mass of people with a broad range of diversity who understand and struggle with the challenges of difference. "What we're trying to get at is the values, not just the numbers," according to Vega-Marquis. "I still haven't found the right words to describe it. Some boards will put one person on the board and think 'we did our bit for people of color' or for women."

The CEO, however, has the day-to-day management responsibility and is the one who has to keep up the pressure, stress the values the foundation holds, find ways with both board and staff to keep the issues on the table, and especially instill the values of difference so deeply into the culture of the foundation that it does not fall to one or two isolated people of color or white women to raise the issues. According to his staff, Gary Yates is such a leader. He is also someone who tunes in to needs of diverse employees. Vice president for communications Magdalena Beltrán-Del Olmo praises Yates for sticking with her: "When I've pushed back at him, it's sometimes been hard, painful, and he's hung in there with me. He's a tall white guy, but I can talk to him about some issues I can't talk with people of color about. It's been among the most supportive experiences."

Intentional inclusion and constant vigilance are values the whole staff now shares. A white staff member, Annette Drake, says,

Diversity wasn't spoken of [where I worked before]. That profession didn't attract people of color. So I'd never faced the need for diversity before. I'm not someone who sees color, never have been. But it's become very important to me. We all came to the understanding that diversity was what we needed to have, and it happened. We now have a very diverse staff, and we all get along, we work toward a common cause.

If TCWF's success with diversity is due in part to the fact that the push to diversify the foundation has been both conscious and intentional, it is also because there has been an informal but firm resolve to achieve diversity at all levels of the foundation. Even when efforts are described as "informal," they are also explicit and involve everyone. And TCWF's emphasis is on core values, not numbers per se, but with conscious efforts to maintain a critical mass sufficient to get beyond tokenism. Magdalena Beltrán-Del Olmo says, "I'm living proof of [the importance of] a conscious decision. . . . I was struck by these two Anglo guys who asked very good questions about issues relating to media and diversity in California." Conscious efforts are also crucial because, as a number of staff people pointed out, diversity-building takes time. Beltrán-Del Olmo recalls, "There was a lot of tension [to overcome]. It took about three years for folks to learn to communicate effectively—across culture, ethnic backgrounds, but even more across sector experience backgrounds." And the process is complex and sometimes messy. Beltrán-Del Olmo recalls, "We were thrust together, joined those already here, and the DNA was still coming together. That's hard, that's real hard. You can't fall back on trying to navigate the organizational culture if the DNA isn't established. It was much more like building new roads, very messy, bulldozers, dirt, no pavements."

Hiring outside Philanthropy and Helping Employees Strengthen Their Skills

One of the reasons diversity works at TCWF is that the foundation has expanded its hiring practices to look for people outside of traditional philanthropy circles. Increasingly, staff and board members come in with previous nonprofit experiences, especially experiences connected to the constituencies they serve in their new roles within the foundation. The foundation's willingness to take risks and search beyond "the usual suspects" turns up new perspectives and expertise that the foundation needs. Gary Yates hired vice president for communications Magdalena Beltrán-Del Olmo from a corporate position: "He took a chance, pulled someone into the field. . . . There's a lesson here for other CEOs. Sometimes it really means taking a chance, not staying within the field."

Because they are willing to bring in people from outside the field, TCWF also provides whatever support employees need to do their work better. Vice president for finance Peggy Minnich says, "We do have in place support for whatever skills need to be worked on. The foundation supports additional training, hiring mentors, helping employees no matter what the skill is they need."

Communication, Cohesiveness, and Valued Relationships

Another important factor in TCWF's efforts to make diversity work is communication: give and take, the ability to argue, to be direct, to talk across ethnic and gender cultures, and promote up-front communication. Annette Drake, director of administration, says, "Communication has been a big issue for us; we work on it every year: presentations, talking to your superior, talking to the employees who report to you. Handling difficult people, time management, everyone gets to take classes, regardless of position." CEO Yates says, "Our goal was to have a group that worked well together, and it was important to learn to ask clarifying questions: e.g., 'what do you mean when you say x, y, or z?' Pushing people to ask clarifying questions was really key." Emphasis on clarity in communication seems to have helped the foundation cohesiveness, with staff members able to find the similarities in differences and celebrate their differences. With cohesiveness comes inclusion and the ability to deal with conflict and change. Director of administration Drake says,

We've also always made sure we have gatherings, lately monthly, combining our San Francisco office and our office down here. We try to involve everybody in decision making by asking for his or her opinions. They don't get to make decisions, but they do have input. So I think everyone feels a part. Cohesiveness does wonders when it comes to changes.

Clear communication also has been important for the board. Chair Vega-Marquis recalls that the biggest issue for her was how to develop trust: "We went through some retreats where we dealt with thorny issues. We always have a dinner before the board meeting, and that's worked really well in getting to know one another as individuals. It's not just enough to put the board together and do our business. We have to find ways to build trust." And this has worked, Vega-Marquis says, "What I like about our board is that we're able to deal with any conflicts up front. We have good people, skilled in people skills and board experience, good at being direct."

Cohesiveness becomes a clearly defined value of the foundation, and it's a value with "teeth," not just lip service, according to director of administration Drake:

Gary talked about it at staff meetings, getting along, being cohesive. And our working climate was really important, making this a good place to work (benefits, hours). Most of our hiring happened by referral. People became happy here and recommended their friends. But we had to remind staff once in a while. And we stopped any grumbling right away, nipped it in the bud, didn't let it go further. . . . Some folks who were sitting on the fence ended up leaving. They just couldn't buy into our philosophy.

The foundation also places high value on relationships among staff: respect, getting along, listening to each other. Drake says, "We value our employees, maybe that's the most important thing. We value each and every one. And I think they know it." Communications officer Julio Marcial says,

Our own diversity is key to why we're so . . . effective. We have leadership willing to listen, take our life experiences into account, every facet of the job. It opens up a dialogue, a continuous exchange of information. . . . We take the time to know each other, each other's history, background. Sometimes we seem so different, but this has taught us we're also so alike.

When Gary Yates thinks back on his history with the foundation, he emphasizes how he learned to listen differently:

Working through the tensions the first several years on the job helped me learn to listen more, act less. I tend to act quickly, want to solve problems right away. Sometimes stuff bubbles up from staff with better solutions, not so much to do with my gender/ethnicity, but organizational power dynamics. What have I learned? It's to listen more. This doesn't mean to do less, but to do things at a slower pace. I wouldn't have said that five or six years ago. I hadn't thought about it until you asked me.

Yates' listening makes employees feel valued. They are consulted often and, although their perspectives may not always be reflected in final decisions, they say they know they have been heard. This is especially true on the grant-making side of the foundation, where Yates is explicit about power-sharing:

It's important that the authority rests with the program people closest to the ground, with quality control at executive and board levels. Most decision making takes place in the program areas by the people who know the most about the communities they are funding. . . . All our program directors have $50,000 in discretionary grants to award and a minimum of $3 million to recommend to the board each year. We have a lot of trust in who the program staff are. And having a significant portion of the board [be] women and minorities helps build that trust. . . . We haven't had a grant turned down at board level in a long time.

It also seems to help staff cohesiveness that the foundation downplays competition. Vice president of finance Peggy Minnich points out, "We actually did away with a more competitive individual process for salary increases. While there are personal performance awards that Gary can give out, everyone pretty much gets the same general salary increases." The foundation structures their goals around people's basic responsibilities and how individual goals fit into the foundation as a whole: "People do get some monetary awards, but it's personal, not announced to the whole world. Their supervisor and Gary would commend them, but there's not a big deal made out of any one person's performance."

Gender As a Key Piece of the Big Picture
Most often mentioned as part of the larger picture of diversity, gender is just one of several lenses foundation staff use to evaluate grantees and the foundation's own work. Vice president of communications Magdalena Beltrán-Del Olmo says, "The gender piece is interwoven with other diversity issues." When asked about TCWF's comfort with using a gender lens compared with other foundations that exhibit discomfort with using such a lens, Beltrán-Del Olmo replies, "This foundation wasn't uncomfortable creating a women's health priority area . . . , and I'm proud we're funding areas not so popular like violence prevention." Vice president of programs

Cristina Regalado describes how "people were astonished by questions" a colleague asked when using a gender lens. "Isn't it enough that we serve women?" they wanted to know. Regalado replies "No, it's the totality of women's lives and their communities that matter. That's what we're trying to do here."

And what about the phenomenon that women sometimes don't feel comfortable advocating for funding women. When asked that question, Gary Yates gave a big laugh and said,

That's not the case here. Senior women on staff in many ways are advocates. Since 1995 that has been the case. But we're looking at two generations of a foundation, with a transition that was tumultuous. . . . Perhaps it's who we happen to hire. Some of these folks are senior people that came from women's foundations or not-for-profits dealing with women's issues. I certainly wouldn't expect them to lay that aside. . . . The women here are not shy about advocating for women's issues.

As important, however, women are not the only ones raising the issues of funding for women and girls. The men interviewed were as likely as the women to raise gender as a concern within the larger topic of diversity. Yet they are not resting on their laurels. Vice president for programs Regalado notes, "Not everyone uses a gender lens where they need to. The challenge we face is how we can institutionalize the concept so that it's more tangible. What's the benefit? It needs to be more institutionalized. We need to find ways to make the concept come alive. So it becomes more automatic." While several staff members noted concerns that the gender issue isn't as strong a concern as ethnic/racial issues, they pointed with pride to the senior women now in place who are comfortable advocating for women's issues and praised the foundation's track record for funding women's organizations and programs as well as for launching a gender-specific women's health priority area.

Deep Diversity Leads to Responsive Grant Making

Regarding the impact of all this diversity work on the foundation's grant making, board chair Vega-Marquis says, "Once the spirit of diversity is unleashed, it's hard to put it back in the box, go back to old models of philanthropy." Gary Yates specifically credits their hiring practices for increasing the effectiveness of their grant making:

I do think that in the hiring of a more diverse program staff there was an effect on grant making. We've been able to make more grants in more diverse regions of the state than we would have without staff with nonprofit experience and ethnic/gender knowledge. And I do believe we can say that we have more sensitivity about women's and girls' issues. I don't have any quantitative evidence, but I'd say we made grants in the past, even before women's health was a priority (which it now is), that targeted women as a priority, so we made more grants to women's and girls' initiatives. Because we've got such a broad diversity in our staff, that gets reflected in the grant making.[8]

Sensitivity to wider constituencies has also led TCWF to a new grant making style: responsive grant making and more partnering with grantees. Because the foundation prides itself on working "close to the ground," where program staff make most of the grant-making decisions, it was not a big stretch for the foundation to trust what it was hearing from grantees. Vice president for programs Regalado says of the change,

It's a paradigm shift. We'd been known as an initiative-driven foundation, targeted, prescriptive, complicated laid-out plans. Moving away from that has required an unlearning or relearning for program officers. I came to the foundation just as the paradigm shifted. The shift led to some internal tension around roles. Program officers had been doing initiatives, but the main focus now is around due diligence, doing all the up-front work, less around monitoring. It's a real power shift.

Most of the people we spoke with would agree: this shift to responsive grant making has resulted in the foundation's being more effective and responding more quickly to needs in the communities the foundation is trying to serve. Communications officer Julio Marcial describes the months of preparation at both board and senior staff levels:

We had strategic planning sessions for eighteen months. Grantees too often are forced into doing the "pretzel dance." Why not fund them to do their strengths, not just to fit our foundation's needs? It was a constant process of communication with staff. Not a cookie-cutter approach. The process empowered our staff, not diminished their power: you will be in charge of developing and writing (with input from everyone else); you will be empowered to develop something from the ground up. We believe in your experience, your understanding. Ok, well now what? Shock. A lot of roadblocks, glitches, but our foundation's culture is "do it whether it's difficult or not." There's an open door there [to senior staff] and feedback mechanisms in place.

The results of this process, according to Marcial, were spectacular:

This process brought us together; now we understood that we were all in this together for the mission. Our work had had more of a silo effect. We had initiative funding, general support, special projects funding, so many different things going on at one time. Now how we do our business is completely different; there's a sense of empowerment that starts with staff.

Without more diversity on the board, especially the diversity of trustees with nonprofit experience, most don't think that paradigm shift could have happened.

One result of this shift has been a shift to core support grants: in response to the success of earlier trial funding strategies, a majority of their grants (56% percent in fiscal year 2001–2002) are now for core support. Instead of doing "the pretzel dance," grantees now have more control over how they spend their money because the foundation now sees that their grantees know how to spend the money most wisely.

Evaluation and Accountability

Due diligence and a sense of accountability to those they are funding also has led the foundation to make a conscious effort to solicit evaluation and feedback from the grantees themselves. Marcial says, "One of our strengths is the evaluation component of our grant making. . . . Whether it's positive or negative, we share what we've learned." If a grant didn't work, they want to know why, not just to note that it didn't work. The foundation is transparent in sharing information, and not just those experiences that make them look good. They also share evaluations that reflect negatively on them because, as Marcial emphasizes, "Evaluation is built into everything we do, and it allows us to be accountable."

The foundation does not have any formal in-house evaluation, although Yates says they've talked about that. But they do solicit evaluations from grantees. Yates describes the process:

Every three years, we use an outside consultant and a questionnaire collaboratively developed by the grants program, executive and communication staff: it's sent to all who submit proposals to us, even those turned down, with a broad range of questions. We've also asked folks who are advocates for small nonprofits; we get their feedback too. We've been doing it consistently since I became president. We have a live person on the reception desk . . . , and I try to meet with applicants and grantees whenever anyone asks. But honest, face-to-face feedback is very hard to get because of the inverse power dynamic. (We have the money.) So we started doing this more formal evaluation of our grant making. We make the reports available on the website unedited except for clarity and typos. Either you put it up or you don't. We got some flak last time because the report mentioned some other foundation names, but it's a way of sharing with people that we're trying. If you start editing, you keep editing. So this is unvarnished.

This kind of "unvarnished" self-assessment is rare in philanthropy.[9] And it may be that a diverse staff and board also make for more courageous funding. The foundation evaluates its own work as well as the work of its grantees, and they are not afraid to take risks. The foundation approaches its evaluation in the spirit of improving, not just proving, the usefulness of their funding. And they take this work seriously enough to provide funding that enables grantees to evaluate their own work—again in the spirit of improving: what went wrong as well as what went right. Most often at TCWF, the funding is right. And effective.

THE HYAMS FOUNDATION

Organized in 1921 as the Godfrey M. Hyams Trust, the assets of this and two companion trusts also created by Mr. Hyams, the Isabel F. Hyams Fund and the Sarah A. Hyams Fund, were combined to create The Hyams Foundation, Inc. in 1993. A private foundation, Hyams's mission is to "increase economic and social justice and power within low-income communities" in Boston and Chelsea, Massachusetts.[10] By the end of 2003, the foundation's assets totaled over $116 million. In its 2003 fiscal year, the foundation made 150 grants totaling $5 million.

The foundation believes that enabling low-income people to increase their economic security, build wealth, and become active participants in their communities will have the greatest social return, and the foundation makes its grants to promote:

• Increased civic engagement, with a special focus on immigrant communities

• More affordable housing, especially for very low-income families

• Increased family economic self-sufficiency

• Enhanced opportunities for low-income teens

These four major program and outcome areas are premised on the following core foundation beliefs:

• A community with strong institutions, clear priorities and strategies to achieve them, active and broad-based leadership, and individuals who participate in the electoral process holds the best promise for influencing the decisions that affect its members

• Access to decent and affordable housing is essential to the health and well-being of every family

• All adults have a right to productive employment

• Youth are a vital resource within our communities whose positive development not only leads to success in school and in the workforce but also to a community better equipped to achieve positive change

The foundation promotes organizational diversity throughout all of its grant-making areas, based on a belief that well-functioning organizations that also have diverse boards and staffs are more effective in serving and empowering local communities. The foundation's grant-making guidelines also mention Hyams's commitment to identifying and drawing increased attention to issues of racial/ethnic discrimination and disadvantage.

The foundation, one of the oldest in the country, grew from the assets of a single donor, Godfrey M. Hyams, who was a metallurgist, engineer, and financier responsible for the growth of the Anaconda Mining Company and the construction of the Virginia Railway, which made available large sources of bituminous coal to the eastern part of the United States. As the foundation describes his life, Hyams "acquired great wealth but always maintained a simple style of living and chose not to seek the attention of the public usually attendant upon a man of such affluence." This sense of modesty also carried over into his personal life. Although Hyams frequently made large gifts for charitable purposes, he usually withheld his identity, and he lived in a three-decker house in Dorchester, Massachusetts, with his two sisters, Sarah and Isabel, both of whom were active in social-work activities at the time. To assure that his resources would be used for charitable purposes after his death, Hyams established a charitable trust in 1921, and on his death in 1927 this trust received the major portion of his estate. It was one of the largest philanthropic gifts ever made in Massachusetts.

Diversifying the Board

As a case study, the Hyams Foundation offers us insight into how one foundation grew from family trusts into a small but complex organization struggling in interesting ways with its own growth and demonstrating a strong commitment to change both itself and the communities it serves. The foundation began with a simple mandate: to support charitable organizations. One of the Hyams sisters had funded settlement houses in Boston, so it was clearly within easy reach for the foundation to target some of its early support to minority and immigrant communities. But for years, the family trusts were administered out of Mr. Hyams's personal attorney's law firm, with his two sisters, a bank representative, and family friends serving as trustees. As current board chair Jack Clymer describes its history,

The foundation was a trust, and the trustees thought they had responsibility for everything. When Joan Diver came on board [in 1970], she built the position of Executive Director. It was a long and hard process to bring the trustees along to the point where they would give what I regard as appropriate weight to what staff had to say. We gradually started to hire staff to do grant making, but the roles of board and staff were mixed; the trustees had their hands in everything.[11]

But those early trustees had "the wisdom to say they didn't know the community," according to Beth Smith, executive director since 1990. By 1979, the trustees made a conscious decision to change the composition of the board, bringing on younger individuals and others active in the community. Jack Clymer recalls, "I think because of some prodding by Joan, the trustees decided it would be worthwhile to have some younger people on the board. The pattern was to get a young lawyer involved; if the trustees got along with that person, he/she'd become a trustee. That was the situation with me in 1981." Another new addition at that time was the foundation's first African-American trustee, only the second woman to join the board after the two Hyams sisters' involvement in the 1920s and 1930s.[12]

Diversifying the Staff

From these early beginnings, the foundation moved to its current reputation for being a foundation whose peers describe as having institutionalized diversity into its organizational DNA. How? Executive director Beth Smith says,

We wanted to be as effective as possible within communities that were always changing. I came in 1985 when the foundation wanted to do more in the immigration area. We were one of the earliest funders of minority neighborhood organizations, also immigrant organizations. This translated into the need for more internal diversity: there were two staff persons of color out of six when I came (I'm white), and the board had one person of color and two women out of seven.

If the impetus toward diversity on the board came out of the community they were serving, according to Smith, the board also did something important: they examined their trustees.

As she describes herself, Beth Smith is a product of the 1960s, active and aware of civil rights and the ways in which poverty disproportionately affects communities of color and women. She brought to the foundation statewide experience on these issues, and when she was hired (at first as a consultant for special projects), she had what she describes as "a strong interest in thinking about how we could change and evolve and be more diverse. . . . I brought an interest in these concerns, but so did my board. We were really in sync on all of that." In 1987, the foundation took what was to become its most significant step toward an intentional, in-depth exploration of diversity. In 1987, the Hyams Foundation, the Boston Foundation, and the United Way of Massachusetts created the Human Services Personnel Collaborative (HSPC), a joint initiative aimed at helping local nonprofits grapple with staffing crises they all acknowledged facing, including hiring and retaining staff of color. After the collaborative developed their Diversity Initiative, staff of participating foundations and corporations came to realize that they could not promote diversity effectively within the broader nonprofit community without looking inside their own organizations, and the Hyams staff involved in the initiative came away with "a heightened sense that the foundation needed a more conscious and consistent process for becoming a more diverse organization."[13] Over fifty nonprofits currently participate in the Diversity Initiative.[14]

This awareness moved the foundation to bring on new staff and new trustees. By 1990, three of the seven staff members were women of color, and three of the then seven board members were women or men of color. And as of 2004, the foundation's staff of eight included six women (two African-American, one Asian-American, one Latina, two white) and two men (both white). Five out of nine trustees were women (two African-American, one Asian-American, one Latina, one white). The men on the board included one African-American, one Haitian-American, and one white. The board also has continued to stress age diversity, and two of the current trustees are in their 30s.

In spite of success increasing numbers, however, by 1992 the foundation also moved to tackle more complex diversity work. It organized a diversity committee that included the executive director, board members and staff, and the board chair. The committee began to grapple with what it meant to really promote diversity inside their own organization as well as out. A board/staff retreat with a diversity consultant gave everyone a chance to communicate across differences as well as react to a draft statement of diversity principles that the foundation still affirms. What emerged from the retreat was an unambiguous understanding that the foundation's focus on diversity was meant to increase its own and the broader community's effectiveness in addressing social issues, not "just" because it was the right and moral thing to do.

Diversity Is a Process

A key understanding stressed by all those interviewed for this case study is that diversity is not something ever achieved: it's a process. As board chair Jack Clymer describes it, the goal is to build a culture that always will be looking for different points of view, different perspectives, different inputs that "help you understand what it is you're really trying to do, how you're doing it better than you could without those points of view. Initially, we thought of it pretty much in terms of race and gender. Recently, we're also focusing on class and age." Smith says that the foundation tried various kinds of activities, including having a consultant come in to assess issues of diversity within the foundation and give the foundation recommendations for becoming more diverse: "This was very beneficial but also was hard, hard work. Some of the feedback was difficult to hear, even when shared confidentially. We still need to spend more time thinking about how we are really working as a diverse organization." Smith also realizes that there is a "catch-22" involved: "Are we working together as well as we could without being too internally focused all the time?" Process alone is never enough.

Promoting Consciousness of Diversity among Grantees

As the foundation has learned better to foster diversity in its own ranks, its grant making has sharpened awareness of the need to promote more consciousness of diversity among its grantees. The foundation requires diversity data about a grantee's board and staff with all grant applications. But as Sylvia Johnson, an African-American who is Hyams's current associate director, describes, finding effective ways of measuring the difference diversity makes in an organization is still a challenge:

We point out to people that they serve 90 percent people of color, but only have five percent people of color on their staff and none on their board. So we encourage people to increase their organization's own diversity but not by a set number. I think there's an assumption that there shouldn't be such a gap, but there are no hard and fast rules. But sometimes an organization can have good numbers, and they still don't act differently. So where's that balance? Increase the numbers but have people on board or staff serving different roles? How do you get at this? Measure this? How do we get deeper than the numbers?

The foundation struggles with these questions internally as well. The answer so far lies in the various ways people can take formal leadership roles in the foundation. CEO Smith says, "Beyond numbers, the other thing we've tried to do is look at roles within the foundation. We have a white CEO and a white board chair: how do we share leadership? We have three committees on the board, and each has a chair. That's been a way to have other leaders emerge."

Associate director Sylvia Johnson describes Boston itself as another challenge: the complexities of a city that has a lot of diversity within racial groups and also between older and newer communities of color as well as issues of class within communities of color:

How do you address the dynamics between the haves and the have-nots, the insiders and the outsiders, and encourage multicultural cooperation and understanding at the same time? How do we move people toward a new and deeper level of community collaboration? There are no easy answers to these questions. We just keep striving to be sensitive to these dynamics ourselves, and we keep trying different ways to encourage dialogue and facilitate relationships among the various groups.

The foundation is committed to providing advice, technical support, leveraging, and other forms of "more than money" support for the diverse nonprofits it funds. It also encourages organizations to start wherever they are. Johnson describes strategies that work:

You don't have to begin with a diversity initiative. You start small, looking at who you contract with, who you bring onto your staff or board, how you communicate with the community, how welcoming you are. People have to be encouraged to start wherever they are. There are a lot of different models. I've found in life that hitting people over the head is not always the easiest way to get them to cooperate. Diversity's here and it's the wave of the future. Wherever you are, jump in!

Paying Attention to Gender

So where does gender fit into this picture? As we see in other case studies in this chapter, a more diverse approach to diversity—defining diversity in the broadest possible terms—gives gender and other differences more leverage. But like the other foundations, Hyams is not resting on its laurels. The foundation builds in extra measures to ensure that women's and girls' organizations are considered—taking another look, for example, at grants turned down if the proposals are from women's or girls' organizations. And they pay attention to what their successful grantees are doing in regard to gender. As Smith says,

I've tried to struggle with the issue of women and girls. How are programs we fund really sensitive to issues of gender? Our work with Molly Mead, for example, had a huge impact on me and how we looked at youth programs.[15] We now challenge grantees: "You say you're coed, but you're only serving 30 percent girls."

Associate director Johnson points out that whenever they have the opportunity to raise gender as an issue, they do. The foundation always has employed more women than men, so according to Johnson, there is a natural openness and tendency to support women and girls: "We're not where we want to be, but we are definitely sensitive to gender issues. Although we support a fair number of gender-specific programs, we routinely push ourselves to look more closely at our level and pattern of support."

Johnson's observation about "routinely pushing" sums up a large part of Hyams's success. The staff and trustees keep trying new strategies. While they respect their foundation's history and the Hyams family legacy, they have learned to push beyond it in ways that provide a model for other foundations seeking to diversify their boards and staffs. Recognizing also that diversity is a process, they have learned to challenge themselves as a routine, accepted part of their institutional culture. Change is embraced, not resisted, and they expect the same of their grantees. Like other foundation case studies in this chapter, Hyams works to understand gender as one of several key parts of their analysis of diversity, which contributes to their national reputation for doing effective philanthropy.

THE JESSIE SMITH NOYES FOUNDATION

Formed in 1947, the Jessie Smith Noyes Foundation is a New York City–based family foundation that promotes "a sustainable and just social and natural system by supporting grassroots organizations and movements committed to this goal."[16] To encourage cross-issue work and funding, in November 2003 the foundation shifted from more narrowly defined program areas to broader funding priorities that include:

• Protecting the health and environment of communities threatened by toxics

• Advancing environmental justice

• Ensuring quality reproductive health care as a human right

• Fostering an environmentally sustainable New York City

With an endowment of $60 million in 2003, the foundation awarded 120 grants totaling $2.758 million, with an additional $407,000 in discretionary board grants and grants to charities designated in the founder's will: altogether a total of $3.165 million in grants awarded in 2003. As in previous years, the foundation primarily made grants to organizations working at the grassroots level. Half of their grants went to state organizations and another third to regional networks and coalitions. About one third of the grants went to organizations with people of color as primary decision makers and constituents. Thirty-five percent of the foundation's grants went to smaller groups with budgets under $250,000 and another 27 percent to those with budgets between $250,000 and $500,000.

Foundation History

The foundation was established in 1947 by Charles F. Noyes as a memorial to his second wife, Jessie Smith Noyes. Charles Noyes was born in 1878 in Norwich, Connecticut, where his father, Charles D. Noyes, was copublisher of the *Norwich Daily Bulletin,* the sixth-oldest newspaper in the nation. As the foundation describes his youthful commitment and ambition, "Charles at age ten delivered his father's paper to every house on his route on the morning after the famous Blizzard of 1888. At twelve, with earnings from his paper route, he bought the newsstand concession on the summer steamer run from New London to Block Island. He added magazines and dime novels to his stock of newspapers, hired boys with bicycles to speed delivery on the island, and soon had a thriving business which he operated throughout his high school years."

This early entrepreneurial spirit soon led to a partnership in a small real-estate brokerage business. His descendents do not know if he ever obtained his high school diploma, but in 1905, several years after leaving the Norwich Academy, he established his own firm, the Charles F. Noyes Company, which invested in skyscrapers and other New York commercial real estate, prospering until it dominated the lower Manhattan real estate market. Charles Noyes came to be known as the Dean of Real Estate in New York City. His most famous transaction was the sale in 1951 of the Empire State Building, "previously regarded as a white elephant, for the largest price at the time in real estate history. In 1959, he turned over all his stock in Charles F. Noyes & Co. to its employees, but remained active in business until 1965, when he became ill at the age of 88."

The foundation was established with goals that still guide the foundation today: aiding organizations and individuals who share his commitment to fairness, integrity, and hard work. Charles Noyes died in 1969 at the age of 91, leaving the foundation additional resources that then brought its total assets to approximately $30 million, an amount that has more than doubled since his death.

Jessie Smith Noyes was born in 1885 in Brooklyn, New York, where the foundation remembers her as devoting much of her adult life to community needs: "a woman of charm and wit with a deep love of beauty and a sensitivity to people, she was described by a friend as 'an aristocrat and a democrat at one and the same time; she appreciated the fine things of life, yet never lost touch with the human equation. . . .' As vice president of the Brooklyn YWCA for many years, Mrs. Noyes worked hard for religious tolerance and for racial equality long before it became a public and popular cause."

From 1947 through 1959, the foundation primarily supported scholarship and loan programs for individual students to attend any accredited college or professional school in the United States. Half the grants were designated for minority students, mostly black. To control soaring administrative costs and to make more money available for scholarships, in 1960 the foundation shifted its awards to institutions, although still stressing the importance of equal distribution of funds to majority and minority students. A few years later, because of cutbacks in enrollments at the predominantly black colleges that had been the mainstay for black students, the foundation began to channel all future scholarship aid for black students through black colleges. After the federal government and many states in the early 1970s set up student aid programs that substantially increased public financial support of education for the disadvantaged, the foundation changed its focus to programs for students of proven ability working toward specific careers in areas of critical need. From 1974 through 1984, the foundation focused its funding on grants to institutions for student aid in selected areas of the environment, health care (population, family planning, and adolescent pregnancy), and public school education, recognizing these as crucial areas of world need, priority concerns that still drive the foundation's work.

In 1985, conducting a review aimed at sharpening their focus, the foundation both broadened and narrowed its vision, asking questions like "what kinds of irreversible damages to the natural environment are occurring, and among those damages, which are the most important to the most people over the long term?" In response to these issues, the foundation sharpened their funding program to focus specifically on the priorities noted at the beginning of this section: communities threatened by toxics, the broader cause of environmental justice, quality reproductive health care as a human right, and an environmentally sustainable New York City.

In some ways, it is easy to see how this kind of an organizational history laid the groundwork for the foundation's reputation of effectively institutionalizing diversity, but all of those interviewed for this case study stress the importance of intentional, conscious focus. The question for this case study is how a family foundation, albeit a liberal family committed to helping the underserved, evolved toward sharing more control and power with those people they are set up to aid.

Adding Nonfamily Trustees to a Family Board

Vic De Luca, Noyes CEO since 2000, describes his understanding of the process: "I started in 1991 as a program officer at the foundation, a few years after the family had decided to bring more nonfamily members onto the board. There had been two previous CEOs. The second, Steve Viederman, had been in the position for 14 years. A consciousness of race issues streamed through all the early years of the foundation's life, but in the late 1980s, the family moved to broaden the range of experiences of board members, so they hired a consultant who helped them plan for the foundation's future and expand the board. The initial nonfamily trustees were known to the family or were grantees. In fact, one of them was an African-American who was brought on the board primarily for his environmental credentials. The principle of broadening the board allowed us in 1992 to push the board into thinking more about racial diversity too. Diversity was a strong interest of a few board members and the entire staff."[17]

Ann Wiener, one of the "grandfathered in" family members who has been on the board for much of her adult life, describes what was then an all-family board thinking that it was presumptuous to deal with organizations "that were different from us economically, culturally, and racially without having those voices heard in the decision making. Just as there needed to be more women in power positions, there needed to be more diversity." She goes on to say that "I think we've always had a pretty broad view of diversity—rural, urban, racial—though I think we tried to be sensitive so there's not that kind of burden on people of color to feel they have to represent groups. We've looked for age diversity; we've always looked for generalists as well as people with specialized knowledge." One of the foundation's program officers also stresses the foundation's broader understanding of diversity: "When we talk about diversity, we mean diversity on every level, not just race. Rural issues are very much a part of that diversity, for example."

When asked how her family came to that awareness as a board, Wiener describes her grandfather's innate sense of justice: "He felt for Negroes who hadn't had access to education." This sense of justice ran in the family. "So he put his three daughters, their husbands, a lawyer, and an accountant on the board, a way of getting advice as well as keeping the family together." In the beginning, "the husbands did the financial stuff, the wives did the grant making." The foundation's direction was set by women "who had to act in subterranean ways: there was the financial discussion, then lunch with martinis, then the women got to make the grants they wanted." She goes on to describe, "My aunt Edith Muma, one of the original trustees still on the board, felt that the foundation needed a more professional presence when we inherited the rest of my grandfather's estate after his death. By the late 1980s, we were moving into water issues, reproductive rights, and sustainable development—problems that affected the health of the world—and we began to see the importance of listening to all the people involved, seeing often that large entities like business and government didn't have space to hear the voices of those directly affected by policy."

Program officer Wilma Montanez, who came on staff in 1996, notes that the board started opening up to nonfamily members with this perceived need to bring in staff, which became their first step in diversifying themselves. This opened up a whole process of setting expertise criteria they wanted board members to contribute. "That situated the issue of diversity in the broadest context," Montanez points out. "Should the board include people we were supporting, such as grantees? The process began 'organically'; now the process is much more deliberate."

Vic De Luca says, "In one of our conversations about diversity, we used examples of our sustainable agriculture program, the importance of having biodiversity, a natural system that's diverse, how humans participate in that. We argued the same thing needed to be applied to the organization itself. Just like you don't want rows of corn, rows of corn, rows of corn, you don't want rows of white men." De Luca also points out that for board diversity to work, staff "needs to burn some capital here. You're going to make mistakes. Sure there are some things we'd do differently, but board members had an openness, a willingness to take risks." He also describes the importance of a more complex understanding of diversity. "The last thing we wanted to do was to become diverse but homogenize the thinking and action of the board members. We look for people with different experiences who by adding their particular viewpoints or regional perspective make our work better."

Steven Carbó, a nonfamily trustee on the board since 2000 and board chair for 2003 and 2004, describes the process:

The board tries for different approaches and benefits from membership that reflects different experiences with the issues. For example, we have folks who work in academia, folks who come out of faith communities, activists, people who have worked at the community level and understand community perspectives. Our support for sustainable agriculture, for example, is enriched by the fact one of our board members operates a farm.

Diversifying Staff

As well as diversifying the board, diversifying the staff is also crucial. Program officer Millie Buchanan says, "Effective funding isn't going to happen until diversity happens. The more people hired with more lenses, the more complexity they bring to the understanding of diversity and its importance. Because the foundation made a commitment to do that, the commitment feeds on itself." Vic De Luca says, "It's a lot of work, not that easy. You're looking in unconventional places for staff or board members. We didn't advertise in environmental publications for our last staff person. We felt that would have just gotten white applicants. Instead we recruited in ways that would ensure we'd get people of color applying."

Program officer Wilma Montanez points out the importance of bringing in staff with a strong familiarity of their grantees and the kind of work they are doing. With change comes "the risk that the foundation will also change—change both how some things look and how things will be done. You have to assume that things will change."

Roadblocks to Diversity

Both trustees and staff members also have struggled with more subtle assumptions that can undermine effective funding. Buchanan describes pitfalls for the field of philanthropy in general: "There's a cultural presumption that a certain set of people by virtue of their genes and brain power have the ability to make decisions better. If you hold that notion in your bones, even if you're in denial, it will play out. If you want to protect the natural systems on which all life depends, and that's what you believe, it's hard to trust that goal to a collaborative of West Virginia grandmothers. It's not a tough sell now on our board, but I think there are still some in other foundations who would be more comfortable funding people with letters behind their names, who are also more likely to be white men."

Staff members point out another external roadblock to diversity: the pressure in the foundation world (also societal) to want immediate results. As Buchanan describes it, the problem is "a Western white male linear approach to things that doesn't respect the time it takes to do things that involve process. A group of funders was discussing at a meeting a few years ago the importance of long-term grants, and the question was raised: how do you make your mark as a program officer if you just fund organizations that others have funded before you? There's a danger of measuring your foundation against other foundations, not against the greater good that can lead you to ask: why are we funding a group for twenty years trying to stop coal mining in West Virginia? It's hard for some people to be serious about diversity if it gets in the way of expediency. Some others in the foundation world say 'I get diversity, but we don't have time to bring all those people along.'"

Importance of Long-Term Support and Leveraging

Being consistent over "the long haul" is important to the foundation. Montanez points out, "Sometimes it's easy to say to a grantee that when we started this initiative, we had more time, but now we have many more issues that need funding. So it requires discipline to 'walk the talk,' to maintain a long-term focus for our funding priorities. If we're going to expect our colleagues and our grantees to work for change, we have to be a model." Buchanan stresses the importance of core support and multiyear funding: "It's important to keep the faith that given enough time, you'll see fruits for your toil. It's a long-term commitment. Core support and multiyear grants are incredibly important. The board has heard us beat this drum: the gold standard of funding is multiyear, general support."

CEO De Luca says, "We do general support grants for the most part. We fund organizations for a long time (a few for 15–16 years). Our grants are usually $25–35,000. We're solidifying the base of support for the institutions we care about. That strategy has been generally accepted by the board. There's also a parallel concern by board members that we bring in some new groups. So we do both. It's not always easy. Funder fatigue sets in: "You sometimes get tired of looking at proposals, start thinking 'can't we do something bigger'? But social change takes a lot of time, and we don't know the tipping points, so we just have to keep going."

Another dimension of long-term commitment to grantees has been working in coalition with other funders. According to Montanez, "Only through a movement will you bring on the changes we say we want and need. We work closely with other foundations and affinity groups. For myself, it's an important way to have colleagues. Working in philanthropy can be very isolating. You can easily work by yourself most of the time, and it can be lonely and not necessarily a healthy way to work. We at Noyes are very committed to working in coalition with other funders. We've stressed the need for these collaborations to our board, so they can better understand the different facets of our role as grant makers, and we keep trying, with our limited dollars, to help grantees leverage more money."

"Walking the Talk"

The foundation takes being a model grant maker seriously. Montanez calls attention to what she describes as "dissonance reduction":

We started looking at our investment portfolio, and that led us into socially responsible investing. Then we asked what about dissonance within our programs:

for example, what do we do if one of our grantees takes a public position against abortion, even though we are funding them to do environmental work. For a grantee to be anti-choice on a personal level is obviously not anything we can do anything about, but if as an organization they take an anti choice position, we would discontinue their funding. This is all conscious, talked about by the board and staff. We also inform each grantee about this foundation policy now.

Monitoring Grantee Diversity

Because they have come to understand the importance of a broad range of diversity in the foundation itself, Noyes also is clear about the importance of a broad range of diversity in the organizations they fund. Buchanan describes the process: "We put together an elaborate chart every year looking at who's making the decisions in our organizations. We use two different lenses: are the groups run by those most affected by their issues? Which are run by people of color? In my field, we could fund groups that fit our priorities and are all white. Board members look at diversity within a broad framework."

Board chair Carbó says, "The board has been living their approach to issues, always looking for organizations and initiatives that arise from and broadly engage communities of color, women, etc. We look at the extent to which organizations both work in those communities and whose leadership reflect those communities. We look at all those things explicitly, holistically."

Vic De Luca points out that the foundation's grants have changed over time to include more groups of color, poor white groups, and groups without a lot of access to funding as well as groups doing community organizing: "Every year we do an analysis of our grantee pool that's now part of our evaluative processes." Carbó says, "The extent to which a group that we've funded has or has not been willing to be more inclusive has played a role in our deliberations about continued funding. We still need more work, but the commitment's there."

Helping People Grow Is an Organizational Value
Buchanan recalls:

As someone who came to work here after the foundation was already well on its way, I think our complex and conscious commitment to all kinds of diversity has helped me as an individual do a better job here, and it's also made my life more interesting. There are things I notice now. I thought I was a reasonably aware person about both race and gender, but there was so much I didn't know and didn't know I didn't know. I've learned so much more about how to live in the world. It's been a real learning curve to me. Helping people grow is an organizational value.

Carbó, appointed in 2000, describes his own changes from being on the board: "I think I've got a deeper understanding of 'bottom-up' approaches to problem solving and empowerment and the intrinsic importance of community-led solutions to social problems. I had some sense of that before I came onto the board, but I think my knowledge and understanding of that has deepened and been enriched."

Importance of Women and Using a Gender Lens

So where does gender fit into the foundation's institutionalized diversity? Family trustee Ann Wiener points out, "Our grant program has always been female-run. Women trustees and staff worked with individuals, saw women as people who made changes." Buchanan recalls the foundation's history too:

Men made the money, but the women gave it away. This foundation was established in Jessie's name and with her principles. They didn't call it social justice then, but that's what it was. They saw it as ethically right to have everyone at the table. The women were the ones making the decisions about how the money was spent. Early on there was a race lens, not a gender lens as such. In the early years, all the scholarships were almost all white or Negro. Then after WWII, the foundation supported Japanese-Americans. The Noyes women would have fought to have women at the table.

De Luca asks, "How does gender fit in? Constantly. We fund a lot of community organizing. Many have a charismatic leader, but that's not sustainable. It's important that there's secondary leadership. In the groups we fund, there's a great many women in leadership positions. It plays out less in the farm community but still pretty significant. Our board members look for people of color, gender issues. We're not afraid of putting that stuff in when we write up grants."

According to Millie Buchanan:

A lot of our groups are multiissue groups; they didn't form to protect their communities against a particular issue. They formed, usually led by women, to make their communities better. They tend to be run by women. Grandmothers in Kentucky have been the ones getting in front of bulldozers for years. . . . So we pay attention to their needs, day care, for example, so we do more than give lip service about making it possible to get everyone to the meetings.

Wilma Montanez notes that the foundation keeps adding lenses to their screening, a gender lens to look at environmental groups, for example:

How many girl farmers? Where are the women leaders in the environmental justice movement? Is their work recognized, validated, and supported? Do women activists bring something different to the work? Certainly, I think so. This is all a work-in-progress. Also, we look at our investments with a gender lens: are they pro-choice or anti-choice? The work on gender is reflected in so many different areas.

Impact on Grants

Paying close attention to these concerns in their grants has led the foundation to work "closer to the ground." They make special efforts to get to know their grantees up close. They struggle to break through class issues inherent in grantor/grantee relationships, and they empower and trust their grantees. Buchanan points out, "I am one of the strongest proponents in the field saying those closest to the ground know a lot better what's going on."

De Luca confirms this:

Being a funder you tend to live in a unique and sheltered situation. Unfortunately, grantees will not challenge funders for fear of angering them. Here the program officers and I all worked on the nonprofit side, so we know what it's like; we talk a lot about our relationships with our grantees. We recognize there's a power imbalance. I know we say partnership, but I don't think it's real. 'Partnership' sounds good, but a partnership requires equality, and that is not the nature of this business. On the one end, funders have the resources, and on the other end, groups doing the work are competing and appealing for those funds. The key is to make sure that you work to break down any real or perceived barriers. We work hard to make sure we're accessible. We take cold calls. We try to guide grant seekers, even those who do not fit our guidelines. We also just try to be real. I went on a site visit to rural Missouri. . . . I told people that I was going to dress very casually (jeans, etc.), and that my trip was to better understand where and how you live. Sometimes it's like a first date, a little awkward and goofy.

Importance of Evaluation

Finally, all the people interviewed for this case study stressed the importance of evaluation, evaluating the foundation's own work as well as that of their grantees. They ask, "Are we funding the right people?" and that type of questioning is all part of an ongoing process. Nonfamily board member Steven Carbó says:

Well, it's interesting. We've initiated a strategic planning process. Wrapped into that process will be consideration of the foundation's values regarding issues of diversity. I expect that our evaluation of Noyes's granting will include a look at the priority we place upon reaching historically marginalized communities. So we'll have an immediate opportunity to evaluate. It's not the first time that we've done this kind of systemic review. And the board's current consideration of staff grant recommendations includes an accounting of the extent to which the docket and individual grants are reaching communities of color, women, geographically isolated areas, the extent to which the staff and boards of prospective grantees are diverse, etc. That's all spelled out in the analysis the board uses to make decisions about funding. This is another instance of how these issues are institutionalized into our work.

According to family trustee Ann Wiener, "We've just started doing a new strategic plan, and there's a key issue that we keep bringing up, looking at, and turning around: if we get too comfortable, if all our grants are successful, are we taking enough chances?" That ability to take risks, indeed to cite risk taking as an organizational value, is at the heart of Noyes's history of innovation and healthy philanthropy. They have learned that diversity is a process that takes patience, struggling with comfort zones and creating safe spaces to bring new trustees and staff, new visions, into the organization without losing their history. They are candid about their struggles to keep watch on their values, emphasizing personal responsibility on the part of both trustees and staff for "walking their talk" if they expect grantees to do the same. Helping people grow is an organizational value both inside and outside the foundation, and like other foundations interviewed for this chapter, they clearly recognize the importance of understanding gender—both as it plays out in board and staff growth as well as in using a gender lens to make effective grants.

And their grants are effective. They are recognized by many colleagues in philanthropy as a leader in innovative grassroots funding. Perhaps as important as that recognition, however, they do not rest on their laurels. Evaluation is key. To repeat Ann Wiener, "If we get too comfortable, if all our grants are successful, are we taking enough chances?" That ability to question and challenge themselves makes for a vibrant, healthy organization with an impressive track record of both effective philanthropy and thoughtful, collegial impact on the field of philanthropy as a whole.

The Philadelphia Foundation

Founded in 1918, the Philadelphia Foundation is a community foundation that pools over 500 trust funds, most of them aimed at improving the quality of life in a five-county region in Southeastern Pennsylvania's Delaware Valley. As the foundation describes its history, "for more than three generations, people of modest and magnificent means have been turning to The Philadelphia Foundation as their philanthropic partner for investing their charitable dollars."[18] In 2003, the foundation had an asset base of just under $250 million, up from $129 million in 1996. In 2003, the foundation awarded 935 grants totaling some $24.1 million to nonprofit organizations in Bucks, Chester, Delaware, Montgomery, and Philadelphia Counties.

Typical of other community foundations around the country, the Philadelphia Foundation's trust funds are created by individuals and families as well as corporations. The foundation also manages the endowment funds for many community-based organizations. The foundation's funds themselves are diverse, with over sixty from the African-American community, another dozen each from Asian and Latino communities, and several specifically serving the area's gay, lesbian, bisexual, and transgender communities. The foundation aims to help people establish charitable funds and trusts "without having to cope with the complexities of setting up a special-purpose nonprofit corporation." They offer perpetuity, "the assurance of knowing that the name of the charitable donor, or the person in whose name the fund is established, will be honored forever."

The foundation describes its first obligation in grant making as supporting the wishes of the donors who have created the funds. With unrestricted assets, however—assets not part of donor-advised funds—the foundation gives highest priority to "low-budget, constituent-controlled organizations where local residents define their own agendas for change and seek their own solutions to community problems." The foundation also stresses diversity in all their work and actively promotes cultural pluralism, specifically targeting systemic causes of social and economic inequities. The foundation cites three primary goals in its grant making:

- Empowering people and groups within the community
- Building community assets
- Managing current issues or preparing for future trends

CEO Andrew Swinney thinks the stability and longevity of the foundation has enhanced its commitment to diversity: "There have only been four executive directors in 84 years. I'm the fourth. I think the foundation's reputation for diversity and inclusiveness came out of my predecessors' and previous boards' truly believing in, having a passion for a community foundation embracing the whole concept of inclusiveness and diversity." While most community foundations in this country have reputations for serving a range of diverse needs in their communities, the Philadelphia Foundation has a reputation for making diversity itself a priority, both within the foundation's own institutional culture as well as in the grants it makes.

A History of Emphasizing Diversity

The Philadelphia Foundation was one of the first community foundations on record to adopt a values statement that includes a commitment to diversity—in 1963. As CEO Swinney describes the commitment: "It's been a living values statement for the organization ever since. Anybody who comes onto the board or on staff early on 'gets it' because the values statement is part of everyday discussions in all aspects of the work that we do." These values extend throughout the foundation: "Even on the financial side, in our investments, we're very conscious of being diverse. It's our history and a living, operating value of the foundation."

Diversity as living history is something all of those interviewed, board and staff, pointed to with pride. And like other foundations described in this chapter, most of the people we spoke with were knowledgeable about the specifics of the foundation's history. Vice president for programs Lynette Campbell says, "In the early 1930s, the foundation decided they were going to take on all the underrepresented groups in Philadelphia, women's suffrage, antislavery, colored people, immigration issues, and settlement houses, for example." The foundation took it upon itself to work with donors to help them understand the needs of all these groups: "We supported advocacy and the rights of people to stand up for their own beliefs and convene collective action." Over time, the foundation strengthened its commitment to embrace community advocacy and leadership development—areas Campbell says more traditional foundations shy away from. In 1963, in response to riots that devastated minority communities, the board adopted empowerment criteria that formalized thirty years of its prior work. Campbell describes the foundation's continuing efforts after the riots to encourage all kinds of neighborhood people to step up to the table:

In a convening role, we brought together different advocacy groups so they could learn to work together without killing one another. We formalized this work with African-American, Asian, and Latino groups, and we also recognized that we needed to be more reflective of those people on our board and staff: there have been conscious efforts made by nominating committees to diversify both board and staff. Essential to the ongoing success of these efforts, there have also been "guardians" on the board who passed these values down to the newest tier of leadership.

These guardians, experienced board members, take it on themselves to make sure new board members are oriented to the foundation's history of commitment to diversity.

An Expanding Definition of Diversity

The Philadelphia Foundation is an especially interesting case study because of this history of conscious diversity—and also because they expanded their knowledge and awareness to include what they describe as a more complex understanding of diversity. Because of its history in a city with a predominantly black minority population, the foundation had garnered the reputation of effectively serving a wide range of needs of local black communities. But as the foundation took a look at itself in the late 1990s, many felt that the foundation was not reaching working-class white communities or other minority populations as effectively as they were serving the needs of the black communities. So some significant soul-searching went on, among both trustees and staff members, to take another look at how they were implementing their historic values statement. CEO Andrew Swinney describes some of their process:

We had a wonderful, rich discussion the first year I was here. What does being inclusive and diverse mean? We were in essence excluding other segments of the community we were supposed to be serving. We needed to be more balanced in implementing that operating statement. How do we make philanthropy accessible to the whole community? From a development perspective, what can we offer to bring people together, donors and nonprofits, as well as our grant making?

Campbell says, "I had a phone call from a white, Irish male, age maybe 38–45, who asked me, 'Well, what does the foundation stand for? I'm not represented. We have difficult problems here in North Philadelphia that aren't being addressed.'" Campbell pointed out to him that the foundation's guidelines read "underrepresented populations, particularly African-Americans, Asians, and Latinos." But the white Irishman had a point and

Campbell was listening. "I calmed him down. We wanted language in the guidelines specific to African-Americans, Asians, and Latinos so those folks who don't usually see themselves in foundation guidelines could see themselves, but this guy's issues are important too and deserve our funding." Still, according to Heather Gee, vice president of development services and who has worked for the foundation since 1999, "When we talk about diversity, we're specifically talking about people of color, people with handicaps, gender identity issues, but we use the broadest brushes. We say we are committed to people who've been underserved. That's who we are."

All the board members interviewed for this case study remain thoughtful about their understandings of diversity and keep asking questions in order to sharpen how the foundation defines and implements its commitments. Ellen Foster, vice chair of the board and a trustee since 2001, says, "We define diversity as representing the entire community we serve, as many constituencies as we can. By economic bracket as well as race, sex, and sexual preference." Ignatius Wang, a former trustee, points out, "We're [also] conscious about having diversity on the board. . . . I served on the board development committee. When we talked about diversity, in addition to race, we talked about skill sets: lawyers, investment skills, CPAs, people more connected to grassroots, etc. So we're not just talking about skin color." Wang also talked about some of the board's struggles to take responsibility themselves for diversity. He described a board development committee meeting where, when he pointed out the need for more people connected to the grassroots community on the board, another board member said, "Well, we have the staff to do that. The board's job is to manage the organization." Wang was taken aback. "Apparently that person didn't know what we meant by having people from diverse groups in policy positions," he said. When asked how he countered that, Wang replied, "I kept raising the issue. I suggested candidates. You don't have to hit people with a stick. But I'm pretty persistent. And it's not just me. People on the board generally are conscious, and they listen." He also described the importance of recognizing different definitions of being connected to grassroots communities and the need for more subtle thinking: "A solution to 'just get more minorities on the board' is a simplistic answer. There are minorities who are not connected to grassroots communities. And people connected to grassroots communities don't have to be minorities or poor either. It's the sensitivity that's sometimes difficult to come by."

In addition to raising consciousness among themselves about the meaning(s) of diversity, however, the foundation board tackled head-on another complex dimension of their commitment to diversity: how to serve all constituencies in the community—including white Irishmen whose problems needed to be addressed—and raise considerably larger endowments to support their work without diminishing their historical commitment to diversity. Board chair Craig Lewis, a trustee since 1996, recalls, "When I first came onto the board, many people in the community were feeling the foundation had tilted overboard in its focus on empowerment and diversity. If we wanted to assure our future ability to serve the community in its broadest sense, we were moving in the wrong direction." As a result one of the challenges Lewis described was finding the right balance, making sure the foundation's commitment to diversity and empowerment did not create roadblocks for their second, equally important function of creating a vehicle for philanthropy in the community.

In 1998, the board set out to make major changes in the foundation's character and culture. That required taking a hard look at how they could attract, educate, and serve the needs of a wider field of donors—including more people of wealth, many of whom were also white—while at the same time maintaining the foundation's commitment to serving traditionally underserved racial and ethnic communities in their geographical area. As Lewis describes it, "One change was to add a second pontoon to this boat equal to the commitment we'd become known for in our grantee interaction. Not done easily." The foundation had to change attitudes within the board and staff, and in the communities they served. Shifting the focus to include more donor-advised funds also meant moving around some staff positions to serve the needs of an increased number of donors. Lewis explained how they expanded to accommodate these new priorities of donor cultivation:

We set goals for ourselves: we would need to be donor-friendly, maintain commitments to our grantees, and not establish a sense of anxiety for grantees that they'd be put into a second-class category. Immediately we understood that we needed to change how we made grants. In order to do that, we suspended one full cycle of grant making (we're semiannual). We just wrote checks to everyone we'd funded before, and that gave our staff a chance to look at everything. We knew we could never perform that kind of analytical process in the midst of our grant cycle, and we needed to convince grantees that we wanted to improve our relationships with them.

Intentionality Key for Institutionalizing Understanding of Diversity

Careful and continued attention to rethinking and dealing with broader definitions of diversity requires considerable intentionality. CEO Swinney says,

> At the board level, our board development committee keeps tabs on gender, ethnicity, sexual orientation (not religion) as well as skill sets and geography. The board committee responsible for replacing new members looks at the balance. We look for all the criteria, including skills needed. This is reviewed and set up in an ongoing process of board appointments and retention. That's been in place a long time. So we not only have the commitments on paper, but a committee is set up to ensure that the composition of the board represents the community as much as possible. It's a live document, a live process.

The same is true for staff diversity, Swinney says. "In any of the foundation's departments, we look at the current composition of the foundation overall—we use the same criteria we do for trustees. Gender and ethnicity are straightforward, and although we don't ask questions about people's sexual orientation, we're conscious of it."

And the foundation keeps looking; it does not "settle" for less than what it wants. Swinney says that if they can't find people in the first round of searching, they have a responsibility to develop more diversity within certain categories: "When we need more diverse board members, we develop and groom new board members through committees. At the staff level, we work outside the foundation with nonprofits and educational institutions; we try to be sure they're more diverse, grow them up in those worlds." Swinney and others at the foundation recognize the need to encourage those among populations underrepresented on their staff to go to school, to get jobs in nonprofits to get ahead.

Vice president Lynette Campbell says, "In my seven years here, I've seen board members struggle as individuals but over time begin to understand what and how important diversity values are to the community. The foundation has been tested; it's had its challenges." And some of those challenges have been internal:

> You really have to work at it, find folks to maintain the balance. Here's an example: after all the work this foundation had done, we fell short in our investment management pool, only to find out some board members didn't think people of color do this work. Some folks challenged the investment committee, said all the people who worked in this area didn't have to have Fortune 500 experience. They were told, "Maybe your lens is unreasonable." I'll never forget a staff person and a board person say, "Where are they?" when we knew there were people of color in foundations across the country. It took a while to get them into compliance. That area took quite a bit of prodding, but it cleaned up.

This kind of intentionality is just as important in other dimensions of the foundation's work, according to Campbell. "The whole issue of diversifying our vendors has also been hard. There are goodwilled people who just don't know how to find vendors of color." Often there is a covert message, according to Campbell, a fear of substandard service if you use a person of color. That must be dealt with and Campbell describes how foundation staff worked on the issue: "The senior management team kept the issue on the table until it got resolved. You need to keep up the pressure. I personally was committed to keeping this on the table, not walking around it. I try to help staff in my department do the same thing. I need to help, but I also don't want to be the only one raising this banner."

Vice president Heather Gee speaks to the same question of intentionality among leaders in the foundation: "It seems to me it's always been a conscious decision among leadership in the organization, starting with the president years ago, continuing with the current leadership on the board." And having watched the organization evolve over the past three years, she knows the difficulty of sustaining diversity as a priority for a diverse staff: "It slips by, and they just don't think about it." Yet when their diversity awareness has started to wane, she has seen the foundation consciously put it back onto their list of highest priorities. She says, "In terms of both our grant making decisions and policies and practices at the board level, that commitment is just as strong if not stronger. I can't tell you the number of times I've sat in our board meetings and heard the board raise these issues, not prompted by staff." She expresses a lot of pride in a board that speaks out and is conscientiously committed to serving people in the community, even if it's not always been the most popular position: "From a fairly new staff person's perspective, I'd say it's in the fabric of the organization: sometimes it's a soft fabric; other times we need to be reminded that this fabric is beautiful because of the richness that's woven in there." Board chair Craig Lewis also expresses pride in how important these issues are to the board: "I'd say diversity as an institutional attitude and priority is more here than with any other organization I'm involved with. Should you be breathing to be a member of the board? Commitment to diversity is right up there with being able to maintain breath and a heartbeat."

Gee points to the intentional planning process that keeps these issues at the forefront, which is primarily a strategic-planning process. When the management team asks themselves, "What are our values?" diversity is one of the core values, along with equity and inclusiveness as fundamental values of community, that are included in their mission statement. So they look at their planning in all departments through lenses of diversity and inclusiveness: "What do we look like when we're doing an event? Publishing materials? Hiring caterers for an event? Doing radio spots? Setting up the entry fee that it takes to create a fund? These are just some of the ways the issues show up." For some, according to Gee, this planning process can be a struggle. "To have to keep looking through these lenses when you've never had to before can make some people dizzy. So we had to keep reiterating their importance because at first, people couldn't always see the purpose." When asked what it takes to bring people around who feel discomfort with these perspectives, Gee says, "Some people never came around. I have seen and heard of colleagues struggling with this. They are willing to see diversity as something they could embrace as a concept, but they couldn't do that in their work with potential donors." For others, however, "It's as easy as breathing. No struggle, no effort—it's just part of who they are, what this organization is about."

Board member Ellen Foster describes how this intentional institutional commitment to diversity works to keep a collective board committed even when individual members disagree. She describes a difficult discussion about funding organizations that support abortion rights. Despite some board members' personal anti-abortion stance, the board decided that in keeping with their mission of reaching every constituency, they had to provide grants to pro-choice organizations: "That was a good example of a collective commitment to diversity overruling beliefs that some of us had. We had a similar discussion about funding a gay rights group that had done some controversial demonstrations." The group had been radical and aggressive in their work, although not in the funded program, and the foundation decided they needed to support the group because it was representative of the community: "We have to support the community, put our own issues on the back burner sometimes."

Board member Foster also describes how the foundation achieved nuance in their institutionalization process and recognized the importance of having different voices at the table: "Whenever I think of institutionalizing, I think of a policy manual, which doesn't work. The real question is how you change the culture." What does work is an Asian-American board member reminding them they have forgotten a group and a black trustee who bluntly tells other board members, "You don't get it." The reality is, according to Foster, that if diverse constituents were not at the table, the foundation would lose its commitment—because of ignorance, not lack of inclination. These are cultural differences, and if different voices are not represented and heard on the board, the foundation would lose what Foster calls "real diversity" in the institution. In another example Foster cites, the board was considering a project with best of intentions until one of their African-American board members said to the rest of board, "You don't get it; there's a pride issue here." Without his input, the project just wouldn't have worked. Diversity may be in the culture of the foundation, but without the board being aware of its own limited knowledge, and without having diverse board members raise questions, good intentions may be all they have. "If this board were all white males, it wouldn't fulfill its mission, as much as these guys would try," according to Foster. "I don't think you ever really 'institutionalize' because leaders change. All you can institutionalize is a commitment to diversity in your ranks." Board chair Craig Lewis would agree. According to Lewis, the board's process gave them a chance to look at the foundation's role for donors and their work with grantees, and they modernized their financial capacity, but they still need to be vigilant about board governance. Lewis says that although the board had no written allocation or quota system in place, "I think it's fair to say that each board member has an absolute commitment to diversity, to reflect all the constituencies we're serving. It's not easy to meet diversity objectives, and it's very easy for our board composition to get out of balance. It's a full-time project to keep looking for qualified candidates."

Earlier in the foundation's history, the board functioned more as a distribution committee. All their threshold governance decisions were made by the banks that held their trusts, so there were only narrowly focused expectations from people who served on the board. That changed a dozen years ago when members of the board took on full governance responsibilities. And, Lewis recalls, "That meant we needed board members with a wider variety of skills and real experience in the community. When the board assumed a commitment to these broad-range governance responsibilities and still maintained its commitment to diversity, it was no small challenge." According to Lewis, they met that challenge: "If I'm not being too presumptuous to toot our horn, I think we've succeeded in doing all of these things, and we've increased the respect we've gotten in the entire community. I think we assuaged a lot of people's fears at the same time that we've strengthened the organization and its commitment to diversity. . . ." Their success, no small feat, is due in part to board members' own hard work. Lewis says, "We've worked very hard assembling a group of board members who reflect a lot of different perspectives in the community, are well respected for their professional achievements, personal ethics, and their commitments to community." These new board members, he points out, "aren't unknown folks just popping up on an issue, never to be seen again in the community. Board action is taken by well-respected folks in the community. I think that's one reason the foundation has the stature it does."

Lewis alludes to how these commitments to community also played out in the foundation's organizational transition, a crucial "right of passage" for the foundation that shifted the racial/ethnic composition of their leadership but not the foundation's core values. The former president of the foundation had been an African-American woman, and Lewis' predecessor as board chair was an African-American man, both of whom were replaced by white males. These new appointments created fear in both the community and on the board itself, especially when the new appointees started to talk about changing the way the group worked. The board quelled these fears:

A lot of people on the board talked about the importance of our commitment to diversity. We made our way through those conversations and proved to everybody, people on our board and in the community, when we said the best way to improve our capacity to the grantee community was to improve our effectiveness as a vehicle for philanthropy.

And the board continues to provide assurance of their commitment to diversity through "good healthy discussions," Lewis said: "If we ever want to get a little complacent, there's someone on the board right there ready to snap us to order. And that's one reason those individuals were appointed as desirable board members in the first place."

Intentionality Also Key for Diversifying Grant Making

In the same way board members are in place to raise questions about the foundation's commitment to diversity, program officers also raise questions. Vice president Lynette Campbell describes both the importance and the process of intentionality in the foundation's grant making. There are program officers who reach out and say, "We don't have any Latino groups in this round, people with disabilities, we've got to go out and find them," according to Campbell. The foundation was the first one in its community to support AIDS groups, she claims, but she also describes her frustration with groups not finding the foundation to apply for grants: "If you don't come in the door, why do I have to go get you if you're not here?" Nonetheless, the foundation is committed to doing outreach, and Campbell says, "Our program officers work to make it happen."

Board member Ellen Foster echoes the importance of extra effort in making diversity happen. She praises the organization's culture and its strong belief in reaching out to the nonprofit community: "Workshop with them, have them in to speak to us, educate us, not just wait for them to come to us." She cites an interesting example, a community art gallery in the foundation's office that changes its exhibits regularly: "Every three months, a different nonprofit hangs their art, and we have an opening. This art is extremely diverse. When you live with this, it becomes a part of your life. I think you have to expose yourself to new ideas, new themes on a regular basis, not just sit in an ivory tower reading books." Lewis also talks about the importance of this arts initiative: "We've now had fifteen different community-based arts organizations offered the chance to display their constituents' artwork: children, mentally impaired, mural artists, a broad variety." When making these simple, tangible efforts like using their office facilities as a gallery and as a convener for diverse groups who otherwise never get opportunities for display, Lewis says, "you're helping folks understand that you're 'walking the talk.' Sometimes the most basic, simple, obvious things do more than any grand plan."

At times, "walking the talk" also can mean taking controversial stands. Lewis points out that any organization publicly supporting gay and lesbian issues fifteen years ago was most likely ostracized by people in mainstream Philadelphia society. But that sort of criticism did not stop the Philadelphia Foundation from becoming involved in what Lewis describes as "empowering people and organizations." He gives the example of the board's rethinking grants made to the Boy Scouts with discretionary donor-advised funds: "Several years ago, we notified the Boy Scouts in this region that we'd no longer provide discretionary funds if they adhered to their national policy of excluding homosexuals." The board expected a fair amount of criticism for stating that position in the community, but they felt strongly about diversity and took that position without regard for re-action. "That's how we manifest our commitment to diversity," according to Lewis. "Interestingly, we got no negative feedback on that decision at all, only two or three comments from people supporting our position."

These values and understandings about diversity are becoming "institu-tionalized," even if not all agree it's a smooth process. When asked how he would assess the foundation's success to date at institutionalizing diversity, former board member Ignatius Wang says, "I think we are successful, and I experience it everywhere I go," having been the first and only Asian on several boards. Appointed to the Board of Trustees of the local community college, for instance, he found no other Asians on the board, but after he served six years and rotated off, the board decided they needed another Asian: "Sometimes you have to get people used to keeping funny-looking faces around." The same is true for the Philadelphia Foundation. Wang de-scribes the time when the board transitioned from the chair and president (both African-Americans) to "a white-haired tall Caucasian chair, and both the president and the COO spoke with a British accent. I was the board treasurer, and I also talk a little funny. It got the grantee community a little bit concerned." That concern may still exist, Wang thinks, espe-cially because the board put its emphasis in the past two or three years on servicing donors. But when asked what the foundation has done to ame-liorate that concern, he says, "I think it was our program officers out there in the field. Lynette Campbell, vice president for programs at the founda-tion, has been here for a long time and carried a lot of the burden, but everyone has helped with the process."

How Gender Plays Out

The vice president for development services, Heather Gee, stresses the im-portance of including gender in both personnel and grant-making deci-sions: "Gender is woven into other lenses. It makes such a difference when the leadership of the organization itself is diverse. They're the ones whose voices, opinions are the strongest." She stresses the importance of having Lynette Campbell, an African-American woman, in a leadership position along with a former female COO in the finance department. They both took part in dialogues with the grant-making committee and were influ-ential in helping all the staff members keep their focus on the broadest understanding of diversity, including gender. "Diversity, including an understanding of gender, couldn't happen without that depth. It's not just three people, it's the whole organization."

According to Campbell, it's also important to be explicit about gender. "As a woman, I'm not going to say I have a hidden agenda: it's a conscious, cautious, caring one." She stresses that it is important that everyone in the foundation "gets" gender, even as the organization goes through management and board transitions: "Culture changes, values don't. Board members and staff both pass those values on." She says, "I've got two white males, one board chair and one president; the other senior manager is a white male. We used to be all women; that's now changed. The values haven't." She points out that the foundation still embraces hiring women and supporting women and girls through their grants, but when the current president was hired, a white Scotsman, the foundation was seeking someone different. "We'd had a black president, a Latina president. This was a shift that needed to be made. Andrew's done well here, and his values totally match the values of this foundation. That's how this work gets institutionalized."

Commitment to Diversity Pays Off, Creates New Sources of Funds for Foundation

When the foundation shifted more of its focus to soliciting and servicing donor-advised funds in the 1990s, many people in the communities the foundation serves expressed concern that the foundation's historical commitment to diversity would take a back seat to aiding donors. CEO Andrew Swinney says, "Certainly on the staff there were a few who believed that we were not being true to how we defined our values statement. In some instances, they decided to leave."

The board also had interesting decisions to make regarding its role as a grant maker. When Swinney took over the presidency in 1998, 60 percent of the total grant money awarded was through competitive cycles using unrestricted funding. By 2004, that amount represented only one third of the total funds the foundation distributed. The rest came from donor-advised funds. Swinney says, "We try to engage and educate donors. This allows us the opportunity to advance causes, introduce donors to institutions that need help." He too cites the example of the Boy Scouts: "Where the board has responsibility for grant making through unrestricted funds, we have policies around things we don't fund: e.g., Boy Scouts. We take positions about monies we are responsible for. But if a donor wanted to support the Boy Scouts, we would try to educate the donor that perhaps that isn't a good idea. . . ."

Working with donors is sometimes a delicate balancing act. Vice president Campbell says that the foundation tends to attract donors who come to them with a vision, and at times foundation staff find themselves needing to expose those donors to other views of community life. The foundation "can't be amoeba-like," she says, "or we'd lose our soul. There are some donors we just can't serve. I don't think we'd sell the soul of the foundation to meet their needs." Educating donors is an ongoing process, according to vice president of development services Heather Gee. "We actively try to educate donors, expose them to organizations that are doing incredible work in the community that are not mainstream, that they won't read about in the daily paper. These are not organizations with the million-dollar galas. We make those introductions as often as we can." The foundation also takes donors into communities. A tour bus picks them up, and they do site visits. "People don't show up in record numbers," Gee says, "but for those that come, it's a great experience. We've also talked about taking donors out on site visits with program officers."

Gee also describes the challenges of looking for new donors who can help the foundation keep its endowment up in an unstable economy without losing sight of the foundation's values: "The tendency is to get as much money in as we can, to look at people who have a lot of money as our primary prospect pool. But the reality is that the foundation is not just here to serve rich people." The foundation defines their role as creating a vehicle for philanthropy for everyone: "At times, we've all had to refocus, remind ourselves that we're here so that anyone who wants to be a philanthropist can participate," not just those who have wealth.

Gee goes on to describe how they broaden their donor base by marketing themselves to Philadelphia and the surrounding counties. "We do ads on public radio, interviews on black radio stations, for example." She guesses that most listeners are retirees who never knew they could become philanthropists with their limited money, that they could set up a permanent fund to memorialize someone or a permanent fund for their favorite cause. "If someone establishes a fund with a little money, we promote that like crazy," she says. "We don't do that for a $6 million bequest, but we do promote ways the everyday person making modest income can use us to fulfill their philanthropic goals." The foundation also encourages a variety of ways for setting up funds. Gee says that even though all the foundation funds are pooled for investment purposes, sometimes groups of people set up specific, targeted pooled funds. Before coming to the foundation, for example, one group of women, all of them members of one of the top black sororities in their community, had established a short-term nonprofit to raise money from their members with the specific purpose of finding land and constructing a building. Gee praises the committed efforts of the four women who worked on the project—opening mail, collecting checks, writing thank-you letters—but says that when one of the foundation's board members directed them to the foundation, they jumped at the opportunity. "We now do all that work for them, and when they're ready to build the building, they'll make grants for the building. They call it working smarter, not harder. They've raised a million dollars from less than 300 members, very few of whom are wealthy."

Board chair Craig Lewis says the foundation's credibility and track record of attention to diversity is also paying off with previously unexplored areas with donors to the foundation. "We're seen as a good intermediary for community resolution of issues." He cites an example that he believes is a precedent. The city of Philadelphia had decided to move ahead with construction of a new sports facility, which created a heated debate; many people questioned whether the city would be better off spending those dollars on other projects. Philadelphia made a commitment to the stadium, but in the process the city convinced each of the sports teams that would be using the stadium to commit contributions to a children's fund. Realizing it needed a mechanism for managing the contributions and, fortunately, understanding that the worst place to distribute this money was from the bowels of city government itself, the city turned to the Philadelphia Foundation. Because of the foundation's stature, their reputation for ethical funding, and their commitment to diversity, they were designated as beneficiary of those funds: "Beginning next year, we'll receive one million a year each from the Eagles and the Phillies. Those donor relationships—and the children's fund—would never have happened without our demonstrated track record for diversity."

Evaluation

As described earlier, the foundation took a year off from grant making to enable both board and staff to look more closely at who they were and what they were doing. Most of those interviewed talked about the importance of this kind of planning process and internal evaluation. Vice president of development services Heather Gee joined the foundation staff just as the foundation was completing its analysis of "who we were funding, how we were funding them, and how we were making people ask for grants." As a result, the foundation had developed new guidelines and criteria that opened it up to new opportunities, including proposals from well-funded nonprofits. "For so many years, we used to fund only very-small-budget organizations. If an organization's budget was over $1.5 million, we wouldn't consider funding them. After what someone called our navel-gazing period, we agreed to fund larger organizations too, say an organization with a $5 million budget that wanted a special project." Any organization could now apply for special projects, although not for general operating money, making the Philadelphia Foundation more accessible to larger nonprofits that fell within their grant making criteria.

On the other hand, the foundation also made the criteria more specific regarding those served by the organizations they funded. Proposals now must include information about the makeup of grant applicants' boards, staff, and constituencies on a demographic sheet that includes the categories of sexual identity, race/ethnic, age, and other diversity characteristics. Many organizations are "thrown for a loop," according to Gee, and may ask "If we don't have gay board members, we don't get funded?" But she points out that "these questions give us more information, and it's an important consciousness-raiser for nonprofit organizations. On the one hand we broaden our scope; on the other, we use a microscope. This came from a need to know our grantee community better. We are having more and more donors coming to us with diverse interests, and this helps us help them."

Board member Ellen Foster also talks about measuring the impact of the foundation's grants on the communities they serve: "Our impact is hard to measure. But anything that's measured in any reasonable way is good because it makes you focus; even if the measure is off, it makes you think about what you're doing." Foster also describes the importance of the foundation's taking risks and being flexible in the size of their grants. "A commitment to diversity means we sometimes take more risks than other organizations: we fund people who aren't so sophisticated. We often give more but smaller grants than other organizations." She points out that some foundations would say that "funding small" leads to fragmented programs, but she and others at the foundation think it allows them to meet the more needy and otherwise forgotten organizations. And, Foster says, a small nonprofit often can leverage the foundation's endorsement to gain access to more or larger donors: "I couldn't really say we have a higher loss factor—we don't consider any grant a loss. Some of the organizations we fund may be risky because they are small or young, but we always make sure they are reasonably well-managed and fiscally responsible or we don't give them a grant." She works with many nonprofits in the city and says they're definitely not afraid to come to the foundation for a grant, no matter how small or large the organization. "To me, that's the measure."

Public Welfare Foundation

The Public Welfare Foundation is a private foundation that provides support to organizations that help marginalized people overcome barriers to full participation in society. The foundation's emphasis—local, regional, and international—is democracy building via community building. As the CEO and board chair describe in their 2002 annual report, "Democracy is not about what someone else will do for us or for others. It is about what we do, as a community, in a shared commitment to improving our own and other peoples' lives."[19] For 2004, the foundation targeted eight primary areas for funding:

- Community development
- Criminal justice
- Youth
- Environment
- Health
- Human rights and global security
- Reproductive and sexual health

First incorporated in Texas in 1947 by newspaper publisher Charles Edward Marsh with the mandate to "help people help themselves in a manner which neither destroys their dignity nor initiative," the foundation reincorporated in Delaware in 1951 and moved its offices to Washington D.C., in 1960. Marsh and his family endowed the Foundation by donating three southern dailies: *The Spartanburg Herald & Journal, The Tuscaloosa News,* and *The Gadsden Times,* which in 1985 were sold to The New York Times Company. In 2003, the foundation's endowment was $413 million, up from $350 million in 1996, and it awarded 430 grants worth a total of just over $18 million. About the same number were awarded in 1996, but the combined value of the grants in 2003 was $2.5 million more than the total dollar value of grants awarded in 1996.

From its first grants in 1948 to the present, the foundation's vision and commitment has been consistent: to support organizations that move people toward full participation in society. Like other foundations in these case studies, Public Welfare continues to rely on the vision of its founder, a man convinced that "the people who can most effectively develop and implement solutions to address a problem are those who are most affected by it." The foundation's board and staff pursue a funding strategy of "service, advocacy, and empowerment" through community building, with an emphasis on promoting democratic participation for people around the world: "service that solves specific problems; advocacy to address those needs in a more systemic way; and work to empower people in need so they play leading roles in achieving those remedies." The foundation emphasizes community building that, in addition to their funding priorities, extends to advocacy in the philanthropic world as well as to their relationships with grantees.

The foundation's commitment to community building also manifests itself in the neighborhood where the foundation has relocated its offices. In 2001, Public Welfare moved into new headquarters in the True Reformer Building in Washington's historic Shaw neighborhood. As they describe in their 2002 annual report, "We promised members of the Shaw community that we would not only be faithful stewards of the historic treasure that is theirs in the True Reformer Building, but that we would be a good neighbor, adding to those voices already present for making Shaw 'better, not different.'" Besides renovating the building to fit both their needs and historic preservation guidelines, they partnered with the locally based Manna Community Development Corporation to build affordable housing on property the foundation owns in the heart of the Shaw community. The housing is designated for people with modest incomes who had been displaced by gentrification in the neighborhood. They also contributed to the Shaw community by providing a temporary home for the African American Civil War Memorial Museum and by welcoming neighborhood groups and others to use the foundation's auditorium for meetings.

Intentional Shift to Diversify Staff

Larry Kressley, Public Welfare's executive director, was first hired in 1982 as a program officer and since 1992 has been CEO. Kressley's colleagues outside the foundation as well as staff and trustees within the foundation all cite the importance of his push to diversify staff in making the foundation what it is today. As the board grew more comfortable with Kressley's staff choices, increased board diversity followed. Kressley notes, "When I was asked to be acting executive director in 1991, there were no people of color on our program staff, while our administrative staff was mostly African-American. We had our work cut out for us." Phillipa Taylor, chief financial and administrative officer and an African-American, says, "Larry knows the importance of diversity and how it positively affects our decision making. He's committed and passionate. I think his being gay gives him even more understanding. He doesn't push diversity down our throats. But he makes sure we all understand how important it is." Later in the interview, she came back to the importance of Larry's leadership: "He creates such an open environment for us to say what we need to say. He really welcomes our differences."

By all accounts, however, this move to a more open environment was not an easy shift for the foundation. Kressley's being the first gay CEO in philanthropy to be out probably made his commitment to diversity harder to implement, rather than easier: "The board bought into my vision of a more diverse staff when they hired me, but it was rough at first. I think they were wondering, 'Is Larry ever going to hire another straight white man?' I replied, 'When he's the best qualified for the job.'" Board member Beth Warner—who is white, as is Kressley—credits him for the foundation's reputation for institutionalizing diversity: "In terms of diversity on staff, I think it's Larry's focus, but I've seen it to be a colorless, genderless process. Those doing the hiring try to see who rises up to the top. It's not, 'We should have more women, more men. . . .' They just let the process happen, and somehow that's created this staff that's remarkably diverse. There's this whole sense of 'right place, right time.'"

So how did Kressley's vision prevail? "What I immediately did was work to get rid of the 'screens' that usually exclude people who are 'different' from consideration." These screens, another example of Norm at work, are the blind spots described in chapters 1 and 2 that get in the way of seeing diversity as assets: stereotypes that make it difficult to recognize that a black woman, for example, could be qualified for a position as an executive financial officer. Kressley explains the foundation's choices as *not* a conscious intention to look for race or ethnic or gender characteristics as much as a conscious effort to remove the blinders: "We made a commitment always to hire the best person for the job. We weren't going to be focusing on demographics. I'm convinced that when you hire the best person—in this kind of work that means looking for the judgment and sensibility needed to do the job—you'll end up diversifying the staff."[20] What makes this kind of job search different—and successful—is the commitment to see past stereotypes, to conduct a search with a nuanced understanding of how traditional norms and assumptions so easily blind us to all possibilities different from those we'd usually make.

Program officer Adisa Douglas, an African-American woman, points out that this same commitment to "hiring the best" applies to gender as well. In Public Welfare's case, it's a "reverse" awareness: with only three out of eight program staff being men, some might see the need to hire more men. But the foundation is committed to their "blind" hiring. As Douglas describes, "We recently hired another African-American female program officer. We interviewed a lot of people. This person brings not only her experiences as an African-American woman growing up in Chicago and attending a liberal law school, but she also brings freshness and new ideas. Hiring her did show our continuing commitment to diversity, but she stood up on her own merits, coming out on top." Douglas goes on to point out an important, if sometimes overlooked, part of a foundation's commitment to diversifying their institutional culture: "Diversity means a mixed staff. I consider my white colleagues part of the diversity. In staff meetings, program discussions, the mixture is what really works." The key is "a certain kind of professionalism on a team that pays attention to others in the room. . . . We all help each other. . . . My experience is so multilateral: nothing I do comes just from one vantage point . . . not 'just' because I'm African-American. . . . Our respect for each other, willingness to listen . . . that's why we flourish here." All of which is still one more example of Kressley's hiring strategy: getting rid of the screens also means "hiring for the team."

A Board Learns to Take Risks

So what about the board? The board in 2004 was still predominantly white and male: twice as many men as women, eight whites, two African-Americans, and one Latina. But it is a board that supports and learns from its staff and, by all accounts, works well with staff without violating the board/staff boundary lines that can make for institutional mayhem. Trustee Beth Warner's grandmother was married to Charles Marsh, the founder, and she is one of two family members on the board (the other is the founder's grandson). For those connected by family to the founder, it's a "second generation" board with trustees serving with or replacing their parents. So there is strong board continuity, but continuity sometimes comes at the cost of new blood. Warner observes, "We have term limits, but everybody is voted back on if they want to run. . . . The only way people leave is to die." So how did these long-serving, and by most accounts conservative, board members work to shift their foundation into an organization that institutionalized deep diversity and learned to "name Norm"?

Trustee Warner and others talk of the complex dynamics that have led to what many describe as a board of somewhat conservative people being enormously proud of and supporting funding initiatives that, for some board members at least, seem to be on the far left edge of philanthropy. But their commitment to diversity works and has worked for long enough now that most of those interviewed inside and outside the foundation think that both the foundation's commitment to diversity and their risk-taking philanthropy is "institutionalized." One of the reasons is the board's respect for its own choice of staff leadership in Larry Kressley and its commitment to keep its hands off administrative decisions. By their own accounts, board members are not always comfortable with those decisions, but they have had the wisdom to separate board and staff functions. Board member Warner points out, "I think there's been a nervousness. Sometimes the diversity on the staff makes some board members uncomfortable, marginally uncomfortable. But we leave it up to Larry to run and hire the staff and make sure they're following through with what our mission is."

How did the board come to hire someone so different from most board members? Kressley shares his impression:

In 1992, when I was appointed to the position, I was said to be the first openly gay man to head a large foundation. I think it was a real struggle for the directors at first. It took them a year to decide. They were also concerned about my left worldview. I doubt I would have been selected if I hadn't already been on staff. The foundation did a national search, and the other final candidate was much more like the board than I am. But the board was familiar with me. As one of the family trustees, the founder's daughter, said, "I didn't want a stranger running the foundation." Another family member answered the concern about my being too left: "Larry's been with us nine years, and we've approved 99 percent of his grants. If he's too left, then I am, and I'm very conservative."

This openness on the part of a conservative board to new ideas has historic precedence in the foundation. Trustee Beth Warner describes what was for her an important lesson, a telling incident that opens a small window into the culture of the board: "Even though many of us are conservative, there's an openness. People on the board have learned to see with different eyes. How did we learn to do that? By having programs brought in front of us, we read and learn. We also had to trust the staff, trust Larry." Warner continues, remembering a time when her father was chair of this board:

He went to a Council on Foundations meeting in New York and some of the people in the larger environmental organizations took him aside, warning him, "You'd better be careful because your staff is taking you down the environmental justice road, and you need to think about where you're heading." Initially, my father had a hard time with that kind of admonition: he was a conservative Yale man, and he wanted to be "in the club." But he was open and listened. What he did in response to that "warning" was to sit down with the environmental program officer, an African-American woman, and listen to her talk about the program. And like others on the board, he became an ardent supporter of our environmental justice initiative. Others on the board may also have had some initial discomfort until we read the proposals, heard the staff. So there's an educational piece and openness on the part of the board. That may be backward policy, staff to board, but it works both ways now. And because we've had a history of giving to those who can't get much support from other sources, we've learned to look and think outside the box. We're proud of that. Larry has empowered this wonderful staff, who are pretty darn remarkable.

Kressley's skill in building an effective, diverse staff also has empowered the board. Unlike other foundations described in this chapter's case studies, Public Welfare has not done diversity workshops for the board. Kressley describes relying on his knowledge of the Public Welfare trustees, "Knowing this group of people who are willing to say, 'Let's do what's right. . . .' I do think that they see this as a commitment that I've made. But their support for me includes support for our commitment to diversity. They take pride in the work." And success breeds success: "Trustees saw what our staff practice was—hiring the best for the job—and they began to feel more at ease with it. They came to trust that the agenda really was to take the filters off that keep out others." Another example of "naming Norm" that works.

Both board and staff have learned to listen and learn from each other. Without stepping over board-staff lines, the board appears to be accessible, and program staff and some administrative staff attend the board meetings. Program officer Adisa Douglas describes her favorite example of board-staff interaction:

We have a section in the meetings that I've really come to love. When we finish presenting our dockets, we have the option of giving presentations on something we're working on. We've been doing this for a year now, and it's given us a few minutes of articulation without answering questions. It's shown the level of staff we have here, how we're thinking, how we're leveraging grants, and how we're trying to address current changes in the world. Most boards would not hear from program staff like this. I've found it to be just wonderful; it adds another level of respect for staff. Too often boards just want a staff person to answer their questions, but this is so rich. Board members learn more, and so does the administrative staff. We get to see how we're all thinking.

Effective Philanthropy

Community-Based Solutions   Public Welfare's commitment to diversity also plays out in its grant making through its insistence on community-based solutions to problems. Larry Kressley points out, "We've always prided ourselves on not playing the usual imperious role of grant makers. That's part of the mandate from our founder: people who live the problems are the best ones to solve them. People who know different communities and build trust with them are going to have closer relationships and closer-to-the-ground knowledge of the work that needs to happen." He cites the example of his own work as a program officer and the importance of having staff that can reach communities the foundation is trying to reach: "Before becoming executive director, I was the program officer in our environment program. I used to think we were doing good grant making, but I wanted to focus on environmental justice." To ensure that focus, he hired Dana Alston, a leader of the environmental justice movement. Later, to increase the effectiveness of their funding in reproductive health, he hired Adisa Douglas, an African-American woman who "has done things in our reproductive health program that a white person just couldn't have done, even though we had the priorities. We were funding the larger organizations reaching people of color, but Adisa took us into those communities to fund groups that implemented what we said we were doing."

Chief financial officer Phillipa Taylor says, "My observations are that the program officers here are real advocates for our grantees. We do a lot of grassroots funding, and our program officers are very conscious of balance of power between grantees and grantors. They don't present the 'we are the experts' stance: we want partners."

Risk Taking   Risk taking also is seen as integral to the foundation's success. Kressley emphasizes, "Some of our groups are marginal: I don't think there is anything like a 'failed grant' because just giving people who seldom receive outside support for their work a grant is itself a community-building exercise." Risk taking also requires stretching the definitions of program areas, as Adisa Douglas did for reproductive health:

I extended our international funding of reproductive health to include female genital mutilation (FGM). I wrote a paper that laid out what it was and the perspectives we needed to fund it. We needed to understand there were women in Africa organizing against this, that we should fund their efforts to do this work. It's an interesting way to look at a new issue. Why is this a reproductive health issue? This work has linked our reproductive health with empowerment and rights of women and girls.

After a board review of ten years of foundation-funded programs working to eradicate FGM, Douglas reported the board spoke of their excitement about the progress they had helped to fund and pride in the role the foundation had played in expanding support for the issue. "I tried something new, took the risk, and Larry backed me. And the board has been very supportive," according to Douglas. She adds, "The point here is the importance of leadership at both board and staff levels to try new things with a different perspective."

The board needs to understand its own role as risk takers. Trustee Beth Warner argues, "People, both trustees and staff members, have to be able to go out on a limb . . . and not worry about what others think. It's hard to do the right thing sometimes, even if you know what that is." And Warner knows how hard that is: "In the world of big-money philanthropy, still mostly white and male leadership," she says, "people don't go out on limbs because they're afraid of falling off." But with Public Welfare, Warner sees a history of risk taking: "Fifty years ago, there were two women running the foundation, which in itself was unusual. But they were the kind of funders who went out in jeeps in Haiti to see what was needed. So there's always been a 'take the risk' culture in this foundation: let's try it, see what happens. That's what makes for effective grants."

Funder/Grantee Partnerships   Public Welfare's 2002 annual report also describes their commitment to community-based solutions and funder/grantee partnerships that, while some in organized philanthropy might deem risky, Public Welfare defines as the heart of its funding strategy. For their Fund for Washington's Children and Youth, a five-year effort to support "homegrown" projects to address problems of children and their families in the poorest neighborhoods of Washington. DC:

We began the Fund in 1997 by convening a community meeting to determine the most pressing needs of young people and to support the development of community solutions to address them. To date, we have invested over $2 million in community-based efforts through the Fund. . . . As grant makers, we continue our commitment to supporting the work of organizations as they define it. We believe that organizations, especially those based in the communities they serve, know what they need to do their work. In supporting those efforts, we avoid the meddling that is too often an occupational hazard in our field.

Funder/grantee partnerships are key to their work. The foundation's Welfare Reform Fund, for instance, started in 1997 to respond to what the foundation saw as the inequities of the 1996 federal act. It used an "engine committee," made up of representatives of organizations from across the country that have received grants from the fund since its inception, to set the new funding priorities. And in 2003, the foundation convened meetings of organizations they had been supporting in areas of healthcare reform, countering hate and discrimination, and environmental justice to provide "an opportunity for organizations we support to help us improve our grant making and other support to them, but they are also an all-too-rare opportunity for organizations working on the same issues to meet to share experiences and map out future strategies."

Core Support   In keeping with trust in their own diverse grantees' ability to determine the best course for their funding, the foundation provides core-support grants, claiming "it is the best way to build strong organizations." Larry Kressley says, "Especially in marginalized communities, crises come up. You have to believe in the organizations. Let them set the course." As a result, as much as 70 percent of their grants are for general support.

Responsibility to the Larger Field of Philanthropy
Maintaining Levels of Funding in Hard Times   The foundation extends its mission of community-building to the larger field of philanthropy itself. In 2002, for example, because they felt so strongly the need to maintain their commitment to the community they served, they pledged to maintain their spending level for grants that year, despite the downturn in the economy in general and in their own investment portfolio. In doing so, they set a new standard in philanthropy because, as they said in their 2002 annual report:

We believe that in times like these there is an increased need for the community-building efforts that the Public Welfare Foundation has supported over its 55-year history. Especially since September 11, many groups we support have faced cash-flow problems that have threatened their continued existence. We have stepped in to assist those organizations and secure the investments that they, and we, have made in them.

Staff Participation in Philanthropy Field   The staff members at Public Welfare Foundation also are active in the larger field of philanthropy. Larry Kressley was on the first Council on Foundations' Committee on Inclusiveness and pressed for increased understanding of how the more subtle, unnamed issues of an institutional culture can impact organizations despite resistance, even from people of color. Kressley argues that "people who bring a difference to an organization have to have an effect," but he also recognizes that "in most of philanthropy, the extent to which you assimilate to the dominant culture is the extent to which you are successful." His reaction: "One of our first new hires when I became CEO, program officer Adisa Douglas, a woman of color, warned me she wasn't going to change, and I told her 'I want you to change us.'"

And she has been an effective agent of change. Douglas, like many others interviewed for these case studies, is active in affinity groups, which are groups of funders under the aegis of the Council on Foundations organized according to common funding areas as well as common racial/ethnic/gender identities. Douglas is on the board of the Funders Network on Population and Reproductive Health and Rights and served as cochair of its 2003 annual conference. Douglas's longest leadership role in philanthropy is as a member of the National Network of Grantmakers (NNG). In 1984, she founded NNG's People of Color Caucus and since has served as a mentor to people of color who are new to philanthropy.

Board members not only encourage such activities by Kressley and his staff but take pride in them. Trustee Beth Warner observes:

One of the things we've wanted Larry and our staff to do is pull together different funders and convince them not to be so scared; diversity and grassroots funding can work! We're committed to that. . . . Larry's well-thought-of in the funding community. We're proud that he goes out and talks about being on the edge a bit. That's as important as doing the funding. If you get it, you've got to go out and tell others, be who you are.

Evaluation

The foundation also sees evaluation as an important component of its work. Although they have not solicited independent, outside evaluations, they regularly do comprehensive internal assessments of their program areas, and they make their findings public on the foundation's Web site (www.publicwelfare.org). According to Kressley, "We've always focused our evaluation on getting information that will be useful to both us and the grantees." Kressley also is interested in using the evaluation process as a learning tool through peer evaluations: "We send people to visit each other's projects and do conferences here. This is a friendly process that emphasizes how grantees can improve their work." Or as Douglas points out, "A key thing we mean by evaluation is looking at the whole program area, bringing grantees together. This does a number of things: we get to hear what they see needs to happen in that area of funding. And we are able to articulate the lessons we've learned."

Those lessons learned, and the ability to keep changing and building on them, are what distinguish Public Welfare as an innovative funder. Trustees have enough confidence to trust their staff and establish clear guidelines and processes; staff leaders clearly articulate institutional values and a nuanced understanding of diversity that give staff room to grow and reward change. All these factors produce effective philanthropy.

4

Effective Foundations Fund "Both/And"

In chapter 3 we saw how six foundations developed more subtle understandings of diversities, including gender. The case studies provided examples of how to institutionalize diversity with intentionality, process, and leadership on both boards and staffs. We also saw how institutionalized commitments to deep diversity, naming Norm, and program evaluations translate into improved relationships with grantees and more effective philanthropy overall. This chapter looks at strategies for funding gender *per se* and how foundations that are effective learn to do "both/and" funding. They make grants to gender-specific programs and organizations and also to mixed-gender programs and organizations that have effectively learned how to use a gender lens—to the benefit of all involved. The case studies in the previous chapter show how broad-based diversity is implemented. Although this chapter focuses on gender, the lessons apply for all the categories of diversity we have discussed in this book. The kind of both/and funding we describe and advocate in this chapter can and must be done across all categories of diversity. The situation described below shows how the leaders in at least one organization came to understand the importance of both/and funding.

On an evening in early April 2002, top women leaders in a major city met to talk about their roles as business, government, and nonprofit executives active in the community. The women were part of an organization that had evolved over the years: shifting purposes from a group whose agenda had been to bolster each other in often-hostile work settings to a group whose agenda was to assert themselves as effective civic leaders. The evolution is typical of many U.S.-based women's organizations over the last decade, shifting from defensive organizations with "siege" mentalities to proactive organizations flexing their collective muscles for the civic good. Their evolution also echoes one of the themes of this book: that women, especially women in all their diversity, are a major resource for civil society.

That particular evening, the organization was meeting to focus on women's philanthropy. What the women expected to talk about was the need for women to focus their philanthropy entirely on programs that serve women or girls. But in the course of their meeting, they came to realize something they least expected: their collective failure to target their philanthropy widely enough for the benefit of women or girls. To their surprise, the discussion that evening quickly led them beyond what they expected to be their topic—supporting "just" women and girls by putting all of their philanthropic resources into programs entirely for women and girls—to a more comprehensive focus. If all of the organizations in their city did not actively account for gender in their programs, then were those organizations likely not effective for women and girls? For men and boys? And if these women did not assume leadership roles ensuring that all of the philanthropy in their city benefited women and girls, who would? If the most powerful women in a major city—a group that experientially understands both explicit and implicit gender biases—did not ask these tough questions about who benefits from their philanthropy, then they had no reason to expect any other group would. Over the course of the evening this group of women embraced a much larger and bolder vision for their philanthropy: to be the leaders in their community who ensured that women and girls were well served by every program receiving philanthropic support. In the months to come they succeeded in raising significant new philanthropic dollars in their community—far exceeding their initial fund raising goal. What made the difference for them was the boldness of their new vision.

A major focus of the discussion that evening—and another theme of this book that we saw play out in the six case-study foundations—is that effective grant making and philanthropy must necessarily be both/and grant making, *not* either/or. Both/and grant making and philanthropy is an approach that includes funding for effective universal programs *and* for gender-specific programs. The grant making also actively incorporates deep diversity, including an informed understanding of gender, in all relevant program areas of a foundation's work, which typically include both universal and specific grant programs for women's and girls' issues. This chapter discusses the importance of this both/and approach and offers several examples of foundations that have practiced this effective funding strategy. Despite their many differences, most foundations have one thing in common: they seek to fund nonprofit organizations that are effective, that deliver and accomplish their stated goals and objectives. The most powerful argument for knowledgeable both/and grant making is effectiveness: both/and grant making is an essential funding strategy, one that ensures both foundations and the programs and organizations they fund are fully effective.

Unfortunately, in the last twenty years the trend has been to de-emphasize gender in foundation program designs, a trend arising, ironically, in part from efforts to guarantee gender equity. As we described in chapter 1, efforts to institutionalize equity for women often have been based on the argument that a woman can do anything a man can do and, therefore, should have opportunities to do so. As a strategy to help women gain entrée into previously all-male domains, from jobs to sports programs, this assertion made sense. But its continued use blurs significant systemic disparities between men and women, especially disparities in opportunities and access to resources, and has had the unintended effect of reinforcing many of the unspoken norms and stereotypes we talked about in chapters 1 and 2. Without clear thinking about gender and other diversities, foundations run the risk of setting up white men as the gold standard, the universal norm to which white women and women and men of color should be compared.

On the other hand, as we also described in chapter 1, earlier rationales for paying attention to gender in program design included the supposition that women and men were inherently different and that women, as the subordinate group, needed special programs to compensate for those differences. Significant, reliable research on gender similarities and differences has disproved this rationale, but challenge to "inherent differences" programming often results in the opposite conclusion—that women and men are just the same, and therefore universal programs should work as well for women as they do for men. In practice, this often has resulted in women's admission into formerly all-male programs that were designed to work well for men. But as we also showed in chapter 1, although research has documented few inherent, biological differences between women and men, there are *profound* differences resulting from gender socialization that have major impacts on both women's and men's lives, usually to the detriment of both groups.

The central case, then, for the relevance of gender to program effectiveness rests on the fact that men and women are socialized very differently, with different expectations about appropriate behavior and social roles, and that society holds men and women to different standards of behavior. This different socialization creates different life experiences and opportunities that often result in significant disparities in access to both tangible and intangible resources. Funding programs must pay attention to these differences if they are to be effective, and foundations can increase the effectiveness of the nonprofits they support by including gender criteria in all their relevant grant making evaluations and decisions. As we also saw in chapters 1 and 2, however, gender is a complex quality of human life, and it is not an isolated phenomenon. Lives are shaped profoundly by racial, cultural, and class contexts as well as by gender—these categories of difference have complex impacts on experiences and opportunities. Well-designed nonprofit programs pay attention to this ever-changing kaleidoscope of human experience. Effective foundations do the same.

Although it can be obvious to individuals and foundations that race, class, and gender together shape individual and group experience, it also can be easy to lose sight of this fact in the grant making process because of the prevailing, unexamined stereotype in this country that *woman* is white, professional, and upper-middle class, despite the fact that most U.S. women are not. This misconception obscures the fact that gender, race, and class are inextricable, that one experience is not "lived" without the other. When we lose sight of the interconnections of race, class, and gender, we fall into the trap of thinking that race and gender are oppositional categories, only one of which can be considered at a time. This false separation is evident, for instance, in foundations that include racial criteria in their grant making but not gender, a practice that pits the needs of white women against those of people of color and excludes the special needs of women of color altogether. The way out of this conundrum is to recognize and analyze deep diversity and the intersection of race and class with gender in nonprofit programs and in the funding of those programs.

Gender Differences Matter

Women and men being socialized differently and held to different standards of behavior by society makes it necessary for programs to incorporate gender in program design, implementation, and leadership to be
effective. The following examples document the different ways gender matters, and they all require thoughtfully designed programs that can be either
coeducational or single-sex.

Disproportionate impact.   Because of their gendered socialization and
social roles, women and girls can be affected *more* than men or boys by
specific problems or issues. Significantly more women than men, for example, live in poverty. Researchers attribute this disparity to at least two
factors: labor-market segregation and women's significantly greater role
(and financial responsibility for) raising children. Overall, women work in
jobs that pay less than men are paid, but even when they work in comparable jobs, they are paid less.[1] And because they often work fewer paid
hours in order to handle childcare responsibilities, women are more likely
to fall into poverty. Poverty and all its attendant issues thus have greater
impact on women than on men. Foundation programs concerned with
poverty obviously need to do gender analyses—and to require gender
analyses of any nonprofits they fund—to ensure they are reaching those
most in need with programs that specifically address those needs, e.g.
adequate child care.

Differential impact.   A problem can also impact women and girls *differently* from men and boys. The opportunistic infections that typically
attack women with full-blown AIDS, for example, are largely different
from the opportunistic infections that attack men. Before this difference
was recognized, many women with AIDS were excluded from receiving
benefits of programs designated for *all* people with AIDS but based on
male infection profiles that did not list infections women experienced. Although variations in opportunistic infections obviously stem from biological differences between women and men, the male-centered definition of
AIDS diagnosis is a concrete example of the distortions arising from the
still-widespread practice of making male health the so-called "generic"
norm for everyone. Spending less money for research on women and AIDS
or basing a definition of AIDS only on men's diseases is the result of social

conditioning, not biology. Early programs designed specifically for women with AIDS were at the forefront in advocating for the needs of women with AIDS, pushing the Centers for Disease Control (CDC) to expand its definition of AIDS so that women could receive the federal and state services that accompany an AIDS diagnosis.

Different gender roles.   The roles that women and girls occupy in society (e.g., raising children) also argue for differences in program design. Labor-market segregation, resulting in lower wages for women compared to men, must be addressed in job-training programs for women. Additionally, if women are expected to participate in programs like substance-abuse treatment, those programs must take into account the childcare responsibilities that many women hold.

Different socialization.   Although not as pervasive in recent decades, women and girls still are socialized into caretaking roles and subservience to men and boys. When women and girls are in mixed-gender groups, they may talk less, venture fewer opinions, and be reluctant to engage in verbal conflicts. All of these behaviors influence the success of a nonprofit program. In a coed leadership program, for example, girls may be less willing to engage in behaviors that are traditionally associated with leadership. Such a program will need to design specific approaches to counter this socialization if it expects to work as well for girls as for boys.

Different opportunities.   Gender socialization also can result in fewer opportunities available to women and girls. Despite few documented differences in inherent mathematical ability, for example, the accepted idea that females are not good in math leads girls to take fewer advanced math and science courses than boys, significantly constraining their future career choices.

Single-Sex Organizations and Programs

The examples above make explicit the ways in which gender knowledge and analysis are essential components of program design and implementation and refute the assumptions of foundation professionals who believe that gender is not relevant to their grant making. They do not, however, resolve the debate about whether women and girls are better served in universal or single-sex programs. If universal programs acknowledge the multiple ways gender socialization affects its constituents, they can be effective for both women and men in certain circumstances. However, single-sex programs can offer advantages that universal programs, no matter how well designed, cannot.

Feeling like the "other."   There is considerable evidence that, in many ways, men and boys are viewed as "normal" and women and girls are viewed as "other." For example, an often-repeated study by Broverman[2] shows that men and women rate the qualities generally associated with the *male* role as being identical with the qualities of a psychologically *healthy* person. Conversely, the qualities normally associated with the *female* role were virtually identical with the qualities of a psychologically *unhealthy* person. All too often, girls and women compared to boys and men are found wanting. Being assertive, for example, is a quality that male and female respondents associate with men and view very positively. Being willing to yield to the views of others is scored as a female quality and also is rated less highly than assertiveness. We know, of course, that both qualities can be very positive and that men and women are capable of each. But this research points to gender stereotypes that continue to constrain women and girls. In a program in which every participant is female, the issue of being "other" recedes into the background, and participants can concentrate on being themselves and working to develop their individual capacities and identities, without having to struggle to escape those constraints. It is ironic yet true that in a single-sex program, gender often becomes a nonissue and other concerns then can take precedence.

Feeling safe and being safe.   The issue of safety is hardly trivial. Women and girls often are less safe in their homes than they are in public places, and they are used to feeling unsafe in environments that men and boys perceive as safe. For too many women and girls, unfortunately, men and boys still pose the greatest threat to their safety, and too often this includes men and boys in their homes as well as those enrolled with them in universal programs. For example, women are more likely to be attacked by husbands or male partners inside their homes than by strangers outside their homes. And women who are homeless often report that a homeless shelter is the choice of last resort because of the frequent sexual violence occurring there. Girls in coed youth programs report high levels of sexual harassment by boys in those programs. The physical location of a universal program sometimes can be so unsafe that it presents an overwhelming barrier for women and girls. Programs specifically designed for women and girls characteristically pay particular attention to these safety issues and often, for example, provide transportation for girls so they don't have to walk home on an unsafe street.

Women and girls in charge.   Typically, women and girls run single-sex programs for women and girls. In research on nonprofit programs in Greater Boston, Mead found that every program for women and girls was run by a woman director, and 97 percent of these programs had a female majority on their board.[3] This means two things: programs for women and girls are controlled by women and girls, and programs for women and girls also are an arena for women and girls to develop and exercise their leadership abilities.

Effective Programs for Women and Girls Promote Democracy

Some funders express the concern that programs specifically designed for women are somehow antidemocratic, that they contradict the ideal that everyone should be welcome in every program and able to succeed in every program. In fact, the opposite may be true. Public policy researchers Helen Ingram and Anne Schneider[4] argue that in a truly democratic society, every group would be, at one time or another, the clearly deserving recipients of public policy benefits. In looking at who benefits from public policies, Ingram and Schneider posit the existence of four categories:

• *The advantaged*, those politically powerful and socially acceptable groups that typically benefit from public policies and are regarded as deserving of the benefits

• *Contenders*, those groups that fight for public-policy benefits but are not regarded as automatically deserving such benefits (this includes any interest group, from the auto industry to environmental conservation groups)

• *Dependents*, groups with little political power that are viewed as deserving of assistance but unable to help themselves (this includes groups like the low-income elderly or people with mental disabilities)

• *Deviants*, groups whose behavior is in some ways judged socially unacceptable, and for whom punitive public policies are designed (such as drug addicts or corporate criminals)

If public policy were truly *democratic*, each interest group within society—including social, racial, and employment groups—would receive an equitable share of public policy benefits. When this does not happen, democracy suffers. One could argue that women and girls are seen too often in the *dependents* and even in the *deviants* categories of public policy (such as low-income women who receive financial assistance) and too seldom *contenders* or *advantaged*. Low-income women who receive financial assistance used to be seen as *dependent*, but since welfare "reform" began in the mid-1990s, they are more often regarded as *deviant*. Unlike middle-class or upper-class women who have choices, low-income women who want to raise children and not work outside their homes are deemed unacceptable by public policy. Gender-sensitive programs of both foundations and nonprofits have an important role to play in changing this kind of public-policy perception.

For purposes of discussion in this book, we propose an additional category to the four Ingram and Schneider developed, one that builds on the Norm knowledge talked about in chapter 2: *the invisible*. Invisible people are those who have legitimate concerns but, unlike women in the *dependent* or even *deviant* categories, cannot get their concerns recognized or put on the public policy agenda. For example, those women who for years died of AIDS without being able to receive benefits, which were available almost exclusively to men who received "official" diagnoses. Similarly, women have been the victims of domestic violence for centuries, but only in the past few decades have women's groups and organizations succeeded in bringing that problem to public and legislative consciousness, mandating an appropriate array of public responses.

One important function of programs for women and girls, then, is to move them out of the *invisible* category—to take their problems seriously, to document them, and to define them as public problems—and at the same time to ensure that they are not put into the *deviant* category. At this point in history, many social norms still are used to define poor women who do not work as deviant. They are deemed lazy and lacking in motivation. Recent punitive policies have forced women back into the workplace and even into marriage. Programs for women and girls can play an important role in countering invisibility or perceptions of deviance by demonstrating that women with children to raise and few employable skills are unlikely to succeed in the labor market—at least not without considerable support to solve the problems specific to their needs. And these programs need to make women and girls in these situations visible, and to move them out of both deviants and dependents in the continuum of policy beneficiaries.

The next step is for foundation and nonprofit programs to change public misperceptions of the capabilities of women and girls and to improve their skills such that they are able to take charge of their own lives. Only then can programs for women and girls make them *contenders*. Political organizations focused on the needs of women and girls, advocacy organizations, and networks of women and girls all serve as vehicles for women and girls to contend with other groups for the benefits of public policy. Arguably, democracy would be more vibrant if no group in society were in the *advantaged* category, securing unchallenged rights to benefit from public policies. If every social group were a contender, well equipped to make the public case for the issues that concern them, we would have a democracy the world could envy. Philanthropy has a central role to play in moving U.S. society closer to that ideal democracy.

What to Look for in Effective Programs

If funders are going to do *effective* both/and philanthropy, they need to know how to determine whether a program, particularly a coed program, is working effectively for women and girls. Girls Incorporated, in their report "What's Equal? Figuring Out What Works for Girls in Coed Settings," recommends that funders look at three considerations: *equity of access, equity of treatment,* and *equity of outcome.*[5] The bottom line, Girls Incorporated argues, is that coed programs must be gender sensitive, not gender blind. "Leveling the playing field is more than simply opening more doors for girls and giving equal treatment to girls and boys; it is transforming the way we look at gender as it relates to girls' and boys' development. . . . Effective strategies for working with girls in coed settings will specifically take gender socialization into account."[6]

Equity of access.   An equitable program provides women and girls with opportunities to participate equal to that of men and boys. Equity of access is not achieved simply by opening the door to both genders. Program creators must ask (and answer) several hard questions. For example, what are the subtle (and the overt) messages that invite and encourage women and girls? What messages keep them away? Is the program located in an area where females are comfortable traveling? If the program works with mothers, does it deal with the childcare problems these women face on a daily basis? How do we know when access is not equitable?

Here is a simple example. A coed computer-technology program recently asked itself why there were virtually no girls in the program. A consultant helped them identify that there were safety issues that limited girls' ability to participate. The program is located in an industrial area of town—a location that raised safety issues because the young people had to arrange their own way to get to the program after school and home again at the end of the day. Most girls' parents simply were uncomfortable letting their daughters walk in this area of town. The result: the program was unintentionally inaccessible to girls.

Equity of treatment. Equitable programs offer everyone in them the same level and quality of attention and resources. Some coed programs may argue that they make equal resources available to boys and girls, but that boys take better advantage of those resources. They may need to ask whether the same treatment is enough when groups are unequal to begin with. How do we ensure, for example, that girls have sufficient opportunity and support to become interested and skilled in nontraditional areas such as computers and working with tools—or in sports such as basketball or soccer when we know that "on average girls are two years behind boys in team-sports skills due to differences in informal practice opportunities."[7] And vice versa. Boys develop more slowly than girls academically. The result of this gap is that coed youth programs that treat all the participants identically often prove to be ineffective and unequal. Similarly, a job-training program for unemployed adults that provides one program design for all the participants, women and men, and does not help women understand their different prospects in the labor market or provide strategies for finding and paying for adequate child care probably will miss the mark for the women in the program.

Equity of outcome. The outcome, of course, is the most important measure because it focuses on the bottom line: do women and men, girls and boys benefit equally from a program ostensibly designed to serve all of them? To assess this, the first step in designing programs must be to look at existing gaps between females and males when they begin participating in the program—gaps in achievement, knowledge, or confidence, for example. Then the program should measure factors such as participation (who comes to the program) and persistence (who stays). Due to gender discrimination and inequitable treatment, girls and women may require more time and resources or different strategies to break through barriers and become equal contributors to society in high-status, high-paying, traditionally male areas. Most important, programs must measure the impact they are having on participants and ask whether there are gender gaps in these impacts.

Limits of "Generic" Funding

The distinction between "generic" funding and funding initiatives foundations describe as "universal" is an important one. Linguists decades ago challenged generic pronouns: what had been *he* or *him* or *his*—masculine pronouns—were defined as "generic," representing the whole, subsuming *she* or *her* or *hers*. And "generic" was considered "universal" because individuals within the category were undifferentiated. No more. *They* is a generic pronoun. *He* obviously is not. Linguistics, journalism, editing, and publishing conventions—all are fields where gender consciousness has helped define more equitable language.

Just like generic pronouns, so-called "generic funding" should not subsume the whole either. Funding that does not take into account gender, race/ethnicity, or other socially defining characteristics of the groups being funded does not work. Both nonprofit and philanthropy executives interviewed as background for this book stressed "generic" funding without regard for gender, race/ethnicity, or other group characteristics as a significant roadblock for philanthropy. One foundation executive pointed out that her colleagues will say, "We want to fund community development, poverty, educational programs," but not "women." She said they insist on "generic" categories that take no account of the individual within: "I'm constantly surprised at how real and pervasive this is in the foundation world."

In another instance, the head of a national women's organization described having spoken to a program officer who works on community economic development: "When we talked to him, he indicated that his area of the foundation doesn't do special population groups. Would he say that to a black organization?" Another fundraiser described a program officer in a large regional foundation as telling her, "We work on low-income issues but not women." As the fundraiser observed, this is a "strange worldview problem." In situations like this, "generic" means that funders don't see the people they're *not* funding. One funder observes: "We fund housing so of course we fund women, gays, lesbians, bisexuals, and transgendered people. But in fact this is a smokescreen," she acknowledged. "Effective funders do nuanced analyses of the diverse needs of different groups."

As we have seen in other parts of this book, one reason for resistance to targeting populations as a separate funding strategy is concern that it would be divisive. A program officer who has struggled to make the case for funding women where she's worked says, "These are real philosophical worldview differences, and pushing a gender lens creates resistance. The conversation kind of ends there—nothing happens, no challenge. People do try to make the case, but it doesn't translate into different funding. The arguments have been developed, but they seem to have little effect in most funding contexts." Another long-time foundation executive says these issues are similar to roadblocks she and her staff experience with their board when they have tried to do ethnic-specific program funding:

The board says, "No, you're dividing." They are a generation that bought into immigration and saw fragmenting leading to more divisiveness. We make the argument that this is not an either/or: you can't integrate if people are not up to speed. We start strengthening immigrants; then we help them connect to broader communities. And we don't want women to go off and forsake their families. We want to strengthen women, and we need to target grants to women to do that. Then we can connect them better to their families and the larger society.

Universal and Targeted: A Both/And Approach

Universal programs do not have to be generic—or ineffective. Effective philanthropy funds programs that work well for diverse women and men, girls and boys, in whatever forms those programs take—mixed sex or single sex. The key to effective philanthropy and effective programs is that they acknowledge and account for both the overt and hidden impacts of gender-based discrimination. A both/and approach means funding a range of programs and organizations—some targeted for women and girls and some universal but designed to work for women and girls as well as for men and boys. Before we look at additional evidence supporting this both/and approach, it may be useful to understand how the debate between targeted and universal programs and policies has played out in other public-policy arenas that philanthropy can learn from.

The philanthropy community generally accepts that targeted programs are more cost effective, can have better results, and are able to take into account the distinct needs of recipients. Yet as politicians are quick to note, universal programs garner the most support. One universal program, Social Security, has garnered such widespread support that most measures to alter its makeup meet an early death from voter outcries. Indeed, "universalists" claim that without widespread political support, programs designed to alleviate poverty are pushed aside. Citing past policies that range from the turn of the century to Reagan-era antipoverty strategies of the 1980s, researcher Theda Skocpol[8] points to the declining financial support for targeted programs. Indeed, even supporters of targeted programs readily agree that garnering political support for targeted programs is an uphill battle. Progressives such as Frances Fox Piven and Richard Cloward[9] also strongly support universal programs on the grounds that targeted programs (e.g., food stamps and income-transfer payments) stigmatize recipients. Referring to the punitive attitudes of the Reagan administration, Piven and Cloward explain: "With the President castigating food stamp cheats, it becomes much harder to hand the stamps to a cashier while standing in a supermarket checkout line."[10] William Julius Wilson contends that negative stereotypes of welfare recipients are so ingrained in our culture that people believe that the lowest class of people are those that receive welfare.[11] Indeed, as Michael Katz points out, the image of the "undeserving" poor has infiltrated our policies, creating punitive measures for those who do not fit into our ideas of productive workers.[12]

Although universal programs may be politically savvy, they have serious, acknowledged flaws. Because of their wide-ranging natures, universal programs often provide the most benefit to those who already are succeeding or likely to succeed. Universal programs, therefore, spend a considerable amount of money on members of our society who can find other forms of assistance. Furthermore, providing services for everyone has never been a cost-efficient way of providing services to those who need them most.

Given all these considerations, both/and funding is a way for funders to get the most impact for their funding dollars. As we have seen, the gender-blind approaches do not work. *Gender-blind* programs can be universal or single-sex, but they do not take gender issues into account in the design or delivery of services or activities, and they are seldom effective. Existing funding initiatives that do work are either gender-sensitive or gender-specific. A *gender-sensitive* program is a coeducational or universal program that takes into account different gender needs in the design and delivery of their activities or services. A *gender-specific* program is a single-sex program intentionally designed to respond to specific needs and strengths of the females or males that it serves. Either of these strategies—or both/and—offer funders strategic tools for effective grant making.

Case Study: The Ms. Foundation for Women

The Ms. Foundation for Women, one of the first women's funds established, is an example of a foundation at the cutting edge of innovative approaches to effective grant making. Its move in 2002 to the both/and funding we have been discussing in this chapter is illustrative of the leadership they are providing in the philanthropic community. Since the foundation's inception, its mission has remained constant: to support the efforts of women and girls to govern their own lives and influence the world around them. As the largest women's foundation—measured both by assets and by grant making—and one of the oldest—formally established in 1972—they have played a central role in making the case for funding women and girls. They have also developed grant making practices designed to empower women and girls to take charge of their own lives and make a difference in the world.

Although the foundation's mission has endured—and has as much relevance today as it did thirty years ago—the foundation itself has evolved new language to talk about their work and the eligibility criteria for one of their key grant making programs, which now emphasizes a focus on "creating a just world." The foundation continues to believe in its mission—*supporting the efforts of women and girls to govern their own lives and influence the world around them*—but their new language emphasizes action: *changing the way the world works*. This is not simply a rhetorical shift or new language for marketing purposes. The Ms. Foundation's commitment to "change the way the world works" represents the boldest, most ambitious vision possible for a foundation—doing whatever it takes to change the world. Their new language also signals an important broadening of approach. The Ms. Foundation no longer funds only women and girls. They now include both/and strategies: funding *both* single-sex programs that empower women and girls *and* coed programs that have a clear vision for how boys and men as allies with girls and women can work together to create the equitable and fully democratic world the foundation has set as its goal. This important shift provides a bold model other foundations can learn from—embracing both/and strategies that are focused on effective transformation of women's roles in every society in the world.

The foundation always has been committed to diversity in its many forms—the deep diversity that we talk about throughout this book. Currently, six of the thirteen members of the Ms. Foundation board are people of color—an impressive figure given that many foundations have been slow to achieve significant racial diversity on their boards of directors. Board diversities include lesbian and bisexual women as well as heterosexual women, women of a whole host of national origins, and two men. The board walks its talk: their deep diversity goes significantly beyond superficial attempts to change the way the board looks. Both individually and collectively, board members understand how to name Norm, and the foundation fully embraces the idea that deep diversity is fundamental to effective grant making. Its efforts to represent and grapple with the global diversity in its mission include a process of taking a hard look at every aspect of the foundation's practices. It is not surprising that a progressive women's foundation insists that its board members embody a wide range of racial, ethnic, sexual identity and class diversity. As important however, and echoing the Thomas/Ely analyses described in chapters 1 and 2, the foundation is committed to going beyond "by the numbers" diversity and challenging itself to institutionalize all that they continually learn from each other.

Given its over thirty-year track record as one of the oldest, preeminent women's foundations, in 2000 the foundation took its boldest—and in some circles most controversial—step in diversifying its board: it added men. But it did so only after careful thought and much deliberation. The men invited to join the board—themselves diverse in a number of ways—had been involved with the foundation for years as donors and as allies, and they were not added simply to increase fundraising prospects (though, as with all board members, they have done this) or to legitimize the activities of the foundation. They were added for a much more important and fundamental reason: the foundation believes that men have to work as allies to enable women to overcome structural impediments that prevent them from exercising their share of influence in society. This is an important step forward. Embracing deep diversity can and often must include inviting those with traditional forms of privilege to the newly reconstructed "table" to sit alongside those who historically have been denied full access to all the benefits that any society has to offer its members.

This step also emphasizes that a "just" world for women is also a "just" (and improved) world for men. In a 1999 strategic-planning process, the foundation acknowledged that many women govern their own lives, but in spite of significant strides over the last decades, the influence of women in larger society is still minuscule. Men continue to dominate many of the "public" spheres of political and corporate life, while women disproportionately exercise leadership in the private spheres of family and the community. Although women increasingly have moved into public spheres through their entry into the paid workforce, this change has not been accompanied by commensurate influence in public policy. Women now participate in the labor market in almost equal numbers to men. But the counterbalancing movement of men into the private and community spheres has been much slower. Only when these spheres are in balance, the foundation argues, will the world work as well for women as it does for men.

The Ms. Foundation's decision to add men to the board of the foundation could be interpreted by some as a retreat, a step back rather than a bold move forward. Such a decision raises the risk that people will assume the foundation is less committed to women. Or that the leaders, in a show of weakness, are admitting they do not have the capacity to run a strong, effective grant-making operation. Such risks could be significant for an organization that espouses the need to "empower women and girls to be in charge of their own lives." But the board and the executive leadership believe not only in themselves but in the strengths and capacities of all women, and they talk about their decision to add men to their board as an unapologetic sign of strength, not a sign of weakness. This decision and others the board and staff leadership have made over the years have institutionalized both/and grant making—grant making grounded in a both/and institutional culture that celebrates women for their capacities, that acknowledges the constraints on women's full contributions to society, and that embraces the potential of men to join with women as allies for the benefit of both women and men.

The both/and grant making that the foundation does can best be understood by looking at a specific example. For years, the Ms. Foundation has led a collaborative social-change program for girls. The goals of this program are to build the capacity of girls to analyze social inequities and then develop programs to address those inequities. Since its inception, the foundation has used this program to make innovative and effective grants that position girls at the center of the issues that concern them and to make it possible for the girls themselves to be key resources to address those issues. The foundation always has been committed to evaluating the effectiveness of this grant making, and it has included girls from diverse racial, ethnic, and cultural backgrounds as central players in that evaluation. In the fall of 2001, all of the partners in this collaborative made an important change in the eligibility criteria for this program to allow mixed-gender youth organizations as well as girl-only programs to apply for funding. In part this was prompted by the recognition that most girls are in mixed-gender youth programs. If the foundation continued to fund solely girl-only programs, they were by definition excluding over 90 percent of the existing programs that serve youth. It was also prompted by the same thinking that led the foundation to add men to the board: it will take the efforts of *both* girls *and* boys to address social inequity. The foundation renamed the program, now the *Collaborative Fund for Youth-Led Social Change: Effective Approaches to Gender and Youth*. Here's the language they used to announce the program:

This request for letters of intent is an invitation to girl-only and mixed-gender community-based youth organizations with a vision and agenda for youth-led social change. The Fund will support and strengthen organizations that combine positive youth development and social change action with a gender-conscious approach.

What the foundation has done is to build on their years of experience helping girls play leadership roles in effecting social change, and, while not backing away from that experience or commitment, they have taken a next step in their grant making by involving both girls and boys, even as they actively challenge gender roles. This grants program offers a vision for a new way that girls and women can work alongside boys and men to create the socially just world that the Ms. Foundation is committed to helping create.

The foundation also has made an important change in its best-known program, Take Our Daughters to Work®, by replacing it with a new program known as "Take Our Daughters and Sons to Work®." In 2004, approximately ten percent of employed Americans, an estimated 13.9 million people, participated in the program: 10.1 million took a girl to work and 6.4 million took a boy to work. The thinking behind this change reflects the broader goal of the foundation: to interest and educate boys in family life while interesting girls in public life. The original purpose of Take Our Daughters to Work® was to educate girls about work and career opportunities and thus ensure that girls would be visible, valued, and heard. The new program focuses on work/family issues. When girls and boys accompany their parents to work, the program designers hope, young people will experience firsthand both the opportunities and the challenges of balancing work and family responsibilities. The Foundation provides workplaces with curricular resources (that participants can use if they choose) for stimulating discussion among young people and between adults and youth about work and family lives. This new program recognizes that a new generation is coming to work and that they value full participation in work, family, and community. It capitalizes on the fact that both girls and boys see a different vision for the future.

The Ms. Foundation is committed to continuing to think actively and creatively about gender and to keep asking itself what its grant making programs should look like to ensure their effectiveness. As they continue thirty years of efforts to stop violence against women, for example, they are examining the role of men in stopping that violence. And they have involved men in this new approach in significant ways. One male expert on violence has urged the foundation to talk about ending *men's* violence against women, not the more neutral idea of general violence against women. In many ways it was probably easier for a male researcher to name the fact that most violence against women is done by men and that effective approaches to ending this violence are predicated on an awareness of the distinctively male dimensions to the problem. Naming the problem in this way is not intended to scapegoat men. Rather it is based on a recognition that nuanced understandings of *gender, deep diversity, and Norm knowledge* must be recognized, analyzed, and sometimes simply named to ensure the outcomes and changes the foundation hopes to achieve.

5

Gender in Youth Programs: Ignoring Gender Doesn't Work

Chapter 4 laid out the importance of foundations taking a both/and approach to gender: making grants to gender-specific programs and organizations as well as to programs and organizations that account for gender in the context of all their work with both women and men, girls and boys. This chapter takes a closer look at what are frequently named "universal" youth programs. It provides evidence that programs—and organizations—that ignore or misunderstand gender do not work well for either girls or boys. It also offers guidelines for grant makers about how to assess universal programs to ensure they are effective for everyone—girls and boys, women and men.

"Universal" Grant Making: Funder and Nonprofit Perspectives

In 1993, Molly Mead conducted research on philanthropic giving in Greater Boston, looking at a question that researchers had explored in other regions of the country: what percentage of foundation dollars actually reach programs for women or girls?[1] Mead asked foundations to report their grant making activity, then she interviewed program officers and foundation executives to probe their grant making decisions in greater detail. What Mead found mirrored conditions around the country: approximately 6 percent of foundation dollars went to programs for women and girls, 2 percent of foundation dollars to programs for men and boys, and 92 percent of foundation dollars to what foundations call "universal," or coeducational, organizations.

The numbers were not surprising, given what was already known from other studies conducted around the country, but Mead's study was the first effort to probe the thinking that lay behind those numbers. Foundation staff gave several reasons for their preferences. Mead labeled them: *efficiency*, *democracy*, and *relevance*. The *efficiency* explanation stressed that, with grant making dollars scarce, it made sense to fund a program that works with *everyone*, not just women or girls. The *democracy* analysis reflected philanthropists' uneasiness with the idea of targeted programs they feared might promote exclusivity and create separate worlds. And the *relevance* explanation referred to the fact that, while some grant makers were comfortable with targeted funding for race or class or community, they were not comfortable targeting funds for gender.

Mead also interviewed leaders of nonprofit programs for women or girls who, not surprisingly, had different perceptions of the value of both their own programs and of alternative programs that did not account for gender differences in the people being served. These leaders countered the *efficiency* argument, for example, with questions about effectiveness: a universal program must work reasonably well for *all* its constituents to represent an efficient use of scarce grant making dollars. Leaders of nonprofit programs for women or girls argued that since they could show powerful evidence for their effectiveness reaching and working with a majority constituency (women and girls being over 50 percent of the population), they could not reasonably be judged "inefficient."

Questioning the *democracy* rationale, these same nonprofit leaders offered research documenting the importance of programs designed for separately configured "marginalized" groups. By working within their group designations—for example, all girls—program participants developed strengths that allowed them to function more effectively in larger, more diverse settings, a measurable benefit that actually promotes democratic interactions rather than inhibiting them.

Finally, the same nonprofit executives also countered the *relevance* argument by pointing out that women and girls are found in all of the categories funders consider relevant, but their needs often are different from those of the men and boys in those categories. The executives also took issue with what they saw as stereotypes and lack of accurate information on the part of funders who cited *relevance* as their reason for not funding women and girls directly (targeting grant dollars for race, ethnicity, or socioeconomic status but *not* gender). Consciously or unconsciously, these funders assumed *women* to be *white* and *upper middle-class*. But "male" is a gender, just as "white" is a race. As these nonprofit executives pointed out, commonly held stereotypes about gender and race render invisible the many women of color and low-income women who are served by (and also run) programs for women and girls. And it keeps in place a difficult double-bind for women of color: that women are white and people of color are male. In fact, the boards, staffs, and constituents of most programs for women and girls are racially diverse. In contradiction to some funders' assumptions, these are not organizations exclusively for or run by white women.

In addition to these specific concerns addressed by the nonprofit executives, most grant makers—both women and men—simply seemed uncomfortable with the idea of targeting. Targeting for population groups of any kind clearly challenged their vision for a democratic society and their sense of stewardship. They thought it unnecessary (and perhaps unnecessarily radical) to target women's programs for more than a small share (6 percent) of grant-making dollars. And at least to some funders, it seemed unnecessarily complicated to have to factor in additional "new" knowledge about a whole range of diverse populations.

Do "Universal" Programs Work? New Research

When Mead presented the results of her research to grant makers, she asked all of them the same question: were they correct to put 92 percent of their dollars into universal programs, especially when no specific evidence existed to document the effectiveness of this strategy? One outcome of this question was another round of research. Foundation leaders in Boston asked Mead to document, if she could, whether or not these universal funding strategies did work. She began to answer that question by sampling how existing coed youth programs met girls' needs. Youth programs try to build strengths rather than fix problems. To know whether the programs worked, obviously it was important to know whether this capacity-building strategy worked as well for girls as it did for boys. Mead found that most coed youth programs had not been fully effective for girls. Fortunately, the story has a positive ending: United Way of Massachusetts Bay joined with Mead and others to strengthen both coed and girl-serving youth programs. Mead's findings show how subtle gender differences play out. Learning to recognize these subtle and not-so-subtle patterns and biases is an important tool for improving philanthropy.

Two Examples of After-School Youth Programs

On a typical school-day afternoon, at least seventy-five African-American, Asian-American, Latino, and white young people stream into the Youth Club, a program located in an urban neighborhood in the Greater Boston area. (All agency names are disguised.) The center strives to be an inviting alternative to "hanging out" on the street or going home to an empty house. It offers a myriad of activities, mostly designed to let young people have fun and expend pent-up energy they cannot release at school. While there is much to praise about the Youth Club, a closer look raises some troubling questions. This program has a ratio of about three boys to every girl. Boys cluster in the middle of one room, playing pool and ping-pong, vying for a turn to play a video game and dividing up into knock-hockey teams. They pay little attention to the girls who sit in small groups around the edge of the room, talking with each other and occasionally watching the boys' activities. In the gymnasium next door, boys play basketball on one side and wrestle each other on the opposite side. The girls sit up on the stage, again talking quietly in small groups.

On the other hand, at the Neighborhood House, located in a demographically similar Boston neighborhood, the scene is quite different. This program has an equal number of girls and boys. On one side of the gym, eight girls and two boys play volleyball together. On the other side, a lively basketball game is being played, mostly with boys, but it is clear that the stellar player is one of the girls. In another area, girls and boys are sitting at computers, completing their homework. The computer area is run by one of the older girls in the program—the acknowledged computer expert. If anyone—male or female, young person or adult—needs help with one of the computers, they know she is the one to ask. Both boys and girls in this facility look engaged and content and there are smiles all around. Why? What makes this Neighborhood House program, similar in aims and activities, so different from the Youth Club program in terms of how both the girls and boys participate?

Over the four-year period that Mead studied coed youth programs like the Youth Club and the Neighborhood House, she observed their activities, talked to staff and to many of the diverse young people in the programs. Because these were urban youth programs, participants were from many different ethnicities (many from newly immigrated families) and overwhelmingly from families with low to moderate incomes. The major conclusion she drew was disturbing. As the differences in the experiences at the Youth Club and Neighborhood House reflect, many coed organizations offering programs like those at Youth Club failed to meet their own stated primary goal: to serve girls as effectively as boys. On the one hand, many programs seem to be based on false assumptions about gender differences that did not reflect an accurate assessment of the young people in their own programs. On the other hand, program staff often lacked understanding about how gender differences play out in the lives of boys and girls—differences based on unequal opportunities and experiences—and how those differences affected their participation in these programs. Program staff also failed to examine program activities to ask whether girls and boys might bring different skills and interests to their participation in those activities. Too often the result in programs like those the Youth Club offered was a mismatch between the program's design and the girls' interests and concerns—a mismatch that caused girls to be marginalized, their needs unmet and their potential unrealized.

This mismatch is no small matter for girls. About 71 percent of young people in the United States participate in some type of youth program every week, and an overwhelming number (in some areas, as high as 99 percent) of those programs are coed.[2] And a large portion of that population, at least a third, are girls participating in coed programs. The systematic failure, therefore, by coed programs to work effectively for girls is a major concern.

Trends in Youth Programming

Although there have been positive trends in youth programming in the past twenty years, the net result, unfortunately, has proven detrimental to girls. Most youth programs today focus on identifying and strengthening a wide range of positive characteristics in young people, rather than operating on a deficiency model that isolates and remedies specific negative traits. Most youth programs today have a common goal: namely, helping each individual young person to develop her/his full potential in such areas as physical development, personal skills, and/or job-related skills. This universal approach of developing everyone's potential might be expected to benefit all young people, girls and boys alike, but most often it does not. The second major trend in youth programming, a shift from single-sex to coed programming, has lessened the potential benefit of this developmental approach for girls.

A brief history of how and why this shift occurred suggests why girls lost out. Ironically, the shift toward coed programs was initiated in part by a concern about lack of adequate youth programming for girls. When most programming was single-sex, the majority of programs were available for boys only. And even in areas with girls' youth programs, the boys' programs generally had substantially better funding and physical facilities. To ensure equal treatment, formerly all-boy programs began to open their doors to girls. In addition to improved access, however, a cost-efficiency concern also motivated the move toward more coed programming. Those who funded youth programs and those who ran them were concerned about the need to provide the best programming possible with limited resources. To many of these people, it made no sense to have *separate* programs for girls and for boys because of the cost of providing equivalent facilities. Demands for youth programs to operate more equitably and cost effectively could have been—and in some cases were—met by increased collaborative strategies between single-sex programs. But once the staff of all-boy programs realized they could serve girls also, many sought to offer programs that would supplant the all-girl programs. Programs that chose this strategy usually gained the advantage of becoming the primary youth-serving agency in their area.

This history is important because it exemplifies the way in which much of today's coed youth programming is pasted on top of a formerly all-boys model, and Mead's research shows the results. Most of the coed programs she studied place the needs and interests of the boys first, are better designed for boys, and are more popular with boys. Program participation rates are also revealing. Both a study of youth programs in New York City and a national study of youth-serving agencies found that, on average, coed-youth programs serve three times more boys than girls.[3] Today, this means that as youth programs are converting to a more promising developmental model, most girls are still in coed programs that do not work for them. As young people are developing skills and learning to regard themselves as future contributors to society with exciting options to pursue, girls are missing out.

How Coed Youth Programs Fail Girls

The twenty-five programs Mead studied incorporated what she categorized as four distinct sets of gender practices:

- Differences are fundamental
- Males are the model
- We are all the same
- Equal voices

These different understandings and applications of gender knowledge offer a microcosm of why universal funding all too often does not result in effective philanthropy. Mead's categories are defined by two factors: first, assumptions inherent in the youth program's design about gender differences in girls and boys; and second, ways that youth program activities interact differently with girls' and boys' socialization and life experiences. These categories operate on a continuum from least effective to most effective, but only one category, *equal voices,* is fully effective for girls. As important, *equal voices* programs fostered the healthy development of boys as well as girls.

Twelve of the twenty-five programs Mead studied fall into the *differences are fundamental* category. These programs assume girls and boys are inherently different in temperament, abilities, and interests. Typically, these programs reinforce the most traditional gender stereotypes because their program activities are designed in response to conventional, stereotyped, and uninformed notions about the needs and strengths of boys and girls. In these programs, boys are most often the actors and the doers, engaged in conventional "boy" activities such as sports, playing video games, working with computers, or building mechanical devices. The girls in these programs are often the watchers and the observers—assuming passive roles that do not reflect their development potential. Alternatively, they may be involved in stereotypical "girl" activities like arts and crafts or socializing with each other.

What *is* rare in these programs is finding girls and boys participating equally in any task or activity. When asked about the obvious gender differences in who does what, staff members of these programs generally responded, "That's the way girls are. We try to get them to [play basketball, build a model car, write a computer program, etc.], but they don't want to." In almost every interview conducted with staff in these programs, the staff assumed that the problem (if any) lay in the girls themselves and their lack of interest in participating in boys' activities. They never questioned any of the structures in place that funneled boys toward one set of activities and girls toward another. Nor did they question why the boys were not

participating in the so-called girls' activities. In short, the girls were compared to the boys and found lacking.

Equal voices programs, at the positive end of the continuum, also assume
that there are significant differences between girls and boys, but that these
differences are neither innate nor incapable of being changed. Rather, they
locate the differences between genders in socially created meanings of gender that are limiting to both girls and boys. The two *equal voices* programs
Mead identified in her study recognize that girls often have unequal access
to opportunity relative to boys. These programs work to make *both* genders aware of these social constraints, and, most critically, encourage active questioning of them. So, *equal voices* programs acknowledge that
there may be some need for different programs for girls and boys, but they
believe these programmatic considerations are driven by differences in life
experience, not inherent, genetic differences in males and females. In these
programs, Mead saw young women and young men participating as equals
in many activities, as well as involved in activities that defied gender stereotypes. In one instance, boys agreed to carry out many behind-the-scenes
tasks for a major event, while girls took on the public leadership roles. In
another instance, several girls and boys acted as security monitors for a
youth rally. Previously, only boys would have filled those roles: but the girls
said that they were just as good as boys in defusing a potentially explosive
situation, and it turned out they were right.

The two program types in the middle of the continuum—*males are the
model* and *we are all the same*—assume sameness between the genders.
They are an improvement over *differences are fundamental* programs in
that they offer, at least on the surface, equal opportunity to girls and boys
to participate in all the activities of the programs. They are not grounded
in stereotypes like "boys do" and "girls watch." However, because neither
of these program categories includes an active challenge to assumed male
norms, they operate in ways that benefit young men at the expense of
young women. They privilege male experience over female experience.
Moreover, they don't do their best for boys either, since as we saw in chapter 1, current ideas about appropriate masculine behavior and attitudes
also limit young men's abilities. In the continuum of youth programs Mead
researched, only the *equal voices* programs fully explored these limits.
Only in *equal voices* programs are stereotypically "feminine" ways of be-
having valued highly enough so that both young men and young women

can develop their fullest potential, choosing from the entire range of human behavior and possibilities.

There are important distinctions between the two categories of programs based on the sameness idea. The *males are the model* category is based on a belief that girls can do anything boys can do. A distinctive feature of the four programs Mead identified in this category is that their activities are ones to which the average young man brings more skills and experience than does the average young woman. The activities themselves are also often those traditionally thought of as "masculine" rather than "feminine." (Examples included a bicycle-repair program, a housing-construction program, and a computer clubhouse.) In each of these activities, the typical girl had fewer skills when she started *as well as* the additional challenge of participating in a program that defies gender norms for girls. Girls were allowed (and often even encouraged) to participate in these programs, but they had to participate as *equals,* despite the fact that their skills were not equivalent to those of the boys. As a consequence, young women dropped out of these programs at a much higher rate. They viewed themselves—and were viewed by other participants and staff—as being "less successful" in the program. And when young women fail to do well in these programs, their failure reinforces the myth that girls cannot do everything boys can do.

The seven Mead identified as *we are all the same* programs begin to acknowledge unequal opportunity for girls. They work consciously to involve girls and boys equally and treat them identically. The distinctive feature of these programs—the *only* feature that distinguishes them from *males are the model* programs—is that their activities are neither traditionally male nor female. Even though the activities are not gender-stereotyped, in these *we are all the same* programs, male behavior is still the gold standard and boys and girls are assumed to have the same experiences and value the same male-defined goals. Young women are encouraged to emulate young men, but young men are not taught to emulate young women. On one occasion, the young people decided to develop a set of activities to address youth violence. While everybody agreed that *gang* violence was an important component of their work, the girls could not convince the boys to see that *relationship* violence was equally important. At a youth rally planned by another *we are all the same* program, young women and young men shared the several visible leadership roles at the event. They gave speeches and moderated activities in equal numbers. Yet only the girls got involved with the less glamorous, behind-the-scenes work such as buying food and ordering supplies.

Without Careful Attention to Gender, Programs Simply Are Not Effective

In twenty-three of the twenty-five programs Mead studied, gender practices conflicted with the stated goal of the program to develop young women and young men to their fullest capacities. In the twelve *differences are fundamental* programs, young men and young women were channeled into very different activities within the same program based on untested assumptions staff made about inherent gender differences in interest and ability. Many of these programs began as all-male organizations, and most activities offered by these programs originally were designed solely with boys in mind. This often results in less for girls to do in the programs and few ways for girls to break into the boys' activities.

In the eleven programs that believe in gender sameness and not difference (*males are the model* and *we are all the same*), Mead found that girls often struggled to succeed, but the unacknowledged reality was that their programs tilted success toward boys. In *males are the model* programs, their sameness orientation masked gender differences. The young people generally participated in identical activities with identical structures and supports. But in a career-preparation program, for example, all of the young people were learning skills that the young men (on average) already possessed to some degree *before* they joined the program. Here, the less-skilled young women were disadvantaged by identical treatment. In *we are all the same* programs, an insistence on gender sameness also came at a cost to the girls. Despite best efforts, these programs were unsuccessful in showing how a superficial belief in equality ignored very real underlying inequalities.

All of these youth-development programs have the capacity to make positive and constructive contributions to maximizing the potential of girls—and boys—by learning from the *equal voices* model. First, the organizations bring their program design more in line with actual proven, socialized differences (or lack of differences) in ability and interests between young women and young men. Second, the programs work with both genders to examine and explode limiting assumptions about appropriate gender traits and roles. Third, organizations adjust their program design so both young women and young men can participate effectively in all the program activities. In this way, the programs prepare young people for the multiplicity of roles they will encounter in their adult lives.

Appropriate attention to gender issues does not happen simply because a program for young people *intends* to benefit (or even *equally* benefit) young women and young men. Rather, in important ways, a program is shaped and constrained by the gender ideas it embodies, often unthinkingly—self-fulfilling prophecies that develop into institutionalized practices containing gender bias that is harmful to girls and young women as well as to boys and young men. Having an equal number of young women and men in the program, adding women to the staff, and allowing girls to do everything boys do—while all necessary steps—alone will not result in programs that benefit both genders equally.

6

Gender in International Grant Making: Lessons Learned

Chapters 4 and 5 documented the importance of U.S. foundations taking a both/and approach: funding effective gender-specific programs and organizations in addition to making universal grants that take into account gender and the impact of gender on women and men, girls and boys served by the programs and organizations they fund. This chapter focuses on the role of gender in international grant making and looks at international funders' history of gender awareness.

In a 1992 essay for *Scientific American,* Harvard University President Lawrence Summers, then chief economist at the World Bank, wrote "educating girls quite possibly yields a higher rate of return than any other investment in the developing world."[1] He reasoned that most girls go on to become mothers and "an educated mother faces an entirely different set of life choices. She is likely to have fewer, healthier children and can insist on the development of all her children." Summers's work and that of other economists, like Nobel Prize winner Amartya Sen, whose research showed the same advantages of investing in girls, has had a major impact on international development.[2]

Although Summers's essay was published in 1992, international development agencies had known for years that it was necessary to consider women in their grant making. In fact, they have been focusing on women as a distinct population since the 1950s. More recently, according to Charlotte Bunch, director of the Center for Women's Global Leadership at Rutgers University, global funders have concentrated gender funding in areas such as micro-credit, girls' education, and reproductive rights (in most cases funding aimed at controlling population growth). While these areas are important, they do not necessarily reflect a gender lens in grant making. Instead, they show a breakthrough—in limited ways—of the success of international women's organizations in making the case for the "effi-ciency" of funding women. Bunch sees some funders committed to women's rights, but even here funding has begun to shrink.[3]

Although other experts also raise questions about the current status of international funding for women and girls,[4] the aim of this chapter is to highlight the evolution in both grant-making discourse and practice about why and how some international funders have focused on funding for women and girls. At least on paper, gender as a legitimate funding cate-gory is established in all mainstream international development agencies, including the United Nations, the World Bank, the International Monetary Fund, USAID, and the Inter-American Development Bank.

Why is gender analysis more commonly used in international develop-ment than in the United States? Why do international funding agencies like USAID and the World Bank focus on the needs of women? While far from fulfilling all the needs of women and girls around the world, inter-national funding strategies nonetheless pose a marked contrast to the ma-jority of U.S. grant making. What lessons can this history of international development practice offer funders of U.S. nonprofits? This chapter offers some answers to these questions.

Forty Years of Focus

Women first were specifically included in international grant making in the 1950s and 1960s. This targeted funding was designed to bring women into the development process as better mothers. Unfortunately, there was little recognition in that era of women's multiple roles in society but, instead, a narrow focus on women's role in the family, specifically childbearing and parenting. Women were viewed as passive beneficiaries of development, not seen as active agents of their own lives or as major contributors to their communities or countries. Funders assumed that women needed assis-tance and had little capacity to assist themselves, and these needs were met through the provision of food aid and family planning. Because women were treated as passive recipients of aid and only their reproductive roles recognized, this phase of targeted support for women has come to be known as the welfare approach.[5]

A major drawback of this approach is that women—not lack of re-sources—were identified as the problem. Women were not making "good" choices about family size and thus needed to be offered (or sometimes forced to accept) family-planning services. Women were not providing adequate nutrition for their families and thus had to be supplied additional food. There was virtually no recognition of women's multiple roles in community and economic spheres, nor any acknowledgment that women often lacked access to adequate material resources or political power. Funders also provided assistance in a top-down manner that ensured women's continued dependence on aid, since they were not given resources allowing them to construct adequate lives for themselves or their families. Widespread dissatisfaction with the welfare approach emerged in the 1970s. Scholars in the field of international development attribute this dissatisfaction (as well as alternative approaches that emerged) to a confluence of factors that include the emergence of a diversity of women's organizations in developing countries demanding a larger role for women in the development process; the research efforts of cultural anthropologists, particularly Ester Boserup,[6] who were beginning to make visible not only women's multiple roles in the productive, reproductive, and community spheres of activity but also the negative impact of development on women's lives; and the growth of the women's movement in the United States and elsewhere and its attention to women's conditions in developing countries.[7]

An early outgrowth of these interactive forces was the 1975 U.N. International Women's Year Conference, which formally put women on the international "agenda" and provided legitimacy for a focus on improving the lives of women and recognizing women's integral role in the development process. The conference, in turn, led to the United Nations designating 1976 to 1985 as the "women's decade," which continued to highlight the important—but often invisible—role of women in the social and economic development of third-world countries.

Women in Development (WID)
This new focus on women in international development came to be called Women in Development (WID), a name coined by the Women's Committee of the Washington, D.C., chapter of the Society for International Development. Members of this society had been paying close attention to research documenting the distinct roles occupied by women and men in most developing countries. The work of Ester Boserup,[8] in particular, was eye-opening because it documented how women played a central role in

food production and argued that their status was integrally connected to their agricultural contributions in their respective societies. Especially troubling was her conclusion: modern development was problematic for women. Conventional development typically ignored women's central role in the production of food and marginalized women even as it was supposed to be improving their lives. Boserup documented, for example, the ways in which the introduction of more modern technologies of food production made it almost impossible for women to continue their work in the agricultural sector. This, in turn, reduced women's status in their societies and thus reduced their freedom. Given women's important roles in agriculture, modern technologies should have been made available to them as well as to men. Because of Western notions about appropriate sexual division of labor, however, when new technologies were introduced, only men were trained to use them. Women in the Society for International Development came to realize that the modernization methods they had helped push for had actually set women back, rendering them invisible. Once they understood these impacts, they began to push for a more equitable approach to development.

During this same time period, American women were advocating for more political recognition of women's roles in developing countries. They achieved major legislative success with the passage of the 1973 Percy Amendment, which mandated that U.S. assistance help move women into their national economies in order to improve both women's status and the development process. One direct result of the Percy Amendment was the U.S. Agency for International Development (USAID) adopting WID as part of their official development approach. In addition to implementing WID in their own practices, USAID also, along with the Harvard Institute of International Development, developed a case-study methodology to identify how women were being left out of development. These case studies provided much of the evidence to conclude that a specific and constructive focus on women was necessary to ensure the effectiveness of development programs. USAID and the Harvard Institute were able to demonstrate specifically—country by country and region by region—how women are key actors in economic systems and how their neglect by development plans failed to tap into potentially large contributions.

These case studies provided analyses of women's contributions to the economic growth of their countries; documented women's formal and informal labor-force participation; looked at what happens when women control income; and documented women's contributions to the supply of food. One important finding that emerged in virtually every developing country was recognizing that when women have control over some or all of the household income, they use that income for their children's nutrition and the family's basic needs. This contrasts markedly with the majority of men in developing countries, who used increased income to improve themselves rather than their families.[9] Where women often use additional income to send their children to school, for example, or to buy adequate food for their children or provide health care for themselves and their family, men use additional income to improve their own housing and health care with less attention to the needs of their families. When women control some income, they also have increased decision-making power in their households regarding childbearing, economic issues, and family welfare. What the case study method was able to do, in other words, was provide evidence for the need to consider gender and show the benefits of doing so.

All this documentation resulted in a dramatic shift away from the initial paternalistic approach to international development. Approaches to women in development have taken different forms in different grant-making institutions and have evolved different rationales for why a focus on women is justified. These differences will be highlighted later in this chapter, but first it is useful to understand two consistent themes that characterize all WID approaches: the first is the recognition that women and men occupy different social roles in every society; and the second is that women always are found in subordinate positions. A central element of WID is the recognition that gender is a social construct. As outlined in chapter 1, the idea of gender as a *social construct* means that women and men are understood to have socially defined characteristics shaped by historical, economic, religious, cultural, and ethnic factors. As a result of socially imposed gender identities, women and men have different life experiences, knowledge, perspectives, and priorities. Societies assign different tasks to men and to women—this sexual division of labor cuts across areas often categorized as *productive work, reproductive work,* and *community work.*

Productive work is done by both men and women but is gender segregated. Women are pushed into certain jobs and job categories in a society, men into other categories, and often there is little fluidity between those categories. In developing countries, women's productive work is often unpaid.

Men may be paid for their work in export agriculture, for example, while their wives raise food for their families. The women's work is just as necessary, but typically unpaid. There are two results from these differentiated gender roles: women are denied direct access to income, and their productive labor is not counted in any of the statistics on economic production. *Reproductive work*, the work of the family, particularly caring for children, is done mainly by women. Both men and women are involved in the third and most recently recognized sphere of activity, *community work*, but also in very different roles. Men generally do the more public and high-status tasks; women tend to do the organizing and support work. This sexual division of labor creates women's often-invisible status. *Reproductive work* in the home often is not recognized or valued. *Productive work*, especially if unpaid, is similarly not seen or valued. And *community work*, since women generally operate behind the scenes, does nothing to change the fact that women are unseen and unvalued.

These analyses of gender help development planners more accurately recognize the causes for and structures of women's subordination in society, their inequality with men, and the power relations involved. These gender analyses emphasize the context in which women face their problems and stress the necessity of social change and the need to empower women in the process.[10] In every developing country, women as a group enjoy fewer advantages and work longer hours than men. In many countries women earn less than men, are prevented from owning land, confront numerous obstacles to holding positions of authority, and face many threats of violence just because they are women. Central goals of WID approaches are thus to make women visible, to recognize their many contributions, to acknowledge their different social roles, and to design development projects that are consistent with these gender differences. The defining differences among WID approaches stem from differing rationales for paying attention to women, the extent to which women are involved in the development process, not simply beneficiaries of it, and whether the unit of analysis is women or differences in gender roles and status between women and men. Some approaches treat women as needy aid recipients who have little capacity to improve their own lives. Other approaches involve women more actively in the development process itself, challenge rigid definitions of women's roles in society, and provide women the economic and political resources to improve their own circumstances.

Equity, Antipoverty, Efficiency, and Empowerment

Critiques of the paternalistic welfare approach prompted the development of a number of alternative approaches: *equity; antipoverty; efficiency;* and *empowerment.* These approaches share many origins, were formulated in the same decade, and are not entirely mutually exclusive.[11] At the present time, most mainstream development institutions use the efficiency approach, despite most women's organizations in developing countries arguing for the empowerment approach.

The *equity approach* to development aims to gain equity for women in the development process. Those who advocate an equity approach believe that women must be included as active participants in development. This approach recognizes women's triple role in the productive, reproductive, and community spheres, as well as the different roles women hold within each sphere. The equity approach seeks to meet "strategic" rather than "practical" gender needs through direct state intervention, giving political and economic autonomy to women and reducing inequality with men. This approach challenges women's subordinate position in relation to men and advocates strategies to change that balance of power. The equity approach generally assumes that the best path to equity for women is economic independence. This approach has been controversial because it challenges women's traditionally subordinate position to men and advocates helping women be economically independent from men. Generally it is an approach advocated by women's organizations in the United States and is not always well received by women's organizations in developing countries.

The *antipoverty approach* essentially is a toned-down version of the equity approach, and it has been less controversial because it argues that women's poverty is the result of underdevelopment, not of their subordination. Thus, it does not focus on power relations between women and men, but on women's economic status. Its general approach is to ensure that poor women increase their productivity and receive some of the benefits of that increased productivity. It recognizes the productive role of women and seeks to meet their practical need to earn an income, particularly through small-scale income-generating projects. It is most popular with those nongovernmental organizations (NGOs) that do not favor empowerment because it puts the emphasis on reducing income inequality between women and men instead of power inequality.[12]

Especially popular with the World Bank and other institutions that frame their work in economic terms, *efficiency* is now the predominant WID approach. It aims to ensure that development is more efficient and effective by focusing on women's economic contributions. The shift from equity to efficiency reflects the recognition that half of the human resources available for development were being wasted or underutilized. This approach assumes that increased economic participation for women in developing countries is automatically linked to increased equity. One major drawback of the efficiency approach is that it relies on the elasticity of women's time. Women are expected to make major economic contributions with no concomitant reduction in family responsibilities. When structural adjustment policies force countries to curtail social spending, policy makers assume that women simply can carry more of the burden of taking care of others.

The *empowerment approach* aims to make women more powerful by making them more able to be self-reliant. This approach is favored by women's organizations in developing countries because it gives women the resources they need to improve their lives and because it views women's subjugation to men as, in part, a function of colonial and neocolonial oppression. This approach recognizes women's triple role in the productive, reproductive, and community spheres and seeks to meet strategic gender needs indirectly through bottom-up mobilization around practical gender needs. It acknowledges that women experience oppression differently according to their race, class, colonial history, and current position in the international economic order.[13] It places far less emphasis than the equity approach does on increasing women's status relative to men. Rather it focuses on the capacity of women to increase their own self-reliance and internal strength and manifest the right to make choices in life and influence the direction of change through their ability to gain control over crucial material and nonmaterial resources.

U.S. Agency for International Development, Inter-American Development Bank, and the World Bank

All of the major international development institutions have incorporated one or more of these various WID approaches. Most development organizations now have an official policy or mandate for WID designed to ensure that they take into account both women's and men's needs in the programs they support. They also have an office or an official charged with leading, advising, and reviewing policy implementation.

U.S. Agency for International Development

USAID has been the acknowledged leader in WID analysis and practice, institutionalizing WID as early as the mid-1970s. Since then, the agency has developed an increasing recognition of the ways in which differential access to and control over resources as well as gender specific responses to opportunities must be addressed if programs and projects are to be successful and efficient. They accept that a focus on gender issues is absolutely central to the achievement of the agency's primary objectives. As former agency administrator J. Brian Atwood said in 1996: " . . . Perhaps [our] greatest accomplishment is the increasing realization that for development to be effective, programs must pay attention to the central role of women in the economic and social advancement of a nation."[14]

The Inter-American Development Bank

In 1987, the Inter-American Development Bank (IDB) approved its operating policy on WID and appointed its first WID advisor in 1989. According to an account of WID at the IDB,[15] the underlying motivation for the bank to focus on women is the belief that the goal of economic and social development cannot be achieved unless both women and men are able to participate fully in all spheres of life, unhindered by discrimination. Staff at the IDB have come to accept that understanding gender differences is central to development planning. IDB has an unusually sophisticated understanding of the rationales for WID, acknowledging equity, efficiency, and empowerment rationales. It holds that, to be successful, WID must balance efficiency (stressing women's contributions to development) and equity (stressing women's benefits from development). It also must give women more access to power.

Gender analysis also is seen as an important tool in the promotion of women's and men's participation in development. The objective of IDB's WID policy is to integrate women more fully into all stages of the development process and to improve their socioeconomic circumstances. The IDB is committed to recognizing and enhancing women's actual and potential roles in productive and social activities as well as their contribution to the national development process.

Although a theoretical commitment to WID is well established at the IDB, the practicalities are daunting. According to the bank's own analysis of this issue, WID is difficult at the IDB. There are no sanctions or rewards for WID, and it takes specific training, which often is not available or even assumed to be necessary. Despite these problems, however, there have been some significant successes. In 1991, 6 percent of IDB's loans addressed gender issues in project analysis and included specific actions to improve women's participation as contributors or beneficiaries. By 1994, this figure had increased to 33 percent.[16]

The World Bank

The World Bank has followed, not led, analysis and action on women-in-development issues.[17] Only in 1994 did it come forward with a policy paper on women—nearly twenty years after it established a WID office. The World Bank has a broad objective: enhancing women's participation in economic development. By 1994, the World Bank became seriously committed to mainstreaming gender concerns into all its operations, rather than operating a parallel or separate set of programs focusing on women,[18] although like universal funding in the United States, gender mainstreaming runs the risk of women's concerns being rendered invisible unless funders do the serious work, described earlier in this book, to name Norm.

Analysts inside the World Bank argue it could do much more for women. While considerable gains have been made over the last twenty years, as seen by key social indicators for women, unacceptable disparities in the well-being of women persist, and even less has been achieved with regard to women's participation in economic and political life. While the World Bank's overall efforts to promote economic growth and reduce poverty can benefit women, these measures alone are insufficient to address the many obstacles to women's full participation in their countries' development.[19]

Three important concepts are incorporated in the bank's current thinking: a shift from a focus on women to a focus on gender, a recognition of the need to mainstream gender operations, and an acknowledgment of the importance of participatory project-lending strategies. A gender approach emphasizes the analysis of inequalities between men and women in the family and in society rather than simply focusing on women separate from men. A focus on gender takes the onus off women as "the problem" and recognizes the complex set of interactive factors between women and men.

Models for Applying This Knowledge in the United States

One important evolution within development organizations is a move to mainstream WID. This involves a shift away from separate women's projects or components focused exclusively on women and an integration of WID into every aspect of the organization's activities. Several factors prompted this change. First, the generally small, women-only projects often did not work. Second, WID activities were being marginalized within development institutions to the point where there was a division between the "real" projects of the organization and the relatively "unimportant" women's projects. Finally, the staff that worked on WID projects were themselves becoming marginalized in their organizations. So, for reasons of project effectiveness and institutional visibility, a move toward mainstreaming WID has occurred. Large mainstream programs continue to represent the primary vehicle for promoting gender equity. However, there is still an acknowledged need for separate programs for women in certain strategic areas. Women-targeted and gender-targeted approaches can have a big payoff, especially when undertaken as part of an overall mainstreaming strategy.

What can we learn from the ways in which international development institutions incorporate gender into their programs and their grant making? The most obvious conclusion is that a focus on gender is more accepted, at least on paper, in international development than it is in the United States. Every major player in international development has a stated focus on gender and an institutionalized approach to including gender analyses in its work. WID is accepted for a number of reasons: the documented ineffectiveness of development projects if programs do not think about women and include women; the recognition of a significant but often gender-specific contribution of women to a country's economic development; the acknowledgment of women's different social roles; and the understanding that women, as a group, almost always are in a subordinate position to men in each country. Second, we can learn from international grant making a clarity about *why* to focus on women. As the World Bank documents in its *Engendering Development* report, focusing on women is about moving communities out of poverty.[20] Focusing on women is key to strengthening the health, economy, and general well-being of families, communities, and nations. As the World Bank's summary documents, society as a whole makes progress only when women's status improves. This is not about "women as a special interest group." On the contrary, funding with a focus on women, especially funding through international agencies like the World Bank and USAID, is understood to be essential to the success of development initiatives in countries around the world. We also can learn from the latest approaches within Women in Development that a focus on gender, not simply women, is important. Many, perhaps most, programs always will be universal if by universal we mean serving women and men, girls and boys.

As we have seen in international grant making, mainstreaming is inevitable. But, at least in some international institutions, funders are expected to conduct gender analyses to understand the different gender roles played by women and men in each area of programming and to design programs that work for women and men. In addition, international institutions understand the important role women-focused projects play. *What we need to fine-tune is determining when and how gender is relevant in a particular area of programming and when and how it is not.* But in both international and U.S. funding, the key is to "see" and to not lose gender in mainstreamed and universal programs. And therefore to fund adequately women's and girls' needs. A focus on women is not an inefficient use of scarce grant making dollars; quite the contrary, it is integrally connected to efficiency. A focus on women also is not antimale; a focus on women makes a community work better and be more productive. Finally, although a focus on women is not synonymous with women-only programs, important reasons still exist for concentrating specifically on women.

Of course, important differences exist between domestic and international funding challenges. The situation of women vis-à-vis men is not as stark in the United States as it is in many developing countries. Women arguably have almost as much access to education as men and, in general, take advantage of those educational opportunities. An experienced funder notes, "everyone knows that to build a good society, you need to educate women. But this doesn't translate to the United States where people think women have equal access to education." It's obvious to many funders that you can't do anything in developing countries if women don't have enough education to participate. But in this country, most women are seen as having enough education, or at least enough access to education. "I think it's that simple at core," another nonprofit executive observes. "Just about every discussion in the developing world focuses on the fact that women aren't educated." Or equal. Could it be that educating women in developing countries is less threatening because they are seen as still clearly subordinate?

The reality, however, is that as much as women in the United States do have access to education, inequalities abound. Just one example, the crucial fields of science and engineering, highlight the gaps: fewer than 10 percent of full professors in the sciences are women, despite women earning more than 25 percent of science PhDs over the past thirty years. Only 10 percent of those who take Advanced Placement tests in computer science are girls. In 1996 only 19 percent of physics degrees and 18 percent of engineering degrees were awarded to women. While women constitute 46 percent of the U.S. workforce, they hold just 12 percent of science and engineering jobs.[21]

Women's Problems Are More Obvious Internationally

For some funders, the problems also are more obvious in developing countries than they are in the United States. To make the case that women are at the crux of economic systems in other countries, as the head of one affinity group noted, "Funders will say, 'Ok, I can buy that.' They look here in the United States and see that men still really run the show. So in the United States, they have a hard time seeing how women can be key to economic development." In poor international economies, the role of women in food production, for example, is more visible. As another funder points out, "You can show that if you give money to women vs. men it has a multiplier effect, it goes immediately to children, families."

Internationally, funders have a depth of understanding about the interconnections between gender and violence, gender and economics, gender and human rights. Here that knowledge is compartmentalized. Why? As one funder points out, "Internationally, there are strong grassroots movements that have forced funders to see the connections. And even the most conservative funders can't ignore women." Much of this organizing took place around the U.N. World Conferences on Women and Population Conferences over the last several decades. International organizing around these conferences produced levels of awareness that are much more politically advanced. And women in foundations who fund women internationally often are connected to these movements.

Nongovernmental Organizations Have More Status Internationally   Besides better-organized grassroots movements outside the United States, there

also is the issue of the nonprofits themselves. Internationally, as NGOs, including women-led and women-focused NGOs, more frequently have become central to policy implementation as well as to service delivery, development funders are more likely to discover the importance of women. In some countries, NGOs actually stand in for civil government, so there is more impetus to fund them than there is to fund similarly configured nonprofits working in the United States even if the nonprofits have NGO status.

The U.S. Women's Movement Is Seen As Successful   The lack of gender awareness in the United States may indicate that the women's movement is tired. Or, in some quarters, that the movement is thought to be over. Opportunities for women clearly have improved in ways we could never have dreamed possible in the early 1970s. As described in chapter 1, funders in the 1970s and 1980s put a lot of attention on gender inequity. Federal education programs stemming from those efforts, the Educational Equity Act and Title IX, for example, have had a visible, profound impact on women's sports. As one nonprofit executive pointed out, "As some of these immediate, 'easier' actions have been taken and the complexity and depth of pervasive problems and issues become more apparent, it's harder to get funding. Now people say 'it's been done.' It takes more time to convince funders."

If the women's movement is tired, the generation that produced it is too, and as an educator pointed out, the next generation has yet to pick up the baton.

Conversations with younger women are more issue- than identity-based; they're more interested in the quantitative information; you have to prove it to them. They think the [equality] work has happened. The media reinforces this general perception. They need to hit another life stage—get children in school or hit the glass ceiling themselves or see continuing problems for women in community activities or get direct experiences like elder care responsibilities. They have to get to mid-30s before they see ongoing issues and problems for women.

People in the United States also like to think we've finished with "women's" issues because we're supposed to be a "fair" society. As a senior program officer in a large private foundation points out, "Initially the obstacle was denial of the problem. Now people think it's over, the problems are solved. There are more women around in high positions, and we don't need to support this work anymore." And an experienced funder notes:

People are caught off guard by our statistics on what's left to do; people want to think the United States is better than that. It is an interesting cultural phenomenon, what we think about our country. Then there are those who say men and boys are now being disadvantaged by all the attention going to women. We have to argue that we still have so much work to do for women to have equality.

More Women Are More "Comfortable" in the United States   Because the level of material comfort among many women and men in the United States is so much greater than in developing countries, women have less self-interest in working on what they themselves might see as women's issues. As one former corporate funder notes, "The case gets more difficult to make in the United States—not because there aren't important women's issues in need of funding, but because now fewer people are affected by them. Many women here have advanced, so we need to define who hasn't." Defining those in need isn't as easy here as it is in developing countries. The needs of those who haven't "made it" are no longer considered pressing: "Even though people can say women make up most of the poor," another nonprofit executive points out, "there's still this sense of women as the ones who've made it, who do not have economic need."

The U.S. Myth of Nuclear Families Distorts Community Reality   If people's lives make clear the connections between gender and the well-being of families and communities in developing countries, those connections are not so obvious in the United States. "I think people don't really take a full look at this country," another affinity group head observes. "That reality goes against our predominant myth of nuclear families, which still dominates how we think about our social fabric despite the fact that nuclear families are no longer the norm for the majority of families in the United States."

A Right-Wing Backlash Threatens U.S. Funders   And then there is also the reality that, because of conservative political agendas, gender is seen as a political hot potato in the United States in ways that it is not internationally. "Funders don't want any U.S. right-wing backlash to come crashing down on them. They don't want anything to do with pro-life, pro-choice issues. Unlike grappling with gender politics in the Sudan, where funders are protected by distance, they don't want to do gender politics here, where they're exposed to U.S. right-wing backlash." Internationally, there is also the reality that more ministries abroad support women's issues. So there is more political cover for gender-based funding.

Funders Lack Global Awareness and Knowledge   Finally, disparity between international and domestic understanding of the centrality of women's roles in families and communities is seen as an outcome of a more general lack of global awareness on the part of U.S. funders. Although many respondents interviewed for this book would agree that gender is integrated into many more funding areas than it was a decade ago, those who feel otherwise attribute the gap to a lack of sophistication among U.S. philanthropic and corporate funders on a variety of fronts. "In my experience, and this applies as much to philanthropic as to corporate foundations," one national nonprofit executive says, "there isn't recognition of subtlety or complexity on the issues." A grassroots leader agrees:

We still have a very long way to go. There's little positive news about the way the funding world understands gender. There are some exceptions, but the view is very narrow, not informed by an understanding of global politics, trends, or economies. Generally funders are uninformed and disconnected from the realities of gender in various contexts around the world: there is some funding, but it's not from a very deep place. Funders are trying to respond to political pressures and appear responsive, but there is no depth of understanding of the conditions of women and girls or the connection of their condition to the well-being of communities and to global politics.

In fact, as we have seen throughout this book, a sophisticated understanding of gender is as relevant in the United States as it is internationally, a key piece of deep diversity. Without it, funders will continue to overlook (or ignore) the real needs of women and their families in this country, needs reflected clearly in labor-market statistics and other demographics. The labor market continues to be highly gender-segregated, with women disproportionately represented in the secondary labor market characterized by lower salaries and fewer benefits, and men disproportionately represented in the primary labor market with higher salaries and benefits. Women do not have access to political power in nearly the same degree as men, especially in positions of elected office. Women live longer than men, and thus are disproportionately represented in the older population, with greater reliance on Social Security and other social programs for the elderly. While much of the debate around the privatization of Social Security has focused on age differences (with younger workers seen as favoring privatization more than older ones), most analyses unfortunately fail to include gender, even though women typically live longer and earn less than men and have more at stake in how the Social Security system is reconfigured.

Moreover, as we described in chapter 1, gender does not apply to just women. As international grant making has shown, and as we have stressed throughout this book, gender analyses need to include men, whether, for example, looking at the growing gender gap in higher education or examining the disproportionate number of African-American and Latino men in prison. Gender intertwined with race and class and all the other "not Norm" categories impacts public policy concerns across virtually all foundation program areas and priorities. And funders must grapple with the intertwined impact of complex diversity and Norm. The bottom line is clear: gender as a key piece of deep diversity must be an integral part of effective grant making programs.

7

Effective Philanthropy: Model Funding Initiatives

Chapter 6 focused on the role of gender in international grant making—how international grant makers have learned to use a gender lens in their work but still fall into some of the same "universal" funding traps described in chapters 4 and 5—missing the complex and often hidden gender norms that undermine effective philanthropy. This chapter focuses on six additional funding initiatives, all of which take gender into account. They also illustrate effective funding strategies discussed in chapters 1–3: spotting hidden norms that deaden both organizations and funding initiatives.

These are just a few among a broad range of programs, projects, and organizations we could have chosen to demonstrate effective philanthropy. These six document effective-philanthropy benchmarks outlined elsewhere in this book:

• Funders for Lesbian and Gay Issues, National Lesbian and Gay Community Funding Partnership

• Hispanics in Philanthropy, Funders' Collaborative for Strong Latino Communities

• Los Angeles Urban Funders: Pacoima Neighborhood Initiative

• Ms. Foundation for Women: Collaborative Fund for Women's Economic Development

• National Women's Law Center, New York City Board of Education Vocational Education Project

• United Way of Massachusetts Bay: Today's Girls . . . Tomorrow's Leaders

These funding initiatives include examples designed by funders, designed by nonprofits, and designed by coalitions of funders and nonprofits working together. Three are city-based initiatives: one launched by United Way of Massachusetts Bay to strengthen programs for girls and boys in Boston;

another by the National Women's Law Center in collaboration with the New York City Board of Education to make vocational education more equitable; and a third, the Los Angeles Urban Funders Collaborative, a funder/nonprofit collaborative that targets three inner-city neighborhoods in Los Angeles. The other three are funder collaborations with a national focus, each of which use innovative strategies to build their coalitions: Hispanics in Philanthropy Funders' Collaborative for Strong Latino Communities, which uses national funding to leverage local and regional foundation collaboration and matches; Funders for Lesbian and Gay Issues National Lesbian and Gay Community Funding Partnership, which uses national funding to leverage local foundation and donor funding through a network of community foundations; and the Ms. Foundation Funding Collaboratives, which bring together groups of funders and donors around the foundation's key issue areas to expand knowledge of the issues and support for the nonprofits doing the work.

Across the board, these initiatives draw on innovative collaboration and partnerships among funders, between funders and individual donors, between funders and nonprofits, and among foundations, nonprofit organizations, and public agencies. These philanthropic and nonprofit leaders have learned to use their collaborations and partnerships to share deep diversity analysis and research, economic and other policy analyses, and legal research. They also have used these collaborations to develop more comprehensive analyses of local and regional issues. Most of these initiatives use a variety of national/community-based collaborations to produce learning on both levels—national and local—including bringing national research and policy concerns to local levels and sharing community-based issues with other local and regional funders as well as with national funders. These leaders also have learned to use collaborations and partnerships to develop community and regional grassroots leadership as well as to improve philanthropic leadership. In the process, they have learned to share and recycle funding strategies across localities and regions—they share their successes and, equally if not more important, their failures or near misses.

These groups also have learned to use collaborative partnerships to gain more visibility for the issues they care about within their philanthropic communities as well as among their nonprofit constituencies. And in the process, these leaders have learned to use various media strategically to gain wider visibility for issues, solutions, and positive outcomes locally, region-ally, and nationally. Most also have learned to use national and regional dollars to leverage and expand local funding and develop more sophis-ticated, efficient mechanisms to channel dollars to grassroots organizations where much of the important work gets done—and in the process, the ini-tiatives have learned to respect and utilize grassroots knowledge and to streamline delivery of services. These organizations also have learned to look for the big picture and to share more comprehensive analyses of the problems their communities and the nonprofits themselves face on a day-to-day basis—and to stick with their initiatives for the long haul. They have learned that significant social change does not happen overnight and that there are no easy fixes; most important, these innovators have learned that long-lasting solutions to complex problems not only take time, they also are hard to measure and only can be seen accurately over a committed span of time. That being said, however, these funders and nonprofits also share a common commitment to evaluation. They take evaluation seriously and use their partnerships and collaborative expertise, including the grantees themselves, as key to the evaluation process. What comes through in all six of these examples is the respect both funders and grantees have for each other's knowledge and work.

Finally, these organizations also have learned to leverage power to facil-itate social change, to wield the "power of the purse" strategically, to edu-cate nonprofits about deep diversity and help them become more effective. One key strategy for achieving this is "due diligence," asking hard questions in ways that help everyone learn, not in ways that punish. Nonprofits also have learned to use their power strategically: through media and leveraging of funders and donors to shed light on important changes needed in both so-ciety at large and within philanthropy itself. Taken together, these six model initiatives provide some impressive blueprints for effective philanthropy.

Funders for Lesbian and Gay Issues: National Lesbian and Gay Community Funding Partnership

The National Lesbian and Gay Community Funding Partnership was founded in 1993 and is a project of Funders for Lesbian and Gay Issues, an Affinity Group of the Council on Foundations and the National Network of Grantmakers. Organized as a collaborative funding initiative, national funders partner with local community foundations to support community-based lesbian, gay, bisexual, and transgender (LGBT) programs. In 2003, less than one third of one percent of annual grant-making dollars supported LGBT programs and projects. One of the aims of the partnership is to raise awareness of the chronically limited philanthropy dollars available to non-HIV/AIDS LGBT issues.[1] The partnership created a collaborative funding model, pooling resources from national funders to offer matching grants to community foundations that in turn would fund problem-solving strategies at the local level. In addition to providing crucial dollars for grassroots work, this collaborative model gives national funders the opportunity to impact issues that are best addressed through community-based efforts.

Spearheaded by Robert Crane, then president of the Joyce Mertz-Gilmore Foundation in New York, the creators of the partnership understood the value of inclusiveness from the outset. The partnership convened a national advisory committee to shape the initiative, develop policies and procedures, and provide advice and oversight. Three community foundation representatives, three LGBT community activists, and six national funders comprised the founding committee. Recognizing the importance of involving those who would be directly impacted by the initiative, beginning in the planning and policy-development stages, representatives from community foundations and the LGBT community were asked to serve on the advisory committee along with representatives from the national funding partners. Racial, gender, and sexual-orientation diversity were and continue to be explicit requirements for the selection of committee members.

The partnership's advisory committee set the following primary objectives for the collaborative:

• Increase awareness and understanding of LGBT people and issues within the philanthropic community and the community at large
• Stimulate the establishment and expansion of philanthropic resources available for LGBT programs and services
• Encourage a positive relationship between community foundations and the organizational and philanthropic leadership of the LGBT community

Community input has been and is sought and valued at every stage of the partnership initiative, which issues a request for proposals (RFP) annually to all community foundation members of the Council on Foundations. Matching grants of up to $50,000 per year for two years are offered along with a possible third-year transition grant of up to $30,000. Proposals are reviewed and grants decisions determined by the partnership's National Advisory Grants Committee. As of July 2005, forty community foundations throughout North America have received grants.

To assure broad-based community input, all partnership sites are required to establish local advisory committees comprised of community foundation staff and/or board members, leaders from the LGBT and straight communities, and gay and straight community members at large. Local advisory committee members reflect the communities they serve and are encouraged to be broadly diverse in terms of race, ethnicity, gender, age, ability, and sexual orientation. These local committees oversee the development and implementation of community scans to ascertain the needs of the local LGBT community and determine resources available to meet them. The results of these scans inform the grant-making guidelines for the local site. Local advisory committee members also are actively involved in helping to raise the matching funds, developing the community foundations' RFPs, reviewing grant proposals, and recommending grant awards to the community foundations' board of trustees.

A significant measure of impact of the Partnership initiative is the depth and breadth of local programs receiving grants from the community foundation partners. Over 900 grants have been awarded since 1995 to a wide range of organizations and programs supporting LGBT youth, antihomophobia and antiviolence projects, grassroots-organizing projects, lesbian-health initiatives, arts and cultural programs, and outreach projects to communities of color, transgender communities, and rural populations. As one partner from the HOPE Fund of the Community Foundation for Southeast Michigan described it, "In the past several years, something happened in our community many of us never dreamed possible. . . . It's the first time in Detroit a partnership between a mainstream foundation and the gay and lesbian community has resulted in a substantial investment in organizations serving these communities." While the grants awarded have significant impact, perhaps a more important result of the initiative is the community building that is taking place across the country. The impact is particularly significant in smaller cities and communities where coalitions are forming and relationships developing both within LGBT communities across gender, class, and race and between these and heterosexual communities.

The former director of the Greater Piscataqua Community Foundation in New Hampshire attests to the success of these connections:

A gay/straight alliance emerged from the Affirming Seacoast Community Partnership that reaches beyond the dollars. Our events have brought together people whose paths would otherwise never cross. They have heightened community awareness of the importance of lesbian and gay people and their issues and concerns and are having the effect of "normalizing the conversation."

Over the course of the partnership, thirteen national funders have contributed over \$4.5 million, which has been matched by over \$3.5 million in local funds. While these funds may seem modest when compared with larger funding collaboratives, they represent by far the largest philanthropic initiative focused on LGBT issues in the country. Another measurable outcome as LGBT grassroots foundations begin working in partnership with "traditional" community foundations on this initiative has been expanded visibility for LGBT issues and effective community-funding models. In a win-win situation, nine partnership sites are working collaboratively with both local LGBT foundations, which provide expertise and knowledge of the LGBT community to the community foundation partner, and a community foundation sponsor that provides capacity-building support and visibility for the LGBT foundation. The lasting impact of the partnership initiative is significant. Three-quarters of the community foundation partners have established permanent grant-making funds for LGBT issues at their foundations, ensuring ongoing support of these issues. In addition, lesbians and gay men have been elected to boards of trustees of several community foundation partnership sites across the country.

The Partnership also has had an impact on the levels of giving from the community foundation sector as a whole. A review of the data from *Foundation Giving Trends 2004* published by the Foundation Center shows a fourfold increase (400%) in the number of grants given by community foundations to lesbian and gay issues—from less than one tenth of one percent (0.1%) just a few years ago to one half of one percent (0.5%) in 2002. Four to six new community foundation partners per year will be awarded grants over the next two to three years, resulting in a network of fifty to sixty community foundations in urban and rural areas throughout the country that support LGBT issues and programs. This network provides a solid base in the field from which to expand outreach and development opportunities for other community foundations. Partnership sites also serve as model programs in their regions. Coupled with community foundations that already are serving local LGBT communities, they develop an expanding network of funders informed and responsive to the lesbian, gay, bisexual, and transgender communities. And not insignificantly, the success of the partnership also provides an important and replicable collaborative model for other issue areas interested in linking national funders, community foundations, and grassroots organizations.

Hispanics in Philanthropy: Funders' Collaborative for Strong Latino Communities

Founded in 1983 to promote stronger partnerships between organized philanthropy and Latino communities, Hispanics in Philanthropy (HIP) is a transnational association of grant makers with more than 450 members representing corporate, public, and private philanthropies, nonprofit leadership, and academia. Governed by a twenty-four-member board and staffed by seven professionals, HIP includes representatives from all parts of the philanthropic sector in the United States and elsewhere in the Americas. Programs sponsored by HIP include regional, national, and international conferences and briefings; research and publications; information and referrals for foundations seeking Hispanic staff, trustees, or consultants; and exchanges with Latin-American foundations.[2]

HIP's flagship program is the Funders' Collaborative for Strong Latino Communities. HIP launched the collaborative in 2000 as a strategy for addressing the dearth of foundation dollars reaching U.S. Latino populations, which were feeling the effects of rapid growth driven by larger numbers of immigrants, increased diversity, and all the attendant problems posed for local and regional nonprofits. The collaborative was designed to channel money raised from national and transnational funders through regional collaboratives that could spark local matches. The initial goal of the Funders' Collaborative was to raise $16.5 million over five years to strengthen the infrastructure of the Latino nonprofit sector and to cultivate the next generation of Latino leadership within the United States and Latin America. By 2005, the collaborative succeeded in raising over $21 million, exceeding its target by $4.5 million.

Like the national Lesbian and Gay Community Funding Partnership described earlier, this combination of national and local funding was designed to have an impact on funders and on the grassroots organizations they aimed to strengthen. An early goal was to build stronger partnerships among funders as well as among nonprofits at the local, state, and regional levels. By strengthening the larger Latino nonprofit sector, the collaborative also increases the options, resources, and vehicles for participation available to the larger Latino community. And because of their transnational focus, the collaborative brings important international perspectives to all these local sites. The overall vision of the collaborative includes direct capacity-building grants, technical assistance, peer training and leadership development, convening and networking among small- and medium-sized Latino nonprofit organizations in the United States and Latin America, and opportunities for regional funders to work with each other and with nonprofits in their region. Another important goal is to educate funders who represent private, community, corporate, and international foundations about Latino issues at local and national levels both within the United States and in Latin America. As of July 2005, the collaborative had made more than 320 grants to small and medium-sized Latino nonprofits.

As a project of HIP, the collaborative falls under the fiduciary responsibility of the HIP board of directors, which is represented on each site committee, but the collaborative's day-to-day work is funder-driven and combines local decision making with national governance. An assembly comprised of all collaborative funders sets the broad outlines of grant-making policy. At the local level, once funds have been raised for a site, a site committee disseminates information to Latino nonprofits, invites and reviews proposals, and makes grant recommendations. Most site committees meet monthly. One of the goals of the Collaborative is to allow the Latino community to find its own solutions to its problems. Key to that is a funding criteria established by all funders of the project: empowering and strengthening Latino-led organizations. In regions of the country that may have a growing Latino population but not yet a sufficient number of Latino-led organizations, site committees have the flexibility to find ways of increasing Latino participation and decision making within mainstream organizations that serve Latinos. Direct grants do not go to non-Latino organizations, but it is possible for them to establish a program to assist these organizations in increasing Latino participation, thus leading to the collaborative's goal of greater Latino leadership.

Governance of local site committees is determined by the local funders and is quite flexible. Some sites have opted for cochairs, others for rotating chairs, and others for no chairs. Each funding organization has one vote, in the cases where a vote is needed, but member funders can have more than one representative in the process. Local funding organizations also decide about size of their site committees and whether prospective (but not yet actual) funders can participate. In most sites, prospective funders are invited to participate in the decision-making process (although not allowed to vote until they are officially funders). In some sites, new funders do not come on board until the end of the grant-making process and thus must wait for the next round before participating.

Minimum requirements for a collaborative site are that it have at least $250,000 in local funds committed and that there be at least two local funders involved. The collaborative's sites therefore can encompass part of a state, a whole state, a region, or any other geographically defined area. Local funders participating within the given region determine the specific geographical parameters of the site. Although it began in 2000 with 9 initial funders and 1 demonstration site, the collaborative as of July 2005 included 116 funders who have contributed over $21 million for 15 project sites in Argentina, Colorado, Connecticut, Delaware Valley (Philadelphia), Dominican Republic, Massachusetts/Rhode Island, Milwaukee, New Mexico, New York City, North Carolina, Upper Midwest (Minnesota, North Dakota, South Dakota, and Montana), Northern California and the Central Valley, South Florida, Southern California, and Southeast Wisconsin—who have funded over 320 nonprofits. Along with Magui Rubalcava, who managed the project from 2000–2003, collaborative founders Aida Rodriguez, Barbara A. Taveras, and Luz A. Vega-Marquis received the prestigious national Council on Foundations' Robert W. Scrivner Award for Creating Grantmaking in 2003. At the awards ceremony in Dallas that year, they called up to the stage all collaborative funders sitting in the audience. As those funders trooped from their lunch tables to join the award recipients on the stage, they made a striking, visual statement about the breadth and impact of the collaborative, both in their sheer numbers and in the diversity of foundations they represented.

If national or transnational grants to the national collaborative are geographically restricted, the grants will be directed accordingly. However most funders are flexible in how their funds are matched, so most grants can be distributed outside of the geographic area of the collaborative donor. Because the focus of the collaborative is on larger, multiyear grants, sites do not need a large number of applicants within their geographic areas, but the national collaborative governance process stresses that local sites have well-thought-out requests. In regions where funds are geographically restricted, the local committee has to ensure that sufficient outreach is done to the existing Latino organizations *prior* to the grant-making phase to ensure quality proposals. If too few organizations within a geographic area apply, then funds carry over to the next year of the project, and the site committee works to increase its outreach. The same applies to programming restrictions, which the collaborative also accommodates, with an emphasis on outreach to ensure a sufficient number of applicants.

One of the first steps for local site committee members is to define the breadth of capacity building they will fund in their region. Some, like the local committee in Northern California, for example, can be very flexible, allowing local organizations to define their own capacity-building needs. Time frames for grants also can vary, but the collaborative generally encourages two- to three-year grants. When the Northern California site committee wanted to expand the number of organizations they could fund, for example, they opted for two-year grants as well as planning grants. In round two of its funding, the same committee made third-year commitments for current two-year grantees and sought additional funds to support those organizations that completed their planning grants and wanted to submit larger, multiyear requests. The collaborative aims to be complementary to their funders' support of other Latino causes, not competitive with them, and stresses that investing in the collaborative is not an "either/or" proposition but is "in addition to."

Along with nonprofit capacity building, Latino leadership development is a key component of the collaborative. The project provides leadership training at both local and national levels. Grantees are convened at both levels, with the goal of encouraging peer learning and networking as well as providing formal training for grantees. Because the leadership component of the collaborative aims to tap into and build on the leadership that already exists within Latino communities, they use Latino nonprofit staff and board members as trainers and peer educators throughout. A committee of collaborative funders with knowledge of leadership development, capacity building, and training designed the Leadership Training Institute at Northwestern University in Evanston, Illinois, in 2003, which was the largest convening of all grantees (including those from Latin America). HIP raised separate funds to enable all site grantees to participate in the Institute.

The collaborative also pays attention to evaluation, including evaluation of its own communications and dissemination strategy. With an outside consultant to conduct the formal evaluation of the collaborative, all HIP grantees will be asked to complete a pre- and a post-assessment. Also, because many of the grants are multiyear, grantees submit progress reports prior to disbursement of their second and third payments. The national collaborative also provides sites with help in hiring culturally competent consultants by providing a hiring workshop, for example, for those organizations that previously have not had experience with consultants.

The collaborative is designed to have an impact that extends beyond its projected five-year life span through the ongoing relationships site members develop with Latino organizations they had not known before joining the collaborative. Sustainability of the collaborative itself is still an open question. As the collaborative nears the end of its five-year time frame in 2005, funders are considering other questions of long-term sustainability, including the expansion of HIP's Latino Donors program, which educates Latino and non-Latino donors on how to be more strategic in their giving.

Los Angeles Urban Funders: Pacoima Neighborhood Initiative

Los Angeles Urban Funders (LAUF) is a comprehensive, community-building funders' collaborative that formed in 1996 as a direct result of the area's civil unrest. In 1992, Los Angeles saw its largest domestic disturbance in a generation when rioting followed the acquittal of the police officers charged with the beating of Rodney King (which had been caught on camera). The events dramatically underscored the inadequacy of philanthropy's responses to the underlying serious conditions in low-income urban communities in and around Los Angeles.[3] In spite of attempts to coordinate philanthropic responses in the years following the riots, funders discovered that most traditional grant-making did little more than scratch the surface of the complex interdependence of the social, economic, and physical needs of neighborhood revitalization. After several years of fumbling and few results to show for their philanthropic investments, a group of funders, corporate leaders, and public policy makers began meeting with community leaders to share their knowledge and experience in order to do collaborative neighborhood problem-solving. In 2003 the board of directors, then with thirty-four members and composed of the funders involved in the project, decided to base LAUF as a collaborative project of the Southern California Association for Philanthropy, the Southern California Regional Association of Grantmakers. By December 2001, thirty-three foundations had pooled over $21 million for work in three Los Angeles neighborhoods.

The four goals of LAUF as they have evolved are:

• To encourage funders to gain an in-depth knowledge of three Los Angeles neighborhoods, coordinate their grant making within these communities, and work collaboratively at monthly meetings

• To strengthen the capacity of leaders and organizations to work together within these communities on collaborative research, asset mapping, strategic planning, and decision making

• To create healthier neighborhoods through comprehensive strategies that integrate human services, economic development, and community organizing

• To share lessons learned with other grant makers, neighborhood leaders, and policy makers[4]

One of the three neighborhoods LAUF targeted, the Pacoima Neighborhood Initiative Site, began with an emphasis on workforce development that built on community efforts already underway when LAUF organized. LAUF selected the Pacoima site because of significant collaboration and innovation that went into those community efforts. And rather than reinventing the wheel, LAUF enhanced working networks of existing neighborhood coalitions and exhibited a level of public candor not often seen in funding collaboratives. By their own descriptions, foundations in the four years between the riots and LAUF's formation saw their investments in the community as throwing money down a sinkhole. They had made funding decisions without input from those most affected, and their attempts at solutions had fallen flat.

Pacoima occupies a four-square-mile area situated in the Northeast San Fernando Valley, about thirty miles north of downtown Los Angeles. Pacoima is a port of entry for immigrants from Mexico's northern and western states (primarily the rural areas of Chihuahua, Michoacan, Zacatecas, and Mazatlan), the majority of whom entered the United States between 1970 and 1990, drawn by relatives who had labored as *braseiros* in Pacoima's olive groves, orange orchards, and alfalfa fields. In contrast to similar immigrant communities, Pacoima's population had begun to stabilize, with many families choosing to settle permanently, but demographic transitions had caused tensions to run high between Latinos, who by 2003 constituted 85 percent of the population, and African-Americans, who had dropped from 85 percent to less than 10 percent.

Bordered by three major freeways and two water-drainage canals, the area has a self-contained community identity. Housing, much of it built during a wave of postwar construction in the late 1940s, is in relatively sound condition, but high rental costs have resulted in multiple-family occupation of single dwellings as well as poor maintenance and upkeep. Despite the area's strong industrial and manufacturing base and its designation as a state empowerment zone, which makes it eligible for numerous economic incentives, as of 2003 Pacoima was plagued with nearly 40 percent unemployment because businesses hired largely from outside the neighborhood.

The local educational infrastructure consists of a feeder system comprised of six elementary schools, three middle schools, and one high school. Most children in Pacoima were unable to read at official grade levels, and because of low standardized test scores, two schools were on the list of the one hundred worst schools in Los Angeles. By 1990 however, six years before LAUF became involved, parents and teachers in Pacoima began actively working together to improve children's academic performance through a series of efforts around curriculum reform, new forms of school management, expanded after-school programming, and an annual "College Day" that exposed parents and children to the benefits of higher education.

It quickly became apparent that for children to perform well academically, they needed safe, healthy, and nurturing family environments to go home to, so the Los Angeles Educational Partnership (LAEP) and United Way created a school-based parent center where parents could access a range of family-support services, including parenting classes, health screenings and treatments, mental-health counseling, domestic-abuse interventions, and even food and clothing for those in need. The prototype parent center, established at Vaughn Elementary School, was managed by a professional director and a staff of ten to twelve individuals, many of whom were parents trained as caseworkers. Relations among family-center staff, the school, United Way, and LAEP were facilitated by a small team of organizational specialists, with LAEP responsible for payroll, personnel, fiscal management, and fundraising. In 1995 the model was replicated in five other schools: Maclay Middle, Maclay Primary, Telfair Elementary, Pacoima Elementary, and Montague Elementary. In adapting the model that they named FamilyCare/Healthy Kids (FCHK), planners sought a leaner, more flexible format that required fewer staff and less funding. Parent centers in the collaborative were staffed part-time by parents and backed up by a full-time coordinator and assistant, who staffed a network of service providers. Over time, a comprehensive array of interventions were in place, including curriculum reform, after-school programs, and family-support services.

Beginning in 1996, LAUF started working with the leaders of these school-based programs to expand the economic aspects of their work. Because an FCHK evaluation had revealed that one of the primary predeterminants to student success—family economic opportunity—still was missing in the initiative, the primary purpose of the LAUF partnership was to expand the economic aspects of FCHK's work. LAUF contracted a team of facilitators, economists, researchers, and organizational specialists to develop a variety of capacity-building projects:

• A series of focus groups among principals, teachers, and parents in each school to ascertain interest in undertaking a community economic-development strategy

• A nine-week training series to familiarize parents with the full range of community economic-development strategies and facilitate a process during which parents selected workforce development as their focus

• A mapping process pinpointing through school records the precise residential locations of all families and identifying geographic clusters for door-to-door outreach

• A massive resident-driven survey process with sixty residents reaching out to 1,500 households in order to obtain information about the local labor pool and the barriers to their employment

• A survey of business leaders identifying types and numbers of available jobs, reasons why Pacoima residents were not being hired, and a recommendation that the Valley Economic Development Center be directly involved in the workforce initiative

Through this capacity-building process, the LAUF partnership decided to construct a workforce-development initiative that would build on the platform of the FCHK collaborative, treating parent centers not only as "one-stops" for integrated human services, but also as "intake valves" linking residents with jobs. The partnership chose the Valley Economic Development Center (VEDC) as the natural institutional base for their initiative. After twenty years of providing assistance to businesses in the San Fernando Valley, VEDC had relationships with employers, many of whom needed assistance with workforce issues, and VEDC already had extended itself to Pacoima, operating a satellite business-assistance center there.

In terms of staffing, the partnership designed its workforce initiative to mirror FCHK. Just as parents had been trained as case managers in the parent centers, the workforce initiative enlisted parents as "career coaches" responsible for initial intake and screening of job candidates, and LAUF hired the director of Pacoima's public-housing community center to direct the program. Because resident research had identified numerous barriers to employment, LAUF sponsored a service-provider network of colleges, training centers, trade unions, and childcare providers to help participants overcome barriers. And to ensure a match between individuals' skills and employers' needs, the initiative formed industry networks, grouping similar businesses into teams to develop common training curricula, apprenticeships, and internal working relationships. The first of these networks—a group of hospitals, medical centers, and clinics—created a model career ladder to help parents interested in the burgeoning health-care field learn how to prepare for entry-level jobs.

The LAUF Pacoima Initiative is evaluated using the following strategies:

• Annual community-engagement surveys that maintain resident involvement and generate continuous data to be fed back into the planning process

• Trainings that help all participating agencies by identifying client outcomes, articulating models for how their work feeds into the larger initiative, and setting up common tracking systems

• Annual assessments of the FamilyCare/Healthy Kids collaborative and Pacoima Workforce Development Initiative
• An overall evaluation that checks in with 500 families to assess the cumulative effect of these multiple interventions on student achievement in terms of grades, conduct, homework completed, and standardized-test scores

Ms. Foundation for Women: Collaborative Fund for Women's Economic Development

The Ms. Foundation supports the efforts of women and girls to govern their own lives and influence the world around them. As we saw in the Ms. Foundation's case study in chapter 3, through its leadership, expertise, and financial support, the foundation champions an equitable society by effecting change in public consciousness, law, philanthropy, and social policy. Guided by their vision of a just and safe world where power and possibility are not limited by gender, race, class, or sexual orientation, the foundation believes that equity and inclusion are the cornerstones of a true democracy in which the worth and dignity of every person is valued.[5]

The hallmark of the Ms. Foundation always has been its ability to name the barriers confronting women and respond with crucial grants, technical assistance, and strategic partnerships to leverage resources. It was among the first supporters of organizations that addressed such issues as domestic violence, woman-friendly legislation, and the interrelationship of race, class, and gender. The Ms. Foundation also allied itself with diverse women's organizations, forming bonds to strengthen the national feminist movement and facilitating the mutual exchange of information and resources between organizers and funders on national and local levels. Today, the Ms. Foundation for Women remains the only national multi-issue, multicultural public women's fund and is a nationally recognized leader on women's and girls' issues. Through its groundbreaking Collaborative Funds and Funding Circles, it continues to bring local activists and funders together, and its programs have expanded to address issues such as girls' leadership, welfare reform, and childcare.

Since its inception, the Ms. Foundation has been a pioneer, investing in what others considered either a risky proposition or an unnecessary investment: women and girls. As the foundation moves into the twenty-first century, with the knowledge and experience of almost thirty years of advocating equality for women and girls, the Ms. Foundation for Women continues to share its vision of who women and girls are—and who they can become. In 1991, the foundation launched the Collaborative Fund for Women's Economic Development, a unique and innovative funding mechanism that brings together private foundations, corporations, and individuals to support organizations that assist low-income women to start and expand microenterprises and cooperative businesses in America's underserved areas. The Ms. Foundation took this collaborative approach because it wanted to increase the number of funders committed to women's economic development and willing to collaborate to achieve a common goal. Donors pool resources and make all decisions collectively to create collaborative funds that are designed to leverage new resources, build knowledge about effective grant making, build grantee capacity, and advance learning in a field.

In the first ten years of the collaborative's existence, the Ms. Foundation for Women mobilized $5.6 million dollars to invest in community-based organizations in rural and urban areas nationwide that are helping low-income women gain economic self-sufficiency. As grant makers new to the field join with those more experienced, each donor's resources are leveraged to attain greater scale and impact. Donor members engage in all aspects of grant making, from developing guidelines to making site visits to guiding the fund's learning component. The third round of the Collaborative Fund for Women's Economic Development, in 1999, pooled approximately $5 million from twenty-four donor partners for grants, technical assistance, and "best practice" research. The objectives were:

• To increase funding for economic development projects benefiting low-income women

• To educate funders about women's economic development through a peer-learning model

• To support effective program strategies and promote continued innovation and experimentation

• To advance learning about how to create ladders for women and their families to move out of poverty and attain long-term economic security

Donor partners—including large and small foundations and individual donors such as the Brico Fund, the Annie E. Casey Foundation, the Ford Foundation, the Appalachian Regional Commission, the Jacobs Family

Foundation, and Lindsay Shea—had to contribute a minimum of $150,000 over three years, and the requirement for individuals was a minimum of $75,000. Grantees were chosen from around the country and included Acre Family Day Care in Lowell, Massachusetts; Appalachian by Design in Lewisburg, West Virginia; Good Faith Fund in Pine Bluff, Arkansas; and Native Americans for Community Action in Flagstaff, Arizona.

National Women's Law Center: New York City Board of Education Vocational Education Project

The National Women's Law Center was established in 1972 with the mission of protecting and advancing the progress of women and girls at work, in school, and in most other aspects of their lives. Because of its primary focus on family economic security, the center also works on a broad array of issues like health, employment, and education, especially as they impact low-income women who often face special economic disadvantages when they are the sole or primary support for their families or bear a disproportionate share of unpaid family-caretaking responsibilities.[6]

Founded the same year Congress enacted Title IX—the 1972 federal law prohibiting sex discrimination in education—the center has been a leader in ensuring that women and girls have equal educational opportunities, opportunities which are especially important for helping low-income women and girls achieve more economic security. The center has, for example, spoken out against biased testing that restricts opportunities for female students, policies and practices that block women's access to nontraditional courses such as math and science, and pervasive sex-segregation in vocational schools. The center uses a variety of tools and projects to do its work—public-policy research, monitoring, and analysis; litigation, advocacy, and coalition-building; and public education—all with the aim of improving families' economic security by informing and educating public-policy makers, advocates, and the general public.

The center combines its tools for maximum impact: beginning in 2000, the center had highlighted the need for research and analysis into the barriers that contribute to sex segregation in specific and identifiable career and vocational-education programs. The center focused on New York City because of its large system of career and technical schools separate from its general-studies high school system, making career education–

focused research more feasible. On August 16, 2001, the center fired a shot across the bow of the NYC's Board of Education's Brooklyn office with a letter to then-chancellor Harold O. Levy documenting the "dual system" of vocational high schools for male and female students and the inferior educational opportunities for female students that result: all of which violated Title IX. The center's research showed that of the eighteen vocational-technical high schools in New York City, thirteen were highly sex-segregated, with their programs incorporating "outmoded and impermissible stereotypes on the basis of sex." Most girls were enrolled in schools and programs leading to "traditionally female" occupations like cosmetology, and most boys were enrolled in training for high-tech and higher-paying jobs.[7]

As a result of their letter, the center developed its Vocational Education Project, in partnership with the New York City Board of Education and funders like the AT&T Foundation; American Express Foundation; IBM; the Three Guineas Fund; law firms Skadden, Arps, Slate, Meagher & Flom and Shearman & Sterling; and the National Association of Public Interest Law fellowship program. In its proposals to funders, the center emphasized New York City's large population of low-income women for whom career education is an important route to stable work at living wages. The center already had contacts in New York that it could tap for developing the project, and New York was a model for the rest of the country in terms of policy and media attention to a problem. Because funders like AT&T, American Express, and IBM each had a major presence in New York, the program also was described as a way each of these companies could give back to their community. And finally, because each of these companies relies upon a workforce of people with diverse, high-tech skills (but not necessarily a college degree), the center was able to make the point that encouraging young women to enter programs leading to jobs in computers, math, and technology served the companies' business interests.

Remedies the center suggested for the Board of Education to come into compliance included:

• Providing more Advanced Placement (AP) courses in math and science at the predominantly female schools and offering specific AP courses that would help students succeed in the occupational fields offered by that school: for instance, AP biology and AP chemistry at the schools with health-occupations programs

• Providing high-tech and engineering programs at the predominantly female schools, focusing on skills preparation for high-wage occupations, beyond clerical or administrative fields that typically pay less

• Ensuring that high schools and junior high schools encourage female enrollment in the predominantly male high schools, and revising recruitment materials and methods and counseling tools to ensure that they do not perpetuate gender stereotypes and that they emphasize female students' opportunities in these schools

• Taking the steps outlined in the 1994 and 2000 reports of the Chancellor's Task Force on Sex Equity, including at the vocational schools with a gender imbalance reinstating full-time sex-equity coordinators to focus on recruiting and retaining students of the underrepresented sex

• Undertaking a review and necessary corrective actions to ensure that female students are not subject to sex discrimination in the admissions process, in the classroom (for instance, due to sexual harassment, pregnancy discrimination, or tracking), or in other aspects of their education

The Vocational Education project is the flagship initiative of the center's Career Education Program, funded half from program-specific support and the other half from the center's own general-support grants and donations. To fund this project, the center put together a multipronged approach, seeking targeted grants, particularly from corporate foundations and law firm fellowship programs, but also identifying both large and small foundations with a commitment to equal opportunity in education. The center notes that this mix of funders has been essential to allow it to do its work while reinforcing the importance of the work to the donors involved. And not incidentally, this multipronged funding strategy also is a model example of how an established, effective nonprofit is able to use its own general-support grants and donations to move quickly on a project central to its mission, taking advantage of both timeliness and media opportunities.

United Way of Massachusetts Bay: Today's Girls . . . Tomorrow's Leaders

The first time that Molly Mead presented the results of her research on youth programs, described in chapter 5, was on a panel moderated by the second-in-command at the local United Way. Pat Brandes, chief operating officer, had overseen a number of efforts to ensure that United Way of Massachusetts Bay hired strong women leaders, and she was dismayed to learn that her agency's grant making might not equal her decisions about staff hiring—especially considering that the United Way provides more funds to youth programs than any other institutional source besides the government.[8] One of the outcomes of this panel was a new United Way program called the Gender Sensitivity Initiative. Its goal was to strengthen coed youth programs by ensuring their gender sensitivity and bringing more dollars to girl-serving agencies within the United Way affiliate memberships. Affiliates were offered the opportunity to participate voluntarily in this program-improvement project, and many of the largest agencies chose to participate. Coed youth programs included the YMCA, Boys and Girls Clubs, Federated Neighborhood Houses, and Catholic Charities. The girl-serving agencies included two Girl Scout councils, a YWCA, and one of the area's Girls Incorporated programs. Mead met with each of the coed agencies to help them assess how well they were serving girls and to help them identify goals for program improvement. Mead also worked with the girl-serving agencies to help them put together training or consulting programs they could develop and then offer to other organizations to enhance their coed programs. The purpose was to harness the effectiveness of the girl-serving agencies and use that effectiveness to help build capacity throughout the sector.

The coed agencies often had stark, irrefutable evidence of ineffectiveness—girls' attendance was lower than boys'; girls would come to programs but not actively participate—and staff made changes that responded directly to those concerns. One program that offered coed sports programming clearly was failing. After Mead observed the program for a number of sessions, she noted that there were no women coaches and men coaches regularly spurred the boys to improve their play by yelling, "Juan, you play just like a girl." Women staff who wanted to coach did not have the requisite skills. Once these patterns became obvious, solutions were straightforward: provide coaching clinics for women staff and talk to the men about their blatant, usually unconscious, sexism. Something happened in this program, however, that extended beyond coaching clinics and consciousness raising. The staff let go of their determination to offer every activity on a coed basis at all times and began to ask whether and when to offer some programs just to boys, some just to girls, and some coed. The staff, in other words, became comfortable with applying gender analyses to their programming. The program now has a boys-only drumming class taught by an accomplished woman drummer, a girls-only discussion group, and an improved coed sports program. Girls and boys are attending more and rating the programs much more positively. And what was good for the girls in the program was good for the boys as well.

In another United Way–sponsored program, staff were concerned that when kids in each age bracket were given a choice of activities, the boys always chose the computer room and the girls the art room. For two weeks the staff tried an experiment: only girls were allowed in the computer room, and boys were limited to the art room. There was some complaining by all parties for a brief time, but the bottom line was that the girls became totally involved with the computers, and the boys had so much fun in the art room that the staff had to force them out at the end of each day. But after the girls decided they didn't want to miss out on their time on the computers and the boys came to realize how much fun they could have with their art projects, there soon was much more mixing in each venue. In each of these programs, the goal was positive youth development in all dimensions—physical, social, emotional, and educational.

The girl-serving agencies took a number of approaches to their funded projects. The Big Sister agency in Boston (one of the last remaining Big Sister programs in the country after most were swallowed by Big Brother agencies) developed a national training model for how to work effectively with "little sisters" and offered this training to Big Brother–Big Sister agencies around the country that didn't have the same expertise in mentoring girls. One of the Girl Scout Councils developed coaching clinics for sports programs in their area to train all coaches how to teach sports to girls. The local Girls Inc. agency, using the impressive curriculum and resources developed by their national office in Indianapolis, put together a unit of their program that they now offer in a nearby Boys and Girls Club that did not have the in-house ability to develop programs for girls.

In summary, one funder, the United Way of Massachusetts Bay, was able to recognize and respond to a problem by developing effective both/and approaches in their grant making. Today's Girls . . . Tomorrow's Leaders is helping coed youth programs improve their work with both girls and boys, and they are supporting a set of girl-serving agencies to do what they do best. The end result is that boys and girls in greater Boston have significantly improved choices in the youth programs they attend.

8

Conclusion

Throughout this book we have offered a range of analyses, case studies, and model initiatives to make the case that effective funders know how to institutionalize deep diversity, an essential step in creating agile learning organizations and democratizing philanthropy. To be effective, learning organizations name Norm, unmasking those often-invisible judgments and so-called "neutral" standards that deaden creativity. And in the process of naming Norm, effective learning organizations tease out subtle and not-so-subtle ways that gender stereotypes permeate institutions and collaborations to the disadvantage of women and girls *and* men and boys. Effective funders have come to know in their bones that funding Norm doesn't effectively fund Norma—or anyone else, for that matter.

Whether as "bottom up" grant making and/or thoughtful "top down" grant making, effective philanthropy includes stakeholder input and stresses the importance of responsible, mutually respectful relationships between funders and grantees. As the case studies and model initiatives in chapters 3 and 7 document, such democratized philanthropy makes an effort to include those working closest to the ground in foundation decision making and priority setting.

The case studies and model initiatives in chapters 3 and 7 also demonstrate other benchmarks: risk taking on the part of both funders and grantees; funders making core-support grants and sticking with grantees over time, leveraging support from other funders on behalf of grantees, and building collaboratives with other funders that can publicize for public benefit both grantees' and foundations' expertise. And, not least of all, transparency—clear guidelines and accessibility coupled with internal and external evaluations of the effectiveness and impact of foundations' own grant making as well as evaluations of the quality and impact of grantees' work, all of which enable funders to improve both their own expertise and their accountability.

As we document in the case studies in chapter 3, these benchmarks are intrinsically tied to foundations' ability to look beyond the obvious in both their grant making and their own internal organizational cultures. Effective foundations have learned to name Norm, to recognize the difference between the good norms that protect and help order our organizations and the bad norms that get in the way of the health of our organizations. Throughout this book we have seen examples of hidden assumptions, unspoken expectations, and unyielding attitudes that make Norm so dangerous for deep diversity. Chapters 4 and 5 showed that universal funding can be effective *only* when Norm is exposed. Neither universal nor targeted funding for women and girls works well when Norm assumes the face of neutrality, the appearance of being "universal"—genderless, objective, colorblind, classless—and dictates policies, procedures, and informal cultural interactions and assumed values that in fact are neither neutral nor universal.

And despite international funders' documented history of gender awareness, chapter 6 made clear how international philanthropy also needs to do a better job naming Norm. Success in linking population "control" to improving women's health, education, and the health of their families, for example—essentially *efficiency* funding strategies—has improved the lives of many women, but such strategies also have allowed funders to ignore essential, systemic roots of discrimination. When hard times hit, those strategies are too easily lost, or susceptible to calls for gender mainstreaming, which, like universal funding, risks being ineffective when gender mainstreaming fails to recognize the insidious, invisible Norm.

We wrote this book to help both U.S. and international organizations recognize Norm, the arbiter of "proper and acceptable behavior" that too often becomes the unnamed, undiscussable elephant on the table, that invisible dead center of organizations and collaborations that pushes to the periphery all the categories of group identities included in our definition of deep diversity: gender, race, class, sexual orientation, gender identity, age, disability, geography, nationality, religion, and other diversities—anyone "not Norm." The point here is that organizations and the people who lead them—as well as those who work in sector-wide collaborations and help manage the shape and direction of both national and international philanthropy—all these leaders must spot and avoid comfort zones and "normal" organizational and collaborative imperatives that reproduce "the way it's been done" instead of reaching for effective governance, staffing, and innovative partnerships.

The links between a comprehensive understanding of gender to help name Norm and all our benchmarks for effective philanthropy are clear. Understanding gender in the context of other diversities (race, class, disabilities, and culture)—which also means recognizing the insidious, unconscious, and unacknowledged preference for "normal"—is essential for building healthier institutions and doing more effective grantmaking.

Throughout this book, we have introduced you to funders who developed increasingly sophisticated understandings of gender and deep diversity. A foundation's commitment to deep diversity helps democratize its board and staff, helps create a learning climate, and more effective philanthropy results. We saw examples of organizations succeeding when they incorporated the best ideas and energies of all stakeholders into their institutions. And we saw that without those understandings, "learning organizations" don't learn.

Gender is the thread that, when pulled, unravels the Emperor's old clothes. *Understanding gender is essential for creating agile, effective learning organizations, for understanding difference, and for institutionalizing deep diversity and Norm knowledge. And by definition, understanding gender is essential for practicing effective philanthropy.*

The philanthropic practices that most benefit women and girls are the same practices that strengthen philanthropy generally and help foundations to do effective philanthropy. The awareness that women's rights *are* human rights, accepted practice in at least some international venues, is key to improving philanthropic effectiveness. Understanding how gender, race, ethnicity, disabilities, and culture are defining factors in poverty, labor-force participation, wage disparities, access to capital, child care, aging, health, and politics—as well as in the development of healthy organizations and healthy collaborations that practice deep diversity—all of this knowledge is essential for effective philanthropy.

We have included appendices in this book that offer basic demographics and links to a broad range of information that readers can use to document and expand much of this book's analyses. We also include links to evaluation toolkits that readers can use to test knowledge and applications of deep diversity, including gender knowledge. And not least of all, we include in the appendices talking points readers can use for explaining to colleagues and friends why they need to read this book.

Both the philanthropic and nonprofit communities are filled with vibrant, creative people working long hours to do important, often unheralded work. A major goal of this book has been to highlight some of that good work and provide thoughtful analyses and resources that will enable us all to do our work better. We intend the ideas presented in this book to be part of an ongoing conversation. Our interpretations—even though informed by a wide range of research and diverse perspectives and experiences—are far from the last word on any of these concerns. These analyses and resources are offered as food for thought—and some new language—for what has been a divisive, often contentious subject. Our expectation is that others will join this conversation and help point the way to still more opportunities for effective philanthropy.

Appendix A
The World's Women 2005: At a Glance
A Demographic and Statistical Overview

Over the past decade, United Nations agencies have tracked women's progress in critical areas identified by the 1995 United Nations Fourth World Conference on Women in Beijing. In 2000, the National Council for Research on Women produced a report that, through statistics, mirrored these areas and provided a snapshot of the current status of women in the world. In 2005, the Council released a report that presents another snapshot, five years later. The World's Women 2005: At a Glance *offers an overview of the status of today's women and girls worldwide. We extend a special thanks to the National Council for Research on Women for permission to reprint selected portions of* The World's Women 2005.

Introduction

The National Council for Research on Women (NCRW), a consortium of 100 research, policy, and educational institutions, is pleased to present this abbreviated version of its report *The World's Women 2005*—a data-driven portrait of women and girls. The report tracks progress made by activists, scholars, policy makers, and women and girls themselves and identifies the enormous challenges still facing them today.

The development and production of the report was made possible with the generous support of UBS AG. It was overseen by NCRW Senior Scholar Kristen Timothy and Deputy Director Elizabeth Horton, with research by Gwendolyn Beetham, Tamara Reichberg, and interns Eva Colen, Justina Demetriades, and Julia Rosen. The full report is available at www.ncrw.org.

Where are Women and Girls Today?

Since the Beijing Platform for Action was adopted ten years ago, more than half of all countries have adopted legislation on women's rights, ratified U.N. conventions, or established national commissions for women.[1] Worldwide, women are running for political office in record numbers; they have the right to vote in most countries where free elections are held; more and more girls and young women throughout the world are enrolled in schools; in most parts of the world, they have the right to own land and property; and worldwide, women are playing a visibly larger role in the public economy. Increasingly, policy makers and funders recognize that focusing on women and girls is "the best way to reduce birth rates and child mortality; improve health, nutrition, and education; stem the spread of HIV/AIDS; build robust and self-sustaining community organizations; and encourage grassroots democracy."[2]

These changes have not come about spontaneously but rather as a result of effective advocacy and action by the international community and organizations of civil society, especially those focused on women.

Where Must We Continue to Fight for Women's Rights?

This snapshot also indicates that there is still work to be done. While differences between men and women in political participation, educational attainment, and access to health care have narrowed, the record remains uneven. Gender gaps continue, and in some parts of the world, including sub-Saharan Africa, the Middle East, and South Asia, they have widened. Even in the United States, progress in addressing some issues of importance to women has stalled and even regressed—the U.S. gender wage gap has remained relatively stagnant for the past twenty years, with women earning roughly 76 cents to the male dollar. And although globalization in some ways has empowered the international women's movement, it also has exacerbated poverty and restricted access to resources in many quarters, in effect constraining the possibilities open to women and girls. Most devastating, the epidemic of violence that continues to plague the world means that for many women and girls, basic physical security is beyond reach.[3]

A Call to Action

We at the National Council for Research on Women believe that the data and statistics offered in this selected edition of *The World's Women 2005* help make the case for actively supporting women's rights and empowerment. As researchers, we know that clear, accurate data and comparative analyses are crucial to that work, to identifying problems, assessing progress, and achieving equality. As we work together to build a safer and more just world for women and girls, we ask policy makers, funders, and concerned citizens everywhere to support these efforts—efforts which we believe will help strengthen our nations, fortify our global community, and improve *all* of our lives.

Women, Education, and Literacy

The United Nations recognizes that investment in education for women and girls results in better nutrition for the whole family, better health care, declining birth rates, poverty reduction, and better overall economic performance.[4] According to a survey of 63 countries in 2000, gains in women's education made the single largest contribution to declines in malnutrition in 1970–1995, accounting for 43 percent of the total.[5]

Women and Literacy

Worldwide 18.3 percent of the adult population, 800 million people, is illiterate. Almost two-thirds of them (64 percent) are women.[6]

Literacy rates for girls worldwide have improved over the past three decades, from 55 percent in 1970 to 74 percent in 2000.[7]

The United Nations estimates that 1 in 7 women in Afghanistan can read.[8] In response to fathers banning their daughters from government schools, the Revolutionary Association of Women of Afghanistan (RAWA) runs more than fifty secret schools in Kabul that hold literacy classes for hundreds of women and girls.[9]

The World Education Forum held in Dakar, Senegal, in April 2000 adopted six major goals for education including "achieving a 50 percent improvement in levels of adult literacy by 2015, especially for women."[10]

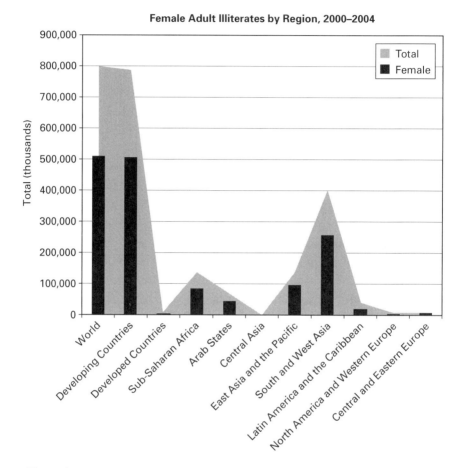

Figure A.1.
Source: United Nations Educational, Scientific and Cultural Organization. 2005. *Education for All: The Quality Imperative. Global Monitoring Report 2005*, table 3.7 [online]. Paris. [Cited 29 April 2005]. Available: http://portal.unesco.org/ education/en/file_download.php/bd3c26824f34f701f7f53b75391c116atable3.7 .pdf.

Adult Illiterates

	Total (Thousands)	% Female
World	799,147	64
Developing Countries	788,999	64
Developed Countries	9,151	62
Sub-Saharan Africa	137,000	61
Arab States	69,298	64
Central Asia	333	70
East Asia and the Pacific	134,978	71
South and Western Asia	402,744	64
Latin America and the Caribbean	39,383	55
North America and Western Europe	6,946	61
Central and Eastern Europe	8,464	77

Figure A.2.
Source: United Nations Educational, Scientific and Cultural Organization. 2005. *Education for All: The Quality Imperative. Global Monitoring Report 2005*, table 3.7 [online]. Paris. [Cited 29 April 2005]. Available: http://portal.unesco.org/education/en/file_download.php/bd3c26824f34f701f7f53b75391c116atable3.7.pd.

School Enrollment

Worldwide the number of girls in primary and secondary schooling is larger than ever before, and more of them are staying in school longer. But compared to boys, fewer girls are enrolled in schools, and girls are frequently removed from school at an earlier age than boys.[11]

In 2000, girls were still 57 percent of school-aged children worldwide who were not in school.[12]

The highest levels of enrollment of school-aged girls outside the developed regions are in Latin America and Southern Africa where more than 90 percent of school-aged girls are enrolled.[13] In Arab countries, enrollments in primary school were 75.6 percent of girls and 91.7 percent of boys in 1995. For secondary school, 58.4 percent of boys and 48.8 percent of girls were enrolled.[14]

In the United States, women have made gains in high school education. In 2003, for the second year in a row, women achieved a higher rate of high school completion (85 percent) than men (84 percent). The 2002 difference between the sexes was the first statistically significant one since 1989.[15]

The United Nations Millennium Development goals include:

➤ Ensuring that all boys and girls complete a full course of primary schooling.

➤ Eliminating gender disparity in primary and secondary education preferably by 2005, and at all levels by 2015.

Figure A.3.
Source: United Nations. "UN Millennium Development Goals" [online]. [Cited 29 April 2005]. Available: http://www.un.org/millenniumgoals/.

In the United States, black women have made large strides in educational attainment over the last twenty-five years. In 1975, 32 percent of black women aged 25 to 34 had completed fewer than four years of high school. By 2000, that percentage had dropped to 13 percent.[16]

College/University Education

Worldwide, an increasing number of women are continuing on to higher education. In the late 1990s, 17 percent of women were enrolled in higher education, compared to 7 percent in 1970. In most countries, however, higher education remains for the elite for both female and male.[17]

In Arab countries, the overall enrollment rate in higher education in 1995 was 12.5 percent, up from 9.2 percent in 1980. In 1995, the enrollment rate was 10.5 percent for females and 14.5 percent for males.[18]

In sub-Saharan Africa, only 2 out of every 1000 women and 4 out of 1000 men have access to higher education.[19]

In many industrialized countries, women now represent a slight majority of all university students. For example, in the United States, 25–29–year–old women outnumber men of the same age in their completion of four years or more of college, as evidenced by the following data:

White women: 35%   White men: 32%
Black women: 17%   Black men: 13%
Hispanic women: 10%   Hispanic men: 8%[20]

Educators

In most regions worldwide, women make up the large majority of primary teachers. At increasingly higher educational levels, however, the percentage of male teachers increases. At the secondary level, for example, women teachers still outnumber men in Latin America (54 percent) and the Caribbean (63 percent), Central and Western Asia (67 percent, 52 percent), and in most of the developed countries, but in higher education, these percentages fall below 50 percent compared to men. For example, women make up only 14 percent of higher education teachers in sub-Sahara Africa (excluding Southern Africa) and 23 percent in Southern Asia.[21]

In the United States, women make up more than half of instructors and lecturers in higher education and nearly half of assistant professors, but only one-third of associate professors and one-fifth of full professors.[22]

Women's Health and Health Security

Everyone has the right to a standard of living adequate for the health and well-being of himself and of his family, including food, clothing, housing and medical care and necessary social services. . . . Motherhood and childhood are entitled to special care and assistance.
—Universal Declaration of Human Rights, Article 25[23]

In the United States, there were 1.4 million more people without health insurance in 2003 than in 2002. Of those newly *un*insured 927,000, or 66.2 percent, were women and girls.[24] Women of color in the United States were estimated to be 28 percent of all women in 1999, but they were 45 percent of the estimated 20 million uninsured women.[25]

Life Expectancy
While women on the whole live longer than men, life expectancy for women in 50 countries is still under 60 years and in 23 countries under 50 years. However, in 2000, life expectancy for women was 80 years in 22 countries, compared to only 14 countries in 1995.[26]

The overall life expectancy in sub-Saharan Africa dropped dramatically in the 1990s, mostly because of the AIDS epidemic. Life expectancy dropped for female babies from 51.1 years to 46.3 years. For male babies, the level dropped from 47.3 years to 44.8 years.[27]

10 Countries with Highest Female Life Expectancy, 2000–2005 (in years)		9 Countries with Lowest Female Life Expectancy, 2000–2005 (in years)	
Japan	85	Rwanda	40
Spain	83	Mozambique	40
Sweden	83	Botswana	40
France	83	Malawi	38
Belgium	82	Lesotho	38
Finland	82	Swaziland	35
Iceland	82	Sierra Leone	35
Norway	82	Zimbabwe	33
Switzerland	82	Zambia	32
Australia	82		

Figure A.4.
Source: Compiled from the United Nations Statistics Division. 2005. "Life Expectancy," table 3a. [online]. [Cited 27 April 2005]. Available: http://unstats.un.org/unsd/demographic/products/indwm/ww2005/tab3a.htm.

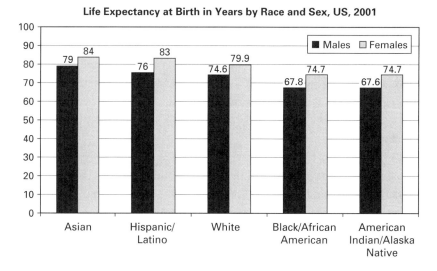

Figure A.5.
Source: United Nations Statistics Division. 2005. "Life Expectancy," table 3a. [online]. [Cited 27 April 2005]. Available: http://unstats.un.org/unsd/demographic/products/indwm/ww2005/tab3a.htm; National Institutes of Health. 2002. Women of Color Health Data Book, p. 55 [online]. [Cited 27 April 2005]. Available: http://www4.od.nih.gov/orwh/wocEnglish2002.pdf.

Reproductive Health

Since the 1994 International Conference on Population and Development, 131 countries have changed national policies, laws, or institutions to recognize reproductive rights. [28]

Sexual and reproductive ill health accounts for one-third of the global burden of disease among women of reproductive age, and one-fifth of the burden of disease among the population overall.[29]

Contraceptive Use

Over 200 million women worldwide have an unmet need for effective contraception. An estimated $3.9 billion would meet these needs and could prevent some 52 million pregnancies each year (half of which would be delayed to a later time, according to stated desires). This prevention or delay would also prevent:

• 23 million unplanned births (a 72 percent reduction)
• 22 million induced abortions (a 64 percent reduction)
• 1.4 million infant deaths
• 142,000 pregnancy-related deaths
• 505,000 children losing their mothers due to pregnancy-related deaths.[30]

In sub-Saharan Africa, 46 percent of women at risk of unintended pregnancy are using no contraceptive method[31] as opposed to 11 percent of women in the United States.[32]

Abortion

An estimated one-third of all pregnancies worldwide are unwanted, but safe abortion services are not universally permitted or accessible to women.[33]

An estimated 46 million women worldwide have induced abortions each year.[34] Of the 19 million unsafe abortions that occur annually, 99 percent of them in developing regions, nearly 70,000 women die from complications—one every eight minutes.[35]

On his first day in office, President George W. Bush reinstated the Reagan-era "global gag rule," which "prohibits foreign nongovernmental groups that receive U.S. family planning funds from any involvement in abortion-related counseling, services, or advocacy, even if they use their own money, and even in countries where abortion is legal."[36]

Women Having Abortions Each Year

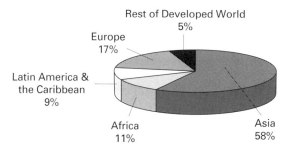

Figure A.6.
Source: The Alan Guttmacher Institute. 1998. *Sharing Responsibility: Women, Society, and Abortion Worldwide*, p. 25 [online]. [Cited 27 April 2005]. Available: http://www.agi-usa.org/pubs/sharing.pdf.

In the United States,

• State legislatures have enacted more than 400 antiabortion measures since 1995.[37]

• In 2003, President Bush signed policy into a federal law that restricts medical abortion. This law has been ruled unconstitutional by three federal court judges on grounds that it lacks a clause that allows exemption in the case of danger to women's health.[38]

• Nine out of ten U.S. counties, primarily in rural areas, now lack abortion services because of violence, harassment, and a lack of training opportunities for providers.[39]

Maternal Mortality

One woman dies every 60 seconds—15,000 women every day—from pregnancy or childbirth-related causes. According to estimates by WHO, UNICEF, and UNFPA, that is at least 529,000 deaths per year—or the equivalent of five 747 jumbo jets crashing and killing all passengers and crew every day.[40]

One million children worldwide die each year because their mother has died. When a mother dies in childbirth, her children under the age of 5 are twice as likely to die.[41]

Providing basic maternal and newborn health services to developing countries would cost an average of $3 per capita per year. However, once complications develop, saving the life of a mother or infant costs about $230.[42]

Medical Causes of Maternal Mortality, 1990s

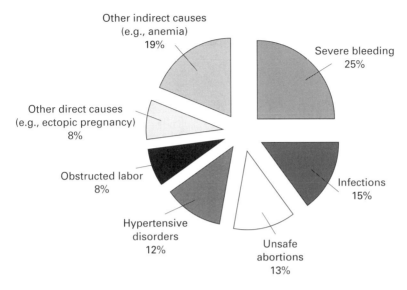

Figure A.7.
Source: Seager, Joni. 2003. *The Penguin Atlas of Women in the World*, p. 38. London: Penguin Books.

Maternal Mortality Estimates by Region, 2000

Region	Number of Maternal Deaths	Lifetime Risk of Maternal Death
World Total	529,000	1 in 74
Developed Regions	2,500	1 in 2,800
Developing Regions	527,000	1 in 61
Africa	251,000	1 in 20
Oceania	530	1 in 83
Asia	253,000	1 in 94
Latin America & the Caribbean	22,000	1 in 160
Sub-Saharan Africa		1 in 6
Northern Africa		1 in 210

Figure A.8.
Source: United Nations Population Fund. 2004. *State of the World Population 2004*, chapter 7: Maternal Health, p. 52 [online]. [Cited 25 April 2005]. Available: http://www.unfpa.org/swp/2004/pdf/en_swp04.pdf. Data compiled by WHO, UNICEF, and UNFPA. 2003. "Maternal Mortality in 2000." Estimates developed by WHO, UNICEF, and UNFPA. Geneva, World Health Organization.

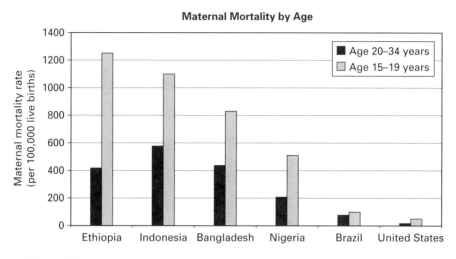

Figure A.9.
Source: International Center for Research on Women. 2003. *Too Young to Wed: The Health, Rights, and Lives of Young Married Girls*, p. 8 [online]. [Cited 27 April 2005]. Available: http://www.icrw.org/docs/tooyoungtowed_1003.pdf.

Girls between 15 and 20 years of age are twice as likely to die from pregnancy or childbirth as are women in their 20s, while girls under 15 face five times greater risk.[43]

According to the United Nations Population Fund, obstetric fistula, caused by prolonged and obstructed labor, is one of the most neglected issues in international reproductive health. Worldwide, more than 2 million girls and women suffer from fistula, especially in sub-Saharan Africa, South Asia, and some Arab states. An estimated 50,000–100,000 new cases are reported annually. Surgical repair for fistula has success rates as high as 90 percent for uncomplicated cases.[44]

In the United States, homicide is the top cause of death among pregnant women.[45]

Female Genital Mutilation

According to the World Health Organization, at least 135 million girls and women now alive are thought to have undergone female genital mutilation (FGM) in more than two dozen African countries, as well as parts of Asia, the Middle East, and some immigrant communities in the West.

Approximately two million girls a year are at risk of mutilation—about 6,000 per day.[46]

An estimated 15 percent of those who undergo genital mutilation suffer the most dangerous and extreme version, infibulation.[47]

In Kenya, an "Alternative Rights of Passage" ceremony, which celebrates female puberty without mutilation, already has saved 1,300 girls since 2000 from the procedure.[48] Meanwhile, in Mali, more than 14,000 people have signed a pledge to combat mutilation.[49]

In the United States:

• According to the Centers for Disease Control and Prevention, an estimated 168,000 immigrant women and girls in the United States have undergone genital mutilation or are still at risk for the procedure.[50]

• Following suit of other Western countries, the United States outlawed genital mutilation in 1996 to prevent immigrants from importing the practice. Makeshift at-home and hospitalized medical procedures, however, still occur.[51]

The Feminization of HIV/AIDS

At its heart, this is a crisis of gender inequality, with women less able than men to exercise control over their bodies and lives. Nearly universally, cultural expectations have encouraged men to have multiple partners, while women are expected to abstain or be faithful. There is also a culture of silence around sexual and reproductive health. Simply by fulfilling their expected gender roles, men and women are likely to increase their risk of HIV infection.

—UNAIDS/United Nations Population Fund/United Nations Development Fund for Women.[52]

Today, women account for nearly half of the 40 million people living with HIV worldwide, up to 48 percent from 35 percent in 1985. In some regions, adolescent girls are five to six times more likely to contract the virus than boys the same age.[53]

Although many countries use early marriage as a poverty reduction strategy, recent studies indicate that young married women are at a higher risk of HIV infection than their unmarried counterparts. In Kenya, 33 percent of married girls were HIV-positive compared to 22 percent of sexually active unmarried girls the same age. In Zambia, 27 percent of married girls were HIV-positive compared to 16 percent of unmarried girls.[54] Worldwide, 82 million girls will marry before their 18th birthday and will be more likely to become infected than their peers who are not married.[55]

In 2004, the U.S. State Department released the *President's Emergency Plan for AIDS Relief: U.S. Five-Year Global HIV/AIDS Strategy*, reflecting President Bush's 2003 pledge of $15 million over five years for AIDS relief to 14 countries (later increased to 15) worldwide. The strategy mandates that 33 percent of all prevention funds be spent on abstinence-only prevention.[56]

The ABC prevention method—Abstain, Be faithful, and use Condoms—has been successful in reducing the spread of HIV/AIDS in some countries, most notably in Uganda. ABC is not an "abstinence only" policy, but a comprehensive approach. Bush Administration Advisor Edward Green notes that Uganda "pioneered approaches toward reducing stigma, bringing discussion of sexual behavior out into the open, involving HIV-infected people in public education, persuading individuals and couples to be tested and counseled, improving the status of women, involving religious organizations, enlisting traditional healers, and much more."[57]

Globally, women and girls provide up to 90 percent of HIV/AIDS care in the home, which can increase the workload of a female caretaker by one third. This increase in social burden combined with the AIDS death toll on working-age women has cut the female labor force in sub-Saharan Africa. In 1995, 50 percent of women were unable to work compared to men, but in 2015, that number will increase to 80 percent.[58]

In sub-Saharan Africa:

• 77 percent of all HIV-positive women worldwide live in sub-Saharan Africa, the worst affected region.[59]

• More than 22 million adults are living with HIV and 11,000 additional people are infected daily—one every 8 seconds.[60]

• Of all HIV-positive adults, 57 percent are women, and 75 percent of young people living with HIV are women and girls.[61]

In the United States:

• Of new HIV cases between 1999 and 2002, 64 percent occurred among women, the majority of whom were ages 13–19.[62] From 1999 through 2003, the annual diagnoses of women with AIDS increased 15 percent, while the diagnoses among men increased 1 percent.[63]

• The rate of AIDS diagnosis for African American women is about 25 times that for white women and 4 times that for Hispanic women.[64]

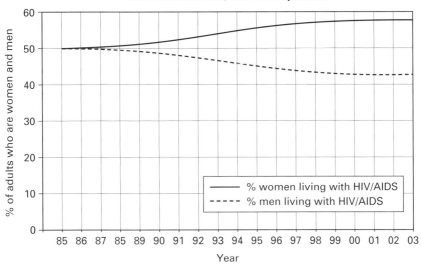

Women and men as a proportion of adults 15 to 49 living with HIV/AIDS, Sub-Saharan Africa, 1985–2003 (percent)

Figure A.10.
Source: International Labor Organization. 2004. "Women, Girls, HIV/AIDS and the World of Work" [online]. [Cited 27 April 2005]. Available: http://www.ilo.org/public/english/protection/trav/aids/publ/women-iloaids-brief.pdf.

Diagnoses of AIDS in US women, by race/ethnicity, 2003

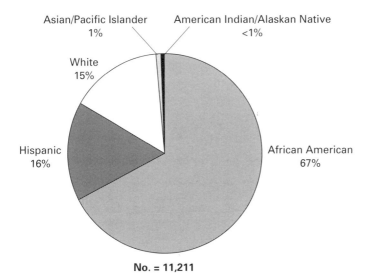

No. = 11,211

Figure A.11.
Source: Centers for Disease Control and Prevention. 2003. "HIV/AIDS among Women" [online]. [Cited 27 April 2005]. Available: http://www.cdc.gov/hiv/pubs/facts/women.htm.

• African American and Hispanic women together account for 83 percent of AIDS diagnoses reported in 2003, yet constitute only 25 percent of all U.S. women.[65]

• AIDS is among the top three causes of death among black and Hispanic women aged 15–34.[66]

Sickness from Unsafe Water and Sanitation

In developing countries, the task of collecting water generally falls to women; it is increasingly more difficult for women in the developing world to secure water as fresh, clean, water sources become scarce due to privatization, conflict, and natural resources depletion.[67]

The World Health Organization estimates that 80 percent of all illnesses are transmitted by contaminated water. Women must take care of those sick from water-related diseases, including malaria, onchocerciasis, shistosomiasis and diarrhea, and replace with their own labor the labor of those who have fallen ill.[68]

It has been estimated that every day, women in South Africa collectively walk the distance to the moon and back sixteen times for fresh water.[69] Over 40 billion work hours are lost in Africa to the need to fetch drinking water.[70]

In Africa and Asia, women carry roughly 20 kg of water at a time, the same amount as the baggage allowance on most airlines. Constantly carrying such heavy weights on the head, back, or hip can result in backache and joint pains, and in extreme cases, curved spines and pelvic deformities, creating complications during childbirth. Long, isolated trips to collect water also expose women to a greater risk of sexual and physical assault since there is an increased incidence of violence against women in these remote locations.[71]

Toilets are unavailable for many poor women who work in urban centers. About 1 in 10 school-age African girls do not attend school during menstruation or drop out at puberty due to the absence of clean and private sanitation facilities in school.[72]

Breast Cancer

Breast cancer is the most common cancer affecting women. Over 1 million new cases are diagnosed each year worldwide. Breast cancer rates have increased 26 percent since 1980.[73]

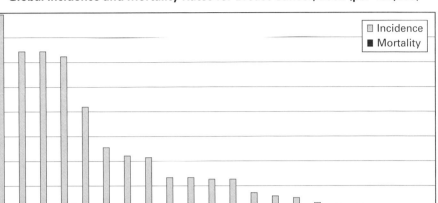

Global Incidence and Mortality Rates for Breast Cancer, 2002 (per 100,000)

Figure A.12.
Source: American Cancer Society. 2002. *Global Cancer Statistics, 2002*, Figure 6 [online]. [Cited 27 April 2005]. Available: http://caonline.amcancersoc.org/cgi/content/full/55/2/74.

Breast cancer is at its highest in developed countries; Europe and North America account for approximately half of the world's breast cancer cases while the lowest rates of breast cancer are found in Asia.[74]

Tobacco Use and Related Illness

Globally, 12 percent of women, or approximately 236 million women, smoke.[75]

Worldwide, overall prevalence of tobacco use is four times higher among men than women (48 percent versus 12 percent).[76] In 2000, smoking killed almost five million people and three times as many men as women.[77]

However, the World Health Organization estimates that the number of women worldwide who smoke will grow in the next generation to more

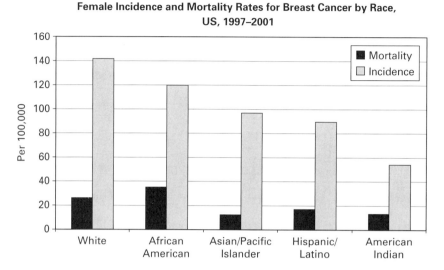

Figure A.13.
Source: American Cancer Society. 2005. "Surveillance Research" [online]. [Cited 27 April 2005]. Available: http://www.cancer.org/downloads/stt/Incidence_and _Mortality_Rates_by_Site,_Race,_and_Ethnicity,_US,_1997-2001.pdf.

than 500 million, or almost triple current rates. More than 200 million of these women will die prematurely from tobacco-related diseases.[78]

In 2025, developing countries are expected to show the greatest growth in smoking rates among women, from approximately 7 percent now to 20 percent. In contrast, smoking among women is expected to decrease in developed countries from 24 percent today to 20 percent in 2025.[79]

Recent studies show that cigarette smoking is more harmful to women than to men, cutting 11 years off a female's life but just 3 years for men.[80] Women develop lung cancer with lower levels of smoking compared to men, and are more at risk of contracting small cell lung cancer (the more aggressive type).[81]

In the United States, lung cancer has overtaken breast cancer as the principal cause of female cancer mortality. In 2005, the American Cancer Society estimates that 73,020 women will die of lung cancer[82] and 40,410 women will die of breast cancer.[83]

• Following an increase in smoking, the death rate from lung cancer in US women rose 600 percent from 1930 to 1997.[84]
• 1 in every 4 American women smokes.[85]

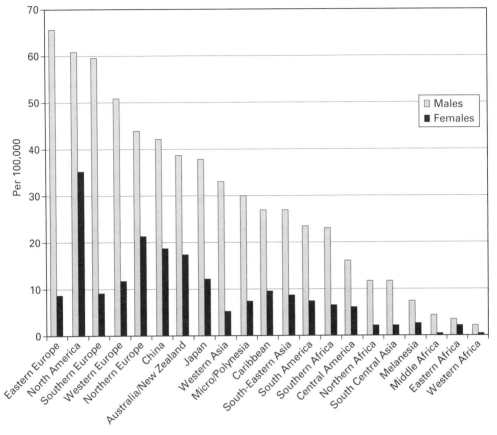

Figure A.14.
Source: American Cancer Society. 2002. *Global Cancer Statistics, 2002*, figure 5 [online]. [Cited 27 April 2005]. Available: http://caonline.amcancersoc.org/cgi/content/full/55/2/74.

Women's Citizenship and Leadership

Voting Rights

In all but four countries (Kuwait, Saudi Arabia, the United Arab Emirates, and Brunei), women have the *formal* right to vote.[86]

• In February 2005, Saudi Arabia held its first election in more than forty years. Women were denied the right to vote although election law does not explicitly ban women. Saudi officials said that the ban on women voters was because of "logistical problems" in a country in which the sexes are strictly segregated, but that in future elections, provisions would be made for women to vote.[87]

• In April 2005, the Kuwaiti parliament took a first step toward giving women the vote and allowing them to run in municipal elections. A second vote by the parliament is required before the law will go into effect. The Kuwaiti cabinet already had approved the bill, but it has been delayed in parliament by the strong Islamist bloc, which has twice defeated similar measures in recent years.[88]

• In the United Arab Emirates and Brunei, neither men nor women have the right to vote.[89]

In Afghanistan, of the nearly 10 million voters registered in the October 2004 election, 41 percent were women.[90]

In the United States's 2004 Presidential election, according to a CNN exit poll, 54 percent women voted compared to 46 percent men.[91]

Heads of Government

In 2004, out of 180 countries, 12 were headed by women: Georgia, New Zealand, Finland, Sri Lanka, Philippines, Ireland, Serbia, Panama, Sao Tome and Principe, Indonesia, Latvia, and Bangladesh.[92]

Women in Parliaments

According to the Inter-Parliamentary Union, women's presence in parliaments and in ministerial positions alters the traditionally male approach to social welfare, legal protection, and transparency in government and business.[93]

Women constitute 15.7 percent of parliamentarians in the world[94] with Rwanda having surpassed Sweden for having the largest percentage of women in parliament, with 48.8 percent.[95]

In the United Kingdom, France, and Japan, women's share of parliamentary or congressional seats is 18.1, 12.2, and 7.1 percent respectively. Notably, these rich countries lag behind 13 developing countries in sub-Saharan Africa, the poorest region in the world. In South Africa and Mozambique, for example, women's share of parliamentary seats is 33 and 34.8 percent respectively, while in Uganda women have 23.9 percent of the seats.[96]

Following the 2004 elections in the United States, women hold 15 percent of congressional seats—14 percent in the Senate and 15.2 percent in the House. A quarter of these seats are held by women of color. Women's percentage of state legislators remained constant at 22.6 percent.[97]

According to the United Nations, quotas were used in all countries that achieved higher than 30 percent representation of women in elected office.[98] For example, in South Africa, women comprise 50 percent of lists submitted by political parties for local-level elections; Rwanda's constitution guarantees women a minimum of 30 percent of parliamentary seats; and 33 percent of local government seats are reserved for women in India.[99] Quotas are not universally accepted as a solution to female under-representation in politics, however. Some argue that quotas should be used in conjunction with other measures, including encouraging more women to stand for election and introducing more family-friendly work practices in parliamentary systems.[100]

In 2000 the Inter-Parliamentary Union (IPU) surveyed 187 women parliamentarians from 65 countries on the difficulties faced by women in politics. The lack of day care for small children in all but the Nordic countries was highlighted as a problem. Notably, 73 percent of the respondents were mothers.[101]

Women in International Organizations

At the United Nations, women headed 6 percent of government delegations in 1991, 14 percent in 1998, and 8 percent in 2001.[102]

As of December 31, 2004, women at the United Nations held 7 out of 40, or 17.5 percent, of the Under-Secretary General–level positions and about 29 percent of the senior management posts, up from 25 percent in 2003.[103]

Women Decision Makers in Corporations and Financial Institutions

In the United States:
• Women represented close to 47 percent of the workforce but held only 15.7 percent of corporate officer positions, according to a 2001 survey of 429 Fortune 500 companies conducted by Catalyst. Women of color made up 1.6 percent of those corporate officers.[104]
• Women were 7.1 percent of those with CFO titles in Fortune 500 companies in 2002.[105]

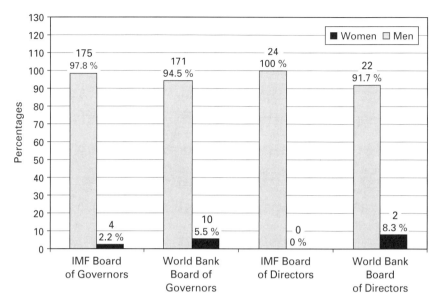

Figure A.15.
Source: Women's Environment and Development Organization. 2002. *The Numbers Speak for Themselves: Women and Economic Decision Making* [online]. [Cited 25 April 2005]. Available: http://www.wedo.org/files/numbersspeak_factsh1 .pdf.

• In 2005, there were a total of 19 women CEOs in the Fortune 1000, 9 of those heading Fortune 500 companies.[106]
• The percentage of Fortune 500 board seats held by women in 2003 was 13.6 percent, up from 12.4 percent in 2001 and 9.6 percent in 1995.[107]

In 2002, Norway's Parliament passed legislation requiring all companies to ensure that women make up 40 percent of their boards. In 2005, the Parliament announced that companies not complying with these standards by 2007 would face closure.[108]

In 48 of 63 countries surveyed by the International Labor Office, women's share of managerial jobs was between 20 and 40 percent. At the higher end of the scale was the United States at 45.9 percent and Brazil at approximately 44 percent. Saudi Arabia had the lowest percent of women "administrative and managerial workers" at 0.9 percent.[109]

Women in the Military

Percentages of women in the military, as well as their level of activity within the armed forces, vary widely from country to country. In Israel, all women and men are required to serve in the Israel Defense Force, but women serve in noncombat positions. A recent study of 26 selected countries with voluntary service showed that women made up 15 percent of the armed forces in the United States, followed by South Africa at 14.4, New Zealand at 14.7, and Australia 12.5 percent. At the low end were Ireland at 1.9 percent and Finland at 1.7 percent.[110]

In United Nations peace-keeping missions, women make up fewer than 3 percent of military personnel and 4 percent of civilian police. These percentages reflect the composition of forces contributed by UN member countries. [111]

In the United States:

• Most active-duty service women in the military are white. They constitute 70.6 percent of female officers and 48 percent of enlisted female personnel in the armed forces overall. In the Army, black women make up the largest percentage of enlisted women, while white women constitute 62.6 percent of the female officers. Enlisted Hispanic women are mostly found in the Marine Corps (17.5 percent) and the Navy (12.2 percent).[112]

Women and the Economy

Women and Poverty

Women represent 60 percent of the **world's** 550 million working poor.[113]

Worldwide, it is estimated that women constitute about 70 percent of the absolute poor—those living on less than a dollar a day.[114]

Approximately 85 percent of the world's single-parent households are headed by women, and they tend to be poorer than dual-parent or male-headed households.[115]

In the United States:

• In 2004, there were 20.1 million women in the United States living below the poverty level.[116]

• More than one-third of all female-headed households fall below the poverty line.[117] Women head 17.7 million households, or 16 percent of all American households.[118]

• Women comprise 84 percent of the homeless clients in families with the Department of Housing and Urban Development but only 23 percent of single homeless clients.[119]

• Between 2000 and 2003, the number of poor children in single-mother families increased by more than 780,000 while Temporary Aid to Needy Families caseloads fell to 253,000.[120]

• Without Social Security, more than half of all women 65 and older would be poor.[121]

Employment

In 2003, out of the 2.8 billion people worldwide working for pay, 1.1 billion were women. While female employment is on the rise, the female unemployment rate is still slightly higher than the male rate (6.4 percent, versus 6.1 percent). This means that 77.8 million women, out of a total of 160 million people, were willing to work and actively looking for work but unemployed.[122]

Differences in unemployment rates are more striking between young females (ages 15–24) and young males. In two-thirds of 97 surveyed countries, more young women than young men were unemployed, and in around half of the countries in Latin America and the Caribbean, unemployment rates for young women were more than 50 percent higher than young men's rates.[123]

Women make up between 60 and 90 percent of the world's part-time workers.[124] Women's share of part-time employment in the United States in 1998 to 2001 was 68 percent.[125]

In the United States, according to Women Employed:

• 63 percent of women work for pay
• 54 percent of women work for pay full-time
• 65 percent of African-American women work for pay
• 63 percent of white women work for pay
• 61 percent of Asian/Pacific Islander women work for pay
• 59 percent of Hispanic/Latina women work for pay[126]

Employment of Women by Sector

In developing countries, the majority of economically active women work in the informal sector—in small-scale, self-owned, usually home-based businesses that operate outside the formal economy. The World Bank estimates that in some countries this activity by women—handiwork, cooking, and other small-scale trade—accounts for 30 to 50 percent of the Gross Domestic Product. But since these businesses are so small and operate outside the formal economy, policy makers seldom take them into consideration in macroeconomic planning.[127]

In the developing world, women also make up the major share of subsistence agricultural workers.[128] Recent research from South Africa and at least 10 other countries in sub-Saharan Africa reveals that women contribute 90 percent of all food processing, water and fuel-wood collection, 90 percent of hoeing and weeding on farms, and 60 percent of harvesting and marketing.[129]

In the industrialized world, women are concentrated in traditional "women's" occupations that often offer lower pay and benefits. For example, in the United States, women ages 24–35 represented 80 percent of all workers in administrative or clerical jobs in 2000.[130]

Snapshot of women's employment in the United States, by sector:
• In 2003, 96.3 percent of secretaries and administrative assistants and 98.3 percent of preschool and kindergarten teachers were women.[131]
• In 2000, women represented 15.6 percent of law partners nationwide and 13.7 of the general counsels of Fortune 500 companies.[132]
• Although women are 46 percent of the workforce, they are about 12 percent of the scientific and engineering labor force in industry, and their representation is much lower at the highest ranks.[133]

Discrimination in the Workforce
Worldwide, women are paid less than men—on average women earn two-thirds of what men earn.[134]

In the United States:
• In 2003 the United States's Equal Employment Opportunity Commission received more than 81,000 employment-discrimination charges, the two most frequent were race based (35 percent) and sex/gender based (30 percent).[135]
• In the ten occupations with the greatest growth in female workers (veterinarians, public administrators, math/science teachers, chemistry teachers, industrial engineers, dentists, car sales people, messengers, physicians assistants, and clergy) wage gaps are either nonexistent or women earn slightly more than men for women aged 25–34 working full-time.[136]

Sex Discrimination in the 21st Century

In the United States, 2004 saw several large sexual discrimination cases brought by women workers across various sectors, from Wal-Mart and Costco to Morgan Stanley and Merrill Lynch. From the highest paid women to the lowest, sex discrimination in pay, promotion, and benefits remains at the forefront of women's struggles in the workplace.

The Wal-Mart case was initially brought by Betty Dukes, a check-out counter assistant who charged in 2001 that Wal-Mart systematically discriminates against women in pay, training, and promotion. 72 percent of Wal-Mart's associates are women, with an average wage of $7.50 an hour. In contrast, only 33 percent of Wal-Mart's managers are women. In 2004, the case became the largest civil rights class action ever certified against a private employer in the US when a federal judge ruled that women employed by Wal-Mart at anytime since 1998 were eligible to participate in the action. About 1.6 million women participants are estimated. In early 2005, Wal-Mart was in the process of appealing the class action decision.

On the other end of the scale, it was a top bond saleswoman at Morgan Stanley, Allison Schieffelin, whose case was taken up by the US Equal Employment Opportunity Commission (EEOC) as a class action for all women at Morgan Stanley in the same circumstances. They alleged that gender bias with regards to training and promotion has limited their status within the company and their pay. The case was settled immediately before trial for $54 million.

Figure A.16.
Source: Featherstone, Liza. 16 December 2002. "Wal-Mart Values." *The Nation*; U.S. Equal Employment Opportunity Commission. 12 July 2004. "EEOC and Morgan Stanley Announce Settlement of Sex Discrimination Lawsuit."

Childcare

Where childcare subsidies are available, there is a dramatic increase in labor force participation among the poor.
—The Century Foundation, 2002, www.ewowfacts.com

Working mothers with children under the age of 6 constituted, on average, 54.7 percent of all mothers with children that age. In 2001, the greatest percentage was in Scandinavia, with Sweden having the highest proportion at 76 percent. France had 59 percent, Japan 34 percent, and the United States 61 percent.[137]

Childcare in Sweden:

• The Swedish parliament determined in 1985 that all children between 18 months and school age should have access to childcare by 1991. This resulted in a highly developed childcare system that has contributed to changes in family patterns and gender roles. The proportion of women in the labor force has approached that of men, and most children in Sweden today grow up with parents who share responsibility for supporting the family.[138]

Wealth and Property Rights
Worldwide, women own only 1 percent of the world's assets.[139]

In the United States, 30 percent of women, compared with 47 percent of men, have private pensions. Women's pension benefits are, on average, less than half of men's.[140]

Land Ownership

In addition to the direct economic benefits of land ownership, property rights may serve to empower women in their negotiations with other household members and with the community and society at large.
—Food and Agriculture Organization of the United Nations[141]

A recent study suggests that women in India who own property are less likely to encounter spousal violence. The study found that nearly 49 percent of the women who owned neither land nor a house experienced long-term physical violence. Comparatively, only 18 percent of those who owned land, 10 percent who owned a house, and 7 percent who owned both, experienced such violence.[142]

In Africa, women are generally not able to own land outright or inherit land. In many African countries, this means that widows are generally denied inheritance of land, often leaving them homeless and destitute. Girl children are also denied a share of their father's inheritance, with preference given to male children.[143]

Single women in the United States buy homes at twice the rate of single men. Twenty-one percent of all first time homebuyers are single women, the second-largest group of homebuyers after married couples.[144]

Business Ownership/Access to Credit and Microfinance
Because land is used as collateral to obtain credit, many women in developing countries are barred from starting a business.[145]

Poor women often rely on micro credit, programs that provide small levels of credit or technical assistance for self-employment and other financial and business services to the very poor.

As of 2002, 2,572 micro credit institutions reported reaching 41,594,778 of the poorest individuals, 79 percent of which were women.[146]

In the United States, 10.6 million firms are majority owned by women.[147] Of these, 21.4 percent were owned by women of color.[148]

Women-owned businesses generated about $2.5 trillion in sales and employed 19.1 million people in 2004. Between 1997 and 2004, the estimated growth in the number of women-owned firms in the United States was nearly twice that of all firms—17 percent compared to 9 percent.[149]

In 2005, in the United States, the President's Fiscal Year 2006 budget proposed cutting the Small Business Administration Micro-Loan program. Fifty percent of the recipients of that funding are women.[150]

Violence Against Women and Girls

[V]iolence against women is a consequence of the gender order established in a society, of the hierarchy and power relations that characterize the relations between the sexes. While certain forms of violence are specific to regions or countries . . . a universal pattern of domination connects them all.

[G]lobally one in three women will be raped, beaten, coerced into sex or otherwise abused in her lifetime.

—The United Nations Development Fund for Women (UNIFEM)[151]

Types of Violence

Domestic Violence

In 2003, 22–33 percent of women across the world said they had experienced physical or sexual abuse by a male intimate.[152] From a mid-90s survey, the percentage of women who stated they had been battered in the past year by an intimate male partner ranged from 3 percent in Australia, Canada, and the United States to 27 percent in Nicaragua, 38 percent in the Republic of Korea, and 52 percent of Palestinian women in the West Bank and Gaza.[153]

In many countries, women believe that it is acceptable for a husband to beat a wife for one or more specific reasons—among them refusing sex, arguing, or burning food—77 percent in Uganda, 52 percent in Turkmenistan, 51 percent in Zimbabwe, 40 percent in Haiti, and 32 percent in Armenia. [154]

Forty-four countries in the world have laws specifically protecting women against domestic violence.[155]

In the United States, between one quarter and one half of domestic-violence victims report that they have lost a job as a result of, at least partly, domestic violence.[156] The annual cost of lost productivity because of domestic violence is estimated at $727.8 million, with over 7.9 million paid workdays lost each year.[157]

Rape

Rape is neither rare nor unique to a specific region in the world. Similar numbers of women have reported being the victim of an attempted or completed sexual assault over their lifetime in London, England (23 percent), León, Nicaragua (21.7 percent), and Midlands Province, Zimbabwe (25.0 percent).[158]

A 2000 United Nations survey of 70 countries across the world reported an average of 15.2 total *reported* rapes annually per 100,000 inhabitants. South Africa had the highest rate in 2000 with 123.9. In 1999 the US rate was 32.1, making it the 9th highest out of 70 countries.[159]

In the United States, the rate of rape for black women in 2002 was 4.0 rapes per 1000, while white women were victims at a rate of 1.5 and Hispanic women at a rate of 0.7 per 1000.[160]

Sites of Violence

Women in Conflict

Gender based violence in times of conflict is part of the continuum of violence that runs through women's lives, from times of peace to times of war. It only deepens with war. In all cases its origins lie in discrimination and inequality. Gender inequality is a seed that, in times of conflict, bears the bitter fruit of concerted and systematic campaigns to destroy the lives of women, families and communities.

—Noeleen Heyzer to the Security Council Open Debate on Women, Peace, and Security, October 2004.

Rape as a War Crime

From 1980 to 2002, there was systematic, widespread rape of women by soldiers or paramilitaries as part of armed conflict in 32 countries. Many of these rapes are related to ethnic persecution:

• 20,000 Muslim women were raped in Bosnia in 2001.

• 168 ethnic Chinese women were gang-raped in Indonesia in the 1998 economic crisis.

• 15,000+ women were raped in Rwanda as part of "ethnic cleansing" in 1994.[161]

Medecins Sans Frontieres (Doctors without Borders) recently reported that about 500 women have been treated for rape in recent months in Darfur, a figure nonetheless underrepresentative of the actual number. Some recent incidences include:[162]

• In January 2003, a woman was raped 14 times by different men.

• In March 2004, 150 soldiers in Janjaweed abducted and raped 16 girls.

• In Kailek, girls as young as 10 were raped by militants.[163]

Ten years ago, it was common to hear the question "Is rape a war crime?" Today, that question, symbolic of the trivialization of sexual violence against women, is settled, at least as a matter of law. The Rome Statute of the International Criminal Court recognizes "rape, sexual slavery, enforced prostitution, forced pregnancy, enforced sterilization and other sexual violence" as war crimes and, where widespread or systematic, as crimes against humanity; crimes against humanity for the first time also include gender-based persecution and trafficking as an enslavement offense.

—Rhonda Copelon, City University of New York School of Law

War-related Deaths and Injuries

Worldwide 2.6 women per 100,000 were killed by war-related injuries in 2000 compared to 7.8 men per 100,000 that same year. Africa had the highest rate of women killed by war injuries at 14.7, with the Americas and Western Pacific having the lowest rate at 0.1. The highest rate of female deaths from war injuries were in the 15–29 age group with a rate of 3.4, with the second highest age group being 0–4 year old females at a rate of 2.6. For male war-related deaths, the 0–4 age group has the second *lowest* rate, with the highest rate being the 60+ age group.[164]

Women and Landmines

In some 80 countries, women and men live with the threat of landmines. Women are particularly affected since they are the majority of the world's farmers and gatherers of food, water, and firewood. In 2003, Landmine Monitor found that roughly 15,000–20,000 landmine casualties occur each year—mainly civilians, with up to 30 percent under the age of 16. There are approximately 200 landmine casualties per month in Afghanistan, one of the most affected countries in the world. The UN Security Council resolution 1325 (2000) calls for gender considerations in its Mine Action Strategy for 2001–2005.[165]

In 1997, Jody Williams and the International Campaign to Ban Landmines (ICBL) received the Nobel Peace Prize. The ICBL represents over 1,000 groups in over 60 countries working locally, nationally, and internationally to ban antipersonnel landmines. ICBL was an important force in advocating for the convention to ban antipersonnel landmines. The Ottawa Convention (Mine Ban Treaty) was signed by more than 120 countries in December 1997.[166]

Women at the Edge

Women Refugees

Worldwide approximately 50 million people seek safety in another country or another region in their own country. Between 75 and 80 percent of refugees are women and children.[167]

An estimated 20 percent of women of reproductive age in a refugee population will be pregnant at any one time.[168] In 2000, reproductive health–related causes were listed as the leading cause of mortality among Afghan women refugees in Pakistan between the ages of 15 and 49.[169] Fifteen percent of all deaths among Burundian refugees were infant and maternal deaths, according to research conducted in Tanzania.[170]

Recent reports indicate that women and children in refugee and displaced camps in Sierra Leone, Liberia, and Guinea are particularly vulnerable to sexual abuse and exploitation by humanitarian workers.[171]

Trafficking in Women and Children

The United States' *Victims of Trafficking and Violence Protection Act 2000* defines trafficking as: "the recruitment, harboring, transportation, provision, or obtaining of a person for labor or services, through the use of force, fraud, or coercion for the purpose of subjection to involuntary servitude, peonage, debt bondage, or slavery."[172]

Estimates on the number of people trafficked internationally vary from 800,000 to nearly 4 million people annually. Experts agree, however, that women and girls are the majority of those trafficked.[173]

The following factors contribute to women's vulnerability to traffickers: feminization of poverty, sex discrimination, and lack of education or employment opportunities. These factors make it more likely for women to take risks to secure their economic well-being.[174] Unemployed single mothers are especially easy targets for traffickers.[175]

The HIV/AIDS epidemic is fueling demand for younger and younger girls, as customers try to find "safe" commercial sex partners.[176]

The powerful global reach of the Internet provides a vast space for trafficking that is unregulated and unrestricted by national borders.[177] According to UNIFEM, the trafficking and sexual exploitation of women is also "inextricably linked to conflict."[178]

In the United States, the statutory maximum sentence for dealing in ten grams of LSD or distributing a kilo of heroin is life, whereas the statutory maximum sentence for engaging in the sale of persons into involuntary servitude is ten years per count.[179]

Payment for a Woman Trafficked from Thailand	
Smuggler's Payment	$13,000–15,000
The Recruiter	$800–1,400
The Escort	$1,000
The Passport/Airline Ticket etc.	$1,500–3,000
Smuggler's Profit	$7,500–9,000

Figure A.17.
Source: Richard, Amy O'Neill. Center for the Study of Intelligence. November 1999. *International Trafficking in Women to the United States: A Contemporary Manifestation of Slavery and Organized Crime* [online]. [Cited 22 April 2005]. Available: http://www.cia.gov/csi/monograph/women/trafficking.pdf.

**Highest rates of female convicted prisoners based on
UN survey of 65 countries, selected day, 2002**

Country	Rate per 100,000 inhabitants
Maldives	104.88
United States	41.75
Belarus	25.73
Myanmar	11.39
Hungary	10.72

**Highest numbers of female convicted prisoners based on
UN survey of 65 countries, selected day, 2002**

Country	Number
United States	120,400
Myanmar	5,557
Mexico	4,697
United Kingdom	3,666
England and Wales	3,354

Figure A.18.
Source: United Nations. 2002. *The Eighth United Nations Survey on Crime Trends and the Operation of Criminal Justice Systems,* table 16.1: Total Convicted Female Prisoners [online]. [Cited 29 April 2005]. Available: http://www.unodc.org/pdf/crime/eighthsurvey/8pv.pdf.

Women in Prison

Based on a worldwide UN survey, on a single day in 2002, 65 countries had an average of 6.14 convicted female prisoners per 100,000 female inhabitants compared to 94.39 convicted male prisoners per 100,000 male inhabitants.[180]

Since 1986, the number of women in U.S. prisons has increased 400 percent. The increase is 800 percent for women of color.[181] The United Kingdom is experiencing a similar trend, with the female prison population rising by 184 percent from 1992 to 2002 with the male prison population growing by only 57 percent in the same time period. [182]

In the United States:
• Between 2002 and 2003, the number of female prisoners nationwide increased 6.3 percent, almost double the percent increase for men.[183]

• Three-fourths of the women in the criminal justice system are African-American or Latina.[184]

• The percent of female inmates who report a history of physical or sexual abuse is up to eight times the percent of male inmates who report such abuse.[185]

• Almost 23 percent of women inmates nationwide are identified as mentally ill, compared to approximately 16 percent of men.[186]

• About 37 percent of women prisoners had incomes of less than $600 per month before their arrest.[187]

Notes

1. United Nations Population Fund. 2004. *State of the World Population.* New York.

2. Coleman, Isobel. 2004. "The Payoff from Women's Rights." *Foreign Affairs,* May/June 2004, p. 80.

3. UNRISD. 2005. *Gender Equality: Striving for Justice in an Unequal World.* New York.

4. United Nations Educational, Scientific and Cultural Organization. 2003. *Education for All Global Monitoring Report 2003/4. Gender and Education for All: The Leap to Equality; Summary Report,* p. 32 [online]. New York. [Cited 20 January 24, 2005]. Available: http://www.unesco.org/education/efa_report/2003_pdf/summary_en.pdf.

5. Smith, Lisa, and Lawrence Haddad, eds. 2000. *Explaining Child Malnutrition in Developing Countries: A Cross-Country Analysis.* IFPRI Research Report 111 [online]. Washington, DC [Cited 29 April 2005]. Available: http://www.ifpri.org/pubs/abstract/111/rr111.pdf.

6. United Nations Educational, Scientific and Cultural Organization. 2005. *Education for All: The Quality Imperative. Global Monitoring Report 2005. Executive Summary,* p. 21 [online]. Paris. [Cited 29 April 2005]. Available: http://www.unesco.org/education/gmr_download/summary.pdf.

7. Seager, Joni. 2003. *The Penguin Atlas of Women in the World,* p. 76. London: Penguin Books.

8. Blanchard, Jessica. "Small Non-profit, Big Goal: Education for Afghanistan." *The Seattle Times.* 9 December 2004.

9. Meo, Nick. "The Taliban Are Gone, but Afghan Women Still Have To Be Taught in Secret." *The Independent.* 20 January 2005.

10. United Nations Educational, Scientific and Cultural Organization. 2003. *Education for All Global Monitoring Report 2003/4. Gender and Education for All: The Leap to Equality;* Summary Report, pp. 1 and 5 [online]. New York. [Cited

20 January 24, 2005]. Available: http://www.unesco.org/education/efa_report/2003_pdf/summary_en.pdf.

11. Seager, Joni. 2003. *The Penguin Atlas of Women in the World*, p. 79. London: Penguin Books.

12. United Nations Educational, Scientific and Cultural Organization. 2003. *Education for All Global Monitoring Report 2003/4. Gender and Education for All: The Leap to Equality. Summary Report*, p. 6 [online]. New York. [Cited 20 January 24, 2005]. Available: http://www.unesco.org/education/efa_report/2003_pdf/summary_en.pdf.

13. United Nations. 2000. *The World's Women 2000: Trends and Statistics*, p. 85. New York.

14. United Nations Development Programme. 2002. *Arab Development Report 2002: Creating New Opportunities for Future Generations*, pp. 152–153. New York.

15. United States Census Bureau. 2004. *Educational Attainment in the United States: 2003* p. 2 [online]. Washington, DC [Cited 29 April 2005]. Available: http://www.census.gov/prod/2004pubs/p20-550.pdf.

16. Costello, Cynthia B., Vanessa R. Wight, and Anne J. Stone. 2003. *The American Woman 2003–2004: Daughters of a Revolution—Young Women Today.* Palgrave Macmillan, p. 71. New York.

17. Seager, Joni. 2003. *The Penguin Atlas of Women in the World*, p. 80. London: Penguin Books.

18. United Nations Development Programme. 2002. *Arab Development Report 2002: Creating New Opportunities for Future Generations.* p. 152–153. New York.

19. Seager, Joni. 2003. *The Penguin Atlas of Women in the World*, p. 81. London: Penguin Books.

20. Seager, Joni. 2003. *The Penguin Atlas of Women in the World*, p. 80. London: Penguin Books.

21. United Nations. 2000. *The World's Women 2000: Trends and Statistics*, p. 92–93. New York.

22. American University Association of University Women. 2004. *Tenure Denied: Cases of Sex Discrimination in Academia.* Washington, DC.

23. Office of the High Commissioner for Human Rights. *Universal Declaration of Human Rights* [online]. [Cited 12 April 2005]. Available: http://www.unhchr.ch/udhr/lang/eng.htm.

24. National Women's Law Center. 2004. "NWLC Analysis of New Census Data Finds that Two-Thirds of Newly Uninsured Americans Are Women" [online]. [Cited 27 April 2005]. Available: http://www.nwlc.org/details.cfm?id=1989&section=newsroom.

25. National Institutes of Health, 2002. *Women of Color Health Data Book*, p. 92 [online]. [Cited 26 April 2005]. Available: http://www4.od.nih.gov/orwh/wocEnglish2002.pdf.

26. United Nations. 2000. *The World's Women 2000: Trends and Statistics*, p. 54. New York.

27. World Health Organization. 2000. "WHO Issues New Healthy Life Expectancy Rankings" [online]. [Cited 29 April 2005]. Available: http://www.who.int/inf-pr-2000/en/pr2000-life.html.

28. United Nations Population Fund. 2004. *The State of the World Population 2004*. New York. And The Population Reference Bureau. 2004. "The 2004 World Population Data Sheet." Washington, DC.

29. United Nations Population Fund. The Alan Guttmacher Institute. 2003. "Adding It Up: The Benefits of Investing in Sexual and Reproductive Health Care" [online]. New York. [Cited 25 January 2005]. Available: http://guttmacher.org/pubs/addingitup/exs_additup.pdf.

30. United Nations Population Fund. 2004. *State of the World Population Report 2004*, p. 39 [online]. New York. [Cited 25 April 2005]. Available: http://www.unfpa.org/swp/2004/english/ch6/page2.htm.

31. United Nations Millennium Project. *UN Millennium Project Reports 2005: Investing in Development*, chapter 5, p. 82 [online]. New York. [Cited 25 April 2005]. Available: http://unmillenniumproject.org/documents/MainReportChapter5-lowres.pdf.

32. The Alan Guttmacher Institute. 2005. "Facts in Brief: Contraceptive Use" [online]. New York. [Cited 25 April 2005]. Available: http://www.guttmacher.org/pubs/fb_contr_use.pdf.

33. European Parliament. 2003. "Report on the Commission Communication on Health and Poverty Reduction in Developing Countries" [online]. [Cited 27 April 2005]. Available: http://wbln0018.worldbank.org/EURVP/ABCDEApplication.nsf/0/21b0f73a142a31c1c1256d5100244d16/$FILE/Health%20and%20Poverty%20Reduction%20in%20Developing%20Countries.pdf.

34. The Alan Guttmacher Institute. 1998. *Sharing Responsibility: Women, Society, and Abortion Worldwide*, p. 25 [online]. [Cited 27 April 2005]. Available: http://www.agi-usa.org/pubs/sharing.pdf.

35. Saving Women's Lives. "Countdown 2015: Sexual and Reproductive Health and Rights for All, From Controversy to Consensus on Abortion" [online]. [Cited 17 March 2005]. Available: http://www.savingwomenslives.org/Countdownabortion.htm.

36. Saving Women's Lives. "Countdown 2015: Sexual and Reproductive Health and Rights for All, From Controversy to Consensus on Abortion" [online]. [Cited 17 March 2005]. Available: http://www.savingwomenslives.org/Countdownabortion.htm.

37. National Abortion and Reproductive Rights Action League. "State and Federal Legislation" [online]. [Cited 25 April 2005]. Available: http://www.naral.org/legislation/index.cfm.

38. Planned Parenthood Federation of America. 2004. "Abortions Bans are Unconstitutional—An Analysis of Stenberg V. Charhart" [online]. [Cited 25 April 2005]. Available: http://www.plannedparenthood.org/pp2/portal/files/portal/medicalinfo/abortion/report-abortion-ban-stenberg-carhart.xml.

39. Saving Women's Lives. "Countdown 2015: Sexual and Reproductive Health and Rights for All, From Controversy to Consensus on Abortion" [online]. [Cited 17 March 2005]. Available: http://www.savingwomenslives.org/Countdownabortion.htm.

40. World Health Organization. 5 October 2005. "WHO says Maternal Mortality Is a Silent Emergency" [online]. [Cited 27 April 2005]. Available: http://www.afro.who.int/press/2004/pr2004100502.html.

41. World Health Organization. 2003. World Health Report 2003 p. 31 [online]. [Cited 27 April 2005]. Available: http://www.who.int/whr/2003/en/whr03_en.pdf.

42. Saving Women's Lives. "Countdown 2015: Sexual and Reproductive Health and Rights for All, Improving Maternal Health, Meeting the MDG Challenges" [online]. [Cited 27 April 2005]. Available: http://www.savingwomenslives.org/Countdownmaternal.htm#end.

43. UNICEF. March 2001. Innocenti Digest: Early Marriage. No. 7, p. 18 [online]. [Cited 27 April 2005]. Available: http://www.unicef-icdc.org/publications/pdf/digest7e.pdf.

44. United Nations Population Fund. 2004. *State of the World Population 2004* [online]. [Cited 25 April 2005]. Available: http://www.unfpa.org/swp/2004/english/ch7/page4.htm.

45. Saving Women's Lives. "Countdown 2015: Sexual and Reproductive Health and Rights for All, Improving Maternal Health, Meeting the MDG Challenges" [online]. [Cited 17 March 2005]. Available: http://www.savingwomenslives.org/Countdownmaternal.htm#end.

46. Amnesty International. 2004. "Making Violence against Women Count: Facts and Figures" [online]. [Cited 27 April 2005]. Available: http://news.amnesty.org/index/ENGACT770342004. And Holland, Kitty. "Genital Mutilation Imposed on 6,000 Girls Daily." *The Irish Times.* 8 March 2005.

47. Rosenberg, Tina. "Mutilating Africa's Daughters: Laws Unenforced, Practices Unchanged." *The New York Times.* 5 July 2004.

48. Holland, Kitty. "Genital Mutilation Imposed on 6,000 Girls Daily." *The Irish Times.* 8 March 2005.

49. Rosenberg, Tina. "Mutilating Africa's Daughters: Laws Unenforced, Practices Unchanged." *The New York Times.* 5 July 2004.

50. Hanson, Jane O. "Ancient Rite or Wrong?; Genital Cutting of Girls Becomes an Issue in Georgia, Nationwide." *The Atlanta Journal Constitution.* 2 March 2005.

51. Hanson, Jane O. "Ancient Rite or Wrong?; Genital Cutting of Girls Becomes an Issue in Georgia, Nationwide." *The Atlanta Journal Constitution.* 2 March 2005.

52. UNIFEM. 2004. *Women and AIDS: Confronting the Crisis* [online]. New York. [Cited 3 February 2005]. Available: http://www.unfpa.org/upload/lib_pub_file/308_filename_women_aids1.pdf.

53. UNIFEM. 2004. *Women and AIDS: Confronting the Crisis* [online]. New York. [Cited 27 April 2005]. Available: http://www.unfpa.org/upload/lib_pub_file/308_filename_women_aids1.pdf.

54. UNIFEM. 2004. *Women and AIDS: Confronting the Crisis*, p. 16 [online]. New York. [Cited 27 April 2005]. Available: http://www.unfpa.org/upload/lib_pub_file/308_filename_women_aids1.pdf.

55. United Nations Populations Fund. "Overcoming Gender Disparities" [online]. [Cited 27 April 2005]. Available: http://www.unfpa.org/adolescents/gender.htm.

56. Planned Parenthood. 2003. "A Planned Parenthood Report on Administration and Congress: The Bush Administration, The Global Gag Rule, and HIV/AIDS Funding" [online]. [Cited 27 April 2005]. Available: http://www.plannedparenthood.org/pp2/portal/files/portal/medicalinfo/abortion/report-030702-AIDS.pdf.

57. Alan Guttmacher Institute. December 2003. Beyond Slogans: Lessons from Uganda's ABC Experience [online]. [Cited 27 April 2005]. Available: http://www.agi-usa.org/pubs/ib2004no2.html.

58. International Labor Organization. 2004. "Women, Girls, HIV/AIDS and the World of Work" [online]. [Cited 27 April 2005]. Available: http://www.ilo.org/public/english/protection/trav/aids/publ/women-iloaids-brief.pdf.

59. UNIFEM. 2004. *Women and AIDS: Confronting the Crisis* [online]. New York. [Cited 27 April 2005]. Available: http://www.unfpa.org/upload/lib_pub_file/308_filename_women_aids1.pdf.

60. Africa AIDS Watch. 2002. "Cold Statistics" [online]. [Cited 27 April 2005]. Available: http://www.africaaidswatch.org/cold%20stats.htm.

61. International Labor Organization. 2004. "Women, Girls, HIV/AIDS and the World of Work" [online]. [Cited 27 April 2005]. Available: http://www.ilo.org/public/english/protection/trav/aids/publ/women-iloaids-brief.pdf.

62. Kaiser Family Foundation. October 22, 2004. *Kaiser Daily HIV/AIDS Report.*

63. Centers for Disease Control and Prevention. 2003. "HIV/AIDS among Women" [online]. [Cited 27 April 2005]. Available: http://www.cdc/gov/hiv/pubs/facts/women.htm.

64. Centers for Disease Control and Prevention. 2003. "HIV/AIDS among Women" [online]. [Cited 27 April 2005]. Available: http://www.cdc/gov/hiv/pubs/facts/women.htm.

65. Centers for Disease Control and Prevention. 2003. "HIV/AIDS among Women" [online]. [Cited 27 April 2005]. Available: http://www.cdc/gov/hiv/pubs/facts/women.htm.

66. Altman, Lawrence K. "Female Cases of H.I.V. Found Rising Worldwide." *The New York Times.* 24 November 2004.

67. WaterAid. "Women's Problems" [online]. [Cited 29 April 2005]. Available: http://www.wateraid.org.uk/other/TextOnly/?ContentID=241&FontSize=0.

68. Women's Environment and Development Organization. "Gender Differences in Water Use and Management" [online]. [Cited 29 April 2005]. Available: http://

www.wedo.org/files/untapped_eng.pdf. And Food and Agriculture Organization of the United Nations. "Women and Water Resources" [online]. [Cited 29 April 2005]. Available: http://www.fao.org/focus/e/women/Water-e.htm.

69. UNIFEM. April 2004. *Women and Water* [online]. [Cited 12 April 2005]. Available: http://www.unifem.org/filesconfirmed/2/351_at_a_glance_water_rights.pdf.

70. World Health Organization. August 2004. "World Facing Silent Emergency As Billions Struggle without Clean Water or Basic Sanitation, Says WHO and UNICEF" [online]. [Cited 29 April 2005]. Available: http://www.who.int/mediacentre/news/releases/2004/pr58/en/.

71. WaterAid. "Women's Problems" [online]. [Cited 29 April 2005]. Available: http://www.wateraid.org.uk/other/TextOnly/?ContentID=241&FontSize=0.

72. Women's Environment and Development Organization. "Gender Differences in Water Use and Management" [online]. [Cited 29 April 2005]. Available: http://www.wedo.org/files/untapped_eng.pdf.

73. Seager, Joni. 2003. *The Penguin Atlas of Women in the World*, p. 46. London: Penguin Books.

74. Seager, Joni. 2003. *The Penguin Atlas of Women in the World*. London: Penguin Books.

75. World Health Organization. 2001. *Women and the Tobacco Epidemic: Challenges for the 21st Century* [online]. [Cited 28 April 2005]. Available: http://www.who.int/tobacco/media/en/WomenMonograph.pdf.

76. World Health Organization. November 2003. "Gender, Health and Tobacco" [online]. [Cited 27 April 2005]. Available: http://www.who.int/gender/documents/en/Gender_Tobacco_2.pdf.

77. Pountey, Michelle. "Addicted to Death; Study Reveals Chilling New Smoking Stats." *Herald Sun.* 27 November 2004.

78. International Network of Women Against Tobacco. 5 August 2003. "A Women's Smoking Crisis Set to Devastate the Developing World." Sweden.

79. International Network of Women Against Tobacco. 5 August 2003. "A Women's Smoking Crisis Set to Devastate the Developing World." Sweden.

80. *The Guardian.* 1 February 2005. "Cigarettes Harm Women More."

81. World Health Organization. November 2003. "Gender, Health, and Tobacco" [online]. [Cited 27 April 2005]. Available: http://www.who.int/gender/documents/en/Gender_Tobacco_2.pdf.

82. American Cancer Society. 2004. "What Are the Key Statistics for Lung Cancer?" [online]. [Cited 27 April 2005]. Available: http://www.cancer.org/docroot/cri/content/cri_2_4_1x_what_are_the_key_statistics_for_lung_cancer_26.asp.

83. American Cancer Society. 2004. "What Are the Key Statistics for Breast Cancer?" [online]. [Cited 27 April 2005]. Available: http://www.cancer.org/docroot/CRI/content/CRI_2_4_1X_What_are_the_key_statistics_for_breast_cancer_5.asp?sitearea=&level=.

84. "Lung Cancer in U.S. Women: A Contemporary Epidemic" [online]. *Journal of the American Medical Association.* vol. 291, no. 14. 14 April 2004. [Cited 28 April 2005]. Available: http://www.inwat.org/pdf/Patel%20-%20women %20and%20Lung%20cancer.pdf.

85. "Lung Cancer in U.S. Women: A Contemporary Epidemic" [online]. *Journal of the American Medical Association.* vol. 291, no. 14. 14 April 2004. [Cited 28 April 2005]. Available: http://www.inwat.org/pdf/Patel%20-%20women %20and%20Lung%20cancer.pdf.

86. Seager, Joni. 2003. *The Penguin Atlas of Women in the World.* London: Penguin Books.

87. "Saudi Arabians Go to Polls Sans Women," *San Francisco Chronicle.* February 8, 2005. "Saudi Women Barred from Voting." BBC News. October 11, 2004.

88. "Kuwait Hastens Women's Vote Bill." BBC news. March 7, 2005.

89. Seager, Joni. 2003. *The Penguin Atlas of Women in the World.* London: Penguin Books.

90. Global News Wire. "Afghan Elections and After." *Financial Times.* October 25, 2004.

91. CNN News. *Election 2004* [online]. [Cited 11 January 2005]. Available: http://www.cnn.com/ELECTION/2004/pages/results/states/US/P/00/epolls.0.html.

92. Women's Learning Partnership. 2004. *Facts and Figures: Leadership* [online]. [Cited 11 January 2005]. Available: http://learningpartnership.org/facts/leadership .phtml#political.

93. Inter-Parliamentary Union. 2000. *Politics: Women's Insights.* Geneva and New York.

94. Inter-Parliamentary Union. 2005. *Women in National Parliaments* [online] [Cited 27 April 2005]. Available: http://www.ipu.org/wmn-e/world.htm.

95. Inter-Parliamentary Union. 2005. *Women in National Parliaments* [online] [Cited 27 April 2005]. Available: http://www.ipu.org/wmn-e/classif.htm.

96. Inter-Parliamentary Union. 2005. *Women in National Parliaments* [online] [Cited 27 April 2005]. Available: http://www.ipu.org/wmn-e/classif.htm.

97. Center for American Women and Politics, Rutgers University. March 2005. *Women in Elective Office 2005* [online]. [Cited 12 April 2005]. Available: http://www.cawp.rutgers.edu/Facts/Officeholders/elective.pdf.

98. United Nations Development Fund. 2002. *Quotable Facts: Human Development Trends.* [online]. [Cited 12 April 2005]. Available: http://www.undp.org/ hdr2002/facts.html.

99. Women's Learning Partnership. 2004. *Facts and Figures: Leadership* [online]. [Cited 11 January 2005]. Available: http://learningpartnership.org/facts/leadership .phtml#political).

100. *International Labor Office. 2004.* Breaking through the Glass Ceiling: Women in Management Update, p. 26 [online]. [Cited 27 April 2005]. Available: http://www .ilo.org/dyn/gender/docs/RES/292/F267981337/Breaking%20Glass%20PDF %20English.pdf.

101. International Labor Office. 2004. *Breaking through the Glass Ceiling: Women in Management Update*, p. 24 [online]. [Cited 27 April 2005]. Available: http://www.ilo.org/dyn/gender/docs/RES/292/F267981337/Breaking%20Glass %20PDF%20English.pdf.

102. Seager, Joni. 2003. *The Penguin Atlas of Women in the World*, p. 91. London: Penguin Books.

103. United Nations Secretariat, Office of the Special Advisor on Gender Issues and Advancement of Women. 31 December 2004. *The Status of Women in the United Nations* [online]. [Cited 27 April 2005]. Available: http://www.un.org/ womenwatch/osagi/fpgenderbalancestats.htm.

104. Catalyst Women. 2002. *Catalyst Census of Women Corporate Officers and Top Earners in the Fortune 500*. [online]. [Cited 25 April 2005]. Available: http://www.catalystwomen.org/knowledge/titles/files/fact/COTE%20Factsheet %202002updated.pdf.

105. Catalyst Women. 2002. *2002 Catalyst Census of Women Corporate Officers and Top Earners in the Fortune 500* [online]. [Cited 27 April 2005]. Available: http://www.catalystwomen.org/knowledge/titles/files/fact/COTE%20Factsheet %202002updated.pdf.

106. *The 2005 Fortune 500: Women CEOs* [online]. *Fortune Magazine*. 18 April 2005. [Cited 27 April 2005]. Available: http://www.fortune.com/fortune/fortune500/ articles/0,15114,1046096,00.html).

107. *Catalyst Women. 2003.* 2003 Catalyst Census of Women Board Directors: A Call to Action in and Era of Corporate Governance [online]. [Cited 12 January 2005]. Available: http://www.catalystwomen.org/knowledge/titles/files/fact/ WBD03factsheetfinal.pdf.

108. CNN International. 6 April 2005. "Women Forced onto Norway Boards" [online]. [Cited 11 April 2005]. Available: http://edition.cnn.com/2005/WORLD/ europe/04/05/norway.women.reut/.

109. International Labor Office. 2004. *Breaking through the Glass Ceiling: Women in Management Update*, p. 2 [online]. [Cited 28 April 2005]. Available: http://www.ilo.org/dyn/gender/docs/RES/292/F267981337/Breaking%20Glass %20PDF%20English.pdf.

110. Women's Research and Education Institute. *Women in the Military Project: Selected Countries Where Women Serve in the Military.* [online]. [Cited 26 April 2005]. Available: http://www.wrei.org/projects/wiu/wim/T7.pdf.

111. Seager, Joni. 2003. *The Penguin Atlas of Women in the World*, p. 101. London: Penguin Books.

112. Women's Research and Education Institute. *Women in the Military: Selected Statistics*, table 3 [online]. [Cited 26 April 2005]. Available: http://www.wrei.org/ projects/wiu/wim/index.htm.

113. International Labor Organization. 2004. *Global Employment Trends for Women*, p. 4 [online]. [Cited 26 April 2005]. Available: http://www.ilo.org/ public/english/employment/strat/download/trendsw.pdf.

114. International Labor Organization. 2004. *Facts on Women at Work.* [online]. [Cited 25 April 2005]. Available: http://www.ilo.org/public/english/bureau/inf/download/women/pdf/factssheet.pdf. (Although this statistic is widely quoted, it is important to note that a lack of gender disaggregated data means that there is no real way of knowing what the percentage of women's poverty compared to men's actually is worldwide. See Institute of Development Studies. April 2001. BRIDGE *Briefing Paper on the "Feminisation of Poverty"* [online]. Available: http://www.bridge.ids.ac.uk/reports/femofpov.pdf.)

115. Seager, Joni. 2003. *The Penguin Atlas of Women in the World*, pp. 20–21. London: Penguin Books.

116. Moving Ideas. 15 March 20005. "Special Report: Beijing +10 U.S. Record Here and Abroad" [online]. [Cited 26 April 2005]. Available: http://www.movingideas.org/content/en/report_content/beijing10.htm.

117. Women's Learning Partnership. 2004. *Facts and Figures: Leadership* [online]. [Cited 25 April 2005]. Available: http://learningpartnership.org/facts/leadership.phtml#political).

118. *Consumer Federation of America. 2004.* Research Shows That Women On Their Own Face Financial Challenges. January 12, 2004. Available: http://www.consumerfed.org/womenfinance.pdf.

119. U.S. Department of Housing and Urban Development. 1999. *Demographic Characteristics of Homeless Clients* [online]. [Cited 27 April 2005]. Available: http://www.huduser.org/publications/homeless/homelessness/ch_2b.html.

120. Center on Budget and Policy Priorities. 2004. *Unemployment Insurance Does Not Explain Why TANF Caseloads Are Falling As Poverty and Need Are Rising* [online]. [Cited 25 April 2005]. Available: http://www.cbpp.org/10-12-04tanf.htm.

121. National Women's Law Center. 2005. *Social Security: Women, Children, and the States*, p. 2 [online]. [Cited 25 April 2005]. Available: http://www.nwlc.org/pdf/sswomen&states2005.pdf.

122. International Labor Organization. 2004. *Global Employment Trends for Women*, p. 4 [online]. [Cited 26 April 2005]. Available: http://www.ilo.org/public/english/employment/strat/download/trendsw.pdf.

123. United Nations. 2004. *World Youth Report 2003: The Global Situation of Young People*, p. 63 [online]. [Cited 25 April 2005]. Available: http://www.un.org/esa/socdev/unyin/wyr03.htm.

124. International Labor Organization. 2004. *Facts on Women at Work.* [online]. [Cited 25 April 2005]. Available: http://www.ilo.org/public/english/bureau/inf/download/women/pdf/factssheet.pdf.

125. International Labor Organization. 2003. *Key Indicators of the Labor Market*, 3rd Ed., Geneva [online]. [Cited 25 April 2005]. Available: http://www.ilo.org/public/english/employment/strat/kilm/kilm05.htm.

126. Women Employed. 2004. *Facts about Working Women.* [online]. [Cited 26 April 2005]. Available: http://www.womenemployed.org/docs/Facts%20about%20Working%20Women.pdf.

127. United Nations. 2000. *The World's Women 2000 Trends and Statistics*, p. 126. And Women in Informal Employment Globalizing and Organizing. *Fact Sheets: The Informal Economy* [online]. [Cited 26 April 2005]. Available: http://www.wiego.org/main/fact1.shtml.

128. International Labor Organization. *The Feminization of Poverty* [online]. [Cited 26 April 2005]. Available: http://www.ilo.org/public/english/bureau/inf/pkits/women3.htm).

129. *United Nations Development Fund for Women. 2002.* Progress of the World's Women 2002, p. 51 [online]. [Cited 27 April 2005]. Available: http://www.unifem.org/index.php?f_page_pid=10.

130. Women's Research and Education Institute. 2004. *The American Woman 2003–2004*, p. 76. Palgrave Macmillan.

131. U.S. Department of Labor, Women's Bureau. 2003. *20 Leading Occupations of Employed Women 2003* [online]. [Cited 26 April 2005]. Available: http://www.dol.gov/wb/factsheets/20lead2003_txt.htm.

132. Catalyst. 2001. *Women in Law: Making the Case* [online]. [Cited 26 April 2005]. Available: http://www.catalystwomen.org/pressroom/press_releases/women _in_law.htm.

133. Catalyst. 1999. *Women Scientists in Industry: A Winning Formula for Companies.*

134. International Labor Organization. 2004. *Facts on Women at Work* [online]. [Cited 26 April 2005]. Available: http://www.ilo.org/public/english/bureau/inf/download/women/pdf/factssheet.

135. Di Tulio, A., and T. Padagano. "Diversity at Work." *Working Mother,* June 2004, p. 49, cited in Evangelina Holvino and Stacy Blake-Beard, "Women Discussing Their Differences: A Promising Trend," *The Diversity Factor,* vol. 12, no. 2, summer 2004 [online]. [Cited 26 April 2005]. Available: http://www.simmons .edu/som/cgo/tdfarticle2004.pdf.

136. Economic Policy Foundation 2001, cited in *Women's Research and Education Institute: The American Woman 2003–2004,* p. 146. 2004. Palgrave Macmillan.

137. Organisation for Economic Co-operation and Development, cited in Nation Master. 2003 [online]. [Cited 25 April 2005]. Available: http://www.nationmaster .com/graph-T/lab_wor_mot#.

138. Swedish Institute. *Child Care in Sweden* [online]. [Cited 25 April 2005]. Available: http://www.sweden.se/templates/cs/BasicFactsheet_4132.aspx.

139. Women's Learning Partnership. 2004. *Facts and Figures: Leadership* [online]. [Cited 25 April 2005]. Available: http://www.learningpartnership.org/facts/leadership.phtml?slashSess=dcc23e435513caae68cdcb34565b082f.

140. Institute for Women's Policy Research. 2005. *Social Security and Women Website.*[Cited 25 April 2005]. Available: www.socialsecurityandwomen.org.

141. Food and Agriculture Organization of the United Nations. 2003. *Food, Agriculture, and Rural Development: Current and Emerging Issues for Economic Analysis and Policy Research,* (CUREMIS II) volume I: Latin America and the

Caribbean [online]. Available: http://www.fao.org/documents/show_cdr.asp?url _file=/DOCREP/006/Y4940E/Y4940E00.HTM.

142. InfoChange News & Features. August 2003 [online]. [Cited 25 April 2005]. Available: http://www.infochangeindia.org/bookandreportsst44.jsp.

143. COHRE. 2004. "Inadequate Inheritance Rights for Women Contribute to Spread of HIV/AIDS." *Africa Housing Rights Bulletin,* vol. 1, no. 2, March [online]. [Cited 25 April 2005]. Available: http://www.cohre.org/library/COHRE _March2004.pdf.

144. National Association of Realtors. 15 July 2003. *New NAR Survey of Home Buyers and Sellers Shows Growing Web Use in a Dynamic Housing Market* [online]. [Cited 27 April 2005]. Available: http://www.realtor.org/publicaffairsweb .nsf/Pages/NewSurveyBuyersandSellers03?OpenDocument.

145. Duddy, J. 11 June 2004. "How Are Land Ownership Laws Changing for Women?" Association for Women's Rights in Development, *Resource Net Friday File,* issue 181.

146. Daley-Harris, Sam. *State of the Microcredit Summit Campaign Report 2003,* p. 3 [online]. [Cited 27 April 2005]. Available: http://www.microcreditsummit .org/pubs/reports/socr/2003/SOCR03-E[txt].pdf. (The poorest families were those who were in the bottom half of those living below their nation's poverty line, or any of the 1.2 billion who live on less than $1 a day adjusted for purchasing power parity (PPP), when they started with a program.)

147. Center for Women's Business Research. 2003. *Top Facts about Women-Owned Businesses* [online]. [Cited 27 April 2005]. Available: http://www .womensbusinessresearch.org/topfacts.html.

148. Center for Women's Business Research. 2004. *Businesses Owned by Women of Color in the United States, 2004* [online]. [Cited 27 April 2005]. Available: http://www.womensbusinessresearch.org/minority/BusinessesOwnedbyWomenof ColorintheUS.pdf.

149. Center for Women's Business Research. 2003. *Top Facts about Women-Owned Businesses* [online]. [Cited 27 April 2005]. Available: http://www .womensbusinessresearch.org/topfacts.html.

150. Olson, Elizabeth. "Fears for a Program That Lends Just a Little: Budget Cuts Imperil S.B.A.'s Microloans." *The New York Times.* 17 March 2005.

151. United Nations Development Fund for Women. 2003. *Not a Minute More: Ending Violence against Women,* pp. 6, 17 [online]. [Cited 22 April 2005]. Available: http://www.unifem.org/index.php?f_page_pid=207.

152. Seager, Joni. 2003. *The Penguin Atlas of Women in the World,* p. 26. London: Penguin Books.

153. World Health Organization. 2002. *World Report on Violence and Health,* chapter 4: Violence by Intimate Partners, p. 89 [online]. [Cited 22 April 2005]. Available: http://www.who.int/violence_injury_prevention/violence/world_report/ wrvheng/en/.

154. Seager, Joni. 2003. *The Penguin Atlas of Women in the World*, p. 27. London: Penguin Books.

155. United Nations High Commission on Refugees. April 2002. "Women Seeking a Better Deal." *Refugees Magazine*, vol. 1, no. 126 [online]. [Cited 27 April 2005]. Available: http://www.unhcr.ch/cgi-bin/texis/vtx/home/opendoc.htm?tbl= MEDIA&id=3cb6ea290&page=publ.

156. Legal Momentum. October 2003. *Fact Sheet: Security and Financial Empowerment Act "SAFE"* [online]. [Cited 28 April 2005]. Available: http:// www.legalmomentum.org/issues/vio/SAFEFactSheet.pdf.

157. Centers for Disease Control. 2003. *Costs of Intimate Partner Violence against Women in the United States* [online]. [Cited 29 April 2005]. Available: http://www.cdc.gov/ncipc/pub-res/ipv_cost/IPVBook-Final-Feb18.pdf.

158. World Health Organization. *World Report on Violence and Health*, chapter 6: Sexual Violence, p. 152. [online]. [Cited 27 April 2005]. Available: http:// www.who.int/violence_injury_prevention/violence/world_report/wrvheng/en/)

159. United Nations Office of Drugs and Crime. 2000. *The Seventh United Nations Survey on Crime Trends and the Operation of Criminal Justice Systems*, table 02.08: Total Recorded Rapes [online]. [Cited 22 April 2005]. Available: http:// www.unodc.org/pdf/crime/seventh_survey/7pv.pdf.

160. Bureau of Justice Statistics. December 2003. *Criminal Victimization in the United States, 2002*, tables 6 and 8 [online]. [Cited 27 April 2005]. Available: http://www.ojp.usdoj.gov/bjs/pub/pdf/cvus0201.pdf.

161. Seager, Joni. 2003. *The Penguin Atlas of Women in the World*, p. 99. London: Penguin Books.

162. "500 Rapes Documented in Darfur." *The Irish Times*. 8 March 2005.

163. Polgreen, Linda. "Darfur's Babies of Rape Are on Trial from Birth." *The New York Times*. 11 February 2005.

164. World Health Organization. 2003. *World Report on Violence and Health*, Statistical Annex, pp. 282–285 [online]. [Cited 28 April 2005]. Available: http:// www.who.int/violence_injury_prevention/violence/world_report/wrvheng/en/.

165. United Nations Development Fund for Women. 2004. *Issue Brief on Landmines* [online]. [Cited 27 April 2005]. Available: http://www.womenwarpeace .org/issues/landmines/landmines_pfv.pdf.

166. NobelPrize.org. 1997. [Cited 22 April 2005]. Available: http://nobelprize.org/ peace/laureates/1997/icbl-history.html

167. United Nations High Commission on Refugees. April 2002. "Women Seeking a Better Deal." *Refugees Magazine*, vol. 1, no. 126 [online]. [Cited 27 April 2005]. Available: http://www.unhcr.ch/cgi-bin/texis/vtx/home/opendoc.htm?tbl= MEDIA&id=3cb6ea290&page=publ.

168. Cited by Reproductive Health Response in Conflict Consortium. November 2004. *General Reproductive Health* [online]. [Cited 27 April 2005]. Available: http://www.rhrc.org/rhr_basics/rh/#11.

169. Cited by Reproductive Health Response in Conflict Consortium. November 2004. *General Reproductive Health* [online]. [Cited 27 April 2005]. Available: http://www.rhrc.org/rhr_basics/rh/#11.

170. Jamieson, D. J. et al. 2000. "An Evaluation of Poor Pregnancy Outcomes among Burundian Refugees in Tanzania." *Journal of the American Medical Association*, vol. 28, no. 3, pp. 397–402.

171. Amnesty International. March 1 2004. *Violence Against Women* [online]. [Cited 27 April 2005]. Available: http://web.amnesty.org/library/pdf/IOR410042004ENGLISH/$File/IOR4100404.pdf.

172. 106th Congress of the United States of America. Second Session 2000. *Trafficking Victims Protection Act* [online]. [Cited 22 April 2005]. Available: http://www.state.gov/documents/organization/10492.pdf.

173. UNIFEM. *Issue Brief on Trafficking: Fact Sheet* [online]. [Cited 22 April 2005] Available: http://www.womenwarpeace.org/issues/trafficking/trafficking.htm#fact.

174. UNIFEM. *Issue Brief on Trafficking: Fact Sheet* [online]. [Cited 22 April 2005] Available: http://www.womenwarpeace.org/issues/trafficking/trafficking.htm#fact.

175. Carpenter, Katherine. January 2003. "Trafficking: A New War on Women" cited in The Zontian. *Globalization and Gender Inequalities*. p. 4. [online]. Available: http://www.zonta.org/site/DocServer/ZontianJan.pdf?docID=878.

176. Seager, Joni. 2003. *The Penguin Atlas of Women in the World,* p. 56-57. London: Penguin Books.

177. Carpenter, Katherine. January 2003. "Trafficking: A New War on Women" cited in "Globalization and Gender Inequalities." *The Zontian,* p. 4. [online]. Available: http://www.zonta.org/site/DocServer/ZontianJan.pdf?docID=878.

178. UNIFEM. *Issue Brief on Trafficking: Fact Sheet* [online]. [Cited 22 April 2005] Available: http://www.womenwarpeace.org/issues/trafficking/trafficking.htm#fact.

179. Richard, Amy O'Neill. Center for the Study of Intelligence. November 1999. *International Trafficking in Women to the United States: A Contemporary Manifestation of Slavery and Organized Crime* [online]. [Cited 22 April 2005]. Available: http://www.cia.gov/csi/monograph/women/trafficking.pdf.

180. United Nations. 2002. *The Eighth United Nations Survey on Crime Trends and the Operation of Criminal Justice Systems,* table 16.1: Total Convicted Female Prisoners [online]. [Cited 29 April 2005]. Available: http://www.unodc.org/pdf/crime/eighthsurvey/8pv.pdf.

181. Moyers, Bill. "Women, Prison, and Children" [online]. Public Broadcasting Station: NOW. 21 May 2004. [Cited 29 April 2005]. Available: www.pbs.org/now/society/womenprisoners.html.

182. Councell, Rachel. 2002. "The Prison Population in 2002: A Statistical Review" [online]. Britain's Home Office Report. [Cited 29 April 2005]. Available: http://www.official-documents.co.uk/document/cm59/5996/5996.pdf.

183. Harrison, Paige M., and Jennifer C. Karberg. Bureau of Justice Statistics, U.S. Department of Justice. May 2004. Prison and Jail Inmates at Midyear 2003 found in the Women in Prison Project, Correctional Association of New York. March 2005. "Women in Prison Fact Sheet" [online]. [Cited 29 April 2005]. Available: http://correctionalassociation.org/WIPP/publications/Women_in_Prison_Fact _Sheet_2005.pdf.

184. Mullings, Leith. March 2004. "Domestic Policy and Human Security in the US." *Peace Review,* vol. 16, no .1, pp. 57, 55.

185. Snell, Tracy L., and Denielle C. Morton. Bureau of Justice Statistics, U.S. Department of Justice. 1991. *Women in Prison, Surveys of State Inmates, 1991* found in the Women in Prison Project, Correctional Association of New York. March 2005. "Women in Prison Fact Sheet" [online]. [Cited 29 April 2005]. Available: http://correctionalassociation.org/WIPP/publications/Women_in_Prison_Fact _Sheet_2005.pdf.

186. Ditton, Paula. Bureau of Justice Statistics, U.S. Department of Justice. July 1999. *Mental Health and Treatment of Inmates and Probationers* found in the Women in Prison Project, Correctional Association of New York. March 2005. "Women in Prison Fact Sheet" [online]. [Cited 29 April 2005]. Available: http:// correctionalassociation.org/WIPP/publications/Women_in_Prison_Fact_Sheet_2005 .pdf.

187. Greenfield, Lawrence A., and Tracy L. Snell. Bureau of Justice Statistics, U.S. Department of Justice. 2000. *Women Offenders* found in the Women in Prison Project, Correctional Association of New York. March 2005. "Women in Prison Fact Sheet" [online]. [Cited 29 April 2005]. Available: http://correctionalassociation .org/WIPP/publications/Women_in_Prison_Fact_Sheet_2005.pdf.

Appendix B
Metasites

These Web sites contain links to other Web sites and resources for demographics, statistical results, and other information about women, girls, gender, and deep diversity.

- Association of College and Research Libraries Women's Studies Section Core Lists in Women's Studies
  www.library.wisc.edu/libraries/WomensStudies/core/coremain.htm
- National Council for Research on Women
  www.ncrw.org
- National Council of Women's Organizations
  www.womensorganizations.org
- Routledge International Encyclopedia of Women's Studies
  www.routledge-ny.com/women/entries/a-e.html
- University of Maryland Baltimore County Women's Studies Online Resources
  www.research.umbc.edu/~korenman/wmst
- University of Maryland Baltimore County The Center for Women and Information Technology
  www.umbc.edu/cwit
- University of Wisconsin Women's Studies Librarian
  www.library.wisc.edu/libraries/WomensStudies

Appendix C
Selected Links

Arranged by topic, this section provides additional links to demographics, up-to-date statistical results, and other research findings related to the lives of women and girls. For more comprehensive links to a wide range of research and policy centers within all of these topic areas and more, see the metasites in appendix B.

Aging and Older Women

- American Association of Retired Persons
  www.aarp.org/research
- Brandeis University National Center on Women and Aging
  www.heller.brandeis.edu/national/index.html
- National Center for Policy Research for Women and Families
  www.center4research.org
- Older Women's League
  www.owl-national.org
- Society for Women's Health Research
  www.womenshealthresearch.org
- Women & Social Security, Institute for Women's Policy Research
  www.womenandsocialsecurity.com/Women_Social_Security

Arts

- Guerrilla Girls
  www.guerrillagirls.com
- Women in the Arts
  www.wiaonline.org

Child Care

- Child Care Bureau
  www.acf.dhhs.gov/programs/ccb
- Child Welfare League of America
  www.cwla.org
- Families and Work Institute
  www.familiesandwork.org
- International Association for Feminist Economics
  www.iaffe.org
- Legal Momentum
  www.legalmomentum.org
- National Child Care Information Center
  www.nccic.org
- National Women's Law Center
  www.nwlc.org/
- Wellesley Centers for Women
  www.wcwonline.org/
- Women and Economy Project, U.N. Platform for Action Committee
  www.unpac.ca

Communications and Media

- About-Face
  www.about-face.org
- Association for Women in Communications
  www.womcom.org
- Aviva
  www.aviva.org
- FAIR Women's Desk
  www.fair.org/womens-desk.html
- Femina
  www.femina.com
- Feminist International Radio Endeavor in Internet
  www.fire.or.cr/indexeng.htm

- Harvard University Women and Public Policy Program at the John F. Kennedy School of Government
  www.ksg.harvard.edu/wappp
- International Women's Tribune Center
  www.iwtc.org
- Journalism & Women Symposium
  www.jaws.org
- Media Report to Women
  www.mediareporttowomen.com
- Mediachannel Issues Guide on Women's Media
  www.mediachannel.org/atissue/womensmedia
- Scribbling Women, A Project of the Public Media
  www.scribblingwomen.org
- University of Pennsylvania Annenberg School for Communication, Public Policy Center
  www.annenbergpublicpolicycenter.org
- Wellesley Centers for Women
  www.wcwonline.org
- White House Project
  www.thewhitehouseproject.org
- Women Make Movies
  www.wmm.com
- Women's Enews
  www.womensenews.org

Deep Diversity

- All India Democratic Women Association
  www.aidwa.org
- Applied Research Center
  www.arc.org
- Asian Nation
  www.asian-nation.org/links4.shtml#Research
- Association for Women's Rights in Development
  www.awid.org

- Chaos Management Ltd.
  www.chaosmanagement.com
- Curricular Crossings: Area Studies and Women's Studies
  www.womencrossing.org
- Database for Expertise on Gender, Ethnicity in European Curriculum
  www.iiav.nl/horizons
- DiversityInc
  www.diversityinc.com
- DiversityWeb
  www.diversityweb.org
- Diversity Initiative of Third Sector New England
  www.diversityinitiative.org
- National Council of La Raza
  www.nclr.org
- National Urban League
  www.nul.org
- Native American Sites
  www.nativeculturelinks.com/indians.html
- Sisterhood Is Global Institute
  www.sigi.org
- Society for Organizational Learning
  www.solonline.org
- U.S. Census Bureau
  www.factfinder.census.gov
- U.S. Department of State, Diversity in the United States
  www.usinfo.state.gov/usa/diversity
- U.S. Equal Employment Opportunity Commission
  www.eeoc.gov/facts/fs-race.html
- Women and Diversity Wow! Facts
  www.ewowfacts.com
- Women of Color Resource Center
  www.coloredgirls.org
- Women of Color Web
  www.hsph.harvard.edu/grhf/WoC

- World Conference Against Racism
  www.un.org/WCAR
- WWW Virtual Library—American Indians, Index of Native American History Resources on the Internet
  www.hanksville.org/NAresources/indices/NAhistory.html

Economic Development

- Association for Women's Rights in Development
  www.awid.org
- Femina
  www.femina.com
- Feminist Majority Foundation
  www.feminist.org
- Harvard University Women and Public Policy Program at the John F. Kennedy School of Government
  www.ksg.harvard.edu/wappp
- Institute for Women's Policy Research
  www.iwpr.org
- International Association for Feminist Economics
  www.iaffe.org
- International Center for Research on Women
  www.icrw.org
- International Women's Tribune Center
  www.iwtc.org
- National Women's Law Center
  www.nwlc.org
- U.S. Census Bureau
  www.census.gov
- Women and Economy Project, U.N. Platform for Action Committee
  www.unpac.ca
- Women in the Economy
  www.womenintheeconomy.org
- World Bank
  www.worldbank.org

Education

- American Association of University Women
  www.aauw.org
- American Council on Education Office of Women in Higher Education
  www.acenet.edu
- Association of American Colleges and Universities Program on the Status and Education of Women
  www.aacu-edu.org/psew/index.cfm
- Association of College and Research Libraries: Women's Studies Section
  www.library.wisc.edu/libraries/WomensStudies
- Center for Women and Information Technology
  www.umbc.edu/cwit
- Feminist Majority Foundation
  www.feminist.org
- Hispanic Outlook in Higher Education
  www.hispanicoutlook.com
- Mills College Women's Leadership Institute
  www.mills.edu/campus_life/womens_leadership_institute/index.php
- National Center for Education Statistics
  www.nces.ed.gov
- National Council of Negro Women
  www.ncnw.org
- National Initiative for Women in Higher Education
  www.campuswomenlead.org
- National Women's History Project
  www.nwhp.org
- National Women's Studies Association
  www.nwsa.org
- State University of New York at Albany Center for Women in Government
  www.cwig.albany.edu
- Twenty-five Year Report on Title IX
  www.ed.gov/pubs/TitleIX

- University LGBT Programs
  www.ku.edu/~lbgt/links.htm
- University of California, Los Angeles Higher Education Research Institute
  www.gseis.ucla.edu/heri/heri.html
- University of Denver Higher Education Resource Services Mid-America
  www.womenscollege.du.edu/chamberscenter/hersmid-america.html
- University of Michigan Center for the Education of Women
  www.umich.edu/~cew
- U.S. Department of Education
  www.ed.gov
- Virginia Tech Science and Gender Equity Program
  www.cis.vt.edu/sage
- Wellesley Centers for Women
  www.wcwonline.org
- Wellesley College Higher Education Resource Services, New England
  www.wellesley.edu/WCW/Hers/Frm_Home.htm
- Women's Educational Equity Act Resource Center
  www.edc.org/womensequity
- Women's Studies Programs, Departments, and Research Centers
  www.umbc.edu/wmst/programs.html

Employment and Labor Force Participation

- Business and Professional Women's Foundation
  www.bpwusa.org
- Catalyst
  www.catalystwomen.org
- Cornell University Institute on Women and Work
  www.ilr.cornell.edu/women&work
- Georgia Institute of Technology Center for the Study of Women, Science, and Technology
  www.wst.gatech.edu
- Institute for Women's Policy Research
  www.iwpr.org

- International Association for Feminist Economics
  www.iaffe.org
- International Center for Research on Women
  www.icrw.org
- Legal Momentum
  www.legalmomentum.org
- National Women's Law Center
  www.nwlc.org
- Rutgers University Center for Women and Work
  www.rci.rutgers.edu/~cww
- Simmons College Graduate School of Management Center for Gender
  in Organizations
  www.simmons.edu/som/centers/cgo
- Social Science Research Network
  www.ssrn.com
- U.N. Population Fund
  www.unfpa.org
- University of Arizona Southwest Institute for Research on Women
  www.sirow.web.arizona.edu
- U.S. Bureau of Labor Statistics
  www.bls.gov
- U.S. Department of Labor Women's Bureau
  www.dol.gov/wb
- Wellesley Centers for Women
  www.wcwonline.org
- Women Employed Institute
  www.womenemployed.org
- Women's Research and Education Institute
  www.wrei.org

Environment

- Girl Scouts
  www.girlscouts.org
- International Association for Feminist Economics
  www.iaffe.org

- International Center for Research on Women
  www.icrw.org
- Society for Women's Health Research
  www.womenshealthresearch.org
- U.N. Environment Programme
  www.unep.org/DPDL/civil_society
- Women Watch
  www.un.org/womenwatch/asp/user/list.asp?ParentID=3011
- Women's Environment and Development Organization
  www.wedo.org

Equity Issues and Affirmative Action

- American Association of University Women Educational Foundation
  www.aauw.org
- Feminist Majority Foundation
  www.feminist.org
- Gender Statistics Users Group, Equal Opportunities Commission, UK
  www.eoc.org.uk
- The Glass Ceiling Commission
  www.digitalcommons.ilr.cornell.edu/keydocs
- ILO Gender Equality Tool
  www.ilo.org/dyn/gender/gender.home?p_lang=en
- Institute for Women's Policy Research
  www.iwpr.org
- International Labour Organization's Gender Equality Tool
  www.ilo.org/dyn/gender/gender.home?p_lang=en
- Legal Momentum
  www.legalmomentum.org
- Rutgers University Center for Women and Work
  www.rci.rutgers.edu/~cww
- Simmons College Graduate School of Management Center for Gender
  in Organizations
  www.simmons.edu/som/centers/cgo
- South Africa Commission on Gender Equality
  www.cge.org.za

- State University of New York at Albany Center for Women in Government and Civil Society
  www.cwig.albany.edu
- University of California, Los Angeles Higher Education Research Institute
  www.gseis.ucla.edu.heri/heri.htm
- University of Washington Libraries: Gay and Lesbian Organizations and Publications
  www.faculty.washington.edu/alvin/gayorg.htm
- Virginia Tech The Science and Gender Equity Program
  www.cis.vt.edu/sage
- We the American Women
  www.census.gov/apsd/wepeople/we-8.pdf
- Women and Economy Project, U.N. Platform for Action Committee
  www.unpac.ca
- Women Employed Institute
  www.womenemployed.org
- Women's Educational Equity Act Equity Resource Center
  www.edc.org/womensequity

Girls and Adolescents

- Girl Scouts
  www.girlscouts.org/research
- Girls Incorporated
  www.girlsinc.org/ic/page.php?id=3.3
- Planned Parenthood Federation of America
  www.plannedparenthood.org
- Wellesley Centers for Women
  www.wcwonline.org
- White House Project
  www.thewhitehouseproject.org
- U.S. Department of Health and Human Services Office on Women's Health
  www.4girls.gov

- Young Women's Christian Association
  www.ywca.org

Global Issues

- Alan Guttmacher Institute
  www.agi-usa.org
- All India Democratic Women Association
  www.aidwa.org
- Amnesty International USA
  www.amnestyusa.org/women/index.do
- Association for Women's Rights in Development
  www.awid.org
- Development Alternatives with Women for a New Era
  www.dawn.org.fj
- FLACSO Gender, Society, and Policies Area
  www.flacso.org.ar/areasyproyectos/areas/agsyp/index.jsp
- Global Fund for Women
  www.globalfundforwomen.org
- Global Information Network
  www.globalinfo.org
- Global Sisterhood Network
  home.vicnet.net.au/~globalsn
- Harvard University Women and Public Policy Program at the John F. Kennedy School of Government
  www.ksg.harvard.edu/wappp
- Institute for Global Communications
  www.igc.org
- International Association for Feminist Economics
  www.iaffe.org
- International Center for Research on Women
  www.icrw.org
- International Women's Health Coalition
  www.iwhc.org

- International Women's Tribune Center
  www.iwtc.org
- International Women's Web Sites
  www.research.umbc.edu/~korenman/wmst/links_intl.html
- Madre: An International Women's Human Rights Organization
  www.madre.org
- Revolutionary Association of the Women of Afghanistan
  www.rawa.org
- Rutgers University Center for Women's Global Leadership
  www.cwgl.rutgers.edu
- Simmons School of Management Center for Gender in Organizations
  www.simmons.edu/som/centers/cgo
- Sisterhood Is Global Institute
  www.sigi.org
- University of Arizona Southwest Institute for Research on Women
  www.sirow.web.arizona.edu
- U.S. Department of State, Office of International Women's Issues
  www.state.gov/g/wi
- Women and Economy Project, U.N. Platform for Action Committee
  www.unpac.ca
- Women's Edge Coalition
  www.womensedge.org
- Women's Environment and Development Organization
  www.wedo.org
- World Bank
  www.worldbank.org/gender

Health

- Alan Guttmacher Institute
  www.agi-usa.org
- Black Women's Health Imperative
  www.blackwomenshealth.org
- Center for Research on Women with Disabilities
  www.bcm.edu/crowd

- Centers for Disease Control
  www.cdc.gov/health
- International Women's Health Coalition
  www.iwhc.org
- National Women's Health Resource Center
  www.healthywomen.org
- National Women's Law Center
  www.nwlc.org
- Society for Women's Health Research
  www.womens-health.org
- U.S. Department of Health and Human Services Initiative to Eliminate
  Health Racial and Ethnic Disparities in Health
  www.raceandhealth.hhs.gov
- U.S. Department of Health and Human Services Office on Women's
  Health
  www.4woman.gov
- U.S. Department of Health and Human Services Office on Women's
  Health, Minority Women's Health
  www.4woman.gov/minority/index.htm
- U.S. Food and Drug Administration Office of Women's Health
  www.fda.gov/womens
- Women's Health Initiative
  www.nhlbi.nih.gov/whi
- World Health Organization
  www.who.org

Human Rights
- American Civil Liberties Union
  www.aclu.org
- Amnesty International
  www.amnesty.org
- Equality Now
  www.equalitynow.org

- Global Information Network
  www.globalinfo.org
- Human Rights Watch
  www.hrw.org
- International Gay and Lesbian Human Rights Commission
  www.iglhrc.org/site/iglhrc
- International Helsinki Federation for Human Rights
  www.ihf-hr.org
- International Women's Tribune Center
  www.iwtc.org
- MADRE: An International Women's Human Rights Organization
  www.madre.org
- Rutgers University Center for Women's Global Leadership
  www.cwgl.rutgers.edu
- Sisterhood Is Global Institute
  www.sigi.org
- University of Minnesota Hubert H. Humphrey Institute Center on
  Women and Public Policy
  www.hhh.umn.edu/centers/wpp
- WILD for Human Rights
  www.wildforhumanrights.org
- Women's Human Rights Net
  www.whrnet.org
- WomensWire
  www.womenswire.net

Law/Legal Issues
- Department of Education, Office of Civil Rights
  www.ed.gov/about/offices/list/ocr/index.html?scr=oc
- Legal Momentum
  www.legalmomentum.org
- National Partnership for Women and Families
  www.nationalpartnership.org

- National Women's Law Center
  www.nwlc.org
- U.S. Civil Rights Commission
  www.usccr.gov

Leadership

- Ann Ida Gannon, BVM, Center for Women and Leadership
  www.luc.edu/orgs/gannon
- Aspen Institute Business and Society Program
  www.aspeninst.org/isib
- Council of Women World Leaders
  www.womenworldleaders.org
- Mills College Women's Leadership Institute
  www.mills.edu/campus_life/womens_leadership_institute/index.php
- Ms. Foundation for Women
  www.ms.foundation.org
- Rutgers University Center for American Women and Politics, Eagleton
  Institute of Politics
  www.cawp.rutgers.edu
- Rutgers University Center for Women's Global Leadership
  www.cwgl.rutgers.edu
- Rutgers University Institute for Women's Leadership
  www.rci.rutgers.edu/~iwl
- State University of New York at Albany Center for Women in
  Government
  www.cwig.albany.edu
- University of Denver Higher Education Resource Services
  Mid-America
  www.womenscollege.du.edu/chamberscenter/hersmid-america.html
- University of Massachusetts, Boston Center for Women in Politics and
  Public Policy
  www.mccormack.umb.edu/cwppp
- Wellesley College Higher Education Resource Services, New England
  www.wellesley.edu/WCW/Hers/Frm_Home.htm

- White House Project
  www.thewhitehouseproject.org
- Women Leaders Initiative, World Economic Forum, Geneva, Switzerland
  www.weforum.org/womenleaders

Pay Equity

- International Association for Feminist Economics
  www.iaffe.org
- National Committee on Pay Equity
  www.pay-equity.org
- Radford University Center for Gender Studies
  www.radford.edu/~gstudies/sources/wage_gaps/wagegap.htm
- U.S. Census Bureau
  www.census.gov

Philanthropy

- National Committee for Responsive Philanthropy
  www.ncrp.org
- Resourceful Women
  www.rw.org
- Wisconsin Women's Studies Librarians Website
  www.library.wisc.edu/libraries/WomensStudies/philanth.htm
- Women & Philanthropy
  www.womenphil.org
- Women Donors Network
  www.womendonors.org
- Women's Funding Network
  www.wfnet.org
- Women's Philanthropy Institute
  www.women-philanthropy.org

Poverty

- Alan Guttmacher Institute
  www.agi-usa.org

- Center for Policy Alternatives Women and the Economy Program
  www.cfpa.org
- Center for Women Policy Studies
  www.centerwomenpolicy.org
- Institute for Women's Policy Research
  www.iwpr.org
- Institute on Race and Poverty
  www.irpumn.org/website
- National Center for Policy Research for Women and Families
  www.center4policy.org
- National Women's Law Center
  www.nwlc.org
- Poverty and Race Research Action Council
  www.prrac.org
- Social Science Research Network
  www.ssrn.com
- United Nations
  www.un.org/womenwatch/daw/beijing/platform/poverty.htm
- University of Connecticut Women's Studies
  www.sp.uconn.edu/~mccomisk/links267.html
- U.S. Bureau of Labor Statistics
  www.bls.gov
- U.S. Department of Labor Women's Bureau
  www.dol.gov/wb

Reproductive Rights

- Alan Guttmacher Institute
  www.agi-usa.org
- Legal Momentum
  www.legalmomentum.org
- National Abortion and Reproductive Rights Action League
  www.naral.org
- National Women's Law Center
  www.nwlc.org

- The Planned Parenthood Foundation of America
  www.plannedparenthood.org
- Women of Color Web
  www.hsph.harvard.edu/grhf/WoC

Sexuality
- Freedom to Marry
  www.freedomtomarry.org
- Human Rights Campaign
  www.hrc.org
- Gay and Lesbian Alliance against Defamation
  www.glaad.org
- The National Gay and Lesbian Task Force
  www.thetaskforce.org
- Queer Resources Directory
  www.qrd.org
- University LGBT Programs
  www.people.ku.edu/~jyounger/lgbtqprogs.html
- University of Washington Libraries, Gay and Lesbian Organizations
  and Publications
  www.faculty.washington.edu/alvin/gayorg.htm
- Women of Color Web
  www.hsph.harvard.edu/grhf/WoC
- Women's Studies Programs, Departments, and Research Centers
  www.umbc.edu/wmst/programs.html

Sports
- Feminist Majority Foundation
  www.feminist.org/sports
- National Association for Girls and Women in Sport
  www.aahperd.org/nagws/template.cfm?template=main.html
- Women's Sports Foundation
  www.womenssportsfoundation.org

Violence

- Family Violence Prevention Fund
  www.fvpf.org
- Legal Momentum
  www.legalmomentum.org
- National Organization for Women
  www.now.org/issues/violence
- Office of the United Nations High Commissioner for Human Rights
  www.unhchr.ch/women/focus-violence.html
- United Nations
  www.un.org/rights/dpi1772e.htm
- U.S. Department of Health and Human Services Office on Women's Health
  www.4woman.gov/owh/violence.htm

Women in Business

- Association of College and Research Libraries
  www.csulb.edu/~sbsluss/Women_and_Business.html
- Center for Women's Business Research
  www.nfwbo.org
- Office of Women's Business Ownership, Small Business Administration
  www.onlinewbc.gov
- Simmons School of Management, Center for Gender in Organizations
  www.simmons.edu/som/cgo
- U.S. Small Business Administration
  www.sba.gov/financing/special/women.html
- Women in Diversity Wow! Facts
  www.ewowfacts.com

Women in Politics

- American University Women and Politics Institute
  www.american.edu/oconnor/wandp
- Center for Legislative Development
  www.cld.org

- Center for Women Policy Studies
  www.centerwomenpolicy.org
- Council of Women World Leaders
  www.womenworldleaders.org
- EMILY's List
  www.emilyslist.org
- Global Information Network
  www.globalinfo.org
- International Institute for Democracy and Electoral Assistance
  www.idea.int/gender
- The Inter-Parliamentary Union
  www.ipu.org/iss-e/women.htm
- Rutgers University Eagleton Institute Center for American Women and Politics
  www.rci.rutgers.edu/~cawp
- State University of New York at Albany Center for Women in Government
  www.cwig.albany.edu
- University of Minnesota Hubert H. Humphrey Institute Center on Women and Public Policy
  www.hhh.umn.edu/centers/wpp
- White House Project
  www.thewhitehouseproject.org
- Wish List
  www.thewishlist.org
- Women's Edge Coalition, Global Issues Action Toolkit
  www.womensedge.org/pages/getinvolved/action_materials.jsp?id=241
- Women's Research and Education Institute
  www.wrei.org

Working Families

- Alfred P. Sloan Foundation
  www.sloan.org/programs/stndrd_dualcareer.shtml
- Corporate Voices for Working Families
  www.cvworkingfamilies.org

- Families and Work Institute
  www.familiesandwork.org
- Labor Project for Working Families
  www.laborproject.org
- National Partnership for Women and Families
  www.nationalpartnership.org
- Project on Global Working Families
  www.hsph.harvard.edu/globalworkingfamilies
- U.S. Census Bureau
  www.census.gov

Appendix D
Selected Philanthropy Infrastructure Organizations

- ARNOVA (Association for Research on Nonprofit and Voluntary Associations)
  www.arnova.org
- Association of Small Foundations
  www.smallfoundations.org
- BoardSource (formerly National Center for Nonprofit Boards)
  www.boardsource.org
- Conference Board
  www.conference-board.org
- Consortium of Foundation Libraries
  www.foundationlibraries.org
- Council on Foundations
  www.cof.org
- Council on Foundations Affinity Groups
  www.cof.org/index.cfm?containerID=72&menuContainerName=&navID=0
- European Foundation Centre Orpheus Program
  www.efc.be/projects/orpheus
- Forum of Regional Association of Grantmakers
  www.givingforum.org
- Foundation Center
  www.fdncenter.org
- Independent Sector
  www.independentsector.org

- International Funders for Indigenous Peoples
  www.internationalfunders.org
- Joint Affinity Groups
  - Asian Americans/Pacific Islanders in Philanthropy
    www.aapip.org
  - Association of Black Foundation Executives
    www.abfe.org
  - Disability Funders Network
    www.disabilityfunders.org
  - Funders for Gay and Lesbian Issues
    www.lgbtfunders.org
  - Hispanics in Philanthropy
    www.hiponline.org
  - National Network of Grantmakers
    www.nng.org
  - Native Americans in Philanthropy
    www.nativephilanthropy.org
  - Women & Philanthropy
    www.womenphil.org
  - Women's Funding Network
    www.wfnet.org
- National Council of Nonprofit Associations
  www.ncna.org
- Nonprofit Academic Centers Council
  www.naccouncil.org
- Philanthropy Roundtable
  www.philanthropyroundtable.org

Appendix E
Selected Philanthropy Research and Resource Organizations and Projects

- Alliance for Justice
  www.allianceforjustice.org
- Alliance for Nonprofit Management
  www.allianceonline.org
- Arizona State University Center for Nonprofit Leadership and Management
  www.asu.edu/copp/nonprofit
- Aspen Institute
  www.aspeninst.org
- Aspen Institute Nonprofit Sector Research Fund
  www.nonprofitresearch.org
- Aspen Philanthropy Letter (formerly the Philanthropy Information Retrieval Project)
  www.comnetwork.org/downloads/apl.htm
- Association of Fundraising Executives
  www.nsfre.org
- BoardSource (formerly National Center for Nonprofit Boards)
  www.boardsource.org
- Boston College Center on Wealth and Philanthropy
  www.bc.edu/research/swri
- Brookings Institute
  www.brook.edu
- Case Western Reserve University Mandel Center for Nonprofit Organizations
  www.cwru.edu/mandelcenter

- Center for Community Change
  www.communitychange.org
- Center for Effective Philanthropy
  www.effectivephilanthropy.com
- Center for Policy Alternatives
  www.stateaction.org
- Changemakers
  www.changemakers.net
- City University of New York Center on Philanthropy and Civil Society
  www.philanthropy.org
- CompassPoint Nonprofit Services
  www.compasspoint.org
- Duke University Center for the Study of Philanthropy and Volunteerism
  www.pubpol.duke.edu/centers/philvol
- Georgetown University Center for Public and Nonprofit Leadership
  www.cpnl.georgetown.edu
- Grand Valley State University Dorothy A. Johnson Center for Philanthropy and Nonprofit Leadership
  www.gvsu.edu/philanthropy
- Grand Valley State University Dorothy A. Johnson Center for Philanthropy and Nonprofit Leadership Nonprofit Good Practice Guide
  www.npgoodpractice.org
- GrantCraft
  www.grantcraft.org
- Grantmakers for Effective Organizations
  www.geofunders.org/
- Groundspring
  www.groundspring.org
- GuideStar
  www.guidestar.org
- HandsNet
  www.handsnet.org

- Harvard University John F. Kennedy School of Government Hauser Center for Nonprofit Organizations
  www.ksg.harvard.edu/hauser
- Hudson Institute's Bradley Center for Philanthropy and Civic Renewal
  www.pcr.hudson.org
- Idealist
  www.idealist.org
- Imagine Canada (formerly Canadian Centre for Philanthropy)
  www.ccp.ca/splash.asp
- Indiana University Center on Philanthropy
  www.philanthropy.iupui.edu
- Innovation Network
  www.innonet.org
- Institute for Gay and Lesbian Strategic Studies
  www.iglss.org
- Institute for Policy Studies
  www.ips-dc.org
- Johns Hopkins University Center for Civil Society Studies
  www.jhu.edu/~ccss
- Johns Hopkins University International Society for Third Sector Research
  www.jhu.edu/~istr
- London School of Economics Centre for Civil Society
  www.lse.ac.uk/collections/CCS
- London School of Economics Centre for Voluntary Organisations
  www.lse.ac.uk/collections/CCS/publications/cvo/cvo_pubs.htm
- National Committee for Responsive Philanthropy
  www.ncrp.org
- National Center for Family Philanthropy
  www.ncfp.org
- New School for Social Research New School for Social Research Nonprofit Management Program
  www.newschool.edu/milano/nonprof/descript.htm

- PACE—Philanthropy for Active Civic Engagement
  www.pacefunders.org
- The Philanthropy Initiative
  www.tpi.org
- Rainbow Research
  www.rainbowresearch.org
- Seton Hall University Nonprofit Sector Resource Institute
  nsri.shu.edu
- Support Center for Nonprofit Management
  www.supportctr.org
- Third Sector New England
  www.tsne.org
- University of Minnesota Humphrey Institute of Public Affairs
  www.hhh.umn.edu
- University of San Francisco Institute for Nonprofit Organization
  Management
  www.inom.org
- University of Southern California Center on Philanthropy and Public
  Policy
  www.usc.edu/schools/sppd/philanthropy
- Urban Institute Center on Nonprofits and Philanthropy
  www.urban.org/content/PolicyCenters/NonprofitsandPhilanthropy/
  Overview.htm
- Urban Institute National Center for Charitable Statistics
  nccsdataweb.urban.org/FAQ/index.php?category=31
- Venture Philanthropy Partners
  venturephilanthropypartners.org

Appendix F
Evaluation Toolkits

- *Building on a Better Foundation: A Toolkit for Creating an Inclusive Grantmaking Organization.* Donors Forum of Chicago, Minnesota Council on Foundations, Northern California Grantmakers, and the New York Regional Association of Grantmakers, 2001. www.mcf.org/mcf/resource/diversitytoolkit.htm
- ClearSighted: A Grantmaker's Guide to Using a Gender Lens. Chicago Women in Philanthropy, 1997. www.womenphil.org/info-url_nocat3910/info-url_nocat_show.htm?doc_id=208981
- *Cross-Currents in the Mainstream: Including Disability in Foundation Funding Priorities.* www.disabilityfunders.org/xcurrnts.html
- *Discrimination and Inclusiveness at a Crossroads.* Model Policy, Donors Forum of Chicago, Group on Funding Lesbian and Gay Issues. www.donorsforum.org/pubs/pubs.html
- Funding Advocacy: The Philanthropy of Changing Minds. www.grantcraft.org/catalog/guides/advocacy
- *Grant Making with a Gender Lens: Using Gender Analysis.* The Ford Foundation, 2004. www.grantcraft.org/catalog/guides/gender
- *A Screening Tool for Disability-Inclusive Grantmaking* www.disabilityfunders.org/screen.html

Appendix G
Selected Philanthropy Research Reports Online

- *The 21st Century Foundation: Building upon the Past, Creating for the Future, 2004*. Jed.Emerson.
  www.blendedvalue.org
- *Agile Philanthropy: Understanding Foundation Effectiveness*. Joel J. Orosz, Cynthia C. Phillips, and Lisa Wyatt Knowlton, Grand Valley State University Dorothy A. Johnson Center for Philanthropy and Nonprofit Leadership, 2003.
  www.nonprofitbasics.org/PDF/Article42.PDF
- *Aging in Equity: LGBT Elders*. Funders for Lesbian and Gay Issues, 2004.
  www.lgbtfunders.org/lgbtfunders/pubsprog.htm
- *Attitudes and Practices Concerning Effective Philanthropy*. Francie Ostrower, The Urban Institute Center on Nonprofits and Philanthropy, 2004.
  www.urban.org/UploadedPDF/411067_attitudes_practices_FR.pdf
- *Building to Last: A Grantmaker's Guide to Strengthening Nonprofit Organizations*. Paul Connolly, The Conservation Company, 2001.
  www.tccgrp.com/know_brief_building.html
- *The Case for Better Philanthropy: The Future of Funding for Women and Girls*. Women & Philanthropy, 2004.
  www.womenphil.org
- *CGO Insights*. Simmons College Center for Gender in Organizations.
  www.simmons.edu/som/centers/cgo/resources/insights.shtml

- *Chicago Philanthropy: A Profile of the Grantmaking Profession.* Louis T. Delgaldo, Lucia E. Orellana-Damacela, and Matthew J. Zanoni, Loyola University Chicago Center for Urban Research and Learning Philanthropy and Nonprofit Sector Program, 2001. www.luc.edu/philanthropy/research/grantmake/philanthro.pdf
- *Community Change Makers: The Leadership Roles of Community Foundations.* Ralph Parzen and Prue Brown, Chapin Hall Center for Children at the University of Chicago, 2004. www.chapinhall.org
- *Engendering Development Through Gender Equality in Rights, Resources, and Voice.* Elizabeth M. King and Andrew Mason, The World Bank, 2001. www.worldbank.org/gender/prr/module7ekam.pdf
- *Fostering Effective Funding for Women and Girls: A Next Stage Strategy.* Mary Ellen S. Capek and Molly Mead, with Foreword and Next Steps by Chicago Women in Philanthropy, 2002. www.wfnet.org/documents/CWIPreportSIfinal.pdf
- *Foundation Effectiveness: A Report on a Meeting of Foundation CEOs, Senior Executives, and Trustees October 9–10, 2003.* The Center for Effective Philanthropy, 2004. www.effectivephilanthropy.com/images/pdfs/cep03seminar.pdf
- *Goals and Intentions: What Should Today's Philanthropy Aim to Do?* Transcript of March 17, 2005, Dialogues on Civic Philanthropy: Perfecting Our Grants. A Project of Hudson Institute's Bradley Center for Philanthropy and Civil Renewal, Council on Foundations, Pettus-Crowe Foundation, and the Association of Small Foundations. www.civicphilanthropy.net
- *High-Engagement Philanthropy: A Bridge to a More Effective Social Sector: Perspectives from Nonprofit Leaders and High-Engagement Philanthropists.* Venture Philanthropy Partners and Community Wealth Ventures, 2004. www.vppartners.org/learning/reports/report2004/report2004.pdf
- *Lesbian, Gay, Bisexual, and Transgender Grantmaking by U.S. Foundations, Calendar Year 2002.* Funders for Lesbian and Gay Issues, 2005. www.workinggroup.org/lgbtfunders/progb.htm#2002Fdn

- *Lesbian, Gay, Bisexual, and Transgender Youth: Pressing Needs and Promising Practices.* Funders for Lesbian and Gay Issues, 2003. www.lgbtfunders.org/lgbtfunders/youth/youth1.htm
- *Listening to Grantees: What Nonprofits Value in Their Foundation Funders.* The Center for Effective Philanthropy, 2004. www.effectivephilanthropy.com/images/pdfs/listeningtograntees.pdf
- *Looking Out for the Future: An Orientation for Twenty-first Century Philanthropists.* Katherine Fulton and Andrew Blau, Global Business Network and Monitor Institute, 2005. www.futureofphilanthropy.org/project_final_report.asp
- *The Meaning and Impact of Board and Staff Diversity in the Philanthropic Field: Findings from a National Study.* Lynn C. Burbridge, William A. Diaz, Teresa Odendahl, and Aileen Shaw, Joint Affinity Groups, 2002. www.lgbtfunders.org/lgbtfunders/JAG/diversity_study.htm
- *Measuring Social Change Investments.* Deborah L. Puntenney, Women's Funding Network, 2002. www.wfnet.org/documents/dpuntenney-paper.doc
- *Missing: Information about Women's Lives.* National Council for Research on Women, 2004. www.ncrw.org/misinfo/report.pdf
- *Moving Ideas and Money: Issues and Opportunities in Funder Funding Collaboration.* Ralph Hamilton, Funders' Network for Smart Growth and Livable Communities, 2002. www.fundersnetwork.org
- *Philanthropic Connections: Mapping the Landscape of U.S. Funder Networks: Report of a Study by the Forum of Regional Associations of Grantmakers.* Lucy Bernholz, Kendall Guthrie, and Kaitlin McGaw, Blueprint Research and Design, Inc., 2003. www.blueprintrd.com/text/rag.pdf
- *Power to the Edges: Trends and Opportunities in Online Civic Engagement.* Jillaine Smith, Martin Kearns, and Allison Fine, PACE-Philanthropy for Active Civic Engagement, 2005. www.pacefunders.org/pdf/05.06.05%20Final%20Version%201.0.pdf

- *Promoting Philanthropy: Global Challenges and Approaches.* Paula D. Johnson, Stephen P. Johnson, and Andrew Kingman, Bertelsmann-Stiftung, 2004.
  www.tpi.org/clientservices/INSP/PromoPhilanthropy_Font_Ver23Feb 2005.pdf
- *Reflection, Action, and Expansion: Analysis of the Challenges and Opportunities for the Development of Emerging Latino Community in Boulder County, Colorado.* Hispanics in Philanthropy, 2004.
  www.hiponline.org/home/Resources/Publications
- *The Regional Infrastructure in Action: Building Grantmaker Effectiveness and Accountability, 2005–2006 Initiative.* Forum of Regional Associations of Grantmakers.
  www.givingforum.org/cgi-bin/doc_rep/public/file.pl/3180/proposal .overview.doc
- *Short Changed: Foundation Giving and Communities of Color.* Will Pittz and Rinku Sen, Applied Research Center, 2004.
  www.arc.org/Pages/pubs/shortchanged.html
- *Strengthening Transparency, Governance, and Accountability of Charitable Organizations.* A Final Report to Congress and the Nonprofit Sector. Paul Brest and M. Cass Wheeler, co-conveners, Panel on the Nonprofit Sector, Independent Sector, 2005.
  www.nonprofitpanel.org/final/Panel_Final_Report.pdf
- *Transformation through Philanthropy—Theory, Fact, and Fiction.* H. Peter Karoff, The Philanthropy Initiative, 2005.
  www.tpi.org/promoting/Transformation.pdf
- *Transformational Philanthropy: An Exploration.* Duane Elgin and Elizabeth Share. Changemakers/Transformative Philanthropy Project, 2002.
  www.simpleliving.net/awakeningearth/pdf/transformational_ philanthropy.pdf
- *Trends in 21st Century Philanthropy.* Katherine Fulton and Andrew Blau, Global Business Network, 2003.
  www.wfnet.org/news/story.php?story_id=179

- *Trouble in Foundationland: Looking Back, Looking Ahead.* Peter Frumkin. Hudson Institute Bradley Center for Philanthropy and Civic Renewal, 2004.
  www.hudson.org
- *What If? The Art of Scenario Thinking for Nonprofits.* Diana Scearce and Katherine Fulton, Global Business Network, July 2004.
  www.gbn.com/ArticleDisplayServlet.srv?aid=32655
- *The Women's Funding Movement: Accomplishments and Challenges,* vol. 3 of *Women and Philanthropy: Old Stereotypes, New Challenges.* Mary Ellen S. Capek, The W. K. Kellogg Foundation, 1998.
  www.wfnet/news/story.php?story_id=50
- *Women's Philanthropy: Untapped Resources, Unlimited Potential.* The W. K. Kellogg Foundation, 2000.
  www.wkkf.org/pubs/PhilVol/Pub602.pdf

Appendix H
Philanthropy Blogs

- Charity Governance's Insights and Analysis for Directors and Officers
  www.charitygovernance.blogs.com/charity_governance
- Council on Foundations's Emerging Issues
  blogs.cof.org/emergingissues
- The Decembrist
  www.markschmitt.typepad.com/decembrist/2005/05/foundations_and
  .html
- Gift Hub: Blogging Philanthropy
  www.gifthub.org
- The Giving Blog
  www.easyphilanthropy.blogspot.com
- Mile Zero: Wherever You Go, There You Are
  www.milezero.org
- National Committee for Responsive Philanthropy
  www.ncrp.org/blog.asp
- OMB Watch: Nonprofit Issues Blog
  www.ombwatch.org/article/blogs/298/0
- Philanthropica
  www.philanthropica.blogspot.com
- Philanthropy 2225: Research, Analysis, and Provocation on Future
  Directions for Philanthropy
  www.philanthropy.blogspot.com
- Sandra's Prospect Research Blog
  www.larkinresearch.blogspot.com

- Tom Munnecke
  www.munnecke.com/blog
- The Waiting Line: Essays and Articles
  www.waitingline.blogspot.com
- Wealth Bondage: *Serio Ludere*
  www.wealthbondage.com
- The World We Want: Blogging the Work and Themes of H. Peter Karoff
  www.giving.typepad.com/theworldwewant

Appendix I
Talking Points for Using This Book

New Ways of Looking at Gender and Diversity

New Language   As a sector, we long have needed new language and new thinking to address stubborn issues like gender and diversity in philanthropy. New ways of labeling these issues—phrases like "deep diversity" and "naming Norm"—help us all to think differently about how we do our work.

"Intersectionality"   The goal is to think about gender in context of *all* the other ways people are seen as different from each other. It's not "just" about gender, or "just" about race or ethnicity. The bigger picture of "intersectionality" highlights how all our differences—gender, sexual orientation, race, ethnicity, nationality, religion, class, disability, geography, age, learning styles, and all sorts of other physiological, social, cultural, and economically defined differences—combine to make all of us complex human beings.

Importance of "Institutionalizing" These Issues

Learning Organizations   Paying attention to these issues is not about "doing the right thing." "Doing the right thing" is obviously important, but even more important is strengthening our organizations, using all of the "differences that divide us" to teach our organizations to become more effective. Differences help us become "learning organizations," a proven strategy for organizational effectiveness.

"Deep Diversity" We must look differently at issues of diversity within organizations. "Deep diversity" means that we learn to see the breadth of differences among our staff, trustees, and grantees: *all* the ways that we are different from each other. And it also means that we learn how to *institutionalize* that knowledge, make it part of our organization's culture, as "normal" a part of our daily lives as how we answer the telephone.

"Naming Norm" Foundations, nonprofits, and a wide range of other organizations must recognize Norm, the arbiter of "proper and acceptable behavior" that too often becomes an unnamed, undiscussable problem. Norm knowledge, awareness of all the ways differences are locked into how we see people and how organizational culture operates, is essential for effective philanthropy. Not all norms are harmful, but many do get in the way of our health and the health of our relationships and our organizations.

Gender and Norm

Understanding Gender Helps Us Understand "Norm" Gender is a useful resource for understanding all kinds of differences, for understanding how unexamined assumptions about each other and what we think of as "normal" in organizations is key to achieving effective philanthropy.

Norm Undermines Innovation Examples of the social construction of gender help document how Norm undermines innovation and effectiveness, both in foundations and in grantees.

"Funding Norm Doesn't Fund Norma" The same funding strategies that fund women and girls effectively are also practices that strengthen philanthropy, in general, which benefits all.

Funding Objectives

Knowing Where Foundation Dollars Are Spent To be effective, philanthropy has to understand the implications and benefits of how and where its dollars are spent. Knowing *who* actually benefits from foundation grants is an important component of foundation accountability.

Not Just "A Fair Share"   The most appropriate goal for any funder committed to equitable funding is *not* assuring women and girls get a "fair share" of anything. The metaphor is misleading. The goal is "deep democracy," a stronger, more vibrant society in which everyone's diverse contributions are recognized, appreciated, utilized, and funded.

All Issues Are Women's Issues   Virtually *all* issues are women's issues: better understanding how our society "constructs" gender is one avenue into understanding how all differences get in the way of effective philanthropy unless we learn to see through our unexamined assumptions.

Women and Girls Not a "Special Interest" Group   To label a majority of the population as a "special interest group" doesn't make sense. Effective funders have learned that women's and girls' needs seldom are met if women and girls are considered mere "add-ons" to traditional philanthropic programs. Well-designed grants supporting the needs and strengths of women and girls both in this country and internationally are essential to effective philanthropy.

Appendix J
Interview Questions

Foundation Leaders

What's Working?

• Have roadblocks changed over time? How?

• What is working now regarding funding women and girls? What language/ analyses, statistics, other data "make the case" most effectively? What has changed over time?

• What are the characteristics of the women and girls being funded (race/ ethnicity, class, sexuality, etc.)?

• Talk about one or two of your most successful grants. Would you be willing to share a copy of one of your best proposals?

Roadblocks

• What are the roadblocks you are still encountering to funding for women and girls? What do you do to overcome them?

• Have roadblocks changed over time? How?

Institutionalization

• Talk about how funding for women and girls is "institutionalized" in your foundation. Are others in your foundation concerned with gender issues in funding?

• How are discussions of gender framed within your foundation? Are you explicit in talking about gender?

• Are there "new" conversations about gender that you have been part of?

• What would happen to funding for women and girls within your foundation if you left?

Quality of Proposals Received

• How do recent grant proposals you have been receiving compare with proposals from when you first started funding women's and girls' organizations and programs?

• Are you seeing differences in quality between proposals from women's/girls' organizations and other nonprofits that serve needs of women and girls?

• What advice do you have that would help nonprofits be more effective in how they raise funds for women and girls?

Magic Wand and Advocacy Work

• Are you part of any coalitions or working groups (informal or formal) that are particularly interested in funding women and girls? If so, could you describe the groups and how they work?

• Are you aware of advocacy organizations like Women & Philanthropy, the Women's Funding Network, and other "women's funding movement" efforts? If so, do you think their initiatives and resources been helpful?

• What additional pressure and/or resources do you think would be most helpful in the future?

• If you could wave a magic wand to improve funding for women and girls, what would the future look like?

Other Questions and People to Interview

• Are there other questions we should be asking you or other points you want to make?

• Can you give us the names of other funders and nonprofit leaders we should be talking to about these issues?

Nonprofit Leaders

What's Working?

• What is working now regarding funding women and girls? What language/analyses, statistics, other data "make the case" most effectively?

• What has changed over time (e.g. are funders more sophisticated in their understanding of gender)?

• What women and girls are you able to get funded (race/ethnicity, class, sexuality, etc.)?

• What difference has it made, if any, that you are a women's organization?

• Talk about one of the most successful grant proposals you've ever gotten funded. Would you be willing to share a copy?

Roadblocks

• What are the roadblocks you are still encountering in fundraising for women and girls? What do you do to overcome them?

• Have the roadblocks changed over time? How?

• What advice do you have for foundations that would help them be more effective in how they fund women and girls?

Institutionalization

• What is your perception of how funding women and girls is "institutionalized" in the foundations who fund your organization?

• What would happen to funding for women and girls if your program officer(s) left?

Magic Wand and Advocacy Work

• Are you part of any coalitions or working groups (informal or formal) that are concerned with funding women and/or girls? If so, could you describe the groups and how they work?

• Talk about organizations like Women & Philanthropy, the Women's Funding Network, and other "women's funding movement" efforts: do you think their initiatives and resources been helpful?

• What additional pressure and/or resources do you think would be most helpful in the future? If you could wave a magic wand to improve funding for women and girls, what would the future look like?

Other Questions and People to Interview

• Are there other questions we should be asking you or other points you want to make?

• Can you give us the names of other funders and nonprofit leaders we should be talking to about these issues?

Case Study Foundations

• How long have you been on the board/staff? In what capacity? How were you appointed?

• Your foundation is considered to be good at understanding and institutionalizing diversity. To the best of your knowledge, how did that come about? Do you know if that was that a conscious decision or policy?

• If your foundation made a conscious decision to pursue diversity as a priority in your foundation, when and how did the need surface and who was involved in your early conversations and planning sessions?

• How do you define diversity? Did your definitions change as you made more of a commitment to institutionalizing diversity? Where does gender fit in to that definition of diversity?

• What were the roadblocks you faced, if any, in discovering what you needed to learn to be better informed about diversity? In getting buy-in from board and staff?

• Can you share some concrete examples of the learning process you went through and what the foundation did to get buy-in from both board and staff?

• How would you assess the foundation's success to date at institutionalizing diversity? Is diversity in your institutional culture's DNA and if not, what will it take to get it there?

• What have been the consequences of diversity for your funding initiatives/processes/grantees? Have your funding priorities changed? Have your grantees changed?

• Have you changed personally in the course of doing this work? If so, how?

• What processes do you have in place for "tune-ups" and evaluations of progress?

• Are there other questions we should be asking you or other points you want to make?

Notes

Preface

1. W. K. Kellogg Foundation, *Women's Philanthropy: Untapped Resources, Unlimited Potential.*

2. Mary Ellen S. Capek, *Women and Philanthropy: Old Stereotypes, New Challenges;* Molly Mead, *Gender Matters: Funding Effective Programs for Women and Girls.* Available online at www.wfnet.org and www.womenphil.org.

3. See especially Mary Ellen S. Capek, *The Women's Funding Movement: Accomplishments and Challenges.* Available online at www.wfnet.org and www.womenphil.org.

4. See the interview questionnaires reprinted in Appendix J.

5. We use the term "gender" throughout this book to refer to socially and culturally constructed differences between and among men and women that change over time.

6. "Cultural competence" is a term in common use in the medical and nursing professions, social service agencies, counseling, law enforcement, education, and other helping professions. It describes the ability of individuals and organizations to offer and deliver services tailored to the complex needs of the culturally diverse populations they serve. The term "gendered cultural competence" emphasizes the importance of making sure gender—too often ignored in the research and "how-to" literature—is included in any definitions and applications of cultural competence.

7. See, for example, National Council for Research on Women, *Balancing the Equation: Where Are Women and Girls in Science, Engineering and Technology?*

Introduction

1. Loren Renz and Steven Lawrence, *Foundation Growth and Giving Estimates, 2004 Preview.* New York: Foundation Center, 2005, 1, available online at: fdncenter .org/research/trends_analysis/pdf/fgge05.pdf. The Foundation Center updates data on foundations and giving in three annual publications: *Foundation Giving Trends,* published in February, which examines funding interests of 1,000+ larger foundations with data two years prior to publication; *Foundation Growth and Giving*

Estimates, published in April, which provides estimates of overall foundation giving for the previous calendar year; and the *Foundation Yearbook,* published in June, which provides data on U.S. foundations overall and by region and type, also two years prior to publication. Highlights of *Foundation Giving Trends* and the *Foundation Yearbook* are also available on the Foundation Center Web site: fdncenter.org/research/trends_analysis/index/html.

Grant-making foundations can be divided into several distinct types:

• Private foundations that include family foundations created by individuals and families as vehicles for carrying out their charitable vision and independent foundations originally organized as family foundations that over time have grown to include nonfamily leadership

• Community foundations organized to serve specific geographic regions and which receive support from a variety of donors

• Corporate foundations created with gifts from for-profit companies to carry out the companies' charitable activities (in addition to or instead of giving directly to nonprofits through corporate giving programs without using a separate foundation)

• Operating foundations whose primary purpose is to run their own direct charitable programs but which also may make grants

2. The National Committee for Responsive Philanthropy, *Axis of Ideology: Conservative Foundations and Public Policy; 1 Billion for Ideas: Conservative Think Tanks in the 1990; Moving a Public Policy Agenda: the Strategic Philanthropy of Conservative Foundations.* To order, go to www.ncrp.org. See also Mary Ellen S. Capek. *Women as Donors: Stereotypes, Common Sense, and Challenges,* 21–22. Available online at www.womenphil.org and www.wfnet.org.

3. The Foundation Center, *Highlights of the Foundation Center's Foundation Giving Trends,* 2005, 1. Available online at www.foundationcenter.org.

4. *Highlights of the Foundation Center's Foundation Staffing,* 2003, 1. Available online at www.foundationcenter.org.

5. Foundations that are professionally staffed often hire people who have themselves worked in the sectors they fund, equipping foundations with experienced staff who can provide strategic advice and experience as well as monetary support for the nonprofit organizations they fund.

6. See, for example, Charles Taylor, *Deep Diversity and the Future of Canada,* available online at www.uni.ca/taylor.html; Barbara Houston, "Multiculturalism and a Politics of Persistence," available online at www.ed.uius.edu/EPS/PES-Yearbook/96_docs/houston.html; also www.seedsofchange.org.

7. See, for example, Arjun Appadurai, "Deep Democracy: Urban Governmentality and the Horizon of Politics," 21–47.

8. "Gender identity" refers to an individual's self-perception (or perceptions by others) that may or may not be in accord with physical anatomy, chromosomal sex, or sex assigned at birth.

9. *Webster's Third New International Dictionary of the English Language Unabridged,* 1540.

10. See, for example, Robin J. Ely and Debra E. Meyerson, "Theories of Gender in Organizations: A New Approach to Organizational Analysis and Change";

Joyce K. Fletcher, *Disappearing Acts: Gender, Power, and Relational Practice at Work;* Joanne Martin, *Organizational Culture: Mapping the Terrain;* Debra E. Meyerson, *Tempered Radicals: How People Use Difference to Inspire Change at Work;* Evangelina Holvino and Deborah Merrill-Sands, "Social Differences Lens"; Aruna Rao, Rieky Stuart, and David Kelleher, eds., *Gender at Work: Organizational Change for Equality;* Rhona Rapoport, Lott Bailyn, Joyce K. Fletcher, and Bettye H. Pruitt, *Beyond Work-Family Balance: Advancing Gender Equity and Workplace Performance.* See also the Simmons College Center for Gender in Organizations Web site, especially their *CGO Insights,* briefing notes available online: www.simmons.edu/som/cgo/publications_resources/briefing_notes.html.

11. Mark Dowie, *American Foundations: An Investigative History,* xl.

12. Angela Bonavoglia, *Getting It Done: From Commitment to Action on Funding for Women and Girls,* 111.

13. Michael E. Porter and Mark R. Kramer, "The Competitive Advantage of Corporate Philanthropy," 56–69; Michael E. Porter and Mark R. Kramer, "Philanthropy's New Agenda: Creating Value," 121–131; the Center for Effective Philanthropy, *Toward a Common Language.* See also www.effectivephilanthropy.com.

14. Peter M. Senge, *The Fifth Discipline: The Art and Practice of the Learning Organization,* 3.

15. Michael E. Porter and Mark R. Kramer, "The Competitive Advantage of Corporate Philanthropy," 63.

16. Dennis Collins, panel presentation at the Council on Foundations Annual Conference, April 2001.

17. David A. Thomas and Robin J. Ely, "Making Differences Matter: A New Paradigm for Managing Diversity." See also Robin J. Ely and David A. Thomas, "Cultural Diversity at Work: The Effects of Diversity Perspectives on Work Group Processes and Outcomes."

18. Using a "gender lens" means "examining a particular issue with a focus on the real life conditions of women and girls and acknowledging that gender is a powerful predictor of experience and opportunity" (Chicago Women in Philanthropy, *ClearSighted: A Grantmaker's Guide to Using a Gender Len).*

Chapter 1

1. Grantmakers for Effective Organizations, executive summary, *GEO Theory of Change,* second draft, April 15, 2003.

2. Ibid.

3. Grantmakers for Effective Organizations, *Baseline Member Survey Report,* 1.

4. Ibid., 30.

5. Ibid., 10–11.

6. Ibid., 30.

7. Ibid., 1.

8. See introduction, note 8.

9. Joel J. Orosz, Cynthia C. Phillips, Lisa Wyatt Knowlton, *Agile Philanthropy: Understanding Foundation Effectiveness.*

10. Lisa Wyatt Knowlton, e-mail correspondence, June 23, 2003.

11. For an interesting example of how "everyday leaders" in organizations make good use of organizational cultural knowledge to strengthen their organizations, see Deborah Meyerson's 2001 book, *Tempered Radicals: How People Use Difference to Inspire Change at Work.*

12. See, for example, the Society for Organizational Learning's Web site: www.solonline.org. Organizational learning literature concentrates primarily on systems thinking, values, dialogue, and feedback and also stresses openness and shared vision. Although learning organization thinkers are beginning to build some links to diversity and gender issues, many people working within these management constructs and theories have yet to link the dynamic, creative thinking that informs their writing and practice on learning organizations with the dynamic, creative insights and thinking around deep diversity and gendered cultural competence. This book builds some of those basic bridges.

13. Peter M. Senge, *The Fifth Discipline: The Art and Practice of the Learning Organization*, 3.

14. See, for example, Senge op. cit.; Chris Argyris, *On Organizational Learning*; Peter Kline and Bernard Saunders, *Ten Steps to a Learning Organization.*

15. Anne Fausto-Sterling uses a similar image to different purpose in her groundbreaking book *Sexing the Body* to illustrate the various layers of human sexuality, from the cellular to the social and historical. We arrived at the metaphor independently.

16. David Thomas and Robin Ely, "Making Differences Matter: A New Paradigm for Managing Diversity." See also an expanded analysis of these issues in Robin J. Ely and David A. Thomas, "Cultural Diversity at Work: The Effects of Diversity Perspectives on Work Group Processes and Outcomes."

17. As we describe throughout this chapter, the reality is complex. Experts disagree on "nature vs. nurture" and other dualities (how much of our sexual/gender identity is biologically determined, for example, and how much is a social construction), but as eminent biologist and historian of science Anne Fausto-Sterling points out, labeling someone a man or a woman is fundamentally a social decision (*Sexing the Body,* 3).

18. Ellen A. Fagenson, ed., *Women in Management: Trends, Issues, and Challenges in Managerial Diversity*, 305.

19. Barrie Thorne, *Gender Play: Girls and Boys in School,* 104.

20. Virginia Valian, *Why So Slow? The Advancement of Women.*

21. Valerie Walkerdine, *Schoolgirl Fictions*, 12.

22. For an in-depth, personal account of gender transitioning, see Jennifer Finney Boylan's memoir, *She's Not There: A Life in Two Genders.*

23. Jean M. Twenge, "Changes in Masculine and Feminine Traits Over Time: A Meta-Analysis."

24. Ibid., 316.

25. "Intersex" refers to individuals born with genitals not clearly identifiable as male or female, for which estimates range from 1 in every 2,000 births to 1.7 percent of all live births (an estimated 34 in 2,000); in some newborns, chromosomal sex may not match the appearance of the external sex organs. For an extensive analysis of intersex, related gender-identity issues, and the intersections of biology and cultural overlays on sex and gender, see Anne Fausto-Sterling, *Sexing the Body*.

26. For a discussion of multicultural feminism see the chapter by Maxine Baca Zinn and Bonnie Thornton Dill, "Theorizing Differences from Multiracial Feminism."

27. Kimberlé Crenshaw, Neil Gotanda, Gary Peller, and Kendell Thomas, eds., *Critical Race Theory*.

28. Anne Fausto-Sterling, for example, talks about how all organisms are active processes, what she calls "moving targets, from fertilization to death." *Sexing the Body*, 235.

29. Bob Pease and Keith Pringle, eds., *A Man's World? Changing Men's Practices in a Globalized World*, 6.

30. Ibid., 8.

31. U.S. Census Bureau, American Fact Finder. Sex by Age by Educational Attainment for the Population 18 Years and Over, Census 2000 Summary File 3 (SF 3), 2005.

32. Nancy Lopez, *Hopeful Girls, Troubled Boys: Race and Gender Disparity in Urban Education*, 2.

33. U.S. Census Bureau, American Fact Finder. Sex by Educational Attainment for the Population 25 Years and Over (Black or African American Alone), Census 2000 Summary File 3 (SF 3), 2005.

Chapter 2

1. See, for example, Capek's second Kellogg monograph, *Foundation Support for Women and Girls: "Special Interest" Funding or Effective Philanthropy?* available online at www.womenphil.org or www.wfnet.org.

2. *Webster's Third New International Dictionary of the English Language Unabridged*, 1540.

3. From Lotte Bailyn and Joyce K. Fletcher, *The Equity Imperative: Reaching Effectiveness through the Dual Agenda*.

4. See, for example, Ella L. J. Edmondson Bell and Stella N. Nkomo, *Our Separate Ways: Black and White Women and the Struggle for Professional Identity* and Kathleen Hall Jamieson, *Beyond the Double Bind: Women and Leadership*. See also Felicia Pratto and Penelope Espinoza, "Gender, Ethnicity, and Power."

5. Burbridge, Lynn C. *Status of African Americans in Grantmaking Institutions*.

6. See, for example, Robin J. Ely and Debra E. Meyerson, "Theories of Gender in Organizations: A New Approach to Organizational Analysis and Change"; Joyce K. Fletcher, *Disappearing Acts: Gender, Power, and Relational Practice at Work;* Debra E. Meyerson, *Tempered Radicals: How People Use Difference to Inspire Change at Work;* Evangelina Holvino and Deborah Merrill-Sands, "Social Differences Lens"; Aruna Rao, Rieky Stuart, and David Kelleher, eds. *Gender at Work: Organizational Change for Equality,* Rhona Rapoport, Lotte Bailyn, Joyce K. Fletcher, and Bettye H. Pruitt, *Beyond Work-Family Balance: Advancing Gender Equity and Workplace Performance.* See also the Simmons College Center for Gender in Organizations website, especially their *CGO Insights,* available online: www.simmons.edu/som/cgo/publications_resources/briefing_notes.html.

7. Capek, *Foundation Support for Women and Girls: "Special Interest" Funding or Effective Philanthropy?*, 16.

8. Bell and Nkomo, *Our Separate Ways: Black and White Women and the Struggle for Professional Identity,* 6.

9. The Council on Foundations (COF) reports gender and race/ethnicity data on foundation boards in its biennial *Foundation Management Series* and on grant-making staff in its annual *Grantmaking Salary and Benefits Report.* The latter only covers full-time paid staff.

According to 2003 data from the Foundation Center, only 17 percent of U.S. foundations are staffed. There are 11,733 full-time professional and support staff in these foundations, and the Council has salary information for 55.2 percent of those full-time staff (6,480 of 11,733) and demographics for 52.2 percent (6,126). The foundations reporting to COF, however, do include most of the major foundations in the country (in 2004, the respondents held 45 percent of all foundations assets), so it is reasonable to use these data (the only aggregate data available) to describe gender and racial/ethnic characteristics of foundation leadership in the United States.

10. Molly Mead. *Worlds Apart: Missed Opportunities to Help Women and Girls.*

11. See introduction, note 8.

12. See chapter 6 for more detailed analysis of the World Bank and its gender funding.

Chapter 3

1. See, for example, Aileen Shaw, "Corporate Philanthropy: The Business of Diversity."

2. The Foundation Center listed only 46 foundations (out of 66,398) with assets over $1 billion in 2004. Out of 66,398, 2,549 foundations are corporate. Loren Renz and Steven Lawrence, *Foundation Growth and Giving Estimates: 2004 Preview.*

3. E-mail correspondence, August 19, 2004.

4. Unless otherwise noted, all quotes and background material describing the foundation's history, mission, and priorities are from the Otto Bremer Foundation

Web site, www.fdncenter.org/grantmaker/Bremer, and the corporation's Web site, www.bremer.com.

5. Unless otherwise cited, all quotes from current foundation personnel and grantees are from authors' interviews conducted with those cited.

6. $985.9 million as of Dec. 31, 2001. By Dec. 31, 2003, the TCWF endowment had grown to $1.044 billion.

7. Unless otherwise noted, all quotes describing the foundation's mission and priorities are from the California Wellness Foundation Web site at www.tcwf.org.

8. Forty-six full-time and four part-time employees in March 2003: eight men (six Caucasian, two Hispanic), forty-two women (nineteen Caucasian, seven African-American, nine Hispanic, and seven Asian-American).

9. The evaluation results are posted on the foundation's Web site: www.tcwf.org.

10. Unless otherwise noted, all quotes describing the foundation's mission and priorities are from the Hyams Foundation Web site at www.hyamsfoundation.org.

11. Unless otherwise noted, all quotes from current foundation personnel and grantees are from authors' interviews conducted with those cited.

12. *A Search for the Meaning of Diversity*, 1992 Hyams Foundation Annual Report, 2.

13. Ibid., 2–3.

14. For additional information, see www.diversityinitiative.org.

15. See chapter 7 in this book.

16. Unless otherwise noted, all quotes describing the foundation's mission and priorities are from the Jessie Smith Noyes Web site, www.noyes.org.

17. Unless otherwise noted, all quotes from current foundation personnel and grantees are from authors' interviews conducted with those cited.

18. Unless otherwise noted, all quotes and background material describing the foundation's history, mission, and priorities are from the Philadelphia Foundation's Web site, www.philafound.org. Unless otherwise noted, all quotes from current foundation personnel, trustees, and grantees are from authors' interviews conducted with those cited.

19. Unless otherwise noted, all quotes and background material describing the foundation's history, mission, and priorities are from the Public Welfare Foundation's Web site, www.publicwelfare.org.

20. In 2004, with a staff of twenty-one approved full-time positions, eighteen were women, two men, with two vacancies. Eight were white, seven African-American, one African-Haitian, one Asian-American, one Pacific Islander, one Egyptian-American. Two identify as gay men and two as lesbians.

Chapter 4

1. According to a U.S. Census Bureau report released August 26, 2004, median income for men age fifteen and older who worked full-time, year-round in 2003 was

$40,668, virtually the same median annual income they earned in 2002. Women with similar work experience saw their earnings decline 0.6 percent to $30,724, their first annual decline since 1995. As a result, women working full-time, year-round earned 76 cents for every dollar in 2003, down from 77 cents for every dollar in 2002.

2. Inge Broverman, Susan Vogel, Donald Broverman, Frank Clarkson, and Paul Rosenkrantz, "Sex Role Stereotypes: A Current Appraisal."

3. Molly Mead, *Worlds Apart: Missed Opportunities to Help Women and Girls.*

4. Helen Ingram and Ann Schneider, "Social Construction of Target Populations: Implications for Politics and Policy."

5. Girls Incorporated, *What's Equal: Figuring Out What Works for Girls in Coed Settings.*

6. Ibid., 3.

7. Heather Johnston Nicholson, *Gender Issues in Youth Development Programs.*

8. Theda Skocpol, "Targeting within Universalism."

9. Frances Fox Piven and Richard A. Cloward, *The New Class War.*

10. Ibid., 87.

11. William J. Wilson, *When Work Disappears: The Work of the New Urban Poor.*

12. Michael B. Katz, *The Undeserving Poor.*

Chapter 5

1. Molly Mead, *Worlds Apart: Missed Opportunities to Benefit Women and Girls.*

2. The New York Women's Foundation, 1996.

3. The New York Women's Foundation, 1996; Michelle Alberti Gambone and Amy A. J. Arbreton, *Safe Havens: The Contributions of Youth Organizations to Healthy Adolescent Development.*

Chapter 6

1. Lawrence Summers, "The Most Influential Investment," 132.

2. See, for example, "Women's Agency and Social Change," in Sen's *Development as Freedom.*

3. E-mail correspondence, August 24, 2004.

4. For example, Joanna Kerr, Executive Director of the Association for Women's Rights in Development, points out in e-mail correspondence, August 13, 2004, that:

• Bilateral donors are giving fewer funds specifically to women's rights and empowerment programs and organizations because of funders' shifts to so-called gender mainstreaming that results in minor attention to women

• National security agendas have de-emphasized rights and development initiatives so that fewer government funds are available for gender equality
• An increasing number of large development projects in the public sector are being run by private-sector companies
• Funds have shifted away from some regions (like South America) while other regions like Eastern and Central Europe and NIS continue to be neglected
• Women's funds have emerged and grown but still constitute a "drop in the bucket"
• Several foundations and nongovernmental funding agencies that have been long-standing supporters of gender equality work, and women's rights are shrinking their budgets in these areas
• New competition for funding has been created through mechanisms like consortium or basket funding
• New conditions are being imposed on groups related to results frameworks, including men in organizations or as beneficiaries, organizational structure requirements, and program directives

5. Caroline O. N. Moser. *Gender Planning and Development.* As Summers comments in his *Scientific American* article, even as late as 1992 often there was a disproportionate emphasis on girls' future reproductive roles, with a much smaller emphasis on their roles in the economy.

6. See, for example, Boserup's seminal book *Women's Role in Economic Development*, published in 1970 but recently reissued with a new introduction by Swasti Mitter.

7. See, for example, Anne Marie Goetz, ed. *Getting Institutions Right for Women in Development;* Naila Kabeer, *Reversed Realities: Gender Hierarchies in Development Thought;* and Kathleen Staudt, ed.. *Women, International Development, and Politics: The Bureaucratic Mire.*

8. Moser, *Gender Planning and Development.*

9. Rae Lesser Blumberg. *Gender, Family, and Economy: The Triple Overlap.*

10. Ria Brouwers, *Review of the Integration of Gender Concerns in the Work of the DAC, Theme 1 of the Assessment of WID Policies and Programs of DAC Members.*

11. Moser, *Gender Planning and Development.*

12. Ibid., 66.

13. Ibid., 74.

14. J. Brian Atwood, "Gender Plan of Action," 1.

15. Inter-American Development Bank, *Women in the Americas: Bridging the Gender Gap.*

16. Ibid.

17. Mayra Buvinic, Catherine Gwin, and Lisa M. Bates. *Investing in Women: Progress and Prospects for the World Bank.*

18. Rounaq Jahan, "Mainstreaming Women and Development: Four Agency Approaches."

19. Buvinic, Gwin, and Bates, *Investing in Women: Progress and Prospects for the World Bank*, 19.

20. Elizabeth M. King and Andrew D. Mason, *Engendering Development through Gender Equality in Rights, Resources, and Voice.*

21. National Council for Research on Women. *Balancing the Equation: Where Are Women and Girls in Science, Engineering, and Technology?*

Chapter 7

1. For additional information about the partnership, see www.lgbtfunders.org/lgbtfunders and *Building Community across a Nation: The National Lesbian and Gay Community Funding Partnership.*

2. For additional information about the HIP Collaborative, see www.hiponline.org.

3. A more comprehensive study of Los Angeles Urban Funders is available as a Kennedy School of Government case study written by Christine Letts and Arthur McCaffrey (2003). To order online, see www.ksgcase.harvard.edu/case.htm?PID=1682.

4. Web site description at www.scap.org/laufindex.htm. Unless noted otherwise, all information in this section comes from this Web site.

5. For additional information about the Collaborative Fund for Women's Economic Development, see www.ms.foundation.org.

6. For additional information about the National Women's Law Center's New York City Board of Education Vocational Education Project, see www.nwlc.org.

7. Letter to Chancellor Levy, August 16, 2001.

8. For additional information about the United Way of Massachusetts Bay, see their Web site at www.uwmb.org.

Bibliography

Abernathy, Jim. "Current Trends in Environmental Funding." In *State of Philanthropy 2004*. Washington, DC: National Committee for Responsible Philanthropy, 2004.

Abzug, Rikki. "New Frontiers: Women and Girls Encounter the Nonprofit Sector." *Nonprofit Management & Leadership* 6 (Spring 1996): 311–315.

Abzug, Rikki, and Christy L. Beaudin. *Women on Boards: Parallel and Subordinate Power Structures/Cultures in Voluntarism and Trusteeship*. Project on Non-Profit Organizations Working Paper No. 211. New Haven, CT: Yale University Institution for Social and Policy Studies, 1994.

Abzug, Rikki, and Jeffrey S. Simonoff. *Nonprofit Trusteeship in Different Contexts*. Burlington, VT: Ashgate Publishing Company, 2004.

Acey, Katherine. "Backbone and Bite: The Place of Volunteerism in Women's Giving." In *Women, Philanthropy, and Social Change: Visions for a Just Society*, edited by Elayne Clift. Lebanon, NH: University Press of New England/Tufts University Civil Society Series, 2005.

Acker, Joan. *Revisiting Class: Lessons from Theorizing Race and Gender in Organizations*. Working Paper No. 5. Boston: Center for Gender in Organizations, Simmons Graduate School of Management, 1999.

———. "Hierarchies, Jobs, Bodies: A Theory of Gendered Organizations." *Gender & Society* 4: 2 (June 1990): 139–158.

Adamson, Rebecca. "Native Americans in the 21st Century and Philanthropy's Role." *First Nations Development Institute Business Alert* 8: 3 (May/June 1993).

Agars, Mark D. "Reconsidering the Impact of Gender Stereotypes on the Advancement of Women in Organizations." *Psychology of Women Quarterly* 28: 2 (June 2004): 103–111.

Alvord, Sarah H., L. David Brown, and Christine W. Letts. "Social Entrepreneurship and Societal Transformation: An Exploratory Study." *The Journal of Applied Behavioral Science* 40: 3 (September 2004): 260–282.

The American Prospect and JEHT Foundation. *Bringing Human Rights Home: Why Universal Rights Protect America*. Special Report: U.S. Human Rights. Washington, DC: The American Prospect, 2004.

Anderson, Margaret L., and Patricia Hill Collins. *Race, Class, and Gender: An Anthology,* 4th ed. Belmont, CA: Wadsworth/Thompson Learning, 2000.

Angier, Natalie. *Woman: An Intimate Geography.* Boston: Houghton Mifflin Company, 1999.

Appadurai, Arjun. "Deep Democracy: Urban Governmentality and the Horizon of Politics." *Public Culture* 14: 1 (Winter 2002): 21–47.

Argoff, Jeanne. *A Disability Policy Primer for Funders.* Falls Church, VA: Disability Funders Network, 2001.

Argyris, Chris. *On Organizational Learning,* 2nd ed. Malden, MA: Blackwell Business, 1999.

Atienza, Josefina, and Jennie Altman. *Foundation Giving Trends: Update on Funding Priorities.* New York: Foundation Center, 2005.

Atwood, J. Brian. *Gender Plan of Action.* Washington, DC: United States Agency for International Development, 1996.

Axelrod, Robert. *The Evolution of Cooperation.* New York: Basic Books, 1984.

Badgett, M. V. Lee, and Nancy Cunningham. *Creating Communities: Giving and Volunteering by Gay, Lesbian, Bisexual, and Transgender People.* New York: Working Group on Funding Lesbian & Gay Issues/Institute for Gay & Lesbian Strategic Studies, 1998.

Bailin, Mike. "Philanthropy in Practice: Great Expectations vs. Getting the Job Done." In *State of Philanthropy 2004.* Washington, DC: National Committee for Responsible Philanthropy, 2004.

Bailyn, Lotte, and Joyce K. Fletcher. *The Equity Imperative: Reaching Effectiveness through the Dual Agenda. CGO Insights.* Boston: Simmons College Center for Gender in Organizations, 2003.

Barnett, Rosalind, and Caryl Rivers. *Same Difference: How Gender Myths Are Hurting Our Children and Our Jobs.* New York: Basic Books, 2004.

Barry, David. "Telling Changes: From Narrative Family Therapy to Organizational Change and Development." *Journal of Organizational Change Management* 10 (1997): 32–48.

Bass, Gary, John Irons, and Ellen Taylor. "The Big Squeeze: Impacts of Federal Budget and Tax Policy." *The NCRP Quarterly* 1 (Spring 2004): 6–11.

Bates, Mariette Jane. *An American Phenomenon: A Qualitative Study of a Metropolitan Foundation with a Ten-Year Life Span.* Unpublished doctoral dissertation, The Union Institute, 1995.

Beer, Michael, and Nitin Nohria, eds. *Breaking the Code of Change.* Boston: Harvard Business School Press, 2000.

Bell, Ella L., Toni C. Denton, and Stella Nkomo. "Women of Color in Management: Toward an Inclusive Analysis." In *Women in Management: Trends, Issues, and Challenges in Managerial Diversity,* edited by Ellen A. Fagenson. Vol. 4: Women and Work: A Research and Policy Series. Newbury Park, CA: Sage Publications, 1993.

Bell, Ella L., J. Edmondson, and Stella N. Nkomo. *Our Separate Ways: Black and White Women and the Struggle for Professional Identity.* Boston: Harvard Business School Press, 2001.

Bell, Ella, Debra Meyerson, Stella Nkomo, and Maureen Scully. *Tempered Radicalism Revisited: Black and White Women Making Sense of Black Women's Enactments and White Women's Silences.* Working Paper 13. Boston: Center for Gender in Organizations, Simmons Graduate School of Management, 2001.

Bernholz, Lucy. *Creating Philanthropic Capital Markets: The Deliberate Evolution.* New York: Wiley, 2004.

Bernholz, Lucy, Kendall Guthrie, and Kaitlin McGaw. *Philanthropic Connections: Mapping the Landscape of U.S. Funder Networks:* Report of a Study by the Forum of Regional Associations of Grantmakers. San Francisco: Blueprint Research and Design, Inc., 2003.

Berry, Mindy L. "Native-American Philanthropy: Expanding Social Participation and Self-Determination." In *Cultures of Caring: Philanthropy in Diverse American Communities.* A Special Report. Washington, DC: Council on Foundations, 1999.

Bleier, Ruth. *Science and Gender: A Critique of Biology and Its Theories on Women.* New York: Pergamon Press, 1984.

Blumberg, Rae Lesser. *Gender, Family, and Economy: The Triple Overlap.* Newbury Park, CA: Sage Publications, 1991.

Bolduc, Kevin, Phil Buchanan, and Judy Huang. *Listening to Grantees: What Nonprofits Value in their Foundation Funders.* Cambridge, MA: The Center for Effective Philanthropy, 2004.

Bonavoglia, Angela. *The Trustee Connection: Making a Difference.* New York: Women and Foundations/Corporate Philanthropy, 1994.

———. *Getting It Done: From Commitment to Action on Funding for Women and Girls.* New York: Women and Foundations/Corporate Philanthropy, 1992.

———. *Making a Difference: The Impact of Women in Philanthropy.* New York: Women and Foundations/Corporate Philanthropy, 1991.

———. *Far from Done: The Status of Women and Girls in America.* New York: Women and Foundations/Corporate Philanthropy, 1989.

Bordt, Rebecca L. *The Structure of Women's Nonprofit Organizations.* Bloomington, IN: Indiana University Press, 1997.

Boserup, Ester. *Women's Role in Economic Development.* New York: St. Martin's Press, 1970.

Bowen, William G. *Inside the Boardroom: Governance by Directors and Trustees.* New York: John Wiley & Sons, Inc., 1994.

Bowen, William G., and Derek Bok. *The Shape of the River: Long-Term Consequences of Considering Race in College and University Admissions.* Princeton, NJ: Princeton University Press, 1998.

Boylan, Jennifer Finney. *She's Not There: A Life in Two Genders.* New York: Broadway Books, 2003.

Bradach, Jeffrey L. "Going to Scale: The Challenge of Replicating Social Programs." *Stanford Social Innovation Review* 1: 1 (Spring 2003): 18–25.

Bradshaw, Pat, Vic Murray, and Jacob Wolpin. "Women on Boards of Nonprofits: What Difference Do They Make?" *Nonprofit Management & Leadership* 6 (Spring 1996): 241–54.

Brest, Paul. "Smart Money: General Operating Grants Can Be Strategic—for Nonprofits and Foundations." *Stanford Social Innovation Review* 1: 3 (Winter 2003): 44–53.

Brest, Paul, and M. Cass Wheeler, co-conveners. *Strengthening Transparency, Governance and Accountability of Charitable Organizations.* Panel on the Nonprofit Sector. A Final Report to Congress and the Nonprofit Sector. Washington, DC: Independent Sector, 2005.

Bridging Worlds Apart: Questions and Actions for Grantmaking with a Gender Lens. Medford, MA: Tufts University Lincoln Filene Center, 1995.

Brouwers, Ria. *Review of the Integration of Gender Concerns in the Work of the DAC, Theme 1 of the Assessment of WID Policies and Programs of DAC Members.* Mimeograph prepared for the Operations Review Unit of the Directorate General for International Cooperation of the Netherlands. The Hague, Netherlands: Institute of Social Studies International Services, 1993.

Broverman, Inge, Susan Vogel, Donald Broverman, Frank Clarkson, and Paul Rosenkrantz. "Sex Role Stereotypes: A Current Appraisal." *Journal of Social Issues* 28 (1972): 59–78.

Bunch, Charlotte, and Samantha Frost. "Women's Human Rights: An Introduction." In *Routledge International Encyclopedia of Women's Studies: Global Women's Issues and Knowledge,* edited by Cheris Kramarae and Dale Spender. New York: Routledge, 2000.

Burbridge, Lynn C. *Status of African Americans in Grantmaking Institutions.* Indianapolis: Indiana University Center on Philanthropy, 1995.

Burbridge, Lynn C., William A. Diaz, Teresa Odendahl, and Aileen Shaw. *The Meaning and Impact of Board and Staff Diversity in the Philanthropic Field: Findings from a National Study.* New York: Joint Affinity Groups, 2002.

Business for Social Responsibility Education Fund. "Liz Claiborne—Family Violence Prevention Fund." *Cause Related Marketing: Partnership Guidelines & Case Studies.* San Francisco: Business for Social Responsibility Education Fund, 2001.

Buvinic, Mayra, Catherine Gwin, and Lisa M. Bates. *Investing in Women: Progress and Prospects for the World Bank.* Washington, DC: Overseas Development Council in cooperation with the International Center for Research on Women, 1996. Distributed by the Johns Hopkins University Press, Baltimore, MD.

Caiazza, Amy. *Women's Economic Status in the States: Wide Disparities by Race, Ethnicity, and Region.* Washington, DC: Institute for Women's Policy Research, 2004.

Caiazza, Amy, and April Shaw, eds. *The Status of Women in the States (2004 Series).* Washington, DC: Institute for Women's Policy Research, 2004.

Calás, Marta B., and Linda Smircich. "From 'The Woman's' Point of View: Feminist Approaches to Organization Studies." In *Handbook of Organization Studies*, edited by Stewart R. Clegg, Cynthia Hardy, and Walter R. Nord. Thousand Oaks, CA: Sage Publications, 1996.

———. "Dangerous Liaisons: The 'Feminine-in-Management' Meets 'Globalization.'" *Business Horizons* 36: 2 (March/April 1993): 71–81.

———. "Using the F Word: Feminist Theories and the Social Consequences of Organizational Research." In *Gendering Organizational Analysis*, edited by A. J. Mills and P. Tancred. Newbury Park, CA: Sage Publications, 1992.

Calvert, Linda McGee, and V. Jean Ramsey. "Bringing Women's Voice to Research on Women in Management: A Feminist Perspective." *Journal of Management Inquiry* 1: 1 (May 1992): 79–88.

Canadian Research Institute for the Advancement of Women. *Looking for Change—Documentation of National Women's Organizations Working Towards Inclusion and Diversity.* Ottawa, Ontario: Candian Research Institute for the Advancement of Women, 1996.

Capek, Mary Ellen S. "Documenting Women's Giving: Biases, Barriers, and Benefits." In *Women, Philanthropy, and Social Change: Visions for a Just Society*, edited by Elayne Clift. Lebanon, NH: University Press of New England/Tufts University Civil Society Series, 2005.

———. "Philanthropy." In *Routledge International Encyclopedia of Women's Studies: Global Women's Issues and Knowledge*, edited by Cheris Kramarae and Dale Spender. New York: Routledge, 2000.

———. *Women and Philanthropy: Old Stereotypes, New Challenges*. A Monograph Series, vol.1, *Women as Donors: Stereotypes, Common Sense, and Challenges*; vol. 2, *Foundation Support for Women and Girls: "Special Interest" Funding or Effective Philanthropy?* (Includes a Special Section on Women's Funds); vol. 3, *The Women's Funding Movement: Accomplishments and Challenges*. Battle Creek, MI: The W. K. Kellogg Foundation, 1998. Available online at www.womenphil.org and www.wfnet.org.

———. "Women as Trustees." In *Women in Academe: Progress and Prospects*, edited by Mariam K. Chamberlain. New York: Russell Sage Foundation, 1988.

Capek, Mary Ellen S., ed. *A Women's Thesaurus: An Index of Language Used to Describe and Locate Information By and About Women*. New York: Harper & Row, 1987.

Capek, Mary Ellen S., and Susan A. Hallgarth, eds. *Who Benefits, Who Decides? An Agenda for Improving Philanthropy: The Case for Women and Girls*. New York: National Council for Research on Women, 1995.

Capek, Mary Ellen S., and Molly Mead. *Fostering Effective Funding for Women and Girls: A Next Stage Strategy*. Executive Report, with foreword and next steps by Chicago Women in Philanthropy. Chicago: Chicago Women in Philanthropy, 2002. Available online at www.womenphil.org and www.wfnet.org.

———. "Funding Norm Doesn't Fund Norma: Women, Girls and Philanthropy." In *The State of Philanthropy in America,* edited by Neil Carson. Washington, DC: National Committee for Responsive Philanthropy, 2002.

Cardona, Chris, and Jeanne Argoff. *Disability Funding in California.* Executive Summary. Falls Church, VA: Disability Funders Network, 2001.

———. *Survey of California Grantmakers and Interviews with Disability Non-profits.* Falls Church, VA: Disability Funders Network, 2001.

Carson, Emmett D. *A Hand Up: Black Philanthropy and Self-Help in America.* Washington, DC: University Press of America, 1994.

———. "A Worst-Case Scenario or the Perfect Storm? Current Challenges to Foundation Board Governance." *The NCRP Quarterly:* 1 (Summer 2003): 15–19.

Carson, Emmett. "Patterns of Giving in Black Churches." In *Faith and Philanthropy in America: Exploring the Role of Religion in America's Voluntary Sector,* edited by Robert Wuthnow and Virginia A. Hodgkinson. San Francisco: Jossey-Bass Publishers, 1990.

The Center for Effective Philanthropy. *Foundation Effectiveness: A Report on a Meeting of Foundation CEOs, Senior Executives, and Trustees October 9–10, 2003.* Cambridge, MA: The Center for Effective Philanthropy, 2004.

———. *Foundation Governance: The CEO Viewpoint: A Report on a Survey of CEOs of the Largest 250 Foundations in the US.* Cambridge, MA: The Center for Effective Philanthropy, 2004.

———. *Toward a Common Language.* Cambridge, MA: The Center for Effective Philanthropy, 2002.

Chakravartty, Shona. *Native American Women and Their Communities: Building Partnerships for Survival.* New York: Women and Foundations/Corporate Philanthropy, 1994.

———. *Far From Done: Women, Funding, and Foundations in Wisconsin.* New York: Women and Foundations/Corporate Philanthropy, 1992.

———. *Far From Done: Women, Funding, and Foundations in North Carolina and the Southeast.* New York: Women and Foundations/Corporate Philanthropy, 1991.

Chakravorti, Bhaskar. *The Slow Pace of Fast Change: Bringing Innovations to Market in a Connected World.* Boston: Harvard Business School Press, 2003.

Chamberlain, Mariam, and Alison Bernstein. "Philanthropy and the Emergence of Women's Studies." In *Teacher's College Record.* Montpelier VT: Capital City Press, 1992.

Chambré, Susan M. "Jewish Women's Philanthropy." In *Jewish Women in America: An Historical Encyclopedia,* edited by Paula Hyman and Deborah Dash Moore. New York: Routledge, 1997.

———. "Parallel Power Structures, Invisible Careers, Benevolence, and Reform: Implications of Women's Philanthropy." *Nonprofit Management & Leadership* 4 (Winter 1993): 233–240.

Chang, Patti, and Kavita Ramdas. "Giving Globally: International Perspectives." In *Women, Philanthropy, and Social Change: Visions for a Just Society,* edited by Elayne Clift. Lebanon, NH: University Press of New England/Tufts University Civil Society Series, 2005.

Chao, Jessica. "Asian-American Philanthropy: Expanding Circles of Participation." In *Cultures of Caring: Philanthropy in Diverse American Communities.* A Special Report. Washington, DC: Council on Foundations, 1999.

Chicago Women in Philanthropy. *ClearSighted: A Grantmaker's Guide to Using a Gender Lens.* Chicago: Chicago Women in Philanthropy, 1997.

Clark, Pat. "Risk and Resiliency in Adolescence: The Current Status of Research on Gender Differences." *Equity Issues* 1: 1 (1995).

Clift, Elayne, ed. *Women, Philanthropy, and Social Change: Visions for a Just Society.* Lebanon, NH: University Press of New England/Tufts University Civil Society Series, 2005.

Clohesy, Stephanie, Christine H. Grumm, and Emily Katz Kishawi. *Smart Growth: A Life-Stage Model for Social Change Philanthropy.* San Francisco: Women's Funding Network, 2002.

Clotfelter, Charles, ed. *Who Benefits from the Nonprofit Sector?* Chicago: University of Chicago Press, 1992.

Cohen, Rick. "Advocating for Advocacy." *The NCRP Quarterly* 2003: 4 (Winter 2003–2004): 12–14.

———. "Hearings and Roundtables: NCRP Brings Philanthropy Accountability Standards to Capital Hill." In *State of Philanthropy 2004.* Washington, DC: National Committee for Responsible Philanthropy, 2004.

Cohen, Rick, and Meaghan House. "Community-Based Public Foundations: A Challenge to Mainstream Philanthropy." In *State of Philanthropy 2004.* Washington, DC: National Committee for Responsible Philanthropy, 2004.

Cole, Johnnetta Betsch, and Beverly Guy-Sheftall. *Gender Talk: The Struggle for Women's Equality in African American Communities.* New York: One World/Ballantine Books, 2003.

Coleman, Gill, and Ann Rippin. "Putting Feminist Theory to Work: Collaboration as a Means towards Organizational Change." *Organization* 7: 4 (2000): 573–587.

Collins, Patricia Hill. *Black Feminist Thought: Knowledge, Consciousness, and the Politics of Empowerment.* New York: Routledge, Chapman and Hall, 1991.

Colon, B. *Diversity Internship Programs: A Guide for Grantmaking Organizations.* New York: Women and Foundations/Corporate Philanthropy, 1995.

Congressional Research Service. *A Brief Legislative History of United States Efforts to Promote Women in Development.* Washington, DC: Congressional Research Service, 1994.

Connell, Robert W. *Gender and Power: Society, the Person, and Sexual Politics.* Cambridge, MA: Polity Press, 1987.

Connolly, Paul. *Building to Last: A Grantmaker's Guide to Strengthening Nonprofit Organizations.* A Briefing Paper on Effective Philanthropy. New York: The Conservation Company, 2001.

Connor, Jeffrey C. "It Wasn't About Race. Or Was It?" *Harvard Business Review* 78: 5 (September/October 2000): 37–45.

Cortes-Vazquez, Lorraine, and Erik Paulino. "State of the Latino Community: The Role of the Latino Nonprofit and Philanthropy." In *State of Philanthropy 2004.* Washington, DC: National Committee for Responsible Philanthropy, 2004.

Council on Foundations. "Building Strong and Ethical Foundations: A New Look at Standards, Conflicts of Interest, and Ethical Dilemmas." 2005 *Foundation News & Commentary* (special supplement) 2005.

Council on Foundations. *Cultures of Caring: Philanthropy in Diverse American Communities.* A Special Report. Washington, DC: Council on Foundations, 1999.

Covington, Sally. *Moving a Public Policy Agenda: The Strategic Philanthropy of Conservative Foundations.* Washington, DC: National Committee on Responsive Philanthropy, 1997.

Cox, Jr., Taylor. *Creating the Multicultural Organization: A Strategy for Capturing the Power of Diversity.* San Francisco: Jossey-Bass, 2001.

———. *Cultural Diversity in Organizations: Theory, Research, and Practice.* San Francisco: Berrett-Koehler, 1993.

Cox, Jr., Taylor, and Stella M. Nkomo. "Invisible Men and Women: A Status Report on Race as a Variable in Organization Behavior." *Journal of Organizational Behavior* 11 (1990): 419–431.

Crenshaw, Kimberlé, Neil Gotanda, Gary Peller, and Kendell Thomas, eds. *Critical Race Theory.* New York: The New Press, 1995.

Crocker, Ruth. "From Gift to Foundation: The Philanthropic Lives of Mrs. Russell Sage." In *Charity, Philanthropy, and Civility in American History,* edited by Lawrence J. Friedman and Mark D. McGarvie. New York: Cambridge University Press, 2002.

Croney, Lisa, and Nicole Cozier, eds. *Safety and Violence in Women's Lives: A Community Issue.* Proceedings of Women & Philanthropy's January 2004 California Regional Meeting. Washington, DC: Women & Philanthropy, 2004.

Cunningham, Katie, and Marc Ricks. "Why Measure: Nonprofits Use Metrics to Show That They are Efficient. But What If Donors Don't Care?" *Stanford Social Innovation Review* 2: 1 (Summer 2004).

Cunningham, Nancy. "Myth versus Reality: State of the Lesbian, Gay, Bisexual, and Transgender Community and Philanthropy's Response." In *State of Philanthropy 2004.* Washington, DC: National Committee for Responsible Philanthropy, 2004.

D'Emilio, John, and Estelle B. Freedman. *Intimate Matters: A History of Sexuality in America.* New York: Harper & Row, 1988.

Damon, William, and Susan Verducci, eds. *Beyond Good Intentions: Learning to Do Good, Not Harm, in Philanthropy.* Indianapolis, IN: Indiana University Press, 2006.

Daniel, Audrey Bennett, Juliet L. Gumbs, Erica Hunt, Lorraine C. Holmes Settles, Joe Louis Barrow III, A'Lelia Bundles, and J. Alfred Smith, Jr. *Moving the Agenda Forward: The Proceedings of the Second National Conference on Black Philanthropy,* edited by Rodney M. Jackson. Washington, DC: National Center for Black Philanthropy, Inc., 2000.

Das, Vidhya. "Bilateral Funding and Women's Empowerment." *Economic and Political Weekly* 26 (June 1–8, 1991): 1424.

Deere, Carolyn, and Mark Randazzo. "Globalization and Grantmakers: The Case for a Social Change Approach." In *State of Philanthropy 2004.* Washington, DC: National Committee for Responsible Philanthropy, 2004.

Delgaldo, Louis T., Lucia E. Orellana-Damacela, and Matthew J. Zanoni. *Chicago Philanthropy: A Profile of the Grantmaking Profession.* Chicago: Loyola University Chicago Center for Urban Research and Learning Philanthropy & Nonprofit Sector Program, 2001.

Diaz, William A. "The Behavior of Foundations in Organizational Frame: A Case Study." *Nonprofit and Voluntary Sector Quarterly* 25: 4 (December 1996): 453–469.

Dees, J. Gregory, Beth Battle Anderson, and Jane Wei-Skillern. "Scaling Social Impact: Strategies for Spreading Social Innovations." *Stanford Social Innovation Review* 1: 4 (Spring 2004).

Disability Funders Network. *Cross-Currents in the Mainstream: Including Disability in Foundation Funding Priorities.* Brochure. Falls Church, VA: Disability Funders Network, 2004.

———. *Emergency Preparedness for People with Disabilities: What Grantmakers Need to Know.* Falls Church, VA: Disability Funders Network, 2004.

Dowie, Mark. *American Foundations: An Investigative History.* Cambridge, MA: The MIT Press, 2001.

Draper, Lee. "Achieving Impact without Giving Cash." *Foundation News & Commentary* (September/October 2004): 28–32.

Dreger, Alice Domurat. *Hermaphrodites and the Medical Invention of Sex.* Cambridge, MA: Harvard University Press, 1998.

Eads, Marci L., and Matthew C. Brown. *An Exploratory Look at the Financial State of the Lesbian, Gay, Bisexual, and Transgender Movement.* Denver, CO: Gill Foundation, 2005.

Eisenberg, Pablo. *Challenges for Nonprofits and Philanthropy: The Courage to Change.* Lebanon, NH: University Press of New England/Tufts University Press Civil Society Series, 2004.

Elgin, Duane, and Elizabeth Share. *Transformational Philanthropy: An Exploration.* San Francisco: Changemakers/Transformative Philanthropy Project, 2002.

Ely, Robin J. *Feminist Critiques of Research on Gender in Organizations.* Working Paper No. 6. Boston: Center for Gender in Organizations, Simmons Graduate School of Management, 1999.

————. "The Power in Demography: Women's Social Constructions of Gender Identity at Work." *Academy of Management Journal* 38: 3 (June 1995): 589–634.

————. "The Effects of Organizational Demographics and Social Identity on Relationships Among Professional Women." *Administrative Science Quarterly* 39: 2 (June 1994): 203–238.

Ely, Robin J., and Debra E. Meyerson. "Advancing Gender Equity in Organizations: The Challenge and Importance of Maintaining a Gender Narrative." *Organization* 7: 4 (2000): 589–608.

————. "Theories of Gender in Organizations: A New Approach to Organizational Analysis and Change." *Research in Organizational Behavior* 22 (2000): 103–151.

————. *Theories of Gender in Organizations: A New Approach to Organizational Analysis and Change.* Working Paper No.8. Boston: Center for Gender in Organizations, Simmons Graduate School of Management, 2000.

Ely, Robin J., and David A. Thomas, "Cultural Diversity at Work: The Effects of Diversity Perspectives on Work Group Processes and Outcomes." *Administrative Science Quarterly* 46: 2 (June 2001): 229–273.

————. *Cultural Diversity at Work: The Moderating Effects of Work Group Perspectives on Diversity.* Working Paper No.10. Boston: Center for Gender in Organizations, Simmons Graduate School of Management, 2000.

Ely, Robin J., Erica Gabrielle Foldy, Maureen Scully, and The Center for Gender in Organizations, Simmons School of Management, eds. *Reader in Gender, Work, and Organization.* Boston: Center for Gender in Organizations, Simmons Graduate School of Management, 2003.

Emerson, Jed. *Reflections on Philanthropic Effectiveness.* Conference Summary. Heidelberg, Germany: Bertelsmann Foundation and the International Network on Strategic Philanthropy, 2004.

————. *The 21st Century Foundation: Building upon the Past, Creating for the Future,* 2004. Available online at www.blendedvalue.org.

————. "Where Money Meets Mission: Foundations Must Bridge the Social and Financial Investment Gap." *Stanford Social Innovation Review* 1: 2 (Summer 2003): 38–47.

Epstein, Cynthia Fuchs. *Woman's Place: Options and Limits in Professional Careers.* Berkeley: University of California Press, 1980.

Fagenson, Ellen A., ed. *Women in Management: Trends, Issues, and Challenges in Managerial Diversity.* Newbury Park, CA: SAGE Publications, 1993.

Fairfax, Jean E. "Black Philanthropy: Its Heritage and Its Future." In *Cultures of Giving: How Heritage, Gender, Wealth, and Values Influence Philanthropy,* edited by Charles H. Hamilton and Warren Ilchman. San Francisco: Jossey-Bass, Publishers, 1995.

Faludi, Susan. *Backlash: The Undeclared War Against American Women*. New York: Anchor Books, 1992.

Farrington, Arin. "'Family Matters' in the Amazon: Minga Peru Reaches Out to Women—and Men—to Rebuild Spiritual, Mental, and Physical Health." *Ford Foundation Report* 34: 4 (Fall 2003): 10–15.

Fausto-Sterling, Anne. *Sexing the Body: Gender Politics and the Construction of Sexuality*. New York: Basic Books, 2000.

Featherman, S. *Statements from the Grassroots: Women Breaking the Continuum of Poverty: A Report on a Regional Conference on Race, Gender, and Poverty*. New York: Women and Foundations/Corporate Philanthropy, 1989.

Feminist Majority Foundation. *Empowering Women in Philanthropy*. Arlington, VA: Feminist Majority Foundation, 1991.

Ferree, Myra Marx, and Patricia Yancy Martin, eds. *Feminist Organizations: Harvest of the New Women's Movement*. Philadelphia: Temple University Press, 1994.

Fischer, Lee, Martha S. MacDonell, Nicanor Perlas, and Henry Ramos. "Reactions to the State of Nonprofit America." *The Nonprofit Quarterly* 9: 4 (Winter 2002).

Fischer, Sunny. "Women's Values, Women's Vision: The Power of Giving Women." In *Women, Philanthropy, and Social Change: Visions for a Just Society*, edited by Elayne Clift. Lebanon, NH: University Press of New England/Tufts University Civil Society Series, 2005.

Fletcher, Joyce. *The Paradox of Post Heroic Leadership: Gender Matters*. Working Paper No.17. Boston: Center for Gender in Organizations, Simmons Graduate School of Management, 2003.

———. *Disappearing Acts: Gender, Power, and Relational Practice at Work*. Cambridge, MA: The MIT Press, 1999.

———. "Relational Practice: A Feminist Reconstruction of Work." *Journal of Management Inquiry* 7: 2 (June 1998): 163–186.

———. "Castrating the Female Advantage: Feminist Standpoint Research and Management Science." *Journal of Management Inquiry* 3: 1 (1994): 74–82.

Florida, Richard. *The Rise of the Creative Class and How It's Transforming Work, Leisure, Community, and Everyday Life*. New York: Basic Books, 2002.

Folbre, Nancy, and Robert E. Goodin. "Revealing Altruism." *Review of Social Economy* 62: 1 (March 2004): 1–24.

Foo, Lora Jo. *Asian American Women: Issues, Concerns, and Responsive Human and Civil Rights Advocacy*. New York: The Ford Foundation, 2002.

The Ford Foundation. "Now It's a Global Movement." *Ford Foundation Report* 31: 1 (special issue on women, Winter 2000): 2–35.

———. *Financial Support of Women's Programs in the 1970's: A Review of Private and Government Funding in the United States and Abroad*. New York: The Ford Foundation, 1979.

————. *That 51 Per Cent: Ford Foundation Activities Related to Opportunities for Women*. New York: The Ford Foundation, 1974.

Ford, Jeffrey D., and Laurie W. Ford. "The Role of Conversations on Producing Intentional Change in Organizations." *Academy of Management Review* 20: 3 (July 1995): 541–570.

Forum of Regional Associations of Grantmakers. *The Regional Infrastructure in Action: Building Grantmaker Effectiveness and Accountability, 2005–2006 Initiative*. Washington, DC: Forum of Regional Associations of Grantmakers, 2005.

The Foundation Center. *Grants for Women and Girls*. New York: The Foundation Center, 2004.

————. *Highlights of the Foundation Center's Foundation Giving Trends*. New York: The Foundation Center, 2005.

————. *Highlights of the Foundation Center's Foundation Staffing*. New York: The Foundation Center, 2003.

————. *Highlights of the Foundation Center's Foundation Yearbook*. New York: The Foundation Center, 2005.

Frumkin, Peter. *Trouble in Foundationland: Looking Back, Looking Ahead*. Washington, DC: Hudson Institute Bradley Center for Philanthropy and Civic Renewal, 2004.

————. *On Being Nonprofit: A Conceptual and Policy Primer*. Cambridge, MA: Harvard University Press, 2002.

Fry, C. *Sex Related Differences in Mathematical Achievement: Learning Style Factors*. Paper Presented at the Annual Meeting of the American Educational Research Association, Boston, 1990.

Frye, Marilyn. *The Politics of Reality: Essays in Feminist Theory*. Trumansburg, NY: The Crossing Press, 1983.

Fulton, Katherine, and Andrew Blau. *Looking Out for the Future: An Orientation for Twenty-first Century Philanthropists*. Cambridge, MA: Global Business Network and Monitor Institute, 2005.

————. *Discovering Philanthropy in the 21st Century*. Draft for Review. San Francisco: Global Business Network, 2003.

————. *Trends in 21st Century Philanthropy*. San Francisco: Global Business Network, 2003.

Funders for Lesbian and Gay Issues. *Lesbian, Gay, Bisexual, and Transgender Grantmaking by U.S. Foundations, Calendar Year 2002*. New York: Funders for Lesbian and Gay Issues, 2005.

————. *Aging in Equity: LGBT Elders*. New York: Funders for Lesbian and Gay Issues, 2004.

————. *Lesbian, Gay, Bisexual, and Transgender Youth: Pressing Needs and Promising Practices*. New York: Funders for Lesbian and Gay Issues, 2003.

————. *The Grantmakers' Guide to Lesbian, Gay, Bisexual, and Transgender Issues*. New York: Funders for Lesbian and Gay Issues, 2002.

————. *Building Community Across a Nation: The National Lesbian and Gay Community Funding Partnership.* New York: Funders for Lesbian and Gay Issues, 2000.

————. *Expanding Opportunities: A Grantmaker's Guide to Workplace Policies for Lesbian, Gay, and Bisexual Staff.* New York: Funders for Lesbian and Gay Issues, 1999.

Funding Infrastructure: An Investment in the Nonprofit Sector's Future. The Nonprofit Quarterly 12 (special infrastructure issue, 2004).

Furnari, Ellen, Carol Mollner, Teresa Odendahl, and Aileen Shaw. *Exemplary Grantmaking Practices Manual.* San Diego: National Network of Grantmakers, 1997.

Gale Research Encyclopedia of Associations CD-ROM, *Gale Global Access: Associations.* Chicago: Gale Research, 2002.

Galvin, Katherine. *Far from Done: The Challenge of Diversifying Philanthropic Leadership.* New York: Women and Foundations/Corporate Philanthropy, 1990.

Gambone, Michelle A., and Amy J. Arbreton. *Safe Havens: The Contributions of Youth Organizations to Healthy Adolescent Development.* Philadelphia: Public/Private Ventures, 1997.

Garofalo, Gitana. *Women Taking Power: The Quest for Equality.* New York: Women and Foundations/Corporate Philanthropy, 1993.

Gary, Tracy. "Lessons Learned: Strategies for Success in Education and Endowment." In *Women, Philanthropy, and Social Change: Visions for a Just Society,* edited by Elayne Clift. Lebanon, NH: University Press of New England/Tufts University Civil Society Series, 2005.

Gelb, Joyce. *Feminism and Philanthropy in the United States and England.* Working Paper. New York: Center for the Study of Philanthropy at the City University of New York Graduate School and University Center, 1990.

George, Susanna. "Why Intersectionality Works." *Women in Action.* 2 (2001).

Gherardi, Silvia. *Gender, Symbolism and Organizational Cultures.* Thousand Oaks, CA: SAGE Publications, 1995.

Gibson, Cynthia, and Ruth McCambridge. "Why Every Foundation Should Fund Infrastructure." *The Nonprofit Quarterly* 12 (special issue, 2004): 8–15.

Girls Inc. *What's Equal: Figuring Out What Works for Girls in Coed Settings.* New York: Girls Incorporated, 1993.

Gittell, Marilyn, Jill Gross, and Kathe Newman. *Race and Gender in Neighborhood Development Organizations.* New York: Howard Samuels State Management and Policy Center, City University of New York Graduate School and University Center, 1994.

Gittell, Marilyn, Sally Covington, and Jill Gross. *The Difference Gender Makes: Women in Neighborhood Development Organizations.* New York: Howard Samuels State Management and Policy Center, City University of New York Graduate School and University Center, n.d.

Gladwell, Malcolm. *The Tipping Point: How Little Things Can Make a Big Difference.* Boston: Back Bay Books, Little, Brown and Company, 2002.

Glass Ceiling Commission. *Good for Business: Making Full Use of the Nation's Human Capital.* A Fact-Finding Report of the Glass Ceiling Commission. Washington, DC: U.S. Department of Labor, 1995.

Goetz, Anne Marie, ed. *Getting Institutions Right for Women in Development.* London: Zed Books, 1997.

Goleman, Daniel. *Emotional Intelligence: Why It Can Matter More Than IQ.* New York: Bantam, 1997.

Goleman, Daniel, Annie McKee, and Richard E. Boyatzis. *Primal Leadership: Realizing the Power of Emotional Intelligence.* Cambridge MA: Harvard Business School Press, 2002.

Grantmakers for Effective Organizations. *GEO Theory of Change,* second draft, April 15, 2003. Unpublished paper.

———. *Baseline Member Survey Report.* Prepared by LaFrance Associates, LLC. Washington, DC: Grantmakers for Effective Organizations, 2003.

———. *Statement on Guidelines for the Funding of Nonprofit Organizations.* Washington, DC: Grantmakers for Effective Organizations, 2003.

Green, Laura. *Shortchanged: Chicago Foundations' and Corporations' Funding of Women's Organizations.* Chicago: Donors Forum of Chicago, 1985.

Grumm, Christine H., Deborah L. Puntenney, and Emily Katz Kishawi. "Women's Biggest Contribution: A View of Social Change." In *Women, Philanthropy, and Social Change: Visions for a Just Society,* edited by Elayne Clift. Lebanon, NH: University Press of New England/Tufts University Civil Society Series, 2005.

Guinier, Lani, Michelle Fine, and Jane Balin. "Becoming Gentlemen: Women's Experience at One Ivy League Law School." *University of Pennsylvania Law Review* 143 (November 1994): 1–110.

Guthrie, Kendall, Alan Preston, and Lucy Bernholz. *Transforming Philanthropic Transactions: An Evaluation of the First Five Years at Social Venture Partners Seattle.* San Francisco: Blueprint Research & Design, Inc., 2003.

Grumm, Christine, and Emily Katz Kishawi."Opening Doors: How Women's Funds Have Transformed Money and Willpower into Community Capital." In *State of Philanthropy 2004.* Washington, DC: National Committee for Responsive Philanthropy, 2004.

Hales, Dianne. *Just Like a Woman: How Gender Science is Redefining What Makes Us Female.* New York: Bantam Books, 1999.

Hall-Russell, Cheryl, and Robert H. Kasberg. *African-American Traditions of Giving and Serving: A Midwest Perspective.* Indianapolis: Indiana University Center on Philanthropy, 1997.

Hamilton, Ralph. *Moving Ideas and Money: Issues and Opportunities in Funder Funding Collaboration.* Coral Gables, FL: Funders' Network for Smart Growth and Livable Communities, 2002.

Harquail, Celia V., and Taylor Cox, Jr. "Organizational Culture and Accultura-tion." In *Cultural Diversity in Organizations*, edited by Taylor Cox, Jr. San Francisco: Berrett-Koehler Publishers, 1993.

Hartnell, Caroline. "Kavita Ramdas Interview." *Alliance* 9: 3 (September 2004).

Hartmann, Susan M. "Financing Feminism: The Ford Foundation." In *The Other Feminists: Activists in the Liberal Establishment*, edited by Susan M. Hartmann. New Haven, CT: Yale University Press, 1998.

Harvard Business Review on Managing Diversity. Cambridge, MA: Harvard Business Review Paperback, 2002.

Heifetz, Ronald A., John V. Kania, and Mark R. Kramer. "Leading Boldly: Foundations Can Move Past Traditional Approaches to Create Social Change through Imaginative—and Even Controversial—Leadership." *Stanford Social Innovation Review* 2: 3 (Winter 2004): 21–31.

Hernandez, Aileen C. *National Women of Color Organizations: A Report to the Ford Foundation*. New York: The Ford Foundation, 1991.

Hine, Darlene Clark. "We Specialize in the Wholly Impossible: The Philanthropic Work of Black Women." In *Lady Bountiful Revisited: Women, Philanthropy, and Power*, edited by Kathleen McCarthy. New Brunswick, NJ: Rutgers University Press, 1990.

Hispanics in Philanthropy. *Reflection, Action, and Expansion: Analysis of the Challenges and Opportunities for the Development of Emerging Latino Community in Boulder County, Colorado*. San Francisco: Hispanics in Philanthropy, 2004.

Holvino, Evangelina. *Complicating Gender: The Simultaneity of Race, Gender, and Class in Organization Change(ing)*. Working Paper No.14. Boston: Center for Gender in Organizations, Simmons Graduate School of Management, 2001.

Holvino, Evangelina, and Deborah Merrill-Sands, "Social Differences Lens." In *Reader in Gender, Work, and Organizations*, edited by Robin Ely, Maureen Scully, and Erica Foldy. London: Blackwell Publishers, 2003.

Holvino, Evangelina, Deborah Merrill-Sands, Bridgette Sheridan, and Robin Stone. *Gender at Work: Beyond White, Western, Middle-Class, Heterosexual, Professional Women*. Report of an International Conference, June 28–29, 1999. Boston: Center for Gender in Organizations, Simmons Graduate School of Management, 2000.

Hood, Jacqueline N., and Judith Kenner Thompson. "Care and Connection: A Study of Gender Differences in Charitable Contributions of Small Businesses." *Journal of Business & Entrepreneurship* 6 (July 1994): 73–89.

Horowitz, Bethamie, Pearl Beck, and Charles Kadushin. *Power and Parity: Women on the Boards of Major American Jewish Organizations*. New York: Ma'yan, The Jewish Women's Project, 1998.

Horrocks, Roger. *Masculinity in Crisis: Myths, Fantasies, and Realities*. New York: St. Martin's Press, 1994.

Houston, Barbara. "Multiculturalism and a Politics of Persistence." *Philosophy of Education* (1996).

Howe, Matt. "Workplace Giving and the Public Trust." In *State of Philanthropy 2004.* Washington, DC: National Committee for Responsible Philanthropy, 2004.

Hudson Institute's Bradley Center for Philanthropy and Civil Renewal, Council on Foundations, Pettus-Crowe Foundation, and the Association of Small Foundations. *Goals and Intentions: What Should Today's Philanthropy Aim to Do?* Transcript of March 17, 2005 Dialogues on Civic Philanthropy: Perfecting Our Grants. Washington, DC: Council on Foundations, 2005.

Hunt, Helen LaKelly, and Kanyere Eaton. "We Are Our Sister's Keeper: Role Models, Success Stories, Inspiration." In *Women, Philanthropy, and Social Change: Visions for a Just Society,* edited by Elayne Clift. Lebanon, NH: University Press of New England/Tufts University Civil Society Series, 2005.

Hurtado, Aida. *Disappearing Dynamics of Women of Color.* Working Paper No.4. Boston: Center for Gender in Organizations, Simmons Graduate School of Management, 1999.

The Hyams Foundation. *A Search for the Meaning of Diversity,* Annual Report. Boston: The Hyams Foundation, 1992.

Ianello, Kathleen P. *Decisions Without Hierarchy: Feminist Interventions in Organization Theory and Practice.* New York: Routledge, 1992.

Ingram, Helen, and Anne Schneider. "Social Construction of Target Populations: Implications for Politics and Policy." *American Political Science Review* 87: 2 (1993): 343–347.

Institute for Women's Policy Research. "The Status of Women in the States 2004 Overview." *Research—in-Brief,* IWPR #R265.

Inter-American Development Bank. *Women in the Americas: Bridging the Gender Gap.* Washington, DC: The Johns Hopkins University Press, 1995.

International Center for Research on Women. *Women's Issues in Development Cooperation: A Call for Action.* Washington, DC: International Center for Research on Women, 1993.

Jahan, Rounaq. "Mainstreaming Women and Development: Four Agency Approaches." In *Women, International Development, and Politics,* edited by Kathleen Staudt. Philadelphia: Temple University Press, 1997.

Jamieson, Kathleen Hall. *Beyond the Double Bind: Women and Leadership.* New York: Oxford University Press, 1995.

Johnson, Paula D., Stephen P. Johnson, and Andrew Kingman. *Promoting Philanthropy: Global Challenges and Approaches.* Gütersloh, Germany: Bertelsmann-Stiftung, 2004.

Kabeer, Naila. *Reversed Realities: Gender Hierarchies in Development Thought.* London: Verso, 1994.

Kanter, Rosabeth Moss. *Men and Women of the Corporation.* New York: Basic Books, 1977.

Karoff, H. Peter. *Transformation through Philanthropy—Theory, Fact, and Fiction.* Fitchberg, MA: The Philanthropy Initiative, 2005.

————. *Just Money—A Critique of Contemporary American Philanthropy.* Fitchberg, MA: The Philanthropy Initiative, TPI Editions, 2004.

Katz, Michael B. *The Undeserving Poor.* New York: Pantheon Books, 1989.

Keating, Daniel P. "Adolescent Thinking." In *At the Threshold: The Developing Adolescent,* edited by Shirley Feldman and Glenn R. Elliott. Cambridge, MA: Harvard University Press, 1990.

Kegan, Robert, and Lisa Laskow Lahey. *How the Way We Talk Can Change the Way We Work: Seven Languages for Transformation.* San Francisco: Jossey-Bass, 2001.

W. K. Kellogg Foundation. *Women's Philanthropy: Untapped Resources, Unlimited Potential.* Battle Creek, MI: The W. K.Kellogg Foundation, 2000.

Kessler, Suzanne J. *Lessons from the Intersexed.* New Brunswick, NJ: Rutgers University Press, 2002.

Kessler, Suzanne J., and Wendy McKenna. *Gender: An Ethnomethodological Approach.* Chicago: University of Chicago Press, 1978.

Kibbee, Barbara. *Funding Effectiveness: Lessons in Building Nonprofit Capacity.* San Francisco: Jossey-Bass, 2004.

Kilduff, Martin, and Ajay Mehra. "Postmodernism and Organizational Research." *Academy of Management Review* 22: 2 (April 1997): 453–481.

King, Elizabeth M., and Andrew D. Mason. *Engendering Development Through Gender Equality in Rights, Resources, and Voice.* Washington, DC: The World Bank, 2001.

Klausner, Michael. "When Time Isn't Money: Foundation Payouts and the Time Value of Money." *Stanford Social Innovation Review* 1: 1 (Spring 2003): 51–59.

Klausner, Michael, and Jonathan Small. "Failing to Govern: The Disconnect between Theory and Reality in Nonprofit Boards, and How to Fix It." *Stanford Social Innovation Review* 3: 1 (Spring 2005): 42–49.

Kline, Peter, and Bernard Saunders. *Ten Steps to a Learning Organization,* 2nd ed. Marshall, NC: Great Ocean Publishers, 1998.

Kochan, Thomas, Katerina Bezrukova, Robin Ely, Susan Jackson, Aparna Joshi, Karen Jehn, Jonathan Leonard, David Levine, and David Thomas. "The Effects of Diversity on Business Performance: Report of the Diversity Research Network." *Human Resource Management* 42: 1 (Spring 2003), 3–21.

Kolb, Deborah M. *Negotiation Through a Gender Lens.* Working Paper No.15. Boston: Center for Gender in Organizations, Simmons Graduate School of Management, 2002.

Kolb, Deborah M., and Deborah M. Merrill-Sands. *Waiting for Outcomes: Anchoring Gender Equity and Organizational Change in Cultural Assumptions.* Working Paper No. 1. Boston: Center for Gender in Organizations, Simmons Graduate School of Management, 1999.

Kramarae, Cheris, and Dale Spender, eds. *The Knowledge Explosion: Generations of Feminist Scholarship.* New York: Teachers College Press, 1992.

Kramarae, Cheris, and Dale Spender, eds. *Routledge International Encyclopedia of Women's Studies: Global Women's Issues and Knowledge*. New York: Routledge, 2000.

Krehely, Jeff. *Axis of Ideology: Conservative Foundations and Public Policy*. Washington, DC: National Committee for Responsive Philanthropy, 2004.

Krehely, Jeff, and Meaghan House. "How Political Wars Are Won: What Mainstream and Progressive Foundations Can Learn from the Right." In *State of Philanthropy 2004*. Washington, DC: National Committee for Responsible Philanthropy, 2004.

Krehely, Jeff, with Heidi K. Rettig. "Alternatives to Perpetuity: Foundations That Decide to Spend Down." In *State of Philanthropy 2004*. Washington, DC: National Committee for Responsible Philanthropy, 2004.

———. "Corporate Philanthropy: Giving to Get?" In *State of Philanthropy 2004*. Washington, DC: National Committee for Responsible Philanthropy, 2004.

Krieg, Iris. *Inclusiveness: Foundation Boards and Corporate Contributions Commitees*. A Report Prepared for The Donors Forum of Chicago Inclusiveness Committee. Chicago: Iris Krieg and Associates, Inc., 1998.

Krishnamurthy, Kalpana. "The Next Wave: Feminism, Philanthropy, and the Future." In *Women, Philanthropy, and Social Change: Visions for a Just Society*, edited by Elayne Clift. Lebanon, NH: University Press of New England/Tufts University Civil Society Series, 2005.

Kwak, Christine, Gail D. McClure, and Anne C. Petersen. "The Future of Funding: E-philanthropy and Other Innovations." In *Women, Philanthropy, and Social Change: Visions for a Just Society*, edited by Elayne Clift. Lebanon, NH: University Press of New England/Tufts University Civil Society Series, 2005.

Kwak, Mary. "The Paradoxical Effects of Diversity: A Variety of Complex Factors Determines Whether Corporate Diversity Efforts Help or Hinder a Firm's Bottom Line." *MIT Sloan Management Review* 44: 3 (Spring 2003): 7–8.

Lagemann, Ellen Condliffe, ed. *Philanthropic Foundations: New Scholarship, New Possibilities*. Bloomington, IN: Indiana University Press, 1999.

———. *The Politics of Knowledge: The Carnegie Corporation, Philanthropy, and Public Policy*. Middletown, CT: Wesleyan University Press, 1989.

Lakoff, George. *Don't Think of an Elephant: Know Your Values and Frame the Debate—The Essential Guide for Progressives*. White River Junction, VT: Chelsea Green Publishing Company, 2004.

Lawrence, Steven, Josefina Atienza, and Asmita Barve. *Foundation Yearbook: Facts and Figures on Private and Community Foundations*. New York: Foundation Center, 2005.

Lawrence, Steven, Robin Gluck, and Dia Ganguly. *Foundation Giving Trends*. New York: The Foundation Center, 2001.

Letts, Christine, and Arthur McCaffrey. *Los Angeles Urban Funders*. Cambridge, MA: Harvard University John F. Kennedy School of Government Case Studies in Public Policy and Management, 2003.

Letts, Christine W., and William Ryan. "How High-Engagement Philanthropy Works." *Stanford Social Innovation Review* 1: 1 (Spring 2003): 26–33.

Letts, Christine W., William Ryan, and Allen Grossman. "Virtuous Capital: What Foundations Can Lear from Venture Capitalists." *Harvard Business Review* 75: 2 (March–April 1997): 36–43.

Leman, Christopher. "Patterns of Policy Development: Social Security in the United States and Canada," *Public Policy 25* (1977): 26–29.

Lindsey, Jr., Handy, "Philanthropy's Record on Diversity and Inclusiveness: An Inconvenient Truth." In *State of Philanthropy 2004*. Washington, DC: National Committee for Responsible Philanthropy, 2004.

Linn, Marcia C., and Janet Shibley Hyde. "Gender, Mathematics and Science." *Educational Researcher* 18: 8 (1989): 17–19, 22–27.

London, Ted, and Dennis Rondinelli. "Partnerships for Learning: Managing Tensions in Nonprofit Organizations' Alliances with Corporations." *Stanford Social Innovation Review* 1: 3 (Winter 2003): 29–35.

Lopez, Nancy. *Hopeful Girls, Troubled Boys: Race and Gender Disparity in Urban Education,* New York: Routledge, 2002.

Lowell, Stephanie, Brian Trelstad, and Bill Meehan. "The Ratings Game: Evaluating the Three Groups That Rate the Charities." *Stanford Social Innovation Review* 3: 2 (Summer 2004): 39–45.

Lyman, Jing. "Afterword." In *Women, Philanthropy, and Social Change: Visions for a Just Society,* edited by Elayne Clift. Lebanon, NH: University Press of New England/Tufts University Civil Society Series, 2005.

Malhotra, Anju, and Rekha Mehra. *Fulfilling the Cairo Commitment: Enhancing Women's Economic and Social Options for Better Reproductive Health.* Washington, DC: International Center for Research on Women, 1999.

Mantila, Kathleen. *Down But Not Out: The Nonprofit Sector in Native America and the New Federalism: Survey Results.* Lumberton, NC: Native Americans in Philanthropy, 1999.

Martin, Joanne. *Organizational Culture: Mapping the Terrain.* Thousand Oaks, CA: Sage Publications, 2002.

———. *Cultures in Organizations: Three Perspectives.* New York: Oxford University Press, 1992.

Martin, Joanne, and Debra Meyerson. "Women and Power: Conformity, Resistance, and Disorganized Coaction." In *Power and Influence in Organizations,* edited by Roderick M. Kramer and Margaret A. Neale. Thousand Oaks, CA: SAGE Publications, 1998.

Marting, Leeda. *What We Know Now.* New York: Women and Foundations/Corporate Philanthropy, 1977.

Maurrasse, David J. *Race, Culture, Power, and Inclusion in Foundations.* Baltimore, MD: The Annie E. Casey Foundation, 2005.

Mayer, Steven E. *Building Community Capacity: The Potential of Community Foundations.* Minneapolis, MN: Rainbow Research, 1994.

Mayers, Dara. "Our Bodies, Our Lives: Microbicides Offer Vulnerable Women the Power to Protect Themselves from Sexually Transmitted Diseases." *Ford Foundation Report* 35: 3 (Summer 2004): 8–13.

McCarthy, Kathleen D. *Women's Culture: American Philanthropy and Art.* Chicago: University of Chicago Press, 1994.

McCarthy, Kathleen D., ed. "Women and Philanthropy." *Voluntas* 7: 4 (special issue, 1996).

———. *Lady Bountiful Revisited: Women, Philanthropy, and Power.* New Brunswick, NJ: Rutgers University Press, 1990.

———. *The Ms. Foundation: A Case Study in Feminist Fundraising.* Working Paper. New York: Center for the Study of Philanthropy at the City University of New York Graduate School and University Center, n.d.

McGregor, Alan, and David Schenck. "'Homegrown,' Innovative, and On the Move: The State of Rural Philanthropy." In *State of Philanthropy 2004.* Washington, DC: National Committee for Responsible Philanthropy, 2004.

Mead, Molly. *Gender Matters: Funding Effective Programs for Women and Girls.* Battle Creek, MI: The W. K.Kellogg Foundation, 2001. Available online at www .womenphil.org and www.wfnet.org.

———. *A Model of Gender Practices in Youth Development Programs.* Nonprofit Sector Research Fund Working Paper Series. Washington, DC: The Aspen Institute, 2001.

———. "Why Girls?" *Leading the Way,* 1: 1 (2000): 10–14.

———. *Why Such Low Funding for Programs for Women and Girls? Contrasting Views of Foundation Staff and Program Staff.* Unpublished Paper, 1997.

———. *Worlds Apart: Missed Opportunities to Help Women and Girls.* Boston: Women in Philanthropy/Boston Women's Fund, 1994.

Mead, Molly, and The Young Sisters for Justice. *Integrating Vision and Reality: Possibilities for Urban Girls Programs.* Boston, MA: The Boston Women's Fund, 2000.

Meadows, Donella. "Places to Intervene in a System." *Whole Earth Review* 91 (Winter 1997).

Mehra, Rekha, Simel Esim, and Marjorie Sims. *Fulfilling the Beijing Commitment: Reducing Poverty, Enhancing Women's Economic Options.* Washington, DC: International Center for Research on Women, 2000.

Merrill-Sands, Deborah, and Evangelina Holvino, with James Cumming. *Working with Diversity: A Focus on Global Organizations.* Working Paper No. 11. Boston: Center for Gender in Organizations, Simmons Graduate School of Management, 2000.

Merrill-Sands, Deborah, Joyce K. Fletcher, Anne Starks Acosta, Nancy Andrews, and Maureen Harvey. *Engendering Organizational Change: A Case Study of Strengthening Gender Equity and Organizational Effectiveness through Transforming Work Culture and Practices.* Working Paper No. 3. Boston: Center for Gender in Organizations, Simmons Graduate School of Management, 1999.

Meyer, John W., and Brian Rowan. "Institutionalized Organizations: Formal Structure as Myth and Ceremony." *American Journal of Sociology* 83: 2 (September 1977): 340–363.

Meyerowitz, Joanne. *How Sex Changed: A History of Transsexuality in the United States*. Cambridge, MA: Harvard University Press, 2002.

Meyerson, Debra E. "The Tempered Radicals: How Employees Push their Companies—Little by Little—to be More Socially Responsible." *Stanford Social Innovation Review* 2: 2 (Fall 2004): 14–23.

———. "Radical Change, The Quiet Way." *Harvard Business Review* 79: 9 (October 2001): 92–101.

———. *Tempered Radicals: How People Use Difference to Inspire Change at Work*. Boston: Harvard Business School Press, 2001.

Meyerson, Debra E., and Richard L. Daft. "Feeling Stressed and Burned Out: A Feminist Reading and Re-Visioning of Stress-Based Emotions within Medicine and Organization Science." *Organization Science* 9: 1 (January/February 1998): 103–119.

Meyerson, Debra E., and Joyce K. Fletcher. "A Modest Manifesto for Shattering the Glass Ceiling." *Harvard Business Review* 78: 1 (January–February 2000): 127–136.

Meyerson, Debra E., and Deborah M. Kolb. "Moving Out of the 'Armchair': Developing a Framework to Bridge the Gap between Feminist Theory and Practice." *Organization* 7: 4 (2000): 553–571.

Meyerson, Debra E., and Maureen A. Scully. "Tempered Radicalism and the Politics of Ambivalence and Change." *Organization Science* 6: 5 (September–October 1995): 585–600.

Michigan Women's Foundation. *Investing in Michigan Women*. Lansing MI: Michigan Women's Foundation, 1993.

———. *Women and the Future of Michigan: Strengthening Partnerships for the 21st Century*. Lansing, MI: Michigan Women's Foundation, 1990.

Miller, Clara. "Risk Minus Cash Equals Crisis: The Flap about General Operating Support." In *State of Philanthropy 2004*. Washington, DC: National Committee for Responsible Philanthropy, 2004.

Mindell, Arnold. *The Deep Democracy of Open Forums: Practical Steps to Conflict Prevention and Resolution for the Family, Workplace, and World*. Charlottesville, VA: Hampton Roads Publishing Company, Inc. 2002.

Minnich, Elizabeth Kamarack. *Transforming Knowledge*, second edition. Philadelphia: Temple University Press, 2005.

Mollner, Carol, and Marie C. Wilson. "History as Prologue: The Women's Funding Movement." In *Women, Philanthropy, and Social Change: Visions for a Just Society*, edited by Elayne Clift. Lebanon, NH: University Press of New England/Tufts University Civil Society Series, 2005.

Moore, Jo Gruidly, and Marianne Philbin. "Women as Donors: Old Stereotypes, New Visions." In *Women, Philanthropy, and Social Change: Visions for a Just So-*

ciety, edited by Elayne Clift. Lebanon, NH: University Press of New England/Tufts University Civil Society Series, 2005.

Morrison, Anne. *The New Leaders: Guidelines on Leadership Diversity in America*. San Francisco: Jossey-Bass Publishers, 1992.

Moser, Caroline O. N. *Gender Planning and Development*. London: Routledge, 1993.

Mulhern, Kymberly, and Kathleen Odne. "The Culture of Small: Rethinking Small Foundation Philanthropy." In *State of Philanthropy 2004*. Washington, DC: National Committee for Responsible Philanthropy, 2004.

Mullis, Ina V. S., and others. *The State of Mathematics Achievement: NAEP's 1990 Assessment of the Nation and the Trial Assessment of the States*. Washington, DC: National Center for Education Statistics, Office of Educational Research and Improvement, U.S. Department of Education, 1991.

Murningham, Marcy. "Women and Philanthropy: New Voices, New Visions." *New England Journal of Public Policy* (February 1990).

National Committee for Responsible Philanthropy. *Social Justice Philanthropy: The Latest Trend or a Lasting Lens for Grantmaking?* Washington, DC: National Committee for Responsible Philanthropy, 2005.

————. *1 Billion for Ideas: Conservative Think Tanks in the 1990*. Washington, DC: National Committee for Responsive Philanthropy, 1999.

National Council for Research on Women. *Missing: Information about Women's Lives*. New York: National Council for Research on Women, 2004.

————. *Balancing the Equation: Where Are Women and Girls in Science, Engineering, and Technology?* New York: National Council for Research on Women, 2001.

————. "Philanthropy: Do 'Universal' Dollars Reach Women and Girls? A Special Report." *Issues Quarterly* 1: 2 (1994).

National Council of Women's Organizations. *The ABCs of Women's Issues: Vote As If Your Life Depended on It—Because It Does!* Washington, DC: National Council of Women's Organizations, 2004.

National Network of Grantmakers. *Evaluation Guide: What is Good Grantmaking for Social Justice?* San Diego: National Network of Grantmakers, 1993.

National Network of Women's Funds. *Changing the Face of Philanthropy, 1985–1992*. St. Paul, MN: National Network of Women's Funds, 1993.

National Science Foundation. *Assessing Student Learning: Science, Mathematics, and Related Technology Instruction at the Precollege Level in Formal and Informal Settings. Program Solicitation and Guidelines*. Washington, DC: National Science Foundation, 1990.

The New York Women's Foundation. *The Status of Programming for Girls Aged 9–15 in New York City*. New York: The New York Women's Foundation, 1996.

Newman, Diana S. "The Role of Community Foundations in Establishing and Growing Endowment Funds by and for Diverse Ethnic Communities." In *Cultures of Caring: Philanthropy in Diverse American Communities.* A Special Report. Washington, DC: Council on Foundations, 1999.

Newman, Diana S., and Joanne B. Scanlon. *Inclusive Practices for Small and Mid-sized Foundations.* Washington, DC: Council on Foundations, 2004.

Newman, Diana S., Mindy Berry, Jessica Chao, Henry A. J. Ramos, and Mary-Frances Winters. *Opening Doors: Pathways to Diverse Donors.* San Francisco: Jossey-Bass, 2002.

Nicholson, Heather Johnston. *Gender Issues in Youth Development Programs.* A paper commissioned by the Carnegie Council on Adolescent Development, 1992.

Nicholson, Linda J., ed. *Feminism/Postmodernism.* New York: Routledge, 1990.

Nilles, Kathleen M., Douglas B. L. Endreson, Amy Locklear, and Jeffrey A. Trexler. *Giving with Honor: A Legal Reference on Charitable Activities of American Indian Tribes.* Washington, DC: Native Americans in Philanthropy and Council on Foundations, 1998.

Nkomo, Stella. "The Emperor Has No Clothes: Rewriting 'Race in Organizations.'" *Academy of Management Review* 17: 3 (1992): 487–513.

The Nonprofit Quarterly. Funding Infrastructure: An Investment in the Nonprofit Sector's Future, (special issue,) 2004.

Nonprofit Sector Research Fund. *Competing Visions: The Nonprofit Sector in the Twenty-First Century.* Perspectives from a Conference Convened by the Nonprofit Sector Research Fund, July 1995. Nonprofit Sector Research Fund Dialogue Series. Washington, DC: The Aspen Institute, 1997.

Odendahl, Teresa. *Charity Begins at Home: Generosity and Self-Interest Among the Philanthropic Elite.* New York: Basic Books, 1990.

Odendahl, Teresa, and Michael O'Neill, eds. *Women, Power, and the Nonprofit Sector.* San Francisco: Jossey-Bass, 1994.

Odendahl, Teresa, and Sabrina Youmans. "Women on Nonprofit Boards." In *Women and Power in the Nonprofit Sector,* edited by Teresa Odendahl and Michael O'Neill. San Francisco: Jossey-Bass, 1994.

Odendahl, Teresa Jean, Elizabeth Trocolli Boris, and Arlene Kaplan Daniels. *Working in Foundations: Career Patterns of Women and Men.* New York: The Foundation Center, 1985.

Open Society Institute Network Women's Program. *Bending the Bow: Targeting Women's Human Rights and Opportunities.* New York: Open Society Institute, 2000.

Orosz, Joel J., Cynthia C. Phillips, and Lisa Wyatt Knowlton. *Agile Philanthropy: Understanding Foundation Effectiveness.* Philanthropic and Nonprofit Knowledge Management Series Monograph No. 1. Grand Valley, MI: Dorothy A. Johnson Center for Philanthropy and Nonprofit Leadership, Grand Valley State University, 2003.

Ostrander, Susan A. "Moderating Contradictions of Feminist Philanthropy: Women's Community Organizations and the Boston Women's Fund, 1995 to 2000." *Gender & Society* 18: 1 (February 2004): 29–46.

———. *Money for Change: Social Movement Philanthropy at Haymarket People's Fund*. Philadelphia: Temple University Press, 1995.

———. *Women of the Upper Class*. Philadelphia: Temple University Press, 1984.

Ostrower, Francie. "The Reality underneath the Buzz of Partnerships: The Potentials and Pitfalls of Partnering." *Stanford Social Innovation Review* 3: 1 (Spring 2005): 34–41.

———. *Foundation Effectiveness: Definitions and Challenges*. Washington, DC: The Urban Institute Center on Nonprofits and Philanthropy, 2004.

———. *Attitudes and Practices Concerning Effective Philanthropy*. Executive Summary. Washington, DC: The Urban Institute Center on Nonprofits and Philanthropy, 2004.

Otis, Kimberly. "Partners and Stewards: Fostering Healthy Collaboration." In *Women, Philanthropy, and Social Change: Visions for a Just Society*, edited by Elayne Clift. Lebanon, NH: University Press of New England/Tufts University Civil Society Series, 2005.

Palmer, Colin. *Topics in Black American Philanthropy since 1785: A Curriculum Guide*. New York: City University of New York Center for the Study of Philanthropy, 1999.

Pandolfi, Joyce. *That 51% . . . Plus: A Ford Foundation Report*. New York: The Ford Foundation, 1979.

Parker-Sawyer, Paula, and Cheryl Hall-Russell. "African American Women's Philanthropy: A Tradition of Sharing." *Women's Philanthropy Institute News* (July 1997): 3–4.

Parzen, Ralph, and Prue Brown. *Community Change Makers: The Leadership Roles of Community Foundations*. Chicago: Chapin Hall Center for Children at the University of Chicago, 2004.

Pease, Bob, and Keith Pringle. "Studying Men's Practices and Gender Relations in a Global Context." In *A Man's World? Changing Men's Practices in a Globalized World*, edited by Bob Pease and Keith Pringle, London: Zed Books, 2001.

Pease, Katherine. *Inclusiveness at Work: How to Build Inclusive Nonprofit Organizations*. Denver, CO: The Denver Foundation, 2005.

———. *Inside Inclusiveness: Race, Ethnicity, and Nonprofit Organizations: A Research Report on Nonprofit Organizations in Metro Denver*. Denver, CO: The Denver Foundation, 2004.

Pfeffer, Jeffrey. "Putting People First: How Nonprofits That Value Their Employees Reap the Benefits in Service Quality, Morale, and Funding." *Stanford Social Innovation Review* 3: 1 (Spring 2005): 27–33.

Phillips, Barbara Y. "The Ford Foundation: A Model of Support for Women's Rights." In *Women, Philanthropy, and Social Change: Visions for a Just Society*, edited by Elayne Clift. Lebanon, NH: University Press of New England/Tufts University Civil Society Series, 2005.

Pifer, Alan. *Speaking Out: Reflections on 30 Years of Foundation Work*, rev. ed. Washington, DC: Council on Foundations, 2001.

Pittz, Will, and Rinku Sen. *Short Changed: Foundation Giving and Communities of Color.* Oakland, CA: Applied Research Center, 2004.

Piven, Frances Fox, and Richard A. Cloward. *The New Class War.* New York: Pantheon Books, 1982.

Pleck, Joseph H., F. Lund Sonenstein, and L. C. Ku. "Masculinity Ideology and Its Correlates." In *Gender Issues in Contemporary Society*, edited by Stuart Oskamp and Mark Costanzo. Newbury Park, CA: SAGE Publications, 1993.

Porter, Michael E., and Mark R. Kramer. "The Competitive Advantage of Corporate Philanthropy." *Harvard Business Review* 80: 12 (December 2002): 56–69.

———. "Philanthropy's New Agenda: Creating Value." *Harvard Business Review* 77: 6 (November/December 1999): 121–131.

Powell, Walter W., and Paul J. DiMaggio, eds. *The New Institutionalism in Organizational Analysis.* Chicago: University of Chicago Press, 1991.

Prager, Dennis J. *Organizing Foundations for Maximum Impact.* Washington, DC: The Aspen Institute Nonprofit Sector and Philanthropy Program, 2003.

Pratto, Felicia, and Penelope Espinoza. "Gender, Ethnicity, and Power." *Journal of Social Issues* 57: 4 (2001): 763–780.

Prewitt, Kenneth, Stefan Toepler, and Steven Heydemann, eds. *Philanthropic Foundations and Legitimacy: U.S. and European Perspectives.* New York: Social Science Research Council and Russell Sage Foundation, 2005.

Prothrow-Stith, Deborah, and Howard Spivak. *Sugar and Spice and No Longer Nice: How We Can Stop Girls' Violence.* San Francisco: Jossey Bass, 2005.

Proudford, Karen L. *Viewing Dyads in Triadic Terms: Toward a Conceptualization of the In/Visible Third in Relationships Across Difference.* Working Paper No. 16. Boston: Center for Gender in Organizations, Simmons Graduate School of Management, 2003.

Puntenney, Deborah L. *Measuring Social Change Investments: A Research Project of the Women's Funding Network.* San Francisco: Women's Funding Network, 2002.

Ramdas, Kavita. "A Different Vision." *Race, Poverty, & the Environment* XI: 1 (Summer 2004): 70.

———. "Empowering Women: The Best Vaccine Against AIDS." *The Commonwealth* 98: 10 (May 15, 2004): 16.

———. "We Would All Have a Say." In *If Women Ruled the World: How to Create the World We Want to Live In—Stories, Ideas, and Inspiration for Change*, edited by Sheila Ellison. Maui, HI: Inner Ocean Publishing, 2004.

Ramos, Henry A. "Nonprofit Diversity: An Asset We Can No Longer Ignore." *The Nonprofit Quarterly* 11: 1 (Spring 2004): 34–39.

Ramos, Henry A. J. "Latino Philanthropy: Expanding U.S. Models of Giving and Civil Participation." In *Cultures of Caring: Philanthropy in Diverse American Communities*. A Special Report. Washington, DC: Council on Foundations, 1999.

Ramsey, V. Jean, and Linda McGee Calvert. "A Feminist Critique of Organizational Humanism." *Journal of Applied Behavioral Science* 30: 1 (March 1994): 83–97.

Ramsey, V. Jean, and Jean Kantambu Latting, "A Typology of Intergroup Competencies." *Journal of Applied Behavioral Science*, 2005.

Rao, Aruna. "Engendering Institutional Change." *Signs* 22: 2 (Autumn 1996): 218–221.

Rao, Aruna, Rieky Stuart, and David Kelleher, eds. *Gender at Work: Organizational Change for Equality*. West Hartford, CT: Kumarian Press, 1999

Rapoport, Rhona, Lotte Bailyn, Joyce K. Fletcher, and Bettye H. Pruitt. *Beyond Work-Family Balance: Advancing Gender Equity and Workplace Performance*. San Francisco: Jossey-Bass, 2001.

Raymond, Susan U. *The Future of Philanthropy: Economics, Ethics, and Management*. Hoboken, NJ: John Wiley & Sons, 2004.

Reich, Rob. "Philanthropy and Its Uneasy Relation to Equality." In *Beyond Good Intentions: Learning to Do Good, Not Harm, in Philanthropy*, edited by William Damon and Susan Verducci, Indianapolis, IN: Indiana University Press, 2006.

Remington, Judy. *The Need to Thrive: Women's Organizations in the Twin Cities*. St. Paul, MN: Minnesota Women's Press, 1991.

Renz, Loren, and Steven Lawrence. *Foundation Growth and Giving Estimates: 2004 Preview*. New York: The Foundation Center, 2005.

Rhode, Deborah L., ed. *The Difference "Difference" Makes: Women and Leadership*. Stanford, CA: Stanford University Press, 2003.

Rhode, Deborah L. *Speaking of Sex: The Denial of Gender Inequality*. Cambridge, MA: Harvard University Press, 1997.

Rich, Andrew. "War of Ideas: Why Mainstream and Liberal Foundations and the Think Tanks They Support Are Losing in the War of Ideas in American Politics." *Stanford Social Innovation Review* 3: 1 (Spring 2005): 18–25.

Ridgeway, Cecilia L. "Interaction and the Conservation of Gender Inequality: Considering Employment." *American Sociological Review* 62 (April 1997): 218–235.

———. "The Social Construction of Status Value: Gender and Other Nominal Characteristics." *Social Forces* 70: 2 (December 1991): 367–386.

Rose, Marsha Shapiro. "The Other Hand: A Critical Look at Feminist Funding." In *Women, Philanthropy, and Social Change: Visions for a Just Society*, edited by Elayne Clift. Lebanon, NH: University Press of New England/Tufts University Civil Society Series, 2005.

———. "Philanthropy in a Different Voice: The Women's Funds." *Nonprofit and Voluntary Sector Quarterly* 23 (Fall 1994.): 227–42.

Roughgarden, Joan. *Evolution's Rainbow: Diversity, Gender, and Sexuality in Nature and People.* Berkeley, CA: University of California Press, 2004.

Russell, John. *Funding the Culture Wars: Philanthropy, Church, and State.* Washington, DC: National Committee for Responsive Philanthropy, 2005.

Ryan, Cynthia. "From Cradle to Grave: Challenges and Opportunities of Inherited Wealth." In *Women, Philanthropy, and Social Change: Visions for a Just Society,* edited by Elayne Clift. Lebanon, NH: University Press of New England/Tufts University Civil Society Series, 2005.

Salamon, Lester M. *The Resilient Sector: The State of Nonprofit America.* Washington, DC: Brookings Institution Press, 2003.

Salamon, Lester M., and Richard O'Sullivan. *Stressed but Coping: Nonprofit Organizations and the Current Fiscal Crisis,* Communiqué No. 2. Baltimore, MD: Johns Hopkins University Center for Civil Society Studies, Institute for Policy Studies, 2004.

Salamone, Rosemary C. *Same, Different, Equal: Rethinking Single-Sex Schooling.* New Haven: Yale University Press, 2003.

Salbi, Zaineb. "Think Big, Spend Small: The Impact of Woman-to-Woman Small-Scale Support." In *Women, Philanthropy, and Social Change: Visions for a Just Society,* edited by Elayne Clift. Lebanon, NH: University Press of New England/Tufts University Civil Society Series, 2005.

Sax, Leonard. *Why Gender Matters: What Parents and Teachers Need to Know about the Emerging Science of Sex Differences.* New York: Doubleday, 2005.

Scearce, Diana, and Katherine Fulton. *What If? The Art of Scenario Thinking for Nonprofits.* Cambridge, MA: Global Business Network, 2004.

Schambra, William A., "In a World of Bloggers, Foundations Can Expect More Scrutiny." *The Chronicle of Philanthropy* 17: 15 (May 12, 2005): 46.

Schambra, William. "Can There Be a New Politics of Philanthropy?" In *State of Philanthropy 2004.* Washington, DC: National Committee for Responsible Philanthropy, 2004.

Schambra, William, with Krista Shaffer. "Grassroots Rising: A Conservative Call for Philanthropic Renewal." In *The State of Our Union: Nonprofits and Government. The Nonprofit Quarterly* 11: 3 (special issue, Fall 2004).

Schein, Edgar H., and Diane L. Coutu. "The Anxiety of Learning: An Interview with Edgar H. Schein (Everyone Touts Learning Organizations, but Few Actually Exist). *Harvard Business Review* 80: 3 (March 2002): 100–107.

Schenk-Sandbergen, Loes. "Empowerment of Women: Its Scope in a Bilateral Development Project." *Economic and Political Weekly* 26 (April 27, 1991): 27–35.

Schuerman, Matthew. "Attention Campers: How Girls Inc. Put the Power of Lancôme to Work in Support of Mission." *Stanford Social Innovation Review* 21 (Summer 2004): 62–63.

Schur, Edwin M. *Labeling Women Deviant: Gender, Stigma, and Social Control.* New York: Random House, 1984.

Scott, Joan Wallach. *Gender and the Politics of History.* New York: Columbia University Press, 1988.

Sen, Amartya Kumar. *Development as Freedom.* New York: Alfred A. Knopf, 1999.

Sen, Gita, and Caren Grown. *Development, Crises, and Alternative Visions: Third World Women's Perspectives.* New York: Monthly Review Press, 1987.

Senge, Peter. *The Fifth Discipline: The Art and Practice of the Learning Organization.* New York: Currency Doubleday, 1990.

Servatius, Mary. *Short Sighted: How Chicago-Area Grantmakers Can Apply a Gender Lens to See the Connections Between Social Problems and Women's Needs.* Chicago: Chicago Women in Philanthropy, 1992.

Sharp, Marcia. "Grantmakers in a New Landscape," *Foundation News & Commentary* 33: 2 (March/April 2002).

Shaw, Aileen. "Corporate Philanthropy: The Business of Diversity," in *The Meaning and Impact of Board and Staff Diversity in the Philanthropic Field: Findings from a National Study,* edited by Lynn C. Burbridge, William A. Diaz, Teresa Odendahl, and Aileen Shaw. New York: Joint Affinity Groups, 2002.

Shuman, Michael H. "Why Progressive Foundations Give Too Little to Too Many." *The Nation* 266: 2 (January 12/19, 1998): 11–15.

Skloot, Edward. *Slot Machines, Boat-Building, and the Future of Philanthropy.* Inaugural address to the Waldemar A. Nielsen Issues in Philanthropy Seminar, Georgetown University, Washington, DC. October 5, 2001.

Skocpol, Theda. *Social Policy in the United States: Future Possibilities in Historical Perspective.* Princeton, NJ: Princeton University Press, 1995.

———. "Targeting within Universalism," in *The Urban Underclass,* edited by Christopher Jencks and Paul E. Peterson. Washington, DC: Brookings Institute Press, 1991: 411–435.

Smith, Dorothy E. *The Conceptual Practices of Power: A Feminist Sociology of Knowledge.* Boston: Northeastern University Press, 1990.

Smith, Jillaine, Martin Kearns, and Allison Fine. *Power to the Edges: Trends and Opportunities in Online Civic Engagement.* Berkeley, CA: PACE—Philanthropy for Active Civic Engagement, 2005.

Smock, Kristina. *Democracy in Action: Community Organizing and Urban Change.* New York: Columbia University Press, 2004.

Sprenger, Ellen, and Bisi Adeleye-Fayemi, eds. "Focus on . . . Investing in Women." *Alliance* 9: 3 (special issue, September 2004).

Stahl, Rusty M. "Foundations for a Framework: A New Generation of Grantmakers Seeks Big Picture and Deep Impact." In *State of Philanthropy 2004.* Washington, DC: National Committee for Responsible Philanthropy, 2004.

Stark, Mallory. "Women Leaders and Organizational Change." *Organizations— HBS Working Knowledge* (December 15, 2003).

Staudt, Kathleen, ed. *Women, International Development, and Politics: The Bureaucratic Mire*. Philadelphia: Temple University Press, 1997.

Stone, Douglas, Bruce Patton, and Sheila Heen. *Difficult Conversations: How to Discuss What Matters Most*. New York: Penguin Books, 1999.

Stoneman, Dorothy. "Philanthropy's Role in National Service and Civic Engagement." In *State of Philanthropy 2004*. Washington, DC: National Committee for Responsible Philanthropy, 2004.

Summers, Lawrence. "The Most Influential Investment." *Scientific American* (August 1992): 132.

Sutton, Robert I. "Sparking Nonprofit Innovation: Weird Management Ideas That Work." *Stanford Social Innovation Review* 1: 1 (Spring 2003): 42–49.

Talburtt, Peg, Judy Bloom, and Diane Horey Leonard. "Putting Our Money Where Our Mouths Are: Sharing Earned Income." In *Women, Philanthropy, and Social Change: Visions for a Just Society*, edited by Elayne Clift. Lebanon, NH: University Press of New England/Tufts University Civil Society Series, 2005.

Taylor, Charles. *Deep Diversity and the Future of Canada*. Available online at www.uni.ca/taylor.html.

Tchozewski, Chet. "A World of Missed Opportunity in Environmental Philanthropy." In *State of Philanthropy 2004*. Washington, DC: National Committee for Responsible Philanthropy, 2004.

Thomas, David, and Robin Ely. "Making Differences Matter: A New Paradigm for Managing Diversity." *Harvard Business Review* 74: 5 (1996): 79–91.

Thomas, Dorothy Q., and Krishanti Dharmaraj. *Making the Connections: Human Rights in the United States*. A Report of the Meeting at Mill Valley, California, July 7–10, 1999. San Francisco: WILD for Human Rights and the Shaler Adams Foundation, 2000.

Thomas, R. Roosevelt, Jr. *Beyond Race and Gender: Unleashing the Power of Your Total Work Force by Managing Diversity*. New York: American Management Association, 1992.

Thorne, Barrie. *Gender Play: Girls and Boys in School*. New Brunswick, NJ: Rutgers University Press, 1993.

Transken, Si. "Dwarfed Wolves Stealing Scraps from Our Masters' Tables: Women's Groups and the Funding Process." *Alternate Routes* 11 (June 1994): 31–36.

Twenge, Jean M. "Changes in Masculine and Feminine Traits Over Time: A Meta-Analysis." *Sex Roles* 5: 6 (1997): 305–325.

The Twenty-First Century Foundation. *Time, Talent, and Treasure: A Study of Black Philanthropy*. New York: The Twenty-First Century Foundation, 2004.

Valian, Virginia. *Why So Slow? The Advancement of Women*. Cambridge, MA: The MIT Press, 1998.

Venture Philanthropy Partners and Community Wealth Ventures. *High-Engagement Philanthropy: A Bridge to a More Effective Social Sector. Perspectives from Nonprofit Leaders and High-Engagement Philanthropists.* Washington, DC: Venture Philanthropy Partners and Community Wealth Ventures, 2004.

Villers, Kate. "The New Health Philanthropy: A Force for Social Justice in Health System Change?" In *State of Philanthropy 2004.* Washington, DC: National Committee for Responsible Philanthropy, 2004.

Walders, Davi. "Dear Mrs. Bethune." In *Women, Philanthropy, and Social Change: Visions for a Just Society,* edited by Elayne Clift. Lebanon, NH: University Press of New England/Tufts University Civil Society Series, 2005.

Walders, Davi. "Working Wonders." In *Women, Philanthropy, and Social Change: Visions for a Just Society,* edited by Elayne Clift. Lebanon, NH: University Press of New England/Tufts University Civil Society Series, 2005.

Walkerdine, Valerie. *Schoolgirl Fictions.* New York: Verso, 1990.

Waring, Marilyn. *If Women Counted: A New Feminist Economics.* San Francisco: HarperSanFrancisco, 1988.

Weber, Lynn. "A Conceptual Framework for Understanding Race, Class, Gender, and Sexuality." *Psychology of Women Quarterly* 22 (1998): 23–32.

Webster's Third New International Dictionary of the English Language Unabridged. Springfield MA: Merriam-Webster Inc., 1981.

Weick, Karl E. "Emergent Change as a Universal in Organizations." In *Breaking the Code of Change,* edited by Michael Beer and Nitin Nohria. Boston: Harvard Business School Press.

———. *Making Sense of the Organization.* Malden, MA: Blackwell Publishers Inc., 2001.

Weitzman, Murray S., Nadine T. Jaladoni, Linda M. Lampkin, and Thomas H. Pollak. *The New Nonprofit Almanac 2000.* San Francisco: Jossey-Bass, 2002.

Wells, Ronald Austin. *The Honor of Giving: Philanthropy in Native America.* Indianapolis: Indiana University Center on Philanthropy, 1998.

Whitt, J. Allen. *The Inner Circle of Local Nonprofit Trustees: A Comparison of Attitudes and Backgrounds of Women and Men Board Members.* Project on Non-Profit Organizations Working Paper No. 192. New Haven: Yale University Institute for Social and Policy Studies, 1993.

Wilson, William J. *When Work Disappears: The Work of the New Urban Poor.* New York: Alfred A. Knopf, 1997.

Winkelman, Lee. "Funders Support Grows as the Impact of Community Organizing Grows." In *State of Philanthropy 2004.* Washington, DC: National Committee for Responsible Philanthropy, 2004.

Winters, Mary-Francis. "Reflecting on Endowment Building in the African American Community." In *Cultures of Caring: Philanthropy in Diverse Communities.* Washington, DC: Council on Foundations, 1999.

Wittstock, Laura Waterman, and Theartrice Williams. *Changing Communities, Changing Foundations: The Story of the Diversity Efforts of Twenty Community Foundations.* Minneapolis, MN: Rainbow Research, 1998.

Women and Foundations/Corporate Philanthropy. *New Ways to Lead: A Discussion by Native American, African American, Latino, and Appalachian Grantees.* New York: Women and Foundations/Corporate Philanthropy, 1987.

———. *Funding of Programs for Women and Girls by a Selected Sample of Major Corporations.* New York: Women and Foundations/Corporate Philanthropy, 1980.

———. *Survey of Six Foundations That Derive Their Assets Primarily from the Sales of Cosmetics to Women.* New York: Women and Foundations/Corporate Philanthropy, 1978.

Women and Foundations/Corporate Philanthropy, Los Angeles Women's Foundation, and Southern California Association for Philanthropy. *A Report on the Proceedings of The Challenge of Being Female: A Conference on Philanthropy and Women's Issues in Southern California.* New York: Women and Foundations/ Corporate Philanthropy, 1990.

Women & Philanthropy. *The Leading 100 New Foundations Funding Women and Girls.* Washington, DC: Women & Philanthropy in partnership with Jankowski Associates, 2005.

———. *The Case for Better Philanthropy: The Future of Funding for Women and Girls.* Washington, DC: Women & Philanthropy, 2004.

Women Working in Philanthropy. *Doubled in a Decade, Yet Still Far from Done: A Report on Awards Targeted to Women and Girls by Grantmakers in the Delaware Valley.* Philadelphia: Women Working in Philanthropy, 1990.

Women's Funding Network. *Making the Case: A Learning and Measurement Tool for Social Change.* San Francisco: Women's Funding Network, 2004.

Women's Funding Network and Women & Philanthropy. *Donor Circles: Launching and Leveraging Shared Giving.* San Francisco: Women's Funding Network, 2004.

———. *Making a Difference: New Wealth, Women, and Philanthropy: Partnerships for Supporting Women and Girls.* San Francisco: Women's Funding Network, 2003.

Working Group for Funding Lesbian and Gay Issues. *Reaching Out: A Grantmakers' Guide to Lesbian and Gay Issues.* New York: Working Group on Funding Lesbian and Gay Issues, 1994.

Yang, Stephanie. "Voices of Young Women: The Development of Girls' Funds." In *Women, Philanthropy, and Social Change: Visions for a Just Society,* edited by Elayne Clift. Lebanon, NH: University Press of New England/Tufts University Civil Society Series, 2005.

Zinn, Maxine Baca, and Bonnie Thornton Dill. "Theorizing Differences from Multiracial Feminism." In *Reconstructing Gender: A Multicultural Anthology,* edited by Estelle Disch. Mountain View, CA: Mayfield Publishing Company, 2000.

Index